Virtual Technologies and E–Collaboration for the Future of Global Business

Jingyuan Zhao
University of Toronto, Canada

Joseph Richards
California State University, Sacramento, USA

A volume in the Advances in E-Business Research
(AEBR) Book Series

Published in the United States of America by
    IGI Global
    Business Science Reference (an imprint of IGI Global)
    701 E. Chocolate Avenue
    Hershey PA, USA 17033
    Tel: 717-533-8845
    Fax: 717-533-8661
    E-mail: cust@igi-global.com
    Web site: http://www.igi-global.com

Library of Congress Cataloging-in-Publication Data

Names: Zhao, Jingyuan, 1968- editor. | Richards, Joseph, 1966- editor.
Title: Virtual technologies and e-collaboration for the future of global
  business / Jingyuan Zhao, and Joseph Richards, editors.
Description: Hershey, PA : Business Science Reference, [2022] | Includes
  bibliographical references and index. | Summary: "The book focuses on
  emerging technologies and tools for collaboration in virtual
  environments, and includes the most new findings in in Automation,
  Computing and Intelligent Information Systems, as well as
  state-of-the-art solutions covering various issues and challenges"--
  Provided by publisher.
Identifiers: LCCN 2022014009 (print) | LCCN 2022014010 (ebook) | ISBN
  9781668450277 (hardcover) | ISBN 9781668450291 (paperback) | ISBN
  9781668450307 (ebook)
Subjects: LCSH: Business enterprises--Computer networks. | Business
  networks. | Communication--Technological innovations. | Organizational
  change.
Classification: LCC HD30.37 .V57 2022 (print) | LCC HD30.37 (ebook) | DDC
  658.4/0220285--dc23/eng/20220502
LC record available at https://lccn.loc.gov/2022014009
LC ebook record available at https://lccn.loc.gov/2022014010

This book is published in the IGI Global book series Advances in E-Business Research (AEBR) (ISSN: 1935-2700; eISSN: 1935-2719)

British Cataloguing in Publication Data
A Cataloguing in Publication record for this book is available from the British Library.

The views expressed in this book are those of the authors, but not necessarily of the publisher.

For electronic access to this publication, please contact: eresources@igi-global.com.

Advances in E-Business Research (AEBR) Book Series

In Lee
Western Illinois University, USA

ISSN:1935-2700
EISSN:1935-2719

MISSION

Technology has played a vital role in the emergence of e-business and its applications incorporate strategies. These processes have aided in the use of electronic transactions via telecommunications networks for collaborating with business partners, buying and selling of goods and services, and customer service. Research in this field continues to develop into a wide range of topics, including marketing, psychology, information systems, accounting, economics, and computer science.

The **Advances in E-Business Research (AEBR) Book Series** provides multidisciplinary references for researchers and practitioners in this area. Instructors, researchers, and professionals interested in the most up-to-date research on the concepts, issues, applications, and trends in the e-business field will find this collection, or individual books, extremely useful. This collection contains the highest quality academic books that advance understanding of e-business and addresses the challenges faced by researchers and practitioners.

COVERAGE

- Interorganizational information systems
- Electronic Supply Chain Management
- Economics of e-business
- Virtual Collaboration
- Valuing e-business assets
- E-Services
- Mobile Business Models
- Trends in e-business models and technologies
- E-Business Management
- Global e-business

IGI Global is currently accepting manuscripts for publication within this series. To submit a proposal for a volume in this series, please contact our Acquisition Editors at Acquisitions@igi-global.com or visit: http://www.igi-global.com/publish/.

Titles in this Series

For a list of additional titles in this series, please visit: http://www.igi-global.com/book-series/advances-business-research/37144

Navigating Digital Communication and Challenges for Organizations
José Gabriel Andrade (University of Minho, Portugal) and Teresa Ruão (University of Minho, ortugal)
Business Science Reference • © 2022 • 325pp • H/C (ISBN: 9781799897903) • US $230.00

Handbook of Research on Smart Management for Digital Transformation
Belem Barbosa (University of Porto, Portugal) Sandra Filipe (University of Aveiro, Portugal) and Claudia Amaral Santos (University of Aveiro, Portugal)
Business Science Reference • © 2022 • 614pp • H/C (ISBN: 9781799890089) • US $325.00

Handbook of Research on Digital Transformation, Industry Use Cases, and the Impact of Disruptive Technologies
Martin George Wynn (University of Gloucestershire, UK)
Business Science Reference • © 2022 • 487pp • H/C (ISBN: 9781799877127) • US $360.00

Handbook of Research on Pathways and Opportunities Into the Business of Esports
Sharon Andrews (University of Houston-Clear Lake, USA) and Caroline M. Crawford (University of Houston-Clear Lake, USA)
Business Science Reference • © 2021 • 473pp • H/C (ISBN: 9781799873006) • US $380.00

Complex Systems and Sustainability in the Global Auditing, Consulting, and Credit Rating Agency Industries
Michael I. C. Nwogugu (Independent Researcher, Nigeria)
Business Science Reference • © 2021 • 320pp • H/C (ISBN: 9781799874188) • US $215.00

Handbook of Research on Management and Strategies for Digital Enterprise Transformation
Kamaljeet Sandhu (University of New England, Australia)
Business Science Reference • © 2021 • 443pp • H/C (ISBN: 9781799850151) • US $305.00

Multidisciplinary Approaches to Crowdfunding Platforms
Carla Sofia Vicente Negrão (University of Coimbra, Portugal) and João António Furtado Brito (University of Cape Verde, Cape Verde)
Business Science Reference • © 2021 • 303pp • H/C (ISBN: 9781799832263) • US $230.00

Impact of Globalization and Advanced Technologies on Online Business Models
Ree C. Ho (Taylor's University, Malaysia) Alex Hou Hong Ng (INTI International University, Malaysia) and Mustafa Nourallah (Mid Sweden University, Sweden)
Business Science Reference • © 2021 • 399pp • H/C (ISBN: 9781799876038) • US $250.00

IGI Global
PUBLISHER of TIMELY KNOWLEDGE

701 East Chocolate Avenue, Hershey, PA 17033, USA
Tel: 717-533-8845 x100 • Fax: 717-533-8661
E-Mail: cust@igi-global.com • www.igi-global.com

Table of Contents

Detailed Table of Contents

Chapter 1

Rabie Barhoun, Ministry of Education National, Morocco

In recent years, collaborative environments play a significant role in collaboration work. The keys element of these environments is the process of collaboration. The calculation of the collaboration does not depend on the current collaboration but also on the past-time collaboration value. The value of collaboration is affected by time-invariant factors, as well as time. The time factor is a crucial element in determining the value of collaboration. This chapter discusses the effect of time on collaboration value, which influences the variation over time of the level of reliability of a collaborative environment. The proposal is based on the ability to measure the temporal variation of the reliability of a collaborative environment. Existing collaborative environments do not take this measurement time into account to determine the level of reliability of the collaboration. The simulations show that the approach offers more flexibility in interpreting the decay of collaboration over time.

Chapter 2

Luis Mariano Bibbo, LIFIA, Argentina
Claudia Pons, National University of La Plata, Argentina
Alejandro Fernandez, National University of La Plata, Argentina

Building groupware is a complex task. This chapter presents the use of the domain-specific language CSSL v2.0 collaborative software system language. CSSL provides simplicity, expressiveness, and precision to model the main concepts of collaborative systems, especially collaborative processes, protocols, and awareness. Models of collaborative systems are created via visual editors that support the concrete syntax of CSSL. According to the MDD methodology, models are independent of the implementation platform and are formally prepared to be transformed. In this implementation, the target of the transformation is a web application that provides a set of basic functions that developers can refine. Evaluation, validation, and verification of the language is performed, determining that the CSSL tools allow developers to solve central aspects of collaborative systems implementation in a simple and reasonable way. The evaluation determined that the CSSL metamodel has low complexity, with semantics strongly associated with UML and with good configuration possibilities.

### Chapter 3

In September 2021, the Government of India approved the extension of a guarantee worth INR 30.6 billion (US$4.1 billion) to the National Asset Reconstruction Company Ltd. (NARCL), also called a bad bank. In a move to address the mountain of NPAs in the banking sector, bad banks may bring some relief to banks or rather defer the crisis. However, historically bad banks have not been successful for countries like Mexico, Greece, South Korea, Argentina, and Italy. Technology can help manage the challenges posed by the mountain of NPAs in the Indian banking sector through emerging technologies like blockchain for transparency and artificial intelligence for streamlined processes. This chapter explains the FinTech way through new emerging technologies to resolve the problem of high non-performing assets and the role of introduction of bad banks to alienate illiquid and risky assets held by banks and financial institutions to clean their balance sheets by transferring their bad loans so that the banks can focus on their core business of taking deposits and lending money.

Social media-supported academic Apps such as Google Classroom, Zoom, ClassIn can simplify teaching and learning, even after the COVID-19 pandemic. Student engagement is a challenging task for educators in internet-enabled technology-enhanced learning platforms. This chapter investigates the role of various SNS platform to ensure sustainable learning. Quantitative data were collected (n = 285) using an online survey technique with the students from a recognized university in China. All the proposed hypotheses were supported. The findings indicated that constructs such as affective engagement (AE) and social engagement (SE) are significant forecasters of social interaction (SI) that may lead to achieve authentic learning task (ALTask) post COVID-19. Further, lack of attention (LAN) was found to significantly moderate social interaction and authentic learning tasks post COVID-19.

This chapter's goal is to identify the teacher mental framework oriented to knowledge management (KM) and compatible to the ubiquitous Nonaka's model, regarding the sharing and collaboration practices found in the EU platform eTwinning. The pilot-study shows that when information and communication technology (ICT) skills become standardized, teachers' behavioral attitudes related to sharing and collaboration should be observed from a more holistic perspective. The first part provides a general description of Nonaka's model in connection with the education sector. The second part offers a bird's eye view of the European context framed by EU Acts and frameworks of reference to identify the roots of an emerging teaching profile linked to the awareness of knowledge flow. The third part presents a pilot research involving the idea of innovation related to the growing attitudes of digital collaboration and sharing. Within the eTwinning practice-context, this chapter proposes to switch the general approach from a teacher learning perspective to a teacher "knowledge management" standpoint.

The COVID-19 pandemic has affected countries economically due to lack of documented guidance; it has also resulted in increased spread and mortality rate. This motivated the authors to design a disaster preparedness system to enable countries to plan strategically and strengthen their efforts in future events. Web-scraping technique is used for crowdsourcing both past and current information such as government policies, associated cost, the spreading and mortality rate, and the medicines used; the results are stored in a database. The framework aims to enable the government bodies and other stakeholders to detect, prevent, and respond to future novel pandemics. Thus, the proposed model aids as a reference tool and can be used for predictive analysis. This information collectively helps countries to acknowledge their strength, weakness, opportunity, and threat (SWOT) ranking and allows them in their national capacities to improve their strategies, infrastructure, and to draft plans in line with the most updated guidance.

### Chapter 7

The variety of opportunities offered by the internet makes it attractive for publishing, especially for developing nations previously unable to distribute publications on a global scale. However, Nigerian publishers striving to seize the moment are grossly under-reported in literature, notwithstanding that their innovations could create opportunities globally. This study, therefore, describes the progression of e-publishing in Nigeria with emphasis on e-publishing capacity building, collaboration, and outsourcing. Data were collected from publishers and their websites by means of in-depth interviews, website observation, and survey, and findings indicate that publishers are building e-publishing capacity by launching websites, e-book clubs, online bookshops, and e-libraries in schools and by collaborating with foreign e-book distribution firms. This study, therefore, provides updated information on an emerging market with huge investment and collaboration potential.

The recent decade has been witnessing an increasing number of studies committed to the use of Twitter in education. It is necessary to determine the effect of Twitter use on education through a meta-analytical review since related meta-analyses are scanty and previous findings are inconsistent. By searching a number of databases, the authors selected 23 publications to examine the effect of the use of Twitter in education. It is concluded that the use of Twitter exerts a significant and positive effect on general education, that the use of Twitter exerts a significant and positive effect on academic achievements in education, and that there are no significant gender differences in the effect of Twitter use in education. Other social media could also be considered in terms of their use in education.

### Chapter 9

The most important cause to the difficulties many freshmen feel to learn programming is their lack of generic problem solving skills and programming debugging skills on their own. On this basis, this chapter introduces a new learner's self-assessment environment as CEHL. The proposed system helps the learner to take full responsibility for learning and completing his work by relying on him to correct his mistakes. CEHL developed so-called S_Onto_ALPPWA in its current second version allowing comparing learners' productions with those elaborated by the teacher. The authors conducted to analyze the effectiveness of two developed versions of an automated assessment scoring tool. Version 1 and Version 2 of this tool are detailed in authors previously published articles by comparing them with the expert scoring. So to achieve this objective, the researchers use a correlational research design to examine the correlations between S_Onto_ALPPWA and expert raters' performances.

    Samuel O. Oladimeji, University of Calabar, Nigeria
    Idongesit E. Eteng, University of Calabar, Nigeria

This research study aimed at developing a distributed system of web-based collaboration that would create a research and innovation ecosystem for university-industry partnership. Based on in-depth literature review, the focus-group approach to qualitative research was conducted with key stakeholders in university-industry partnership coming together to understand the research problem and system requirements. The requirements gathered at the project initiation stage guided the system design and implementation of a distributed collaborative research and innovation system that runs on three separately located servers: two for two different universities and one for all industry players. The system developed was modeled to describe how it works and to demonstrate how it would meet the identified functional requirements. Recommendations were given to guide further research and development that would improve the impact of this research study.

    Rohit Vashisht, ABES Engineering College, Ghaziabad, India

Code smellings are not bugs or errors; rather, they are a fundamental deviation in software design that lowers code quality. Code smells don't always mean the software won't work; it will still provide a result, but it can slow down processing, increase the risk of failure and errors, and make the programme more vulnerable to future flaws. The conceptual theory behind code smell and its various kinds are discussed in this chapter. Identifying and eradicating code smells is a time-consuming and endless process with no guarantee that the software will be smell-free. Also, because it's very hard to uncover and eliminate all smells by hand, adopting automated code review techniques that can detect smells becomes essential. Code refactoring is one method of restructuring written code to reduce the effects of bad code smell on generated software code. A novel three-phase code refactoring framework has been proposed in this study. The effectiveness of Python code smell detection using Pysmell tool and refactoring using the rope automation tool are also studied in this chapter.

Short-form video sharing services (SVSs), such as TikTok, have rapidly grown in popularity in the recent years. Some evidence suggests that because SVSs allow users to quickly and easily create and consume on-demand content, they are addictive, and they appeal to a wide audience. The available literature attempting to explain this phenomenon remains scant. In order to fill this gap, the current study aims to examine the roles of habit and compatibility on SVS continuance intention and the interaction of these relationships with user experience, using TikTok as a context. To this goal, data collected from 157 university-student TikTok users are analyzed using structural equation modeling to determine whether these factors shape their continuance decisions. The findings show that habit and compatibility positively affect continuance intention while experience does not. This study enhances SVS continuance research by theorizing and empirically confirming that habit and compatibility are important influences in the context of continuing SVS usage.

Preface

Collaboration is working with others to achieve shared and explicit goals. Collaboration is a strategy that can be used in any type of workplace, including non-profits, corporations, government agencies, service providers, and educational institutions. All employers and employees in the organization can benefit from learning about different types of collaboration. According to LumApps, the employee experience platform, various types of collaborative working include team collaboration, community collaboration, network collaboration, cloud collaboration, video collaboration, internal collaboration, external collaboration, and strategic alliance. Recent advances in inter and intra organizational software and communication technologies have led to the development of what may be called as the e-collaboration concept. E-collaboration in its essence is a communication process between different parties through electronic devices to accomplish work goals. E-collaboration can be broadly defined as collaboration among individuals engaged in a common task using electronic technologies (Kock et al., 2001). Synchronous electronic collaboration technologies allow all participants from the same or different locations, time zones or organisations to collaborate on the same task in real time, while asynchronous collaboration is used when participants wish to share information, but simultaneous interaction is not necessary (Sundaravej, 2013; Akinsola & Munepapa, 2021). The impact of e-collaboration technologies on organizational forms and functions can be significant (Zammuto et al., 2007; Garrigos-Simon et al., 2012; de Vreede, et al., 2016). Organizations rely increasingly on e-collaboration tools to optimize performance (Cassivi, et al., 2004; Shannak, 2013; Wohlrab, et al., 2018; Akinsola & Munepapa, 2021). For example, growth in marketing communication has been observed with e-collaboration by sharing of information to a target audience in order to create a favorable and receptive scenario for certain a product, service or idea; the sharing is extended further to involve sharing of market information among organizations (IvyPanda, 2021). Through such sharing organizations are able to leverage their own areas of competence and gain a competitive advantage by acquiring richer content and better solutions in a creative and cost-effective way.

Effective collaboration technologies and tools are critical to the development of contemporary business landscapes, especially for the future of global business. Individuals and businesses can benefit from research on the design, execution, and assessment of collaboration applications that occur increasingly in the virtual environment. A virtual environment is a networked application that allows a user to interact with both the computing environment and the work of other users. Simply put, it is a networked common operating space. Once the fidelity of the virtual environment is such that it "creates a psychological state in which the individual perceives himself or herself as existing within the virtual environment" (Blascovich, 2002, p. 129), then the virtual environment (VE) has progressed into what could be described as the realm of immersive virtual environments (IVEs). Virtual environments both immersive and otherwise would be the realm in which all spheres of global business will operate, at least to a certain degree, going forward.

The book focuses on emerging technologies and tools for collaboration in virtual environments, including the cutting-edge areas of Automation, Computing and Intelligent Information Systems, as well as the state-of-the-art solutions covering various issues and challenges. Researchers and practitioners working in these areas discuss and share their views on new methods and techniques, including various collaboration and communication technologies. This book contributes to a fuller understanding of emerging collaboration technologies and tools for organizations and society in virtual environments, and provides insight for how to develop technologies and tools for collaboration, in particular, for global business in the post pandemic era. Furthermore, this book assesses the importance of technologies and tools for e-collaboration in the realm of global business in dealing with future crises similar to such as pandemics like the COVID -19. The book is organized into 12 chapters. A synopsis of each chapter is given below.

Chapter 1 (Temporal Variation of Collaboration in a Collaborative Environment) discusses the effect of time on collaboration value, which shows the reliability over time of a collaborative environment. The research proposal is based on the ability to measure temporal variation of the reliability of a collaborative environment. Existing collaborative environments do not track the level of reliability over time during the period of collaboration. The simulations show that the proposed approach offers more flexibility in interpreting the decay of collaboration over time.

Chapter 2 (Evaluation of A Model Driven Proposal to the Development of Groupware Systems) presents the use of the domain specific language CSSL v2.0 Collaborative Software System Language. CSSL provides simplicity, expressiveness, and precision to model the main concepts of collaborative systems, especially collaborative processes, and protocols. Models of collaborative systems are created via visual editors that support the concrete syntax of CSSL. Using the MDD methodology, models are independent of the implementation platform, and are formally prepared to be transformed for particular applications.

Chapter 3 (The Study of Fintech Way of Resolving Indian Banking's High Non-Performing Assets Through Emerging Technologies) explores the new emerging technology of Fintech to resolve the problem of high non-performing assets. The study uses the role of "Bad Bank" to alienate illiquid and risky assets held by other banks and financial institutions. These other banks can clean their balance sheets by transferring their bad loans to the "Bad Bank" so that the banks can focus on their core business of taking deposits and lending money.

Chapter 4 (Investigating the Role of Social Media on Student Engagement and Authentic Learning: Post COVID-19) investigates the role of social media to ensure sustainable learning. The findings indicated that constructs such as affective engagement (AE) and social engagement (SE) are significant forecasters of social interaction (SI) that may lead to achieve authentic learning task (ALTask) in the post COVID-19. Further, lack of attention (LAN) was found to significantly moderate social interaction and authentic learning tasks during post COVID-19.

Chapter 5 (Redefining Teachers' Interactions and Role Awareness: From a Learning Perspective to a Focus on Knowledge Management) is to identify a teacher's mental framework oriented to knowledge management (KM), and is compatible with the ubiquitous Nonaka's model, as applied to the sharing and collaboration practices found in the EU platform eTwinning. The pilot-study shows that when information and communication technology (ICT) skills become standardized, teachers' behavioral attitudes related to sharing and collaboration should be observed from a more holistic perspective. Within the eTwinning practice-context, this chapter proposes to switch the general approach from a teacher learning perspective to a teacher "knowledge management" standpoint.

Chapter 6 (Impact of COVID-19 on the Indian Economy and Future Disaster Preparedness System Using Web Scraping) aims to enable the government bodies and other stake holders to detect, prevent, and respond to future novel pandemics. Thus, the proposed model aids as a reference tool, and can be used for predictive analysis. This model helps countries to acknowledge their Strength, Weakness, Opportunity and Threat (SWOT) ranking, and allows them under their own national capacities to improve response strategies, infrastructure, and to draft plans in line with the most current guidance.

Chapter 7 (Progression of E-Publishing Capacity Building in Nigeria) describes the progression of e-publishing in Nigeria with emphasis on e-publishing capacity building, collaboration and outsourcing. Data were collected from publishers and their websites by means of in-depth interviews, website observation and survey, and the findings indicate that publishers are building e-publishing capacity by launching websites, e-book clubs, online bookshops and e-libraries in schools, and by collaborating with foreign e-book distribution firms. This study, therefore, provides updated information on an emerging market with huge investment and collaboration potential.

Chapter 8 (Exploring Academic Achievements and Gender Differences in Twitter-Assisted Education) is a study of 23 publications to examine the effect of the use of Twitter in education. The finding is that the use of Twitter exerts a significant and positive effect on general education and on academic achievements in education, and that there are no significant gender differences in the effect of Twitter use in education. Other social media could also be considered in terms of their use in education.

Chapter 9 (Computer Programming Practical Works Activities From Human to Automatic Scoring) introduces a new learner's self-assessment environment described as CEHL. The proposed system helps the learner to take full responsibility for learning and completing their work by relying on them to correct mistakes. The authors analyzed the effectiveness of two developed versions of an automated assessment scoring tool, and examined the correlations between variables such as experts raters' performance and other relevant variables by using a correlational research design.

Chapter 10 (Building a Distributed Web-Based Research and Innovation Ecosystem for University-Industry Partnership) develops a distributed system of web-based collaboration that creates a research and innovation ecosystem for University-Industry partnership. The system developed is modeled to describe how it works and to demonstrate how it will meet the identified functional requirements. Recommendations are given to guide further research and development that would improve on the impact of this research study.

Chapter 11 (An Empirical Analysis of Code Smelling and Code Restructuring in Python) discusses the conceptual theory behind code smell and its various kinds. Code refactoring is one method of restructuring written code to reduce the effects of bad code smell on generated software code. A novel three phase code refactoring framework has been proposed in this study. The effectiveness of Python code smell detection using the Pysmell tool and refactoring using the Rope automation tool is also studied in this chapter.

Chapter 12 (The Roles of Habit and Compatibility in the Continued Use of Short-Form Video Sharing Services: A Study of TikTok) aims to examine the roles of habit and compatibility on short-form video sharing (SVS) continuance intention and the interaction of these relationships with user experience, using TikTok as a context. The findings show that habit and compatibility positively affect continuance intention, while experience does not. This study enhances SVS continuance research by theorizing and empirically confirming that habit and compatibility are important influences in the context of continuing SVS usage.

Jingyuan Zhao
University of Toronto, Canada

Joseph Richards
California State University, Sacramento, USA
2022 June

REFERENCES

Akinsola, S., & Munepapa, J. (2021). Utilisation of e-collaboration tools for effective decision-making: A developing country public-sector perspective. *South African Journal of Information Management*, *23*(1), 1–7. doi:10.4102ajim.v23i1.1099

Blascovich, J. (2002). Social Influence within Immersive Virtual Environments. In R. Schroeder (Ed.), *The Social Life of Avatars: Presence and Interaction in Shared Virtual Environments* (pp. 127–145). Springer. doi:10.1007/978-1-4471-0277-9_8

Cassivi, L., Lefebvre, É., Lefebvre, L. A., & Majorique Léger, P. (2004). The Impact of E-collaboration Tools on Firms' Performance. *International Journal of Logistics Management*, *15*(1), 91–110. doi:10.1108/09574090410700257

de Vreede, G. J., Antunes, P., Vassileva, J., Gerosa, M. A., & Wu, K. (2016). Collaboration technology in teams and organizations: Introduction to the special issue. *Information Systems Frontiers*, *18*(1), 1–6. doi:10.100710796-016-9632-3

Garrigos-Simon, F. J., Lapiedra Alcamí, R., & Barberá Ribera, T. (2012). Social networks and web 3.0: Their impact on the management and marketing of organizations. *Management Decision*, *50*(10), 1880–1890. doi:10.1108/00251741211279657

IvyPanda. (2021, February 23). *E-Collaboration: Strategic and Competitive Opportunities*. https://ivypanda.com/essays/e-collaboration-strategic-and-competitive-opportunities/

Kock, N., Davison, R., Wazlawick, R., & Ocker, R. (2001). E-collaboration: A look at past research and future challenges. *Journal of Systems and Information Technology*, *5*(1), 1–8. doi:10.1108/13287260180001059

Shannak, R. (2013). The Impact of Using E-collaboration Tools on Company Performance. *European Scientific Journal*, *9*(10), 1–18.

Wohlrab, P., Knauss, E., Steghöfer, J., Maro, S., Anjorin, A., & Pelliccione, P. (2018). Collaborative traceability management: A multiple case study from the perspectives of organization, process, and culture. *Requirements Engineering*, *25*(0), 21–45.

Zammuto, R. F., Griffith, T. L., Majchrzak, A., Dougherty, D. J., & Faraj, S. (2007). Information technology and the changing fabric of organization. *Organization Science*, *18*(5), 749–762. doi:10.1287/orsc.1070.0307

Chapter 1
Temporal Variation of Collaboration in a Collaborative Environment

Rabie Barhoun
Ministry of Education National, Morocco

ABSTRACT

In recent years, collaborative environments play a significant role in collaboration work. The keys element of these environments is the process of collaboration. The calculation of the collaboration does not depend on the current collaboration but also on the past-time collaboration value. The value of collaboration is affected by time-invariant factors, as well as time. The time factor is a crucial element in determining the value of collaboration. This chapter discusses the effect of time on collaboration value, which influences the variation over time of the level of reliability of a collaborative environment. The proposal is based on the ability to measure the temporal variation of the reliability of a collaborative environment. Existing collaborative environments do not take this measurement time into account to determine the level of reliability of the collaboration. The simulations show that the approach offers more flexibility in interpreting the decay of collaboration over time.

INTRODUCTION

Recently, the covid 19 epidemic shows the importance and usefulness of collaborative environments in different sectors (Loda, et al., 2020). It is not the covid 19 epidemic the only reason that shows the need for a collaborative environment but also the case where collaborators are geographically distant from each other. Collaborative work in such an environment is teamwork aimed at achieving a common goal (Montebello, 2003; Aggarwal et al., 2020; Duque, et al., 2012; Haliloğlu, 2021). It is clear that the main element of these environments is collaborative work Formally, we can say that collaborative work is an essential process in the chain of realization of collaboration work to reach a common objective (Kotsopoulos, et al., 2010; Chen, et al., 2019). Barhoun (Barhoun, 2021a) has been proposed a reli-

DOI: 10.4018/978-1-6684-5027-7.ch001

able collaboration model during a collaborative activity in order to achieve a common goal. Yusri et al. (yusri, et al., 2020) have proposed a collaborative learning platform to help teens become more aware of privacy. (Mora, et al., 2020) have been proposed a collaborative work model to improve the learning process of science and engineering students. In (Barhoun, 2021b), Barhoun proposes collaboration as a trust assessment component of a collaborative environment.

The use of a distributed and collaborative environment is justified by several factors: (1) facilitating the sharing of information between distributed users; (2) enabling reliable collaboration between multiple users to make an important decision; and (3) coordinating and improving the collaborative process to accomplish shared tasks. Barhoun et al. (Barhoun, et al., 2019) discussed an emergency care case of a hospital where many remote actors involved, such as a doctor, specialist, nurse, etc., have to work together to care for the patient. In this case study, the authors assert that collaboration is an obligation, and all collaborators must have this goal to end this collaborative activity. In a collaborative environment, there are many factors influencing collaboration. Therefore, collaboration is a subjective and dynamic concept. Indeed, it is necessary to establish an effective collaboration model. Firstly, to formalize temporal variation of collaboration in a reliable and collaborative environment. Secondly, allowing better control of the temporal variation of collaboration value over time by manipulating a decay parameter. In a collaborative environment, there are many factors influencing collaboration. Therefore, collaboration is a subjective and dynamic concept. Indeed, it is necessary to establish an effective collaboration model. Firstly, to formalize temporal variation of collaboration in a reliable and collaborative environment. Secondly, allowing better control of the temporal variation of collaboration value over time by manipulating a decay parameter.

The proper functioning of the collaborative environment makes it possible to achieve an objective during a collaborative activity. Then this founded an idea of the reliability of the environment, which is now progressively concerned with the behavior of the protected environment is discussed by (Avizienis et al., 2004). Take the example of a hospital emergency care unit, before an emergency occurs, the emergency unit manager may want to know that all staff (remote or present) are ready to collaborate as reliably as they did last time. Over time, an emergency unit may experience performance degradation for certain reasons: (1) some collaborators are gone or absent, (2) staff experience in teamwork or collaboration, (3) some soft entities require maintenance, (4) certain energy sources require recharging, etc. This example shows that the collaborative reliability of the emergency cell would guide the reliability of the environment. Indeed, a collaborative environment is more reliable and stable for a user, tends to be perceived as more reliable in collaboration. Reliable collaboration gives an entity a guarantee or an assurance that the other collaboration entities behave or act by the expectations of the former entity according to a collaboration charter. Thus, in our example, the collaboration reliability of the emergency unit would guide the reliability of the environment.

The above shows that collaborators need collaborative environments, in which the raised the demand for measuring reliability level, the greater the collaboration. Nevertheless, the notion of collaboration reliability in a collaboration environment is well explored in the different fields: fault tolerance, computer security, etc. Defining and measuring the collaboration of a collaborative environment is based on the following elements: availability, trust, maintainability, … and time. However, we believe that the concept of collaboration inherent in the notion of reliability.

The most suitable collaborative models are based on the numerical representation of collaboration that changes over time. We hypothesize that the perceived value of collaboration is an intuitive measure of the degree of reliability of a reliable collaborative environment. Therefore, to serve our purpose goal, we consider the models that represent collaboration in a numeric interval (0, 1). We observe that it is reasonable and practical to model the temporal variation of collaboration when it is represented as a numerical value in a continuous range. In this sense, very few models have been proposed to address the issue of collaboration change over time. Unfortunately, no study has been proposed a collaboration model that addresses the question of how collaboration has evolved over time. In this chapter, collaboration is defined as a collaborative relationship between one entity and another entity in a specific context. We build on the above work to present a model of temporal variation of collaboration value in a reliable collaborative environment.

The rest of this chapter is structured as follows. Section 2 presents a model for temporal variation of collaboration that emphasized the varying the collaboration value over time, then the discussion and simulation are covered in this section. Section 3 concludes the chapter and discusses the scope for future work.

TEMPORAL VARIATION OF THE COLLABORATION MODEL

Collaboration Model

We focus on the collaboration model above, which represents collaboration as a value in a range (-1, 1). Consider the following definition:

Definition 1: *In a reliable collaborative environment, the collaboration value represents the ability to provide a reliable collaborative service that collaborators can trust.*

Where a collaboration value is between the interval (-1, +1), with a positive range indicating a collaboration, a negative range indicating a non-collaboration, and 0 indicating a neutral level. We neglect the negative range of collaboration, i.e. the non-collaboration aspect. Our goal is to use "collaboration value" as a measure of "reliability". If we were to adopt the notion of "non-collaboration" then this would represent an "unreliable" scenario. In this study, we are not looking to measure how "unreliable" a collaborative environment is, but rather we want to measure how reliable the collaborative environment is. In the model proposed above, the value of collaboration is assessed based on certain parameters such as: experience, time, etc. We borrow the same idea, but let's not focus on how changes in these settings affect collaboration (and reliability). Instead, we discuss how a collaboration value, assessed at a certain point in time, would change over a while without any variation in the underlying metrics. In addition, the model suggests that if a collaborative environment reaches the lower limit of reliability over time without any intervention, a collaboration event must change the contributing factors positively to increase the collaboration value. We also observe that during an activity, the collaboration evaluation relies significantly on the evaluation mechanism of the collaboration. For any collaborative environment whose reliability is assessed by collaboration, the user must have a policy (or policies) for the collaboration assessment process. This policy must answer the questions: what parameters and to what extent the collaboration value is influenced. So, we argue that how time would affect a collaboration value should be controlled by user-defined parameters and should be part of the collaboration evaluation policy. We illustrate this in a general architecture of a collaborative environment whose reliability is under discussion, see Figure 1.

Figure 1. Global architecture of the proposed model

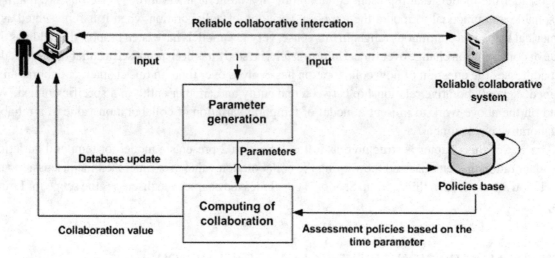

This architecture explains that the collaboration engine assesses the collaboration behavior based on the generated parameters and other policy information, including time variation parameters. In more detail, the control of temporal variation relies on policy from the input of the collaboration engine. Here, we suggest that the user (soft or human) has no possibility to use other parameters for the collaboration evaluation during a specific time. The adopted policy provides only the necessary information (time parameters) to evaluate the collaboration. The variation captured is influencing the reliability of the collaborative environment, as perceived by the user.

Variation of Collaboration Over Time

Based on perceptions of social behavior, we affirm that our general tendency is to neglect past events, regardless of their positive or negative outcome. Hence, if nothing happens, it will affect the user's perception, the collaboration will decrease to a neutral value over time. The decay is initially slow, then over time, the decay rate is faster, and finally, it reaches the neutral value. In other words, we propose that over time $t \circledR +\yen$, the collaboration $C \circledR 0$. This is inferred from the fact that recent collaboration will decrease very slowly, but the process of decrease accelerates as its ages and nothing is occurring to change it. The value of collaboration is almost zero and does not matter after some time. The mathematical modeling of this phenomenon can be done in different ways; however, the exponential-based modeling remains the most relevant. In the next section, we discuss the temporal variation of collaboration based on an exponential approach.

Parameterized Temporal Variation Model

The collaboration mode introduced above supports the change of collaboration over time in an exponential form, where collaboration decreases over time. In this chapter, we present the variation of collaboration over time according to the following modeling:

$$C_p = C_l \times e^{-(C_l \times \Delta t)^{2k}}$$ (1)

Here, C_p is the collaboration value computed at the present time, C_l is the last calculated collaboration value of which no parameter change is observed, Δt is the time difference between the present time and the last time, and k is the decay constant with $k \geq 1$, $k \in \mathbb{N}^*$ ($\mathbb{N}$ is the set of natural numbers).

According to a policy of environmental perception, the environment admin determines the parameter k that represents the rate of change of collaboration over time. We have two major extremes scenarios:

- For $\Delta t = 0$, that is to say at time $p = l$, $e^{-(C_l \times \Delta t)^{2k}} = 1$ and therefore $C_p = C_l$;
- For $\Delta t \to +\infty$, so $e^{-(C_l \times \Delta t)^{2k}} \to 0$. Therefore, $C_p \to 0$.

This confirms that the last known collaboration value decreases asymptotically to zero in infinite time.

Figure 2a. Collaboration value variation over time according to three decay parameters (k=1,2, 3); C_l=0.5

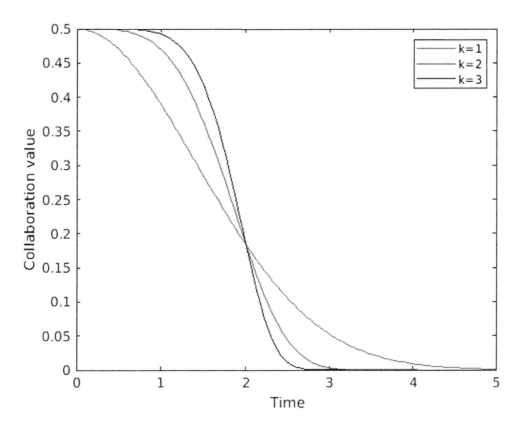

Figures 2a and 2b shows the collaboration value variation over time, according to three values of the decay constant k=1, 2 and 3. It is clear that the parameter k controls the rate of decrease of collaboration over time.

Figure 2b. Collaboration value variation over time according to three decay parameters (k=1,2, 3); C_l=0.9

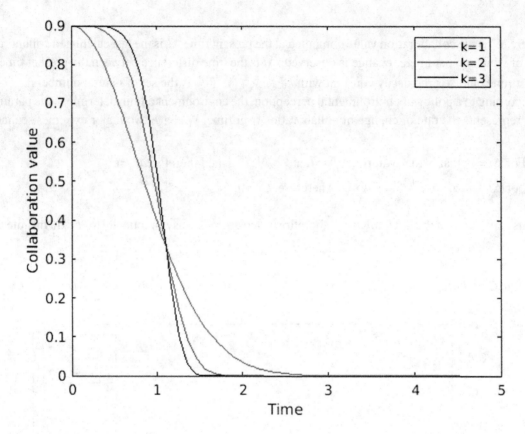

According to Figures 2a and 2b, the higher the value of k, the more rapidly the curve of the collaboration value decreases. Finally, all decay curves converge at some point before asymptotically approaching zero. To understand more the influence of decay parameter on the temporal variation of the collaboration, we define a fixed value for the decay parameter, and then vary the last computed collaboration value.

Figures 3a and 3b show that from a lower value of C_p, the rate of change of collaboration is slower. In other words, the lower of initial collaboration value, the more stable the variation for a longer time, then slowly decreases to approach the zero-value related to the higher initial collaboration value. The problem is more complex when collaboration is taken as a behavior of reliability.

In the following, we discuss the case where the value of the decay parameter does not depend on the initial value of the collaboration. Then, the modeling of collaborative temporal variation over time is formed as:

$$C_p = C_l \times e^{-\left(C_l^{-1} \times \Delta t\right)^{2k}} \qquad (2)$$

Figure 3a. Temporal variation of collaboration values (C_i=0.5, 0.7, 0.9) with fixed decay parameter k=1

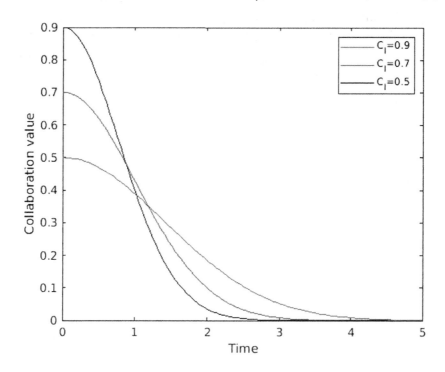

Figure 3b. Temporal variation of collaboration values (C_i=0.5, 0.7, 0.9) with fixed decay parameter k=3

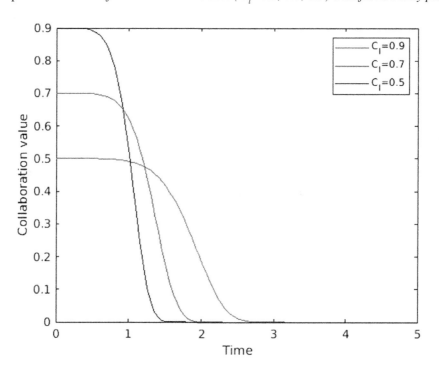

To analyze this representation exponential, we fix the value of the collaboration, and we vary the decay value k from the value 1 to the value 3. A very similar behavior of temporal variation of the collaboration in Figures 4a. and Figure 2a. (resp. Figure 4b. and Figure 2b). However, the decay is faster for equation (2), and the "intersection" is not removed between the curves, see Figures 4a and 4b.

Figure 4a. Collaboration value variation over time according to three decay parameters (k=1, 2, 3); C_i=0.5

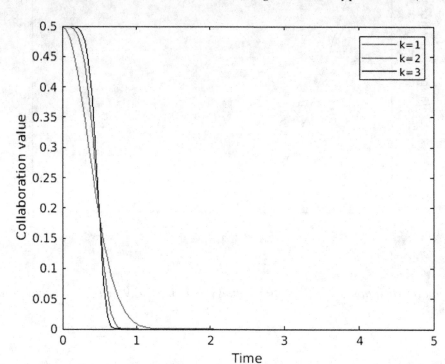

To observe the change from the last form of modeling, we fix the value of decay parameter, and we use the following initial collaboration values: 0.5, 0.7, and 0.9.

Figures 5a and 5b show a decrease in the collaboration value proportional to the initial value of C_i, unlike the previous exponential form. However, Figures 5a and 5b do not overlap like Figures 3a and 3b. The exponential behavior of this model is captured as follows:

- $C_p = C_i$ when $\Delta t \rightarrow 0$;
- $C_p \rightarrow 0$ when $\Delta t \rightarrow +\infty$.

The previous modeling in both forms: (1) the value of the decay constant depends on the initial value of the collaboration, (2) the value of the decay constant does not depend on the initial value of the collaboration, allows a real control over the decrease in collaboration over time.

Figure 4b. Collaboration value variation over time according to three decay parameters (k=1, 2, 3); C_i=0.9

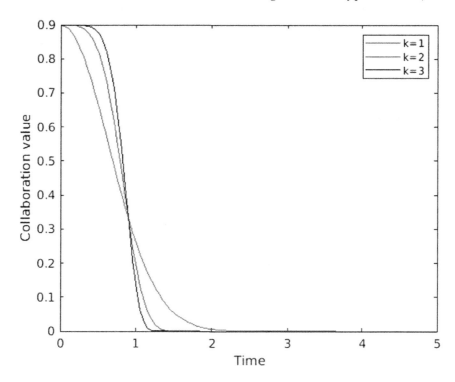

Figure 5a. Temporal variation of collaboration values (C_i=0.5, 0.7, 0.9) with fixed decay parameters k=1

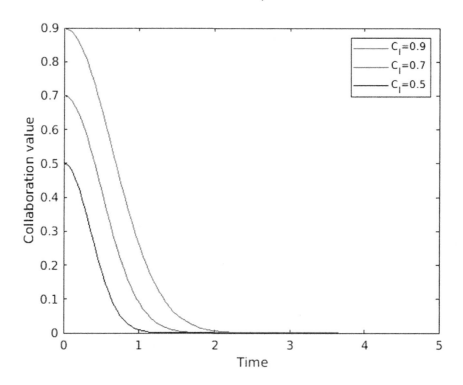

Figure 5b. Temporal variation of collaboration values (C_l=0.5, 0.7, 0.9) with fixed decay parameters k=3

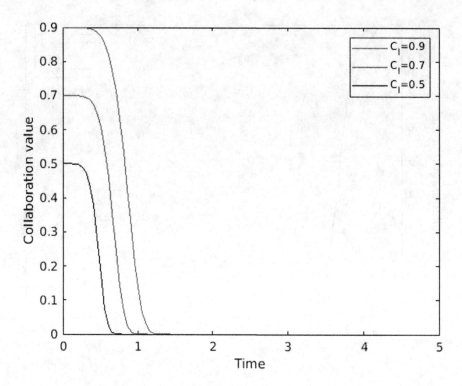

Two-Parameter Temporal Variation Model

In this part, we try to find a solution so that the user has more control over (i) how fast the rate of collaboration value decays and (ii) when the collaboration value will approach zero level. The decay rate, d, satisfies 0<d<1, is a user-defined value. Δ is the user-defined maximum decay time. We can, therefore, propose an exponential model of the decay of the value of collaboration over time using these two parameters:

$$C_p = C_l \times \left(1 + t \times e^{d \times (t - \delta)}\right)^{-1} \tag{3}$$

Where C_p represents the value of the current collaboration, and C_l represents the last value of collaboration after which no changes, in the parameter controlling collaboration, happened.

We consider the time of last collaboration calculation to be the starting point. That is, C_l is the collaboration value at t=0. after t crosses, the collaboration value becomes asymptotic to zero. That is, at t=0, $C_p = C_l$ and $\lim_{t \to \infty} C_c = 0$.

To demonstrate the proposed model with the d parameter, we present an example such as d=0.5, and δ=25, which implies that the collaboration value will decay at a rate 0.5 and the maximum decay will occur rat 25 time. The last collaboration value Cl is varied with values, as before, 0.3, 0.6, and 0.9. We specify here that the user is responsible for assigning the values for the parameter, d, above. The corresponding temporal behavior is illustrated in Figure 6. We observe the similar diminution of collaboration as depicted by equation 2, illustrated in Figure 5a. We also observe that the proposed model does not suffer from anomaly observed in equation 2 that is illustrated in figure 4.

Figure 6. Temporal variation of collaboration values (C_l=0.3, 0.6, 0.9) with fixed decay parameters: d=0.5 and δ=25

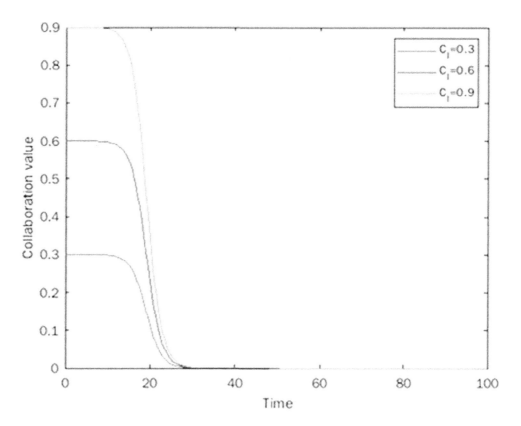

In the following example, we set C_l=0.9 as the last calculated collaboration value. The decay rate d is kept constant with a value of 0.25, but the maximum decay time varying between 25, 50, 75. Figure 7 shows that the same initial collaboration C_l asymptotically approaches zero level at a specified time unit, however, this does not influence the decay significantly as the rate of decay is kept constant.

Next, we examine variation of decay rate with same initial collaboration (C_l=0.9). Figure 8 presents diminution of C_l with time where the rate of decay d is varying but the collaboration value is kept constant at C_l=0.9.

Figure 8 shows that the higher the value of d, the greater the decrease compared to the same starting value of the collaboration. This illustrates that the user can choose, according to his level of "forgetting", an appropriate value for *d* and *δ*.

Figure 7. Temporal variation of collaboration with fixed collaboration value (C_i=0.9) and decay rate: d=0.5.

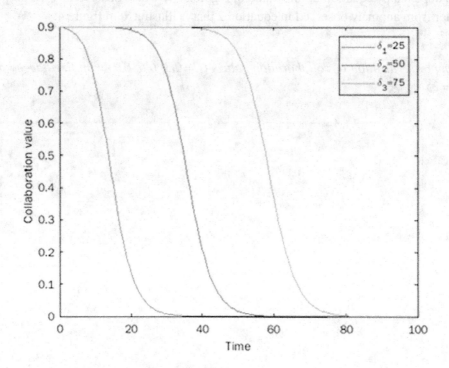

Figure 8. Temporal variation of collaboration with fixed collaboration value (C_i=0.9) and maximum decay δ=50.

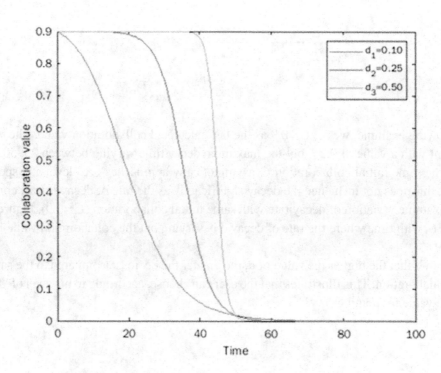

CONCLUSION AND FUTURE WORK

Collaboration is an essential factor in a collaborative environment, used as a reliability criterion of such a environment. The issue that we are trying to resolve is how this measure of reliability, is captured by the value of collaboration, changes over time. However, collaboration is a social behavior, then even if there is no external factor influencing the collaboration value, the time elapsed is sufficient to reduce the last computed collaboration value. In this chapter, first, we have proposed a temporal variation of collaboration model. Second, we have simulated the temporal variation of a collaboration model based on a two-form exponential representation time variation model to control the variation of the collaboration value over time.

The temporal effect in all existing collaboration models is a critical issue. The proposed model allows control of the temporal variation of collaboration over time by manipulating a single decay parameter. The main drawbacks of this model, in both forms of exponential, are: (1) the user has no control over the duration after which the value of the collaboration should be considered negligible, (2) the user cannot predict when the collaboration value will tend towards the neutral value. To camouflage the defects of the proposed first model, we proposed the second model, based on two parameters, to control the collaboration change. This last model allows controlling for declining collaboration behavior but is still not flexible enough. Even with this model, the user still cannot precisely control the retention of old collaboration values in terms of quantity and duration.

In future work, we will try to find a new temporal variation model of collaboration where the user has more control over the temporal variation rate of collaboration with a reduced overhead of increasing the complexity of the model. However, this additional cost would be worth having a fine-grain measure of the reliability of a system.

REFERENCES

Aggarwal, S., Srivastava, M. K., & Bharadwaj, S. S. (2020). Towards a definition and concept of collaborative resilience in supply chain: A study of 5 Indian supply chain cases. *International Journal of Information Systems and Supply Chain Management*, *13*(1), 98–117. doi:10.4018/IJISSCM.2020010105

Al Omoush, K. S. (2018). Web-Based Collaborative Systems and Harvesting the Collective Intelligence in Business Organizations. *International Journal on Semantic Web and Information Systems*, *14*(3), 31–52. doi:10.4018/IJSWIS.2018070102

Avizienis, A., Laprie, J. C., Randell, B., & Landwehr, C. (2004). Basic concepts and taxonomy of dependable and secure computing. *IEEE Transactions on Dependable and Secure Computing*, *1*(1), 11–33. doi:10.1109/TDSC.2004.2

Barhoun, R. (2021a). Reliable Collaboration in a Distributed Collaborative Environment: Modeling and Computing. International Review on Computers and Software.

Barhoun, R. (2021b). A Trust and Activity Based Access Control Model for Preserving Privacy and Sensitive Data in a Distributed and Collaborative System: Application to a Healthcare System. International Review on Computers and Software.

Barhoun, R., Ed-Daibouni, M., & Namir, A. (2019). An Extended Attribute-Based Access Control (ABAC) Model for Distributed Collaborative Healthcare System. *International Journal of Service Science, Management, Engineering, and Technology*, *10*(4), 81–94. doi:10.4018/IJSSMET.2019100105

Chen, B., Hatada, K., Okabayashi, K., Kuromiya, H., Hidaka, I., Yamamoto, Y., & Togami, K. (2019, November). Group Activity Recognition to Support Collaboration in Creative Digital Space. In Conference Companion Publication of the 2019 on Computer Supported Cooperative Work and Social Computing (pp. 175-179). doi:10.1145/3311957.3359471

Dewan, P. (1999). Architectures for collaborative applications. *Computer Supported Cooperative Work*, *7*, 169–193.

Duque, R., Rodríguez, M. L., Hurtado, M. V., Bravo, C., & Rodríguez-Domínguez, C. (2012). Integration of collaboration and interaction analysis mechanisms in a concern-based architecture for groupware systems. *Science of Computer Programming*, *77*(1), 29–45. doi:10.1016/j.scico.2010.05.003

Haliloğlu, E. Y. (2021). Efficiency Assessment of University-Industry Collaboration. In University-Industry Collaboration Strategies in the Digital Era (pp. 155-175). IGI Global.

Innes, J. E., & Booher, D. E. (2016). Collaborative rationality as a strategy for working with wicked problems. *Landscape and Urban Planning*, *154*, 8–10. doi:10.1016/j.landurbplan.2016.03.016

Kotsopoulos, D. (2010). When collaborative is not collaborative: Supporting student learning through self-surveillance. *International Journal of Educational Research*, *49*(4-5), 129–140. doi:10.1016/j.ijer.2010.11.002

Loda, T., Löffler, T., Erschens, R., Zipfel, S., & Herrmann-Werner, A. (2020). Medical education in times of COVID-19: German students' expectations–A cross-sectional study. *PLoS One*, *15*(11), e0241660. doi:10.1371/journal.pone.0241660 PMID:33206678

Montebello, A. R. (2003). Beyond Teams: Building the Collaborative Organization. *Personnel Psychology*, *56*(4), 1070.

Mora, H., Signes-Pont, M. T., Fuster-Guilló, A., & Pertegal-Felices, M. L. (2020). A collaborative working model for enhancing the learning process of science & engineering students. *Computers in Human Behavior*, *103*, 140–150. doi:10.1016/j.chb.2019.09.008

Yusri, R., Abusitta, A., & Aïmeur, E. (2020). Teens-Online: A Game Theory-Based Collaborative Platform for Privacy Education. *International Journal of Artificial Intelligence in Education*, 1–43.

Chapter 2
Evaluation of a Model–Driven Proposal to the Development of Groupware Systems

Luis Mariano Bibbo
https://orcid.org/0000-0003-4950-3605
LIFIA, Argentina

Claudia Pons
https://orcid.org/0000-0003-1149-0976
National University of La Plata, Argentina

Alejandro Fernandez
National University of La Plata, Argentina

ABSTRACT

Building groupware is a complex task. This chapter presents the use of the domain-specific language CSSL v2.0 collaborative software system language. CSSL provides simplicity, expressiveness, and precision to model the main concepts of collaborative systems, especially collaborative processes, protocols, and awareness. Models of collaborative systems are created via visual editors that support the concrete syntax of CSSL. According to the MDD methodology, models are independent of the implementation platform and are formally prepared to be transformed. In this implementation, the target of the transformation is a web application that provides a set of basic functions that developers can refine. Evaluation, validation, and verification of the language is performed, determining that the CSSL tools allow developers to solve central aspects of collaborative systems implementation in a simple and reasonable way. The evaluation determined that the CSSL metamodel has low complexity, with semantics strongly associated with UML and with good configuration possibilities.

DOI: 10.4018/978-1-6684-5027-7.ch002

INTRODUCTION

Groupware also known as Collaborative Systems are applications in which a group of users, following a common goal, develop different joint activities. The collaborative software allows them to share information, communicate, collaborate, and coordinate joint activities. According to (Ellis, Gibbs, and Rein 1991; Grudin 1994), collaboration platforms are "Computer-based systems that support groups of people engaged in a common task (or goal) and that provide an interface to a shared environment".

A main characteristic of the collaborative systems is the equilibrium between the individual work and the effort the users must do to achieve the common goal. To this end, the collaborative system offers coordination mechanisms (Dourish and Bellotti 1992; Grudin and Poltrock 1997) for organizing the activities. For example, a coordination protocol can specify the collaborative tasks to be developed, the order in which they must be developed, and the specific tasks that each role can perform in each state at any time.

Additionally, to take more advantage of the shared environment, the users can be informed regarding the actions that the other users perform and how these actions affect the work environment (Gutwin and Greenberg 2002; Gutwin, Greenberg, and Roseman 1996). This information provided by the system is known as awareness. According to (Dourish and Bly 1992) the awareness is the perception or knowledge of the group and of the activities performed by others that provides context for your own activities. In particular, awareness information allows users to coordinate their work based on knowledge of what others are doing or have done. For example, users are able to see the changes in the shared documents or the degree of progress of the common tasks, as explained in (Collazos et al. 2019).

The most frequent types of awareness are presence, location, density, user data (Age, Nationality, etc.), activity level, actions, places where you were, places where you performed the actions, changes you made, objects you control, objects you can reach, information you can see, intentions, abilities, and influence. Past awareness data is frequently stored, analyzed, and presented. Awareness information can be grouped to increase effectiveness. For example, when the user's presence is displayed, other information such as status, location, or resources can be attached to it, thus improving the effectiveness of awareness.

Without doubt, building collaborative systems with awareness is a complex task that requires specific software modeling (Collazos et al. 2019; Gallardo et al. 2011; Kamoun, Tazi, and Drira 2012). However, traditional approaches, based on mainly coding the applications, are still used in the development process of these software systems. On the one hand, there is no clear documentation of design decisions taken during the coding phase, making the evolution and the maintenance of the systems difficult. When we use general purpose languages (Java, C++, C#, etc.) instead of domain specific languages, the possibility of generalizing concepts - that could be extracted, re-used and applied in different systems - is wasted and the code is written from scratch over and over again. On the other hand, models and diagrams created in the early stages quickly lose their value as coding progresses.

In this context, the goal of our work was to investigate the application of modern technologies for developing collaborative systems, in particular the Model Driven software Development approach (MDD) (Brambilla, Cabot, and Wimmer 2012; Stahl et al. 2006), that proposes to improve quality and efficiency of the software construction processes. In this paradigm, models assume a leading role in the software development process, going from being merely descriptive entities that lose value as the development progresses, to becoming artifacts from which implementations are automatically derived.

The MDD initiative promotes:

○ Abstraction: the use of a higher level of abstraction in both the specification of the problem to be solved and the corresponding solution.

○ Automation: increased confidence in computer-aided automation to support analysis, design, and execution.

○ Standardization: the use of industrial standards to facilitate interaction between applications and technological evolution.

One of the key benefits of applying MDD is the flexibility to face technological changes. High-level models are free of implementation details, which facilitates adaptation to changes to the underlying technology platform or the deployment architecture.

A basic concept used in the MDD field is the idea of creating models for a specific domain through Domain-Specific Languages (DSLs), focused and specialized to that domain (Robert et al. 2009). These languages allow designers to specify the solution using problem domain concepts directly. End products are then automatically generated from these high-level specifications.

Following our goal of finding better tools for developing collaborative systems, we designed and implemented CSSL v2.0 -Collaborative Software System Language-, a DSL built using the metamodeling mechanism as a UML extension. This DSL has been validated and verified.

The rest of the paper is organized as follows. Section 2 describes the most relevant works related to the modeling of collaborative systems. Then. section 3 describes the abstract syntax of CSSL v2.0, using the metamodeling technique and a set of editors implementing its concrete syntax. In section 4 applying the MDD methodology, the language semantics was defined through model-to-text transformations, obtaining executable code from the models expressed in the CSSL v2.0 language. . Section 5 elaborates a case study about the application of the language to model a complex collaborative system. Section 6 compare CSSL with related works. Section 7 shows the evaluation of the DSL using as reference the work of (Robert et al. 2009) to later discuss its validation and verification using as reference the work of (Sargent 2013). Finally, conclusions and lines of future work are presented.

Background

In this section we present inspirational and foundational works related to the design of Collaborative Systems. This information is combined with (Bibbo, Giandini, and Pons 2016), where software engineering resources to design Collaborative Systems in a standardized, efficient and automated way were searched and analyzed.

Firstly, a cluster of documents published by a group of scientists from the Laboratory of User Interaction and Software Engineering of Castilla La Mancha University were analyzed. In these articles (Belkadi et al. 2013; Gallardo et al. 2011; Gallego et al. 2011; Kamoun et al. 2012; Teruel et al. 2011, 2012, 2013, 2014; Vieira, Tedesco, and Salgado 2010), published between 2011 and 2014, the authors progressively define a language to model CSCW systems requirements. Initially, a language named CSRML (Teruel et al. 2011) (Collaborative System Requirements Modelling Language) was proposed as an extension of i* Goal-Oriented specification. The language presents a set of basic elements for modeling the special collaboration features of CSCW systems, such as goal, role, actor, task and awareness. These elements are connected via a set of relationships, for example Playing link, Participation link, Responsibility link. Then, in 2012 the authors conducted various experiments and comparisons with different Goal Oriented techniques (Teruel et al. 2012) (e.g., NFR framework, i* and Kaos) in order to determine which is the most suitable one to specify requirements of collaborative systems. They showed that the understandability was higher for the models specified with CSRML than for those specified with other methods, especially for collaborative aspects. Then they build a CASE tool that provides support for CSRML for specifying CSCW system requirements (Teruel et al. 2013). The tool was implemented as a Visual Studio 2012 extension by using the Visualization and Modeling SDK. Finally, in 2014 they made a usability experiment of the CSRML CASE tool 2012 (Teruel et al. 2014), identifying some usability flaw to be solved in the next releases of the application, as well as giving a general overview on how to develop this kind of tools by means of Visual Studio Modelling SDK.

The CSRML language is based on the abstract concepts of "elements" and "relationships", from which, concrete elements are defined, such as goal, task, role, resource and general awareness. This definition leaves out other important concepts such as Session, Tool and Workspace. The CSRML language is not expressive enough for the specification of collaborative processes seen as a set of ordered tasks in pursuit of a common goal. Several collaborative specifications, such as "which tasks can be performed at any time", "which sessions can be performed at a given time", or "under which conditions a task can be run", cannot be expressed in the language. Because of this drawback, awareness information related to the processes cannot be defined in the model. For example, how far advanced the processes are, how many of them are active or what process is about to begin.

Although a detailed description of the CSRML language features is provided, it fails to define a rigorous metamodel supporting the language. On the other hand, the CSRML CASE tool 2012, is not based on standards and is not integrated with the standard UML, which prevents us from using UML related tools such as plugins, code generators or editors.

In (Belkadi et al. 2013) a detailed literature review about the concept of awareness is presented. This review helps to identify key awareness-related requirements for the development of collaborative systems. Researchers points out that the awareness is a multi-faceted concept, and thus they have proposed different types of awareness and added adjectives to define the key facets of this concept (social, mutual, activity, etc.). They also concluded that collaborative systems which intend to support awareness must meet many requirements. In (Gutwin et al. 1996), a list of questions covering the main facets of awareness was proposed.

Regarding this literature survey, the following concepts have been frequently used and should be the basis of a robust awareness-focused model:

- **Context element:** The context or situation is modeled through a set of elements
- **Task and activity:** Describe what is expected to be done and what the actor is really doing.
- **Resource:** It describes an element of the context. This element contributes to, or is used during, the fulfillment of an interaction.
- **Interaction:** The concept of interaction plays a central role in activity theory, in collaborative design and in Business Process Modeling (BPM).
- **Role:** According to the theories of organization, a generic structure for these interactions can be defined according to the major categories of contributions (or roles). In a normal work situation, functional roles are formally established as particular job positions.

In (Kamoun et al. 2012), FADYRCOS (A Framework for DYnamic Reconfiguration of networked COllaborative Systems) is presented. It supports semantic adaptation enabling the awareness of the presence/absence, roles and tasks of collaborators. This framework is based on a generic multi-level modeling approach that ensures multi-level adaptation. They intend to support collaboration in distributed environments where sessions can be implicit, new mechanisms are needed for managing session evolution and role changes. A multi-level modeling architecture is proposed with 3 levels:

- **Collaboration Level:** The collaboration level provides a session level abstraction. It describes how the members of a group are organized within sessions where they can send and receive data flows.
- **Application level:** The retained model in this level is a domain specific ontology that represents concepts and relations modeling the context of the application. Such ontology depends on the application domain, hence it will be provided by the designer of the collaborative system using the framework. The main generic collaboration elements that will be specialized are: Node, Group, Role and hasSession.
- **Messaging Level:** For this level, two communication paradigms are considered: the Event Based Communication and the Peer-To-Peer communication.

One of the interesting features of the work is the deployment service where adaptation needs related to collaboration are handled. On the one hand, a set of services representing the current state of a session is proposed (Connect, Quit, AddToGroup, AddRole, RemoveRole, etc.) and on the other hand it allows the dynamic creation of spontaneous sessions between participants (createSession, closeSession, joinSession, quitSession). These services allow you to link the specifications made in the design stage with different implementations.

In (Gallardo et al. 2011) an ontology of awareness for modeling collaborative systems is presented. First of all, a review was performed with the aim of elaborating a theoretical foundation, which is useful for an adequate understanding of the work. One of the most outstanding contributions in this field is the Theory of Awareness by (Gutwin and Greenberg 2002), which includes a framework that defines different awareness elements and makes validation of awareness support possible by means of a set of relevant questions ("Who, What, Where").

The ontology presented is divided into three sub-ontologies. First, we have the sub-ontology of the application domain, which includes the application domain concepts, such as entities, properties and relationships, that are content that users will manipulate with the system. Next, the workspace sub-ontology, which deals with the collaborative tasks of the modeling process to be supported and the tools used to implement such tasks. Finally, a new sub-ontology was added, describing the concepts relating to awareness in the scope of collaborative systems for modeling.

The study addresses the awareness problem in collaborative systems in two aspects. On the one hand the concept of awareness appears modeled with two subclasses Workspace and Group Awareness. On the other hand, introduces the concept of Awareness mechanism depicting how the awareness is going to be handled. For example, when you want to inform that a user accesses to a session, the Access Awareness Mechanism is used. In other words, on one hand we specify the "What kind of awareness is reported" and on the other hand, we describe "Which event/action is activated".

In (Gallego et al. 2011) a set of Awareness Support Widgets is described. This proposal is an extension of a previous work of the same authors published in (Gallardo, Bravo, and Redondo 2012; Molina et al. 2013). In this metamodel the connection between the awareness model and the traditional concepts of collaborative systems (e.g., Workspace, Session, Collaborative Process, Tool, etc.) is not clearly defined. Additionally, certain types of awareness are not supported by the metamodel, for example awareness-related activities performed by users cannot be specified and the progress of a collaborative process cannot be displayed.

In (Vieira et al. 2010) a metamodel called Context Metamodel is presented. This work is not specifically about awareness; however, it includes some interesting concepts to specify the awareness in collaborative systems. The main class in the metamodel is ContextualElement class (like collaborative element used in groupware). Awareness information can be attached to this class. In the proposed metamodel there are a set of useful enumeration types, such as the ContextType that lists different kinds of awareness (i.e., the Gutwin's and Greenberg's list: "who", "what", "where" "when" "why"). Another enumeration type is the UpdateType defining when the awareness is updated. And finally, the AcquisitionType determining the mechanism by which awareness information is acquired.

Using the proposed metamodel collaborative processes cannot be fully modeled. Several collaborative aspects, such as "which tasks can be performed at any time", "which sessions can be performed at a given time", or "under which conditions a task can be run", cannot be expressed in the model. Because of this drawback, awareness information related to the processes cannot be defined in the model. For example, how advanced the processes are, how many of them are active or what processes are about to begin.

In (Briggs, Gert-Jan de Vreede, and Kolfschoten 2007) the idea of thinklet is presented as a design patterns for collaborative work practices. Collaboration engineers use thinkLets as building-blocks for creating reusable collaboration process designs to be transferred to practitioners to execute for themselves without the ongoing intervention of professional facilitators. The collection of thinkLets forms a pattern language for creating, documenting, communicating, and learning group process designs. Each thinkLet must specify a set of rules that prescribe the actions that people in different roles must perform using the capabilities provided to them under some set of constraints specified in the parameters.

In (Gallardo et al. 2012) a model-driven method for the development of domain-independent collaborative modeling tools was proposed. This method consists of a methodological framework, a conceptual framework and a technological framework. The methodological framework defines the phases to be carried out when applying the method, whilst the conceptual framework is made up of the meta-models used in the method and the transformation processes established between them. Finally, the technological framework consists of the integration of some plug-ins from the Eclipse Modeling Project with some add-ons which provide collaborative functionality. The work proposes a domain design within the conceptual framework, describing the atomic elements to be edited collaboratively. The collaborative tools that will be used in the system are some specific editors and a few other classic tools of collaborative systems (i.e, chat or news).

Then, in (Greenberg and Gutwin 2016) the work of (Tenenberg, Roth, and Socha 2016) is analyzed. The restrictions and limitations of *Gaze Awareness* were pointed out and focused on how this type of awareness can be sensed, transmitted and displayed through technology. It showed how difficult it is to build groupware with awareness in relation to: technical constraints, reciprocity, design for groups and privacy, plausible deniability and mediating distraction. In summary, designing for we-awareness is non-trivial both for technical reasons and because people may not want others to "know that you know that I know". Greenberg and Gutwin concluded that Tenenberg's article raises some valuable possibilities for the design of distributed awareness systems. And added that they and other researchers have been thinking about supporting these kinds of shared behavior (although not calling it we-awareness) for many years.

Groupware can be also seen to help a face-to-face group or a distributed group. Furthermore, a groupware system can be conceived to support real-time (synchronous) interaction or an asynchronous, non-real-time interaction. In (Handzic 2011) the authors explore which technologies are being most used to share knowledge in organizations and how effective they are in different application contexts.

In (Peters, Lang, and Lie 2011) a groupware system is presented as a communication platform. The system is described and some experience of the use of it is reported. The software was developed on the basis of the open-source content management system/ Web application server ZOPE (Latteicr and Pelletier 2002). They presented an example of a groupware application for the case of a different place and different time. The system works with different roles that have different functionality enabled. They also introduce the concept of protocol, to change the way of using the operations of the activities (open and closed modus).

Finally, in (Molina et al. 2013) the main conceptual frameworks were analyzed and the concepts that are generally used are specified. (Activity, Action / Operation, Agent / User, Group, Role, Tool, Shared Object / Resource, Awareness Rules). Furthermore, it is mentioned that modeling cooperation involves the inclusion of special coordination tasks at the end of the cooperative activity to enable the group to collect their individual contributions in the final product (group solution), as well as decision-making or agreements in this production process. In this latter case, they are talking about the existence of protocols for interaction and coordination among the group members and they come to the following conclusion:

- The language should support the modeling of different levels of abstraction and, in particular, the decomposition of tasks into subtasks.
- It should be able to specify aspects of coordination (one of the basic concepts in CSCW systems).
- The models that specify the work to be done will allow specifying the workflow.

Molina's work presents the abstract syntax of CIAN notation and provides a conceptual framework that encompasses the elements previously identified as relevant to model groupware applications. Like the work in (Gallardo J et al), a model describing the atomic elements to be edited collaboratively is supported; this may be useful in some domains, but it restricts the variety of potential tools to be used.

REQUIREMENTS TO DESIGN COLLABORATIVE SYSTEMS WITH AWARENESS

Based on a the previous section and a systematic literature review (Bibbo et al. 2016), we have elaborated a list of requirements to achieve the adequate design and planning of the awareness in collaborative systems:

Req 1: Having a conceptual model with the concepts intervening in the collaborative systems.

As seen in the present review there are a few works with abstract models that allow software designers to include the concept of awareness in the collaborative systems. One of the first conclusions we may arrive at is that in general there is a coincidence among the studies analyzed regarding the elements found in the collaborative system. These elements, "Shared Object", "Tool", "Session", "Workspace", "User/Role", "Group", are related to the concept of awareness. One of the questions used to identify the social awareness is: "What roles will the other members of the group assume?" in which the concept of role appears. There are also other examples of workspace awareness that ask: How can I help other participants to complete the project? or What are they doing? or Where are they?.

Also, most of the studies incorporate the concept of "Task", which represents the collaborative tasks that users have to perform. However, the studies do not model processes that involve these tasks and that allow giving them a logical order.

Req 2: Having a model that allows expressing the awareness related to the concepts that intervene in the system.

The model has to cover the different alternatives that awareness presents (workspace awareness, social awareness, group awareness, etc). These elements are related to the concept of awareness. In the design of collaborative systems, we must be able to say which type of awareness each of the elements in the system is going to have. For example, we must be able to say that performance of the other users is going to be shown in a given session. We also we must be able to determine somehow in what space the users are.

Req 3: Having a model of the collaborative process as a set of collaborative activities (sessions) developed by users.

This review revealed that there is not a proposal that covers all the needs for modeling the awareness. There is no highlighted model and therefore, there is no standard de fact accepted by the academic community. Most studies show examples of application use that utilizes awareness information in a particular domain (educational situation, health care, etc.). There are a few studies dealing with awareness modeling through the conceptual models, abstractions or meta-models. Some works present formal models considering req 1, which is related to the main concepts. Few of them allow incorporating the awareness of the designs and relate it to the main concepts. As stated above, there are no works that allow modeling collaborative processes giving the tasks a logical order. For example, the design should express which task has to be performed before another one or what conditions have to be fulfilled to progress on a particular task.

Req 4: Allow associating awareness information of the collaborative processes.

Previous requirement reveled that it is necessary to consider the awareness in relation to the collaborative processes. For example, an interesting awareness could be to inform the level of progress that a group of users has in a project or which tasks are in progress and which ones are about to start. To this end, it is necessary to obtain a model that allows modeling the type of awareness and relates it to the collaborative processes.

Req 5: Allow modeling the different status developed during an interaction session (interaction protocols).

On the other hand, it is well known that sessions in the collaborative systems allowed the users to collaborate using different shared tools and objects. The sessions are not static, but change their status when the users perform their activities. For example, in a session in which a user is introducing a topic, another user may want to ask a question. If the system allows the user to ask for authorization to ask questions, then the speaker will be able to call on another user who would like to speak or continue with his/her speech. As can be seen, the session presents a status when the speaker is delivering his speech and another one when the student is asking. During the speech, the system operates in a determined way and allows the users to perform a set of actions. When the user asks for authorization to ask a question the system changes the status. The modeling of these different status describes how the system changes according to the interaction of the users

Req 6: Incorporate different types of awareness associated with the stages of the session.

The previous requirement revealed that it is necessary to model the awareness related to the different status of the session. According to the above example when a user raises his/her hand to ask a question, the system should inform the other participants that someone wants to ask a question. The speaker is the one who may authorize the other user to ask. When the speaker authorizes the user to ask, the other users in the session should receive a particular piece of awareness information indicating the user who is asking a question.

Req 7: utilization of standards in the construction of the involved models

Finally, the use of industrial standards as a mean to facilitate communications among developers is recommended. This standardization makes it possible the interaction among different applications and products that are based on those standards and on the technological specification. If the model is defined from the meta-model of UML, different plug-ins based on the UML meta-model could be used to see some aspects of our products. For example, editors related to UML can be used to describe our collaborative system.

As a general conclusion we note that in addition to the abstract model that considers the main elements of the collaborative systems it is necessary to have some modeling elements that allow associating different types of awareness to the fundamental concepts of the collaborative systems. Also, two aspects of the dynamic modeling of these systems should be considered. On the one hand, incorporation of collaborative process as a consequence of tasks or collaborative activities and on the other hand, the interaction protocols that describe the participation of users/roles in each collaborative task.

THE DOMAIN-SPECIFIC LANGUAGE CSSL

This section presents the design and implementation of the domain specific language CSSL v2.0 - Collaborative Software System Language -built as an extension of UML, using the metamodeling mechanism. CSSL provides simplicity, expressiveness and precision to model the main concepts of collaborative systems, especially collaborative processes, protocols and awareness. This language meets all the requirements defined in the previous section.

Abstract and Concrete Syntax

The abstract syntax specifies the language structure while the concrete syntax, which is usually a graphical notation, defines the way language constructions look like to the user. It is important to note that the same abstract syntax might have several different concrete syntaxes. In the case of the CSSL language, the metamodeling approach is used to express the abstract syntax while a set of graphical editors are applied for implementing the concrete syntax. These editors allow metamodel instantiation.

Metamodeling is a well-established and effective technology in the field of language engineering. The CSSL metamodel was built as an extension of the UML metamodel. Therefore, it includes UML, and all its metaclasses can be used. To give an example, Figure 1, Figure 2 and Figure 3 show in dark gray some UML metaclasses with their CSSL-specific extensions.

Figure 1. CSSL conceptual model

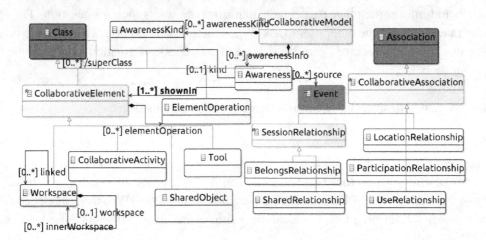

Figure 1 shows the main metaclasses of the CSSL metamodel: CollaborativeElement which is a subclass of UML Class, and CollaborativeAssociation which is a subclass of UML Association. This language allows users to work with the main concepts of collaborative systems: "Shared Object", "Tool", "Collaborative Activity", "Workspace", "User", "Role" and connect them to express the characteristics of the system. For example, an activity involves certain roles and uses some tools (elements are specified and related). In addition, the language allows users to describe the awareness elements that appear in the collaborative system and how they relate to the elements being modeled. This is reflected in the metaclasses Awareness and AwarenessKind that can be connected to any collaborative element by means of the shownIn relationship.

Figure 2. Collaborative processes in CSSL

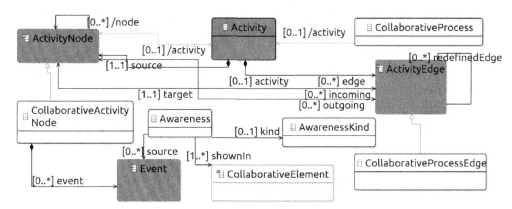

Figure 2 shows that CollaborativeProcess behavior is represented through UML Activity that is composed of nodes (ActivityNodes) and edges (ActivityEdge). The metamodel extends the latter two allowing users to have collaborative activities such as nodes (CollaborativeActivityNode) and edges (CollaborativeProcessEdge) that are activated from the operations that roles carry out. It can also be seen that collaborative nodes are related to a set of events that can trigger awareness information to be displayed in some collaborative element (Workspace, Tool, etc.).

Figure 3 displays the metaclasses to model protocols. The possibility of defining the behavior of a collaborative activity through a protocol is contemplated. The StateMachine metaclass is used to represent the protocol of an activity. The modeling consists in describing the states through which an activity passes, having into account the operations that roles can perform.

In the protocol metamodel, the metaclass CollaborativeActivityState, subclass of UML State, has a set of operations assigned through assignedRoleElementOperation and another set of operations that trigger a transition to another state. It is important to note that operations assigned to roles are related to an event that can cause an Awareness information update to be displayed in some collaborative element.

Figure 3. Protocols in CSSL

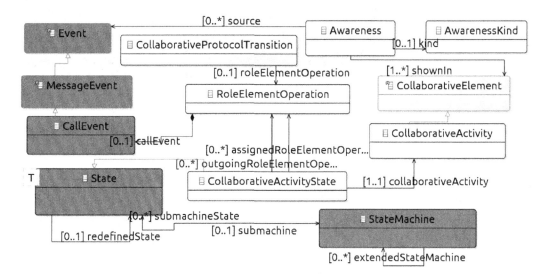

Using the metamodel, users can instantiate the CollaborativeModel metaclass that is a subclass of the UML Model, which contains the elements constituting the system as packaged elements (instances of PackageElement). This allows users to create CollaborativeRoles, CollaborativeActivity, Workspace, and so on.

Creating models from instantiating metaclasses, using a standard UML editor, is a hard and unfriendly work. This style of instantiation would require users to create an instance of CollaborativeModel and from it instantiate the "children" in that model, as shown in Figure 4 where, for example, Workspace is instantiated. In this case, abstract syntax is used as if it were concrete and a tree-shaped listing with all the instantiated classes and associations is displayed.

Figure 4. UML editors

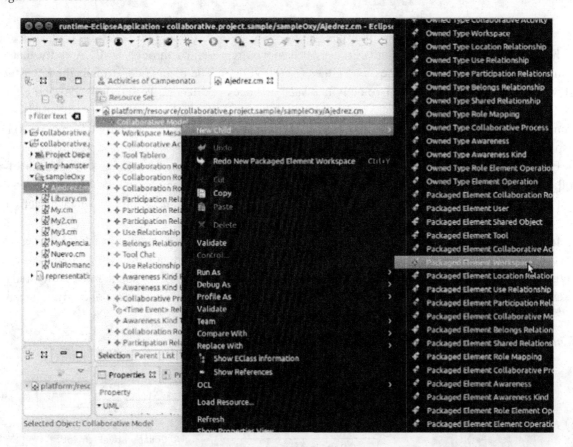

Figure 5. CSSL language-specific editors

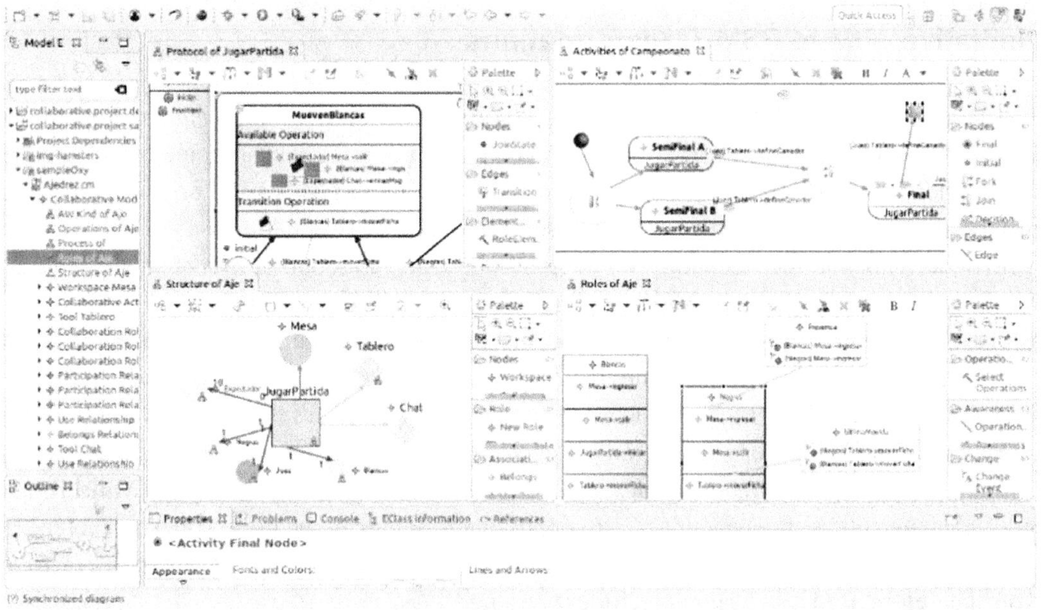

To provide more flexibility and readability to the DSL, different concrete syntaxes (Editors) can be offered. Then users can choose the syntax that is most intuitive for them. This work introduces a concrete syntax, implemented through graphical editors, that was developed using eclipse's Sirius project. It is shown in Figure 5.

Different representations are available according to the needs of the language. The main graphical editors describing the collaborative system with awareness are:

- **System Structure:** this editor allows the user to create and connect the main concepts of the system. Awareness information is also supported.
- **System roles:** this editor allows the user to define which roles are involved in the system and which operations are assigned to them. The actions triggering the awareness are also defined.
- **Process Diagram:** For each process, the collaborative activities that make up it and in what order they are executed are displayed. In this editor, users can indicate how the awareness is updated as the process advances.
- **Activity diagram:** This editor allows the user to specify the states through which a collaborative activity goes. Users can also indicate how awareness information is modified due to the actions of the roles.

Other editors allow users to create processes, awareness types, add operations to spaces, add operations to activities, and other system configuration. Together they provide tools for designers to describe collaborative systems with awareness.

DERIVING CODE FROM THE DOMAIN-SPECIFIC LANGUAGE

MDA Initiative: PIM to PSM Transformations

Model Driven Architecture (MDA) is an approach to software design, development and implementation guided by the Object Management Group (OMG) (Kennedy and Carter 2003)(Kennedy and Carter 2003; Kleppe, Warmer, and Bast 2003). MDA is a pragmatic realization of MDD and provides guidelines for structuring software specifications that are expressed as models. MDA separates business and application logic from underlying platform technology. Platform-independent models (PIM) of an application, built using UML or the other associated OMG modeling standards, can be realized through the MDA on virtually any platform. These platform-independent models document the business functionality and behavior of an application separated from the technology-specific code that implements, which is documented by Platform Specific Models (PSMs). Each one can evolve at its own rate: business logic responding to business need, and technology taking advantage of new developments. Therefore, interoperability both within and across platform boundaries is facilitated (Lidia Fuentes and Antonio Vallecillo 2004).

The CSSL language is independent of any deployment platform because it does not reference any of the features of specific technologies, such as: programming languages, hardware, network topology, and so on. Therefore, CSSL is a language for expressing PIMs.

The key challenge of MDA is in transforming PIMs to PSMs that can be used to generate implementations. Transforming a model into another model means that a source model is transformed into a target model based on some transformation rules, as shown in Figure 6.

Figure 6. Transformation architecture

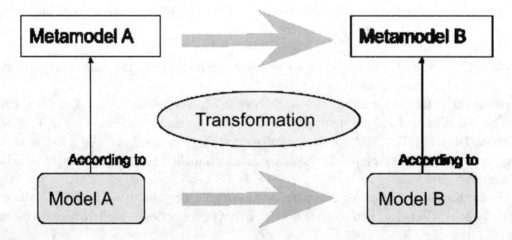

One or more PSMs can be derived from a PIM, depending on the different technologies. In this section we describe a particular transformation from CSSL PIM models to an executable model. The transformation is composed by a set of rules associating each element of the CSSL Metamodel to an element in the target metamodel. In this case, the specific stack of technologies included in the PSM are JavaScript and technologies associated with that language, such as Node.js and client-side frameworks such as Angular and React. The main concepts conforming the PSM are Application, Component, Button, Process, Classes (Types), Permissions, Role, User and Container Component. Table 1 represents how elements of the PIM are transformed to the PSM.

After applying the transformation, the abstraction level is reduced because elements get defined in terms of elements in the chosen specific platform. Notice that not all elements from the PIM are mapped in Table 1.

Table 1. PIM to PSM transformation

Metaclases	Transformaction
CollaborativeModel	Application: A collaborative system or application is created for each model.
CollaborativeElement	Abstract Component: Collaborative elements will be visible components in the system. These elements have operations that appear as buttons in the system interface.
CollaborativeElement: Workspace	Container Component: A component visible on the system that will contain the activities that belong to it and the operations defined in its context.
CollaborativeElement: CollaborativeActivity	Container Component: A component visible on the system that will contain the tools that are used and the operations defined for the activity.
CollaborativeElement: Tool	Container Component: A component visible on the system that will contain the features defined for the tool.
CollaborativeElement: SharedObject	Container Component: A component visible on the system that will contain the operations defined for it.
ElementOperation	Button: the button appears on collaborative items and represents related operations that can be executed on each of them.
CollaborativeAssociation	Maintains relationships between collaborative elements.
CollaborativeAssociation: BelongRelationship	This association indicates that a CollaborativeActivity belongs to a Workspace.
CollaborativeAssociation: UseRelationship	This association indicates that a Tool is used in a CollaborativeActivity.
CollaborativeAssociation: ParticipationRelationship	This association indicates that a CollaborationRole participates in a CollaborativeActivity. This relationship defines which and how each role participates in each activity.
User	User registered in the system.
CollaborationRole	Role within the system. This element controls user permissions.
RoleElementOperation	Enables a role to execute an operation on a collaborative item. Makes the button visible to a particular role. On the other hand, it activates an Event indicating that the operation was executed. This is used to display awareness information somewhere in the system.
CollaborativeProcess	A container component composed of CollaborativesNodes instances, control nodes (initial, fork, join, decision, final), and edges connecting these nodes. It represents a system process.
CollaborativeActivityNode	Represents an instance of an activity within a process.
CollaborativeProcessEdge	The edges of a process that starts when a role executes an operation (RoleElementOperation).
CollaborativeActivityState	Represents a state within a collaborative activity. There is a set of RoleElementOperation assigned to it.
CollaborativeProtocol-Transition	It is a state change within an activity that originates from an operation (RoleElementOperation) performed in the source state.
AwarenessKind	Types of awareness information.
Awareness	A system-visible component that is linked to a component through the shownIn relationship. It defines a set of events that will update the component information.

Model-to-Text Transformation

The final step of the MDA is automatic code generation. By taking information from the PSM, an automatic transformation produces both structural and behavioral code that are compliant with the compilation process of the platform and can be executed on it. A target architecture was chosen to implement the concepts conforming the PSM.

This section introduces a Model-to-Text transformation developed with the Acceleo Eclipse plug-in (https://www.eclipse.org/acceleo/ n.d.). The transformation maps elements from the CSSL language to elements in the PSM model. The resulting PSM consists of a set of files containing code in some programming language and a target architecture; in this case a Web Client-Server architecture was chosen.

Specifically, for each element of the language, the transformation defines which system components must be built; both on the client and on the server side. On the other hand, a lightweight language was chosen that does not require complicated configuration (for example, JavaScript and technologies associated with that language, such as Node.js and client-side frameworks such as Angular or React).

The transformation also defines that the data exchange between the client and the server is performed through a REST API, which functions as an interface between systems that use the HTTP protocol to get the data or warn of the execution of some operation, using an XML or JSON format.

The target code is written in TypeScript, which is a JavaScript-based programming language, with the advantage of being a typed language, which allows the creation of class structures and can run on both the client and server side.

In short, the transformation consists of taking an instance of the CSSL language and producing as a result a Web application implemented in TypeScript, where the developers can then add their own code to adapt the result to their interests.

WebSocket technology was chosen to implement awareness. It establishes a bidirectional connection between the client's browser and the server that lasts as long as the client browser remains open. Both the client and server are able to send and receive messages over the established connection channel using the standard protocol WS or the secure version WSS.

Finally, executable models are obtained, through model transformations, using Javascript-related web technology (Express.js, Angular.js, Node.js), MongoDB and Websockets.

The main concerns of collaborative systems are already built in this preliminary version of the system. That is, user management, roles and operations, collaborative processes, and awareness are already implemented. Then, developers can refine this system according to their own needs.

Transformation Output

The target of the transformation is a web application that provides a set of basic functions that developers can refine to complete the development of the collaborative system. In this section the output of the transformation is analyzed in two steps. First the construction of the system structure is described and afterward the implementation of the system dynamics is explained.

System Structure

The main phases of transforming the structural aspects of the system are presented in this section:

Figure 7. (a) Structure of operations transformations

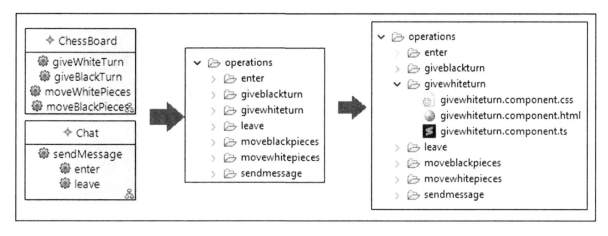

Figure 8. (b) Operation transformation

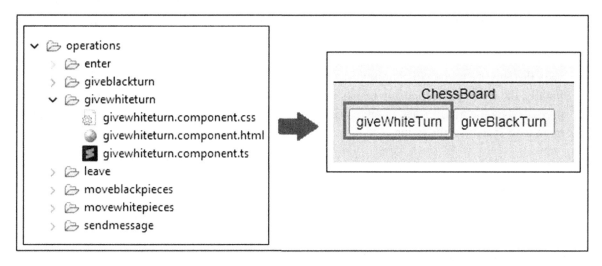

Figure 9. (c) Workspace transformation

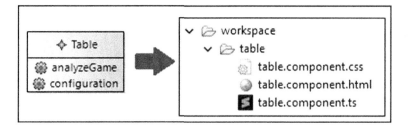

A directory default structure, based on the standards of each technology is obtained as it is shown in Figure 7.

- Transformation of operations. The operations are transformed into buttons in the application.

The Figure 8 shows an example of a target application, a Chess game, that is obtained from two collaborative elements by applying the transformation.

- Workspace Transformation. Workspaces are transformed into containers that give a framework to the execution of activities. Additionally, containers hold their own operations. After the transformation is applied, Angular components are created, and saved in their proper directory ("workspace"). Figure 9 shows an example.
- Transformation of collaborative activities (CollaborativeActivity). Activities are located within workspaces. They are invoked by users within a collaborative process. Activities contain operations and offer tools to the users. Activities are transformed to Angular components that are saved in the "activity" directory within the project as shown in Figure 10.
- The belongRelationship, UseRelationShip, and ParticipationRelationship associations are used to connect the elements, getting the result shown in the Figure 11. The "PlayGame" activity appears in gray, the tools in green, the roles in light-blue color and finally the workspace is shown in orange. The arrows show which elements are linked to each activity. These associations are instances of different associations expressed in the metamodel. The ParticipationRelationship relates the activity to the collaboration roles. The UseRelationship relates the activity to the tools. Finally, the BelongsRelationship relates the activity to the workspaces. All these relationships are processed by the transformation, given rise to the components and containers of the resulting collaborative system in the Figure 12.

Figure 10. (a) Activity transformation

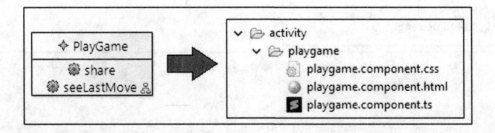

Figure 11. (b) Activity relationships

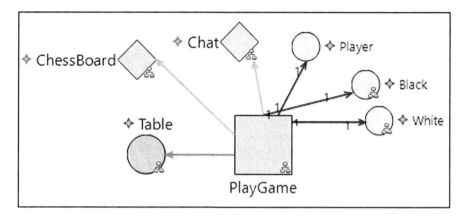

Figure 12. (c) Activity interface

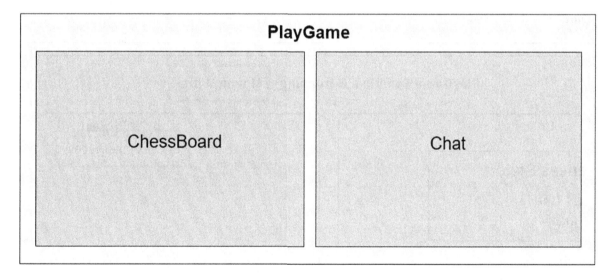

System Dynamics

After finishing the first step of the transformation, a preliminary version of the web system is already available. It allows a group of users to connect to the system to share collaborative activities.

The next step of the transformation consists in implementing the dynamic aspects of the system. This section discusses the transformation of the main dynamic models: protocol construction, collaborative processes, and awareness.

Figure 13. (a) Protocol model

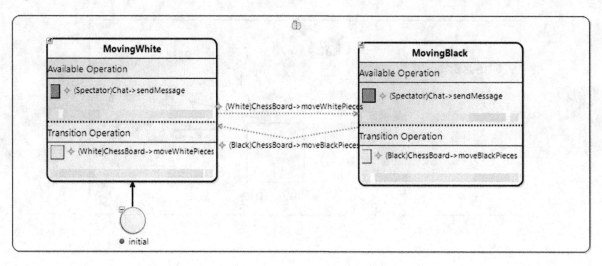

Figure 14. (b) Protocol transformation

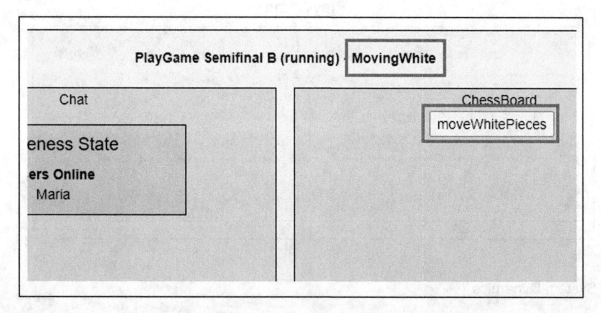

- **Transformation of activities protocols.** Protocols are modeled as state machines, and each state is specified as the set of operations that roles can execute in that state. Some of the operations can cause a state transition. In the example being followed, the "PlayGame" activity goes through the "Moving White" and "MovingBlacks" states. In the first, the Whites role can move a piece, and in the second the Black role is the one that can move, and the states change as the roles run the MovePiece operation, as shown in the Figure 13. In the interface, the user will always see the protocol status to the right of the activity name while the available operations appear as buttons that can be activated as shown in Figure 14.

- **Transformation of Collaborative Processes.** Processes organize a set of collaborative activities by defining in what order each of them is activated. When users enter the system, they will only have access to the processes in which they are enrolled. For example, Figure 15 shows the process that simulates a chess competition, where participants must play three games to win. In this process, three activities of the type "PlayGame" are created. As users enter the system, they are placed in the games they have to play, and the process starts. The system controls which user participates in each game and enables the winners to play the contest final.

Figure 15. Collaborative process transformation

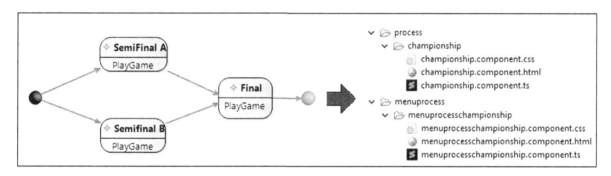

- **Creation of activities and processes.** One of the central decisions to make in the process of transforming from model to text is to define how system instances are to be created. In our example, the design decision was that users can create the activities and processes in which they participate. Once users are logged into the system, they can create Games and Championships from the system home. The example shows the user's games and championships, Figure 16. The system displays and supervises the status of each game as shown in Figure 17.

Figure 16. (a) Main menu

Figure 17. (b) Process instances

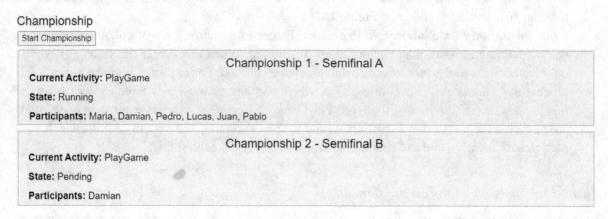

- **Transformation of awareness.** The transformation mechanism defines how those models are transformed into components that display the awareness information in the system, Figure 18. Awareness models will be transformed into components that will be displayed in collaborative elements (Workspace, CollaborativeActivity, Tool). At the same time, a communication channel (Websockets) is created between the awareness originator and the component that displays the information. The second example shows that the awareness "Turn" is displayed in the "Board" element and is updated from the user/role moves and the system clock, Figure 19.

Figure 18. (a) Awareness transformation

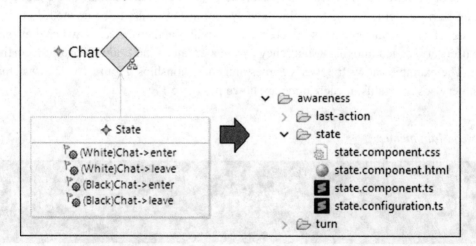

Figure 19. (b) Last action awareness

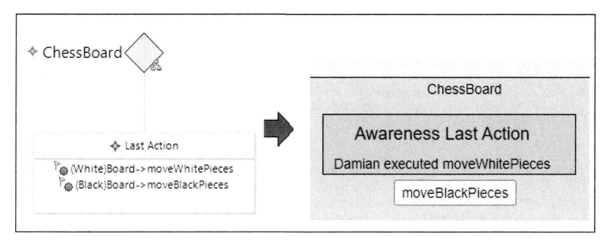

CASE STUDY

Modeling the DimSum Thinklet

ThinkLets (Robert O. Briggs, Gert-Jan de Vreede, Gwendolyn L. Kolfschoten - 2007) are design patterns for collaborative work practices. ThinkLets are used by facilitators and collaboration engineers to design collaboration processes for high-value recurring tasks, and to transfer those designs to practitioners to execute for themselves without the ongoing intervention of professional facilitators. The collection of thinkLets forms a pattern language for creating, documenting, communicating, and learning group process designs.

In (Robert O. Briggs, Gert-Jan de Vreede, Gwendolyn L. Kolfschoten - 2007) a fully documented thinkLet, named DimSum is presented as example. In this thinkLet, the team works to create a specific, precise, statement, in a way that all understand, and that accommodates the interests of all team members. Each member proposes a candidate terminology for the common statement. Participants then get the words and phrases they like best from the candidate statements to create a new common statement. Periodically all participants propose new candidate statements based on the current draft of the common statement. The cycle continues until a version emerges that all participants accept.

Here, the pattern of collaboration is a cycle of generation of concepts, clarification of meaning and consensus building on the final statement.

This collaboration pattern can be easily and accurately modeled by applying CSSL.

Before starting with the design of the interaction among the participants, the environment where the users collaborate should be described. The tools, the roles and the virtual place where the users will meet to develop the collaborative activities involved in the DimSum thinkLet are identified in a first step. Figure 20 displays the complete thinkLet environment. The model specifies two collaborative activities: one for generation of concepts (ContributeSt) and another for clarification of meaning and consensus building (ReviewSt). Both collaborative activities are carried out in the same virtual place called Room. Coordinator and participant are the two roles involved in the task. Finally, the specification describes the set of collaborative tools that users/roles employ to carry out the task. The tool set includes a. statement browser, a statement editor, a voice conference system, and a voting system.

Figure 20. Modeling of the DimSum ThinkLet environment

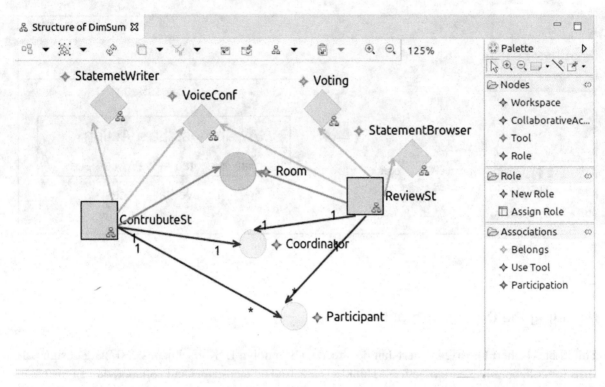

The collaborative process model for the Dimsum Thinklet task is illustrated in Figure 21. The model specifies the ContributeSt and ReviewSt activities and the transitions that define the collaborative process. The activities are labeled with icons of the work of (Solano et al. 2014) that show the type of activity and whether they produce information or not.

Figure 21. Modeling of the DimSum ThinkLet process

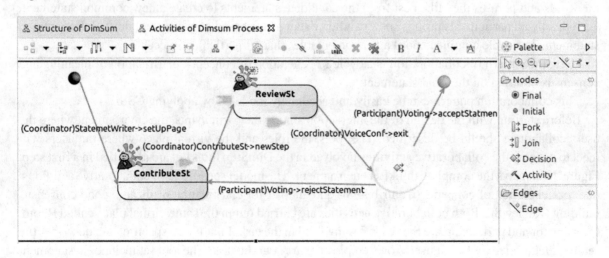

Then, each of the collaborative activities is modeled in CSSL. For this purpose, the protocols are specified. Figure 22 shows the interactions between the participants in the ContributeSt collaborative activitiy. The model is compliant with the DimSum Thinklet specifications where it is described that the activity goes through different states. In each of them, users can perform different operations. The model shows a first state of the activity called Setup where the coordinator explains the objective of the activity. Then, in the following state, called ProduceSt, the participants contributions are generated and collected and finally in the last state, called ReviewSt, the candidate sentences are adjusted. The activity continues cyclically until a consensus is reached among all participants.

Figure 22. Modeling of the DimSum ThinkLet activity

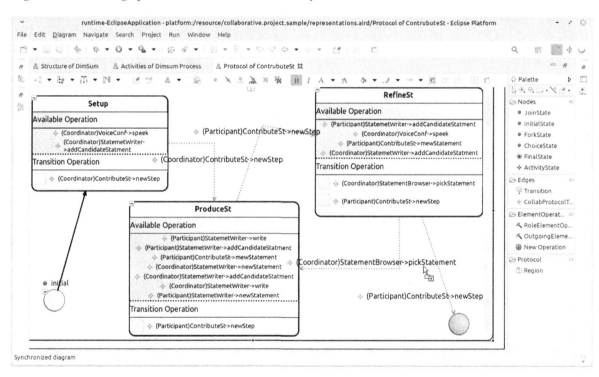

Awareness Modeling

The above models describe the structure and dynamics of the DimSum thinkLet. But another important element in a collaborative process is the awareness specification. And indeed, the modeling of awareness is one of the most important strengths of CSSL since it allows the collaboration engineer to specify where the awareness components should be displayed, and which events trigger the update of each of them.

Although the awareness specification would notably enrich the thinkLet scope, the DimSum thinkLet does not define the types of awareness to apply. Therefore, the following five types of awareness are incorporated to the thinkLet model: Presence, Speaking, Statement, VotingResult, TimeToVote. Figure 23 shows the instances of the awareness types with the details of the events that update them.

It is noteworthy that most of the awareness were defined as synchronous and not transient (not stored in the system). Except in the case of the awareness Statements that must be stored in the system for later retrieval. The Figure 23 also shows that awareness components are linked to different types of elements (Workspace Room, VoiceConf Tool, Vooting Tool, ContributeSt Activity).

Figure 23. Modeling of the DimSum ThinkLet with awareness

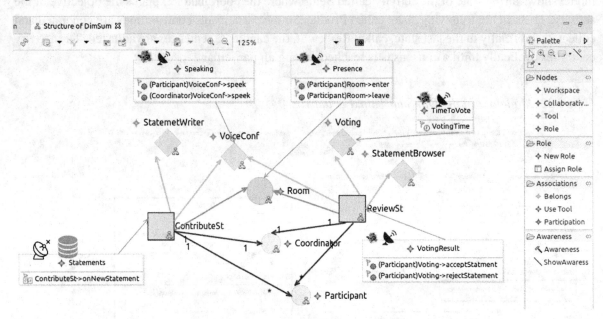

Most awareness updates are based on the actions that users perform. The system is attentive to the operations performed by the roles in the system and activates the update of awareness when appropriate. On the other hand, other awareness types are linked to events not originated by users. For example, the elapsed time, as specified in the Awareness TimeToVote, where there is a UML timeEvent activated to control the amount of time allowed to vote.

Awareness can also be specified linked to events in activities as shown in Figure 24.

Figure 24. Modeling of the DimSum ThinkLet process with awareness

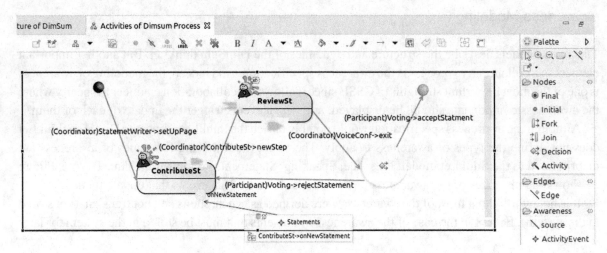

COMPARISON WITH RELATED WORKS

In this section we present a discussion of the most relevant works related to the modeling of collaborative systems with special attention to awareness. The information is an update of a systematic literature review (Bibbo, Giandini, and Pons 2016), where software engineering resources to design Collaborative Systems in a standardized, efficient and automated way were searched and analyzed.

CSSL is a domain specific language built as a UML extension using the metamodeling mechanism. A first version of the language was introduced in (Bibbo, Giandini, and Pons 2017). The current version meets all the requirements stated in the background section.

Unlike de work of (Gallardo et al. 2012) with CSSL, the content of the editors cannot be specifically modeled, but CSSL allows integrating any type of collaborative tool into the design, describing what operations the roles can execute at each time. Regarding the workspace, CSSL allows engineers to design relationships between workspaces such as the inclusion between workspaces. This facility allows covering several collaborative domains (E-learning, Brainstorming, Collaborative games, etc.). It also allows integrating a specific design of the awareness information associated with the different elements of the model.

Although the proposal of using thinklets (Briggs, Gert-Jan de Vreede, and Kolfschoten 2007) is interesting to document the dynamics of collaboration, CSSL provides a more comprehensive view of the system. In addition to modeling the interaction, CSSL defines the collaborative tools (Tools) that will be used at each time, the collaboration environment (Workspace) and especially the awareness modeling, indicating the type of information and in which collaborative element it will be displayed and how it will be kept up to date. An example of a thinklet modeling with CSSL is presented in this article, as a case study.

The difference between CSSL and most related proposals is that CSSL is formally linked to UML. CSSL extends some UML classes that allow modeling collaborative processes (extending Activity) and protocols (extending StateMachine). These designs combine the power of the UML to describe processes and protocols (with their metaclasses of Fork, Join, Decision, etc.) with the actions (operations) performed by the roles in collaborative activities.

The popularity and maturity of UML favors that CSSL can be widely adopted for modeling collaborative systems. Also, it brings the benefits of leveraging the available UML modeling software tools.

Regarding language coverage, the expressive power of CSSL is enough to represent all surveyed concepts. In addition, in CSSL the awareness modeling smoothly integrated into the rest of the models gives rise to a new and powerful design that allows obtaining a concrete implementation automatically through model transformations adhering to the model driven software development approach. And then getting benefits in terms of standardization, code reuse and automation.

EVALUATION, VALIDATION AND VERIFICATION OF THE METAMODEL

Evaluation of the Metamodel

This section performs a metamodel evaluation based on metrics recognized in the academic community. For this analysis, a set of three metrics presented in (Robert et al. 2009) was taken as the main reference. The metrics quantitatively determine how good a UML Profile is. Given their characteristics, these metrics can also be applied to metamodels, measuring a) How close the metamodels is to UML semantics, b) How complex it is, c) How configurable it is.

The metrics are:
- ○ **ANLA** (Average Number Location Application): This metrics calculates the average number of UML elements to which stereotypes in a UML Profile can be applied. It is calculated as:

$$ANLA = 1/n \sum_{i=1}^{n} Mi$$

Where n is the number of stereotypes conforming the profile and Mi is the amount of metaclasses to which the i-th stereotype can be applied. The stereotype can be applied to any subclass of its base metaclasses. Therefore, a larger ANLA will be obtained when the affected metaclasses are closer to the "root" element of the metamodel referenced by the profile than when they are closer to the "leaves". For example, a stereotype that extends the Element metaclass can be applied to 199 metaclasses. The ANLA gives an indication of how much the profile depends on the UML metamodel. A high ANLA represents a profile that extends metaclasses close to the root elements of the metamodel, and because the semantics of them are more general, the resulting profile will not be as dependent on the UML metamodel. In contrast, a low ANLA represents a more dependent profile.

Figure 25. UML metaclasses to calculate ANLA

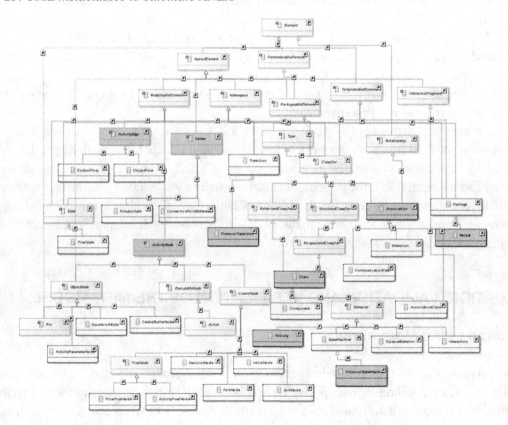

For the metric to be applicable to a metamodel, a variant of the formula was defined. According to the adapted metric each metaclass will be analyzed to determine whether it extends a UML metaclass near the root or closer to the leaves. The distribution of extended metaclases in the hierarchy tree can be seen in the Figure 25, where the main UML metaclasses that are extended by the CSSL language are highlighted. Specifically, for each metaclass, the adapted metric calculates two distances: - RI that is the number of subclasses ranging from the extended metaclass to the farthest leaf and - RS that is the length of the path to the root. For example, for a metaclass that extends the Class metaclass, RI is 3, while RS is 7. The variant of the ANLA formula is as follws:

$$ANLA = \sum_{i=0}^{n} RIi / (RSi + RIi)$$

- ALDIT (Average Leaf Depth of Inheritance Tree): This metric represents the average length of the inheritance tree in stereotypes. To apply the ALDIT metric to the metamodel, the metaclasses that extend a CSSL metaclass are counted and the average is calculated using the following formula:

$$ALDIT = \sum_{i=0}^{n} Li$$

Where n is the number of metaclasses in the CSSL metamodel and for each of them, Li = 1 if the metaclass extends other CSSL metaclass or Li=0 if it extends a UML metaclass.

- ASWA (Average Stereotype with Attributes): This metric calculates the average of stereotypes that have attributes. To apply ASWA to the CSSL metamodel, CSSL metaclasses that have attributes are counted and the formula is defined as follows:

$$ASWA = \sum_{i=0}^{n} Ai$$

Where n is the number of CSSL metaclasses and Ai = 1 if the metaclass has one or more attributes, or Ai = 0 in other case.

Applying the Metrics to CSSL

In this section the results of applying the metrics on the CSSL metamodel are shown. Considering that he CSSL metamodel defines 25 new metaclasses, the index **n is 25**.

- The formula ANLA {ANLA}, where each Mi is calculated as follows.
  - For the 12 metaclasses extending the metaclass "Class", the RI is 3 and the RS is 7. Then Mi = (3/(3+7)) = 0.3
  - For the metaclass that extends "Model" the RI is 0. Then Mi = 0.
  - For the 6 metaclasses that extend"Association" the RI is 1 and the RS is 2. Then Mi = (1/(1+2)) = 0.3333.
  - For the metaclass extending ActivityNode, the RI is 3 and the RS is 3, then Mi = 0.5.

- ○ For the metaclass that extends ActivityEdge, the RI is 1 and the RS is 3, then Mi = 0.25.
- ○ For the metaclass that extends Vertex, the RI is 2 and the RS is 2, then Mi = 0.5.
- ○ For the 3 metaclasses that extend ProtocolTransition, Activity, and ProtocolStateMachine respectively, the RI is 0. Then Mi = 0.
- In summary, **ANLA = 0.274**

This result is relatively low, indicating that the language mostly extends classes close to the leaves of UML metamodel. According to Robert et al.'s work (Robert et al. 2009), this means that the CSSL metamodel relies heavily on UML semantics, allowing the use of tools implemented for the management of UML models in the management of CSSL models, such as editors, code generators, profiles, etc.

- **ALDIT:** calculating this metric, Li = 1 for 9 CSSL metaclasses that extends other CSSL meta-classes, while Li = 0 for the remaining16 classes. Therefore:
  - ○ **ALDIT = 9/25 = 0.36**
- **ASWA:** the amount of CSSL metaclasses that have some attribute is 14, then:
  - ○ **ASWA = 14/25 = 0.56**

The application of ALDIT and ASWA, shows that the CSSL metamodel has a low complexity (**0.36**), with a short inheritance tree. On the other hand, it provides good parameterization possibilities (**0.56**) by users since more than half of the metaclasses have useful attributes for customizing the models to be instantiated from CSSL.

Conceptual Model Validation

According to Sargent (Sargent 2013), conceptual model validity means determining that (1) theories and assumptions underlying the conceptual model are correct, and (2) model representation of the problem, structure, logic, and mathematical and causal relationships of the model are reasonable, for the intended purpose of the model.

Then Sargent in (Sargent 2013) claims that the theories and assumptions underlying the construction of the model are tested using mathematical analyses and statistical methods. And that the opinion of experts on the subject is essential to determine the validity of the conceptual model. For this reason a systematic literature review was carried out to corroborate that experts accept the concepts, structures, and relationships included in the CSSL metamodel.

Through the systematic literature review (Bibbo et al. 2016), different models and ontologies of Collaborative Systems were analyzed, identifying a set of representative conceptual elements., such as "Shared Object", "Tool", "Collaborative Activity","Workspace", "User/Role", "Group". These elements also relate to the concept of awareness. As described in (Belkadi et al. 2013), one of the questions used to identify awareness is: "What roles will the other members of the group assume?" where the association between the concept of role and awareness appears. In other examples of awareness the question to ask is: "How can I help other participants to complete the project?" or "What are they doing?" or "Where are they?" In addition, most works incorporate the concept of "Task", which represents the collaborative tasks that users must perform.

The literature review and the related works corroborates that the CSSL metamodel presented in this paper, contemplates and includes all the concepts presented in the different scientific works. A noteworthy aspect is that the CSSL metamodel contemplates the concept "Awareness" related to "Collaborative Elements", "Collaborative Process" and "Protocol", allowing the creation of designs that include "Awareness" in the models instantiated from the metamodel.

In conclusion, the CSSL conceptual model can be considered correct and reasonable for its purpose, and therefore valid. This claim is supported by the systematic review of the work of numerous experts in the field of collaborative systems with awareness.

Model Verification

Sargent explains in (Sargent 2013) that model verification can be performed through computerized verification. This ensures that the computer programming and implementation of the conceptual model are correct. This means that the models are implementable and that the programs that are developed from these models work. To help ensure that a correct software is obtained, software development techniques found in the field of software engineering should be used in developing and implementing the software.

According to this definition, the CSSL metamodel can be considered verified because the semantics of the metamodel was implemented by means of a model-to-text transformation, as described in section 4. The transformation produces an executable web version of the model that solves central aspects of collaborative systems, as follows:

- Registration of users/roles in the system.
- Security issues, session management, login, and logout.
- Allow users/roles to perform operations provided by the collaborative item.
- Allow users/roles to access collaborative spaces, participate in collaborative activities and use collaborative tools.
- Coordinate user participation within collaborative activities according to protocols.
- Schedule collaborative activities in collaborative processes.
- Manage in-system instantiating.
- Providing an Awareness Platform.
- Construction of a prototype of the Application.

Once the program has been developed and possible bugs have been fixed, the first tests can be performed to determine if the system is working correctly. At this stage, different types of tests ranging from unit test, integration test to user acceptance test are performed. For example, the intuitiveness of the navigation between collaborative spaces, the usefulness of the awareness, and the correctness of the collaborative activities are subjects that can be analyzed at this stage.

At this point the system requirements are validated and design alternatives are considered to achieve a properly functioning application.

When modeling errors are detected, the analysts are able to correct the CSSL models and generate the modified system automatically by re-applying the model-to-text transformation. This demonstrates the advantages of MDD by allowing iterating between modeling and testing several times until obtaining the system that meets the requirements.

CONCLUSION AND FUTURE WORK

Collaborative Systems are applications in which a group of users, following a common goal, develop different joint activities. On the one hand the collaborative software allows users to share information, communicate, and coordinate joint activities and, on the other hand, it provides awareness information, which requires maintaining and informing users about the status of the collaboration on the fly.

Building these systems is a very complex task that requires powerful tools.

In this paper a proposal to apply the Model Driven software Development approach (MDD) to the construction of Collaborative systems was elaborated.

MDD separates business and application logic from underlying platform technology. Models allow designers to specify the solution using problem domain concepts directly. End products are then automatically generated from these high-level specifications.

The proposal consists of a domain specific language, named CSSL v2.0, that defines the main concepts of collaborative systems, especially collaborative processes, protocols and awareness. A concrete syntax is defined via a set of editors through which collaborative systems models are created by instantiating the language concepts. In addition to the static aspects, dynamic aspects such as collaborative processes, protocols and awareness are modeled.

Following the MDD methodology, the language semantics was defined through model-to-text transformations, obtaining executable code from the models expressed in the CSSL v2.0 language.

The target of the transformation is a web application that provides a set of basic functions that developers can refine to complete the development of the collaborative system.

The transformation was implemented in Acceleo and for the target code a lightweight and flexible javascript-based technology was used (Express, Node.js, Angular, MongoDB and Websockets).

The main concepts of the collaborative system were mapped into application components, both on the server and on the client side. The model-to-text transformation allows developers to obtain a draft version of the collaborative system that resolves the management of users, roles and operations, collaborative processes and awareness.

The results obtained corroborate that the CSSL v2.0 language allows defining in a precise, concise, and friendly way the abstract concepts of collaborative systems, including collaborative processes, protocols and awareness. This allows designers to build models that facilitate communication between developers, and executable versions are derived from them. An important aspect to highlight is that the models are built maintaining compatibility with UML, which makes it possible to interchange with other tools, such as editors, translators, or other UML profiles. This allows designers to use tools developed for CSSL and UML in combination.

Finally, evaluation, validation and verification of the language were carried out. The evaluation determined that the CSSL metamodel has low complexity, with semantics strongly associated with UML and with good configuration possibilities. On the other hand, the validity of the metamodel was analyzed based on a systematic review of the work of different experts from the scientific community determining that concepts and relationships of the metamodel are reasonable for its intended purpose. Finally, model verification was performed through computerized verification, demonstrating that the model-to-text transformation allows developers to obtain an executable web system that solves central aspects of collaborative systems.

Future work includes the combined application of other UML profiles complementing the CSSL language, such as Mobile profiles. Additionally, other transformations will be built from the models to obtain implementations on different platforms. This would allow the creation of a factory of collaborative applications for different platforms, exploiting the power of the model transformation tools.

On the other hand, it is intended to incorporate usability evaluation tools. Specially to evaluate the impact of the awareness functionality on the usability of collaborative systems. This will allow, not only, to evaluate the collaborative applications produced (collaborative games, teaching environments, group decision making) but also to evaluate the CSSL language both in its syntax and its semantics.

Another line of future work is the possibility of incorporating collaborative functionality to the editors implemented to support the graphical representation of the language. This challenge will allow building collaborative tools to develop collaborative systems.

Finally. An architecture will be designed to support awareness services for large-scale collaborative systems. The objective of this architecture is to support different types of awareness (presence, location, action, etc.) with their different implementation variants (synchronous/asynchronous, volatile/persistent, etc.). The proposed architecture, oriented to microservices, should provide scalability (vertical and horizontal), improve the maintenance of the developed systems, foster continuous development and integration, and facilitate the experimentation and integration of new technologies.

REFERENCES

Belkadi, F., Bonjour, E., Camargo, M., Troussier, N., & Eynard, B. (2013). A Situation Model to Support Awareness in Collaborative Design. *International Journal of Human-Computer Studies*, *71*(1), 110–129. doi:10.1016/j.ijhcs.2012.03.002

Bibbo, Giandini, & Pons. (2016). Sistemas Colaborativos Con Awareness: Requisitos Para Su Modelado. *XLV Jornadas Argentinas de Informática e Investigación Operativa (45 JAIIO) - Simposio Argentino de Ingeniería de Software (ASSE 2016)*, 111–22.

Brambilla, M., Cabot, J., & Wimmer, M. (2012). Model-Driven Software Engineering in Practice. *Synthesis Lectures on Software Engineering*, *1*(1), 1–182. doi:10.2200/S00441ED1V01Y201208SWE001

Briggs, de Vreede, & Kolfschoten. (2007). *ThinkLets for E-Collaboration.* IGI Global.

Collazos, C. A., Gutiérrez, F. L., Gallardo, J., Ortega, M., Fardoun, H. M., & Molina, A. I. (2019). Descriptive Theory of Awareness for Groupware Development. *Journal of Ambient Intelligence and Humanized Computing*, *10*(12), 4789–4818. doi:10.100712652-018-1165-9

Dourish & Bly. (1992). *Portholes: Supporting Awareness in a Distributed Work Group.* Dl.Acm.Org.

Dourish, P., & Bellotti, V. (1992). Awareness and Coordination in Shared Workspaces. *Proceedings of the 1992 ACM Conference on Computer-Supported Cooperative Work - CSCW '92*, 107–14.

Ellis, C. A., Gibbs, S. J., & Rein, G. (1991). Groupware: Some Issues and Experiences. *Communications of the ACM*, *34*(1), 39–58. doi:10.1145/99977.99987

Fuentes, L., & Vallecillo, A. (2004). *An Introduction to UML Profiles.* Cepis.Org/Upgrade

Gallardo, J., Bravo, C., & Redondo, M. A. (2012). A Model-Driven Development Method for Collaborative Modeling Tools. *Journal of Network and Computer Applications*, *35*(3), 1086–1105. doi:10.1016/j.jnca.2011.12.009

Gallardo, J., Molina, A. I., Bravo, C., Redondo, M. A., & Collazos, C. A. (2011). An Ontological Conceptualization Approach for Awareness in Domain-Independent Collaborative Modeling Systems: Application to a Model-Driven Development Method. Expert Systems with Applications. doi:10.1016/j.eswa.2010.05.005

Gallego, F., Molina, A. I., Gallardo, J., & Bravo, C. (2011). A Conceptual Framework for Modeling Awareness Mechanisms in Collaborative Systems. Lecture Notes in Computer Science (including subseries Lecture Notes in Artificial Intelligence and Lecture Notes in Bioinformatics), 6949. doi:10.1007/978-3-642-23768-3_56

Greenberg, S., & Gutwin, C. (2016). Implications of We-Awareness to the Design of Distributed Groupware Tools. *Computer Supported Cooperative Work*, *25*(4–5).

Grudin, J. (1994). Computer Supported Cooperative Work: History and Focus. *Computer*, *27*(5), 19–26. doi:10.1109/2.291294

Grudin, J., & Poltrock, S. E. (1997). Computer-Supported Cooperative Work and Groupware. *Advances in Computers*, *45*, 269–320. doi:10.1016/S0065-2458(08)60710-X

Gutwin, C., & Greenberg, S. (2002). A Descriptive Framework of Workspace Awareness for Real-Time Groupware. *Computer Supported Cooperative Work*, *11*(3-4), 411–446. doi:10.1023/A:1021271517844

Gutwin, C., Greenberg, S., & Roseman, M. (1996). Workspace Awareness in Real-Time Distributed Groupware: Framework, Widgets, and Evaluation. *Proceedings of HCI '96*. 10.1007/978-1-4471-3588-3_18

Handzic, M. (2011). Groupware. *Socio-Technical Knowledge Management*, 58–68. https://www.eclipse.org/acceleo/

Kamoun, A., Tazi, S., & Drira, K. (2012). FADYRCOS, a Semantic Interoperability Framework for Collaborative Model-Based Dynamic Reconfiguration of Networked Services. *Computers in Industry*, *63*(8), 756–765. doi:10.1016/j.compind.2012.08.007

Kennedy, A., & Carter, K. (2003). *MDA Guide Version 1.0.1*. Object Management Group.

Kleppe, Warmer, & Bast. (2003). The Model Driven Architecture: Practice and Promise. Addison-Wesley.

Latteier & Pelletier. (2002). *The Zope Book*. Academic Press.

Molina, A. I., Gallardo, J., Redondo, M. A., Ortega, M., & Giraldo, W. J. (2013). Metamodel-Driven Definition of a Visual Modeling Language for Specifying Interactive Groupware Applications: An Empirical Study. *Journal of Systems and Software*, *86*(7), 1772–1789. doi:10.1016/j.jss.2012.07.049

Peters, Lang, & Lie. (2011). ITFG. *E-Collaborations and Virtual Organizations*, 252–75.

Robert, S., Gérard, S., Terrier, F., & Lagarde, F. (2009). A Lightweight Approach for Domain-Specific Modeling Languages Design. In *2009 35th Euromicro Conference on Software Engineering and Advanced Applications*. IEEE. 10.1109/SEAA.2009.81

Sargent, R. G. (2013). Verification and Validation of Simulation Models. *Journal of Simulation*, 7(1), 12–24. doi:10.1057/jos.2012.20

Solano, A., Granollers, T., Collazos, C. A., & Rusu, C. (2014). Proposing Formal Notation for Modeling Collaborative Processes Extending HAMSTERS Notation. In Advances in Intelligent Systems and Computing (Vol. 275). Springer Verlag. doi:10.1007/978-3-319-05951-8_25

Stahl, T., Völter, M., Bettin, J., Haase, A., & Helsen, S. (2006). *Model-Driven Software Development - Technology, Engineering, Management*. Pitman.

Tenenberg, J., Roth, W. M., & Socha, D. (2016). From I-Awareness to We-Awareness in CSCW. *Computer Supported Cooperative Work: CSCW: An International Journal*, 25(4–5), 235–278. doi:10.100710606-014-9215-0

Teruel, Navarro, López-Jaquero, Montero, & González. (2011). An Extension of i * to Model Requirements for CSCW Systems Applied to Conference Preparation System with Collaborative Reviews. *5th International i* Workshop (iStar'11)*.

Teruel, M. A., Navarro, E., López-Jaquero, V., Montero, F., & González, P. (2013). CSRML Tool: A Visual Studio Extension for Modeling CSCW Requirements. CEUR Workshop Proceedings.

Teruel, M. A., Navarro, E., López-Jaquero, V., Montero, F., & González, P. (2014). A CSCW Requirements Engineering CASE Tool: Development and Usability Evaluation. *Information and Software Technology*, 56(8), 922–949. doi:10.1016/j.infsof.2014.02.009

Teruel, M. A., Navarro, E., López-Jaquero, V., Montero, F., Jaen, J., & González, P. (2012). Analyzing the Understandability of Requirements Engineering Languages for CSCW Systems: A Family of Experiments. *Information and Software Technology*, 54(11), 1215–1228. doi:10.1016/j.infsof.2012.06.001

Vieira, V., Tedesco, P., & Salgado, A. C. (2010). Using a Metamodel to Design Structural and Behavioral Aspects in Context-Sensitive Groupware. *Proceedings of the 2010 14th International Conference on Computer Supported Cooperative Work in Design, CSCWD 2010*. 10.1109/CSCWD.2010.5472002

Chapter 3
The Study of FinTech:
Way of Resolving Indian Banking's High Non-Performing Assets Through Emerging Technologies

Narinder Kumar Bhasin

https://orcid.org/0000-0001-7167-8730

Amity University, Noida, India

Kamal Gulati

Amity University, Noida, India

ABSTRACT

In September 2021, the Government of India approved the extension of a guarantee worth INR 30.6 billion (US$4.1 billion) to the National Asset Reconstruction Company Ltd. (NARCL), also called a bad bank. In a move to address the mountain of NPAs in the banking sector, bad banks may bring some relief to banks or rather defer the crisis. However, historically bad banks have not been successful for countries like Mexico, Greece, South Korea, Argentina, and Italy. Technology can help manage the challenges posed by the mountain of NPAs in the Indian banking sector through emerging technologies like blockchain for transparency and artificial intelligence for streamlined processes. This chapter explains the FinTech way through new emerging technologies to resolve the problem of high non-performing assets and the role of introduction of bad banks to alienate illiquid and risky assets held by banks and financial institutions to clean their balance sheets by transferring their bad loans so that the banks can focus on their core business of taking deposits and lending money.

INTRODUCTION

On Feb 1, 2021, Union Finance Minister Ms. Nirmala Sitaraman while presenting the Union Budget 2021 lays focus on the seven important pillars for reviving the economy. These pillars are Health and Wellbeing, Reinvigorating Human Capital, Physical and Financial Capital and infrastructure, Minimum

DOI: 10.4018/978-1-6684-5027-7.ch003

Government Maximum Governance. Inclusive development for Aspirational India and the concept of Bad Bank in the country. FM further said that Asset Management Company (AMC) and Asset Reconstruction Company (ARC) will be set up for effective management of the non-performing assets and bad loans of big Public Sector Banks (PSB`s). This announcement was significant to ensure the financial stability in Indian Banking Industry and clean-up of the bank`s book was urgently required because of the high level of stressed assets in Public Sector Banks (PSB`s). A higher level of provisioning created by PSB`S for increasing non-performing assets was an alarming situation that can impact adversely the financial stability. ARC and AMC will be established for taking over the problem loan of the banks and then effectively managed and disposed of as alternative investment funds to potential investors for eventual value realization. A Bad Bank in other countries has been designed as a corporate structure to isolate high-risk and illiquid assets of other financial institutions to improve the health of financial payment systems. The Bad Bank in India is ready to commence operations with 15 cases worth Rs. 50335 Cr to be transferred by the banks . (Verma, 2022)

RBI Governor Mr. Shaktikanta Das said that an overreaching goal of the Indian financial system is to maintain good health and stability of the banking sector as a policy priority. The Financial Stability report has also reflected that the gross NPA ratio may increase to 13.59% by September 2021. The Indian Bank Association (IBA) has also submitted the proposal to the Government for setting up a Bad Bank with contribution from the Government and Banks the Confederation of Indian Industry (CII) had suggested and recommended to setting up multiple bad banks to meet the challenges of the NPA`s of banks to clean their balance sheets.

BACKGROUND

Former RBI Governor Dr. Raghuram Rajan has fundamentally opposed and was not in favor of the introducing "Bad Bank" suggesting that banks must recover their dues themselves. He further said that it will lead to the creation of an entity that would take over bad assets of the banks to clean up their balance sheets to increase the lending and dispose of their NPA`s for recovery by another entity. He had maintained that it will create more issues when the loans are transferred to bad bank and are not priced appropriately. In his opinion, the assets backing of the bank loans in India are viable or can be made viable therefore the concept of a bad bank and a good bank does not be relevant. Recapitalization of Public Sector Banks in the past by the Government of India as a solution for tiding bad loans was a temporary solution to give more life to projects but it could clean up the stressed assets in the system. However, Former Governor Dr. Raghuram Rajan and Former Deputy Governor Mr. Viral Acharya in the co-authored paper suggested the Government to privatize the PSB`s and focus on an overhaul of the bad loan management system. The duo opines that the first step to deal with bad loans in the Indian banking sector is to focus on honest recognition of loan losses. They also suggested that the Government obtains enormous power from direct bank lending and exercised to advance public goals like financial inclusion and infrastructure finance.

The Economic Survey, 2017 suggested Public Sector Asset Rehabilitation Agency (PARA) to buy out the big NPLs from banks in India. Mr. Sunil Mehta`s panel in his proposal Project Sashakt five-point plan recommending new Asset Management Company to take a mammoth and loan of Rs. 500 Crore. Former Finance Minister Mr. Arum Jaitley has also given the green light and said in the post-budget meeting that the Bad Bank is a possible situation to reduce the bad loans and faster recovery as well as fresh lending by banks. With this background, the impending launch of "Bad Bank" has gained momentum after the finance minister`s confirmation during the Union Budget to launch such a bank.

GLOBAL PERSPECTIVES

India's NPA ratio is at 9.1%, slightly behind Russia which is at 9.2%. This was followed by Korea (2000) which had NPA ratio of 8.9%. Other countries like Brazil, South Africa and China had 3.8%, 3.2% and 1.7% NPA ratio. Sanjeev Prasad, Sunita Baldawa and Anindya Bhowmik, analyst at Kotak bank's research arm said "We suggest a combination of 'curative' and 'preventive' measures to address the extant NPL problem and avoid repeat failures." They suggested two key areas, first, approval of specific resolution plans for 20-30 large stressed assets by a government committee, second, conversion of a portion of debt of stressed assets to equity may partly alleviate the problem. "To thwart future NPLs, the government can look at 'preventive' measures such as (1) development of a corporate bond market and (2) empowerment of public banks' management and private banks' boards," they said.

Gross NPAs of gross advances which stood at Rs 1.3 lakh crore as on March 2012, have increased by a whopping 438.46% to Rs 7 lakh crore as on December 2016. As per the Economic Survey, gross NPAs climbed to almost 12% of gross advances for public sector banks at end-September 2016. RBI now has more power to intervene in the NPA resolution and the central bank has issued directions regarding assets under corrective action plan (CAP) on joint lenders forum (JLF). Moody's Investors Services in its recent report said. "Resolution for NPAs is a long process due to two factors - the operating environment in key stressed sectors remains quite challenging and the market value of stressed assets is typically much lower than what the banks currently reflect on their balance sheets." As both government and RBI trying to do all they can, lets have a look at other countries who tackled with the same so-called NPA problems. Some of these methods may help India in their problem as well.

Figure 1. Non performing assets - countrywise

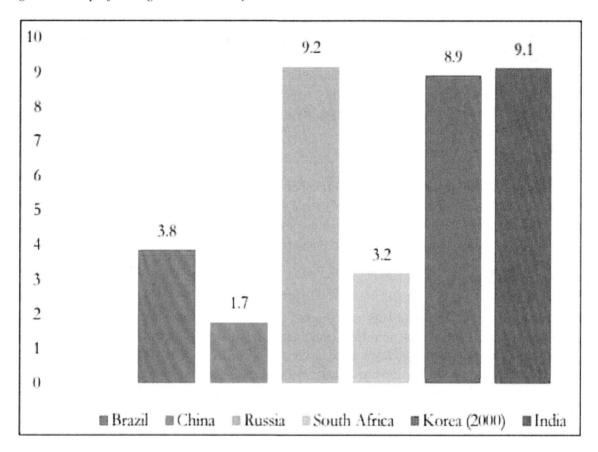

Source: RBI for India. World Development Indicators, World Bank for others.

China

The country being in the list of twin balance sheet has significantly followed four key methods to resolve the issue. Firstly, reducing risk by strengthening banks, raising disclosure standards and spearheading reforms of the state-owned enterprises (SOEs) by reducing their level of debt. Secondly, many laws were passed allowing creation of asset management companies, foreign equity participation in securitization and asset backed securitisation. Moving on, government which bore the financial loss of debt were discounted and debt equity swaps were allowed in case growth opportunity existed. To further strengthen resolution of NPA agenda, the Chinese government also implemented incentives like tax breaks, exemption from administration fees and clearcut asset evaluation norms.

Korea

Just like China, Korea too followed the idea of securitization, debt equity swaps and asset-backed securitization method. Apart from, the Korea government created Korea Asset Management Corp (KAMCO) and a NPA fund to fund and finance the purchase of NPAs. Main objective of central bank of Korea was solely defined as maintaining price stability, which is why they created the Financial Supervisory Commission (FSC) to ensure an effective supervisory system in line with the universal banking practices.

Japan

Japan government made amendment in the foreign exchange control law and the threat of suspension of banking business in case of failure to satisfy the capital adequacy ratio was prescribed. On the corporate front, major business group established a private standard settle vehicle for Japanese accounting standards (2001) in line with the international standards.

Other Countries

Spain and Ireland both developed large state-backed asset management companies under which they bought stressed assets at low valuations from banks and later executed these assets to those specializing in stressed asset investing and recovery. Ireland had further set up a National Asset Management Agency (NAMA) in 2009 for a period of 10 years. So far, NAMA had taken over almost 74 billion euro in bad loans from Irish banks in the aftermath of the crisis. Italy also had followed the securitization move just like China and Korea. It would be wrong to say that India has not done much for NPA resolution compared to the other countries. In fact, powerful norms have been introduced but they lack in legal hindrance, time consuming nature of asset disposal process, postponement of the problem in order to repot higher earnings, manipulation by debtors using political issues. One of the major key hurdle that RBI faces under NPAs resolution are losses that the banks are willing to take on the value of their bad loans. Former Finance Minister Mr. Arun Jaitely said the government is open in providing more funds for bank recapitalisation paring its stake once their health improves. So far, recapitalization has been low compared to other countries. China had injected $127 billion into the banking system during 2004-07, while the US Fed injected $2.27 trillion following the 2008 crisis. In contrast, India injected $17 billion only.

OBJECTIVES

1. To study the purpose of setting up Bad Bank in Indian Economy to resolve the increasing Non-Performing Assets in Indian Banking System
2. To analyse the role of Fintech and emerging technologies like Block chain, Artificial intelligence, Machine learning and Robotic Process automation through risk management software to resolve non-performing assets through Bad Bank

RESEARCH METHODOLOGY

To understand the role of Fintech and Emerging technologies, we used secondary online sources. The following sections were analysed on the basis of this to identify the Research problem. They are as follows:

- Impact of Bad Bank to reduce and resolve NPA problems through Digital Risk Management Software
- Positive and Negative Impact on Fintech stat ups sector and payment category wise.
- Innovative Role of Collaboration between banks and Fintech

The Secondary sources that we used were Online Article, Journals, and Issued Public Interest Booklets.

RESEARCH QUESTION AND NEED OF THE STUDY

Can E Collaboration of Fintech and Bad Bank can avoid the accumulation of NPA`s in the future, is an important research question . However, historically bad banks have not been successful for countries like Mexico, Greece, South Korea, Argentina and Italy, therefore the need of the study was to examine the purpose and success of Introduction of Bad Bank in India with the use of Fintech and emerging technologies in managing and reduce NPA.

LITERATURE REVIEW

Deloitte Report (2017) report on Blockchain Risk Management - Risk functions need to play an active role in shaping blockchain strategy answer the question – is your organization prepared for the new risks posed by the introduction of a blockchain framework? The report explained Blockchain through distributed ledge technologies (DLT) support entrepreneurs and corporates minimize the risks and is viewed as a foundational technology for the future of risk management.

Thales (2020) Report on Biometrics for Financial Institutions explains the digitalization of financials services and the rise for Biometrics from smart phones to new EMV Cards. The paper also attempts to answer the question how Biometrics fits into multi-factor authentication strategies and explains the five main biometrics used for commercial cases are smartphones. Finger or palm veins, finger prints, facial recognition, voice recognition and iris scan .

Sachdev (2021) in her blog "The Fintech way of solving India`s high NPA Situation "explains the various initiatives taken by the three Fintech founders to manage the challenges posed by the increase volumes of high NPA`s . These three Fintech Founders are – Mr Abhishek Pandit, Executive VP- AISECT, Mr Atul Monga, CEO & Co -Founder – Basic Home Loan and Mr. P.T Suresh, Founder and Director, Paycraft Solutions . Three FinTech founders talk about how Blockchain, Artificial Intelligence and Bio Metrics can provide solution to the high mountain of Bad Loans in Indian banking sector.

Chawla (2020) in his article " Top Credit Scoring Start Ups in India that use AI " published in Start Ups explain the process adopted by Indian Fintech Start Ups for calculating borrower`s credit history by designing alternative credit scoring models based on Artificial Intelligence techniques. The paper focus on various data point generated through digital technologies to assess the customer`s financial obligations through advanced AI modelling and data analytics.

Srikanth & Saravanan (2021) . in the article "Bad Bank is a Good Idea "Published in Business Line (last updated 15th FEB, 2021) in their opinion said that " If the bad bank is designed with a good business model, it may address the twin balance sheet problem India and capital adequacy concern also.

Yadav & Chavan (2021) in their research paper "ARC in India: A Study of their Business Operations and Role in NPA Resolution ." explain the evolution of the Asset Resolution Mechanism with special reference to ARCs and comparison of the Indian ARC model with the models in other countries. The paper focus on the main features of ARC Industry in India and stage of operations of ARC IN RESOLUTION OF ASSETS.

Bhasin, N. K., & Rajesh, A. (2022) in their research paper The Role of Emerging Banking Technologies for Risk Management and Mitigation to Reduce Non-Performing Assets and Bank Frauds in the Indian Banking System focussed on the application of new emerging digital banking tools with improved skills of lending managers to mitigate the risks of NPA and frauds. The research design of the study was divided into three sections – classification of risks in bank lending, reasons for increasing NPAs in Indian banking System and role of E Banking technologies to address the bad loans.

Bhorayal (2021) . Analytics India Magazine AIM research published the report "Indian Ai Start Up Funding in 2021" state that the technology driven start ups using various emerging technologies have increased heir funding from $ 1,108 million in 2021 from $ 836.3 million in 2020 reflecting 32.5% YOY increase.

Renuka, R.S . (2021) in their blog at Datamatics "Minimize NPA with integrated loan prediction for NBFCs and Banks." explains the benefits through a loan default prediction system which can significantly help the banks and financial institution to offset the bad loan losses with cost reduction and improved efficiencies. Loan default prediction system work om machine learning algorithms data on historical loans which captures the underlying characteristics of loans and status of payback.

Bhasin, N. K., & Rajesh, A. (2022) in their research paper " Impact of E Collaboration Between Indian Banks and Fintech Companies for Digital Banking and New Emerging Technologies " explain an overview of Fintech Ecosystem in Indian Banking System and top fintech products and services that have influenced Indian banking System. The paper focus on the top fintech trends like peer to peer (P2P) Digital lending services, cryptocurrency, artificial intelligence and machine learning, blockchain and NextGen Chatbot,

Singh et al.(2021) in their research paper " Role of Machine learning in changing social and business ecosystem – a qualitative study to explore the factors contributing to competitive advantage during Covid Pandemic ." explain the impact of AI and ML and improvement in the business operations . The paper also focusses on the market and customer insights and social role of machine learning in social media context.

Baudino, Orlandi & Zamil (2018) in the FSI Insights on policy Implementation 7 – The Identification and measurement of non performing assets: a cross country comparison published by Bank for International Settlements explains the accounting framework related to NPA identification, measurement and treatment of problem assets.

RESEARCH GAP

Various authors and researchers have studied both the topics of Introduction of Bad Bank and Non-Performing Assets in India and Emerging Technologies separately for resolving the problem of large number of bank frauds and non-payment of loans and advances. There was a limited literature review available on this theme of the book chapter. This research theme of the Fintech way of resolving NPA is a new theme which will help Banks and Fintech to E Collaborate and will lead to success of NPA by use of AI, ML and other emerging technologies to achieve its objective to avoid accumulation of bad loans.

RESEARCH DESIGN

To study the objective of the research, answer the research question and to address research gap, the Research has been design into two sections – Section 1 - Introduction of Bad Bank for Resolving Non Performing Assets (NPA) in Indian Banking Sector and Section 2 - Emerging Technologies to Manage the Challenges poised by Increasing NPA in Indian Banking Sector.

SECTION 1: INTRODUCTION OF BAD BANK FOR RESOLVING NON PERFORMING ASSETS (NPA) IN INDIAN BANKING SECTOR

1.1 Global Experience of Bad Bank

There have been countries who have tried to set up the bad bank in the past and nobody have failed. Initially, the bad bank was proposed to set up to resolve the bad loans issues by taking over the and loans from public sector banks and focus on their commercial banking operations. Most of the bad banks have emerged out of the global financial crisis or domestic crisis which have led to a surge in bad loans. Few examples of Bad Bank in other countries are:

Mellon Bank (1988)

The concept of Bad Bank was first used at the Pittsburgh-headquartered Mellon Bank in 1988 to solve the problems in the bank's bad debts in the commercial real-estate portfolios. It holds $ 1.4 billion of bad loans and took no public deposits. Federal Reserve agreed and allowed Mellon Bank to take over the bad loans of Grant Street National Bank (in liquidation).

Figure 2. Country-wise global bad banks

NOT ALL BAD

The first bank to use a bad bank strategy was Mellon Bank in the US, which was created in 1988 to hold $1.4 bn of bad loans. It was dissolved in 1995 after repaying bondholders

Some such banks:

UK: UK Asset Resolution

Nigeria: AMCON

SPAIN: SAREB

IRELAND: National Asset Management Agency (NAMA)

SWEDEN: Retriva & Securum

Finland: OHY Arsenal

UK Asset Resolution (2010)

UKAR, is a British financial service holding company set up as a bad bank to hold the two run-off elements, North Rock Asset Management (NRAM plc) and Bradford & Bengley (Mortgage Express brand). This bad bank was set up in the wake of the financial crisis of 2007-08 had a total mortgage book of £4.7bn (as of 31 March 2020.

AMCON (2010)

The Asset Management Corporation of Nigeria (AMCON) is a Nigeria`s Bad Bank set up on 19th July 2010 to absorb non-performing assets in exchange for government bonds after the Central Bank injected $ 4 billion to protect nine lenders in 2009. AMCON was established to bring stability and revive the financial system by taking on the job of resolving the problem of Non-Performing Loans (NLPs). Non-performing ratio with an upper limit of 5% has been set by The Central Bank of Nigeria whereas this ratio stood at double-digits in 2009 before the bailout. AMCON has recovered 57% of bad debts from 12000 debtors amounting to $ 1.8 trillion in 2015.

SAREB (2012)

In 2012, Spain set up a Bad Bank, known by Spanish language acronym - SAREB (Sociedad de Gestión de Activos procedentes de la Reestructuración Bancaria) to resolve payment crisis of over 100 billion Euros by taking of over bad loan assets and property from the troubled banks and due to collapse in housing markets in Europe. SAREB was set up a non-government and for-profit company to absorb soured assets and investments of private Spanish Banks, Public equity, financial institutions in the ratio of 55:45. SAREM was set for a span of fifteen years. SAREB took over the high-risk assets of the four nationalized Spanish banks BFA-Bankia, Catalunya Banc, NGC Banco-Banco Gallego, and Banco de Valencia) .

National Asset Management Agency (2009)

NAMA – National Asset Management Company was established in Ireland in 2009 as an unusual corporate entity following the global financial crisis – Bad Bank to address the serious crisis in Irish Banking System to which increased to Euro 30 Billion during the period 2008-09. It started with the large balance sheet by acquiring loans, costs, expenditure, and advancing working capital to bring down to zero as commercially practicable. NAMA achieved its recovery objective in October 2017.

Retriva and Securum

Retriva & Securum was set up as Asset Management Company in the year 1992 as a Bad Bank by Swedish Government to take over all the bad loans of two State- owned Nordbanken and Gotabanken respectively. These two banks account for 20% of bad assets in the Swedish Banking System. The six largest banks in Sweden accounted for 90% of bad loans and huge losses close to 12% of GDP. The Government did not save the owners of the banks but saved the banks by recapitalizing and Securum was authorized to take over the high-risk loans of these banks. Securum became one of the world`s largest Bad Banks and ranked as one of the top Europe's largest property owners. Securum acted on behalf of the Swedish Government with the objective to manage its vast holdings to find investors in the open market and recovered 86% of the amount involved. Securum was wound up in 1997.

OHY Arsenal

The collapse of two major banks, the Säästöpankki group/SKOP and STS Bank in the 1990`s caused the Finnish Banking Crisis in 1990s. The Finland Government introduced the two Bad Banks – OHY Arsenal and Sponda (property management companies). Arsenal started the process of winding down by deliberately filing for bankruptcy. 200 million of remaining capital has been collected during the bankruptcy. However, Arsenal is still involved in court cases and may not be disestablished until they are complete. Sponda was privatized and listed in Helsinki Stock Exchange in 1998, and in 2012, all government-held shares were sold by their holder, the government's asset management company Solidium. As of 2016, Sponda operates and remains on the stock market.

The Global experience of the world`s various countries as discussed above reflects that by and large Bad Banks are successful for the objective they have been set up however, there could be many approaches in different countries to resolve the problems of toxic assets. Four such avenues/approaches model by Mckinsey are explained in Table 1.

Table 1. Four avenues / approaches - bank to deal with bad loans

1	Banks ring-fence parts of its portfolios against losses - with second ring-fence that could be offered by the Government
2	Banks can establish a separate internal bad-loan restructuring unit
3	Toxic Loans could be transferred to a special purpose entity, usually sponsored by the Government
4	Bad loans are transferred to a legally separate banking entity

Source: Mckinsey & Company, 2009

1.2 The Necessity of Bad Banks in India

Government of India (GOI) in their Economic Survey 2020-21 focus on the two important issues of the Indian Economy – The Twin Balance Sheet (TBS) problem and the highest degree of stress being faced by both banking and corporates. India`s NPA ratios are higher than any other major emerging market of the world except Russia. Economic Survey reports further explains that Indian Public Sector Banks have a negative return of assets (ROA) which is far below the international norms of 1.5 percent and above for the banks around the world. With Covid Pandemic the volume of bad loans increased due to moratorium and waiver of interest on loans which lead the economy to a technical recession, a contraction for first two quarter of the fiscal year, and economy expected to shrink 7.5% in the year 2021. Figure 2 reflects the increasing NPA and bad loans from Rs. 323335 crores to 899802 crores in 2020.

Figure 3. Total bad loans of banks 2015-2020
Source: Jargajosh .com

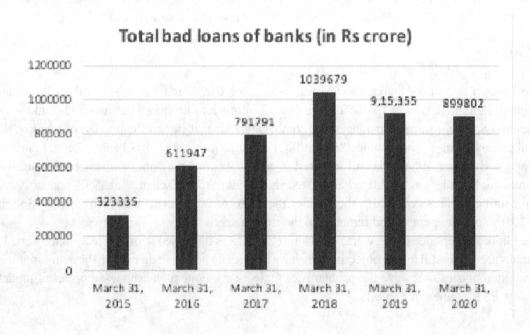

Indian Economy was in boom phased from the year 2000 to 2008 when the non-food or commercial credit doubled, the huge investment into telecom, roads, power aviation, and steel infrastructure projects and was an era of 9% growth. With the global financial crisis in 2008-2009, the Government banned many projects and corporates profit decreased resulting in nonpayment of loans. The direct impact of an increase in NPA lead to the restrictive lending by the banks and RBI placed many banks under prompt correction actions. (PCA). The lenders were required to make excessive provisioning and focus on recovering their bad loans. The primary reasons for the high level of NPA were the absence of a robust credit appraisal process, willful defaults and lack of sound monitoring standards.

Therefore, it became necessary to launch Bad Bank as a structural solution to transfer the NPA`s of PSB`s to one institution having expertise in resolving and restructuring such bad loans. As per the RBI Financial Stability Report and FM announcement of a bad bank, it's the right time for introducing the Bad Bank, taking into consideration the worst scenario of bad loans due to the COVID 19 pandemic and a severe stress ratio expected to 14.8% of its assets as NPA and PSB`s 17.6% by the first half of September, 2021. Table 1 reflects the gross non-performing assets trends during 2019 -2020 0.90% and 36 lakh crore marginal decrease due to massive write-offs by the banks amounting to Rs.2.38 lakh crore in the year 2019-20 and increase in total restructured standard advances to 0.43%. Public Sector banks GNPA stood at 6.78 lakh crore and 10.3% as of 31st March,2020.

Table 2. Gross non-performing assets

	31st March, 2019	**31st March, 2020**
Per Cent	9.10%	8.20%
Amount	9.36 lakh Crore	9 lakh Crore

Source: RBI`s Trend and Progress Report 2020

1.3 ARC`s in India: Business Operations and Role in NPA Resolution

On 19th April,2021 Reserve Bank of India constituted a Committee on the functioning of Asset Reconstruction Companies (ARC`S) for a comprehensive review of regulatory guidelines and working of ARC`s in the financial sector ecosystem. The Committee will be headed by Shri Sudarshan Sen, Former Executive Director, RBI with other five members from ICICI Bank, SBI, Management Development Institute, Ernst and Young, and Chartered Accountant. The terms of the reference of the committee are a review of existing legal and regulatory frame work of ARC`s, resolution of stressed assets under Insolvency and Bankruptcy Code, 2016, review of ARC`S business models, and suggestions for improving the liquidity in the trading of security receipts. The Committee has also invited suggestions and feedback on the terms of references from the ARC`s market participants and stakeholders.

RBI, Bulletin (April,2021) featured the article "ARC`s in India: A study of their Business Operations and Role in NPA Resolution" which explains the features of ARC industry in India, broad contours of the NPA Resolution mechanism, Indian ARC`s models, and future developments.

RDDBFI Act, 1993- Debt Recovery Tribunals

As per Narsimham Committee recommendations, the Recovery of Debts Due to Banks and Financial Institutions (RDDBFI) Act was passed for effective assets resolution in 1993. Debts Recovery Tribunals (DRTs) had a promising start with loan recovery of 81% in 2008-09 but in 2019-20 it reduced to 4% because of considerable delays in settlement, inadequate infrastructure and overstretched capacity.

SARFESI Act, 2002

Another legislative reform The Securitization and Reconstruction of Financial Assets and Enforcement of Security Interest (SARFESI Act) was introduced in 2002 to help financial institutions to ensure asset quality in multiple ways. This act empowers the financial institution and the banks to auction the borrower`s property and collateral without any intervention of the court to recover the secured loans by enforcing the security interest. ARC was set up as an alternative institution regulated and supervised by RBI for NPA resolution for sale of financial assets. An ARC needs to be set up with net owned funds of Rs. 100 crore and 15% Capital Adequacy Ratio (CAR) of its risk-weighted assets. An ARC can raise funds through the issue of bonds, security receipts, and debentures.

IBC Act, 2016

Another important financial sector reform was the launch of the Insolvency and the Bankruptcy (IBC) in 2016 to streamline and speed up the insolvency resolution process and recovery of secured assets for individuals and corporates. The total amount recovered under IBC was 45.5% whereas 26.7% by ARC`s. IBC seeks for making insolvency resolution economically viable process where as ARC`s deal with the recovery of NPA`s.

With the above initiatives and financial reforms, ARC continues to play an important role in loan recovery of the banks and improve quality of assets management post SARFESI and IBC Act. The important stages of the operations of ARC`s are:

1. Acquisition of Assets
2. Resolution of Assets
3. Recovery and Redemption of Security Receipts (SR)

Table 3 reflects the distribution of total resolved assets by a method of resolution. As per the regulatory guidelines, recovery of SRs is a critical indicator of the performance of ARC`s and ARC`s should be transparent in disclosing the NAV of SR`s for investor`s valuation.

Table 3. Distribution of total resolved assets, by method of resolution, in percent

	Resolution Method	Mar-16	Mar-17	Mar-18	Mar-19	Mar-20
1	Rescheduling of payment of debt	37.0	36.5	36.8	35.7	32.0
2	Enforcement of security interest	32.0	35.1	31.5	28.6	26.6
3	Settlement of dues of a borrower	30.0	24.8	25.2	28.4	26.0
4	Taking possession of assets	2.0	3.9	6.2	7.2	1.5
5	By sale of business	0.0	0.4	0.3	0.1	13.9

Source: RBI Supervisory returns

Table 4 reflects three Stages of ARC`S Business Models. Stage 1 The ARC`s acquire Non-Performance Assets from the banks through auctions and bilateral deals. Various subscriptions were formulated and investors subscriptions are invited through Qualified Institutional Buyers. ARC`s are required to invest a minimum of 15% of SR till the redemption under each segment,

Stage 2 focuses on the resolution of assets in different forms like sale or management takeover, lease of a part or whole business, enforcement of security interest, and rescheduling of payment of debts.

Stage 3 relates to the redemption of SR`s during the recovery of debt and work for a period of five years which can be extended up to eight years after the approval of their boards.

Table 4. Stages of ARC`s business models

STAGE 1	ARC`s ACQUISITION - NPA FROM BANKS AND FINANCIAL INSTITUTIONS
STAGE 2	ARC`s PROCESS OF PLANNING FOR RESOLUTION
STAGE 3	RECOVERY OF DEBT AND REDEMPTION OF SR`s

Source: RBI Bulletin, April 2021

SECTION 2: EMERGING TECHNOLOGIES TO MANAGE THE CHALLENGES POISED BY INCREASING NPA IN INDIAN BANKING SECTOR

Criteria for using Blockchain, Artificial Intelligence and other emerging technologies to manage the challenges of Bad Bank are the success of these applications in other commercial banks in India like HDFC Bank, ICICI Bank, Axis Bank, SBI, Bank of Baroda and Canara Bank.

2.1 Blockchain for Improving Business Strategy and Transparency

A Blockchain is a distributed database which stores information electronically in a digital format in groups, known as blocks. Mr. Abhishek Pandit, Executive VP, AISECT – An e-governance service provider involved in implementation of Financial Scheme associated with the two regional rural banks and three nationalized banks in India said that the Blockchain technology can help in improving transparency between market participants. A key advantage of application of Blockchain technology in Banking enhances security, improves efficiency, no third party involvement and quick transaction time. Blockchain technologies mitigate the exposure to banks and financial institutions to various types of risks in current business processes as shown in Table 5.

Table 5.

Type of Risk	Standard Risk Considerations through Blockchain
Strategic Risk	Improve business strategy, peer to peer nature of technology and right network
Buisness Continuity	Blockchain solutions shorten the duration of many business process and business continuity plans accounts for shorter incident response and recovery time
Reputational Risk	Blockchain technology is a part of core infrastructure and work with legacy infrastructure
Inforamtion Security Risk	Provides technology security, prevents corruption of data and cyber security risks
Regulatory Risk	Mitigate cross border& Operatioal risks, Provides data protection, transparency and market efficiency
Operational and IT Risks	Promote new business processes, updated technology, speed and scalibilty
Contractual Risks	Servicel level agreements between particiapting nodes and the administrator of the network
Suplier Riks	Third Party Risks as technology sourced from the external vendors

2.2 Artificial Intelligence (AI) and Machine Learning (ML) for Streamlined Processes

Artificial Intelligence and Machine Learning can play an important role in early detection of frauds and stress loans in Banks and NBFCs with less dependence on human intervention . AI and ML technology will help banks for online dispute resolution and lead to personalization of collection strategy by evaluating date form the past history of the borrowers regarding repayment and traits of individual borrower . (Sachdev,2021). loan default prediction system functionalities are highly useful which can significantly help the banks and financial institution to offset the bad loan losses with cost reduction and improved efficiencies. Loan default prediction system work om machine learning algorithms data on historical loans which captures the underlying characteristics of loans and status of payback. (Renukdas, 2021) . Functional features of lending Web / Mobile Application for Loan Prediction which help lenders to leverage requisite insights and minimize risk for an enhanced customer experience are:

1. Applications and Agent Tracking
2. Prospect Evaluation
3. Custom Business Analysis on Smartphone Data
4. Automated KYC
5. Debt Recovery Reports
6. Analysing existing NPAs
7. Alternative Credit Integration

2.3 Emerging Tech for High Tech Banking

Big Data, AI, ML and Data Sciences are the emerging technologies which are moving traditional method of lending to high tech securities in the banking industry . These Financial technologies (Fintech) enable the banks for early detection of defaults and frauds and create a robust system to take action for recovery and collection in time. Basic Home Loan Start Up and Fintech (2020), CEO Mr. Atul Monga aims to make home loan stress free process and faster through the use of emerging technologies like AI and ML for efficient strategy in monitoring the home loans for disbursement . monitoring timely repayment and collection. Paycraft Solution, Fintech Company set up in 2021 to ease and enable urban mobility and Mr P.T .Suresh, Founder & Director said that using the insights for emerging tech, banks can build a predictive model for early warning signals of loans .

2.4 Biometrics for Authentication

Biometrics for Financial Institutions, White Paper by Thales (2020) explains the digitization of financial services through Biometrics to protect against increase attempt of frauds in banks through strong authentication. Biometrics fit exactly into the multi factor authentication strategies such as facial recognition or finger print verification and are widely used by Government agencies for e-passport border control, electronic id and DNA used for criminal investigation. Banks have also adopt the Biometrics for identification of borrower and tracking in case of bad loans . Aadhar Biometric authentication has made datebase more secure and E KYC documents have reduced the burden of physical carrying documents. Banks are E collaborating and partnering with Fintech partners to develop risk management software for delinquent customers to bring down NPAs and improve customer experience.

2.5 Composite Credit Scoring

Most Fintech companies with the use of Machine Learning have complemented the standard credit rating scores with the new models of composite credit scoring on non- traditional markers of credit worthiness, consumer behaviour and other indices analysed with complex algorithms. Banks have started looking beyond the traditional published indices of credit risk modelling . Examples of Indian Fintech Start ups who have design credit score models based on AI and Ml techniques for credit assessment and partnered with the bank are – Lendingkart, Capital Float, Credit watch, Perfios and CreditVidya. (Chawla, 2020). All these Fintech Start ups make the best use of data science, algorithms, API based systems and AL / ML algorithms for dynamic credit assessment to banks and financial services. Capital Float has raised $ 140 million form the VC Funds like Ribbit Capital, Amazon, Saif Partners and Sequoia where as Credit Watch has raised $ 5 million funding and is trusted by RBL Bank, SBI, Karur Vysya Bank and Aditya Brila Financial Services.

2.6 Digitising Transaction Data

Digital Lending Process is important for the banks and financial institutions from the disbursement of loans to monitoring to collection and to ensure the risk management for loans getting bad. New emerging technology will help banks for faster disbursement of loans and advance and streamline credit loan cycle in small business lending.

Analysis of the Failure of Bad Banks in China

As India gets ready to operationalise a new bad bank, the National Asset Reconstruction Company Ltd. (NARCL), China is struggling with one of its biggest bad banks, the China Huarong Asset Management Co. Ltd. (Huarong). The Hong Kong-listed company, which counts the Chinese government as a principal shareholder, recently stoked financial stability concerns when it skirted a potential bond default. Earlier this year, its former Chairman Lai Xiaomin was executed for soliciting bribes, corruption and bigamy. While such harsh punishment will hopefully remain an outlier in global finance, the Chinese experience should inform Indian policy thinking on bad banks.

Recent research by Ben Charoenwong at the National University of Singapore and others highlights that Chinese bad banks effectively help conceal NPLs. The banks finance over 90 per cent of NPL transactions through direct loans to bad banks or indirect financing vehicles. The bad banks resell over 70 per cent of the NPLs at inflated prices to third parties, who happen to be borrowers of the same banks. The researchers conclude that in the presence of binding financial regulations (for example, on provisioning) and opaque market structures, the bad bank model could create perverse incentives to hide bad loans instead of resolving them

CONCLUSION

The success of Bad Bank depends upon the design aspects like complete segregation of risk from selling banks, fair pricing, investment of external credit, minimizing moral hazards and professional management of new entity with the E Collaboration with Large Fintech Players with the use of next generation emerging technologies. The role of digitalization through new technology can lead to secure loan origination, follow up, closure and enhanced customer satisfaction and experience . The success of this partnership can make Bad Bank Good Bank . The above data analysis reflects that Bad Bank would also give an impetus to India`s economic growth, which has been affected by heightened risk aversion arising from the unbridled growth in NPAs. And the Bad Bank will unlock trapped capital m which will be a net positive for the economy in the long term . Various examples of success of Bad Banks in other countries like US, Finland, Sweden and Indonesia where the same has been institutionalised and have served the purpose of reducing Non Performing Assets.

REFERENCES

Bhasin, N. K., & Gulati, K. (2021). Challenges of COVID-19 During 2020 and Opportunities for FinTech in 2021 for Digital Transformation of Business and Financial Institutions in India. In J. Zhao & J. Richards (Eds.), *E-Collaboration Technologies and Strategies for Competitive Advantage Amid Challenging Times* (pp. 282–299). IGI Global. doi:10.4018/978-1-7998-7764-6.ch011

Bhasin, N. K., & Gulati, K. (2021). A Study of the Readiness of Indian Banks to Absorb COVID-19`s Impact Through New Emerging Technologies and Strategies for Competitive Advantage. In J. Zhao & J. Richards (Eds.), *E-Collaboration Technologies and Strategies for Competitive Advantage Amid Challenging Times* (pp. 50–75). IGI Global. doi:10.4018/978-1-7998-7764-6.ch003

Bhasin, N. K., & Rajesh, A. (2021). Impact of E-Collaboration Between Indian Banks and Fintech Companies for Digital Banking and New Emerging Technologies. *International Journal of e-Collaboration*, *17*(1), 15–35. doi:10.4018/IJeC.2021010102

Bhasin, N. K., & Rajesh, A. (2022). The Role of Emerging Banking Technologies for Risk Management and Mitigation to Reduce Non-Performing Assets and Bank Frauds in the Indian Banking System. *International Journal of e-Collaboration*, *18*(1), 1–25. doi:10.4018/IJeC.290293

Bhorayal, R. (2021). Study: Indian AI Start Up in 2021. *Analytics India Magazine*. https://analyticsindiamag.com/study-indian-ai-startup-funding-in-2021/

Chawla, V. (2020). *Top Credit Scoring StartUps that use AI*. StartUps. https://analyticsindiamag.com/top-credit-scoring-startups-in-india-that-use-ai/

Renukdas, R. S. (2021). *Datamatic Blog Minimize NPA with Integrated Loan Prediction for NBFC`s and Banks*. https://blog.datamatics.com/minimize-npas-with-integrated-loan-prediction-in-nbfc-and-banking-apps

Sachdev, N. B. (2021). *The Fintech Way of solving India`s high NPA situation*. The Tech Panda. https://thetechpanda.com/the-fintech-way-of-solving-indias-high-npa-situation/34589/

Sanil, H.S., Singh, D., Raj, K.B., Choubey, S., Bhasin, N.K.K., Yadav, R., & Gulati, K. (2021). Role of machine learning in changing social and business eco-system – a qualitative study to explore the factors contributing to competitive advantage during COVID pandemic. *World Journal of Engineering*. doi:10.1108/WJE-06-2021-0357

Srikanth, M., & Saravanan, P. (2021). *Bad Bank is Actually a Good Idea*. National Institute of Rural Development and IIM Tiruchirappalli.

Tandon, T. (2021, April). What is Bad Bank? Know its Significance, Role and Benefits. *RBI Bulletin*.

Thalesgrpup.com. (2020). *Report. Biometrics for Financial Institutions*. https://www.sc.pages05.net/lp/22466/795954/fs-wp-biometrics-for-financial-institutions.pdf

Times of India.Com. (2021). *What is Bad Bank and Can It Resolve NPA Woes*. Retrieved from https://timesofindia.indiatimes.com/business/india-business/why-bad-bank-could-be-a-good-move-for-an-ailing-economy/articleshow/80614795.cms

Verma, S. (2022). *Explained: Bad Bank is ready, how will it resolve stressed assets*. Retrieved from https://indianexpress.com/article/explained/explained-bad-bank-stressed-assets-7747007/

Verma, S., & Mathew, G. (2021). *Explained: The Arguments for and Against a Bad Bank*. Indian Express.Com.

Wikepedia.en. (2021). *Bad Bank and U. K. Asset Resolution*. Retrieved from https://en.wikipedia.org/wiki?curid=21296887

Yadav, A., & Chavan, P. (2021, Apr.). *ARC's in India: A Study of their Business Operations and Role in NPA Resolution. RBI Bulletin*.

Chapter 4
Investigating the Role of Social Media on Student Engagement and Authentic Learning during Post COVID-19

Syed Far Abid Hossain
https://orcid.org/0000-0003-0729-1456
BRAC Business School, BRAC University, Dhaka, Bangladesh

Tanushree Karmoker
IUBAT University, Bangladesh

Fm. Asikullah
IUBAT University, Bangladesh

Reefat Arefin Khan
IUBAT University, Bangladesh

Phonebuson Chakma
https://orcid.org/0000-0002-3701-1673
IUBAT University, Bangladesh

Md. Ahmedul Islam Sohan
IUBAT University, Bangladesh

Kazi Khaled Shams Chisty
IUBAT University, Bangladesh

ABSTRACT

Social media-supported academic Apps such as Google Classroom, Zoom, ClassIn can simplify teaching and learning, even after the COVID-19 pandemic. Student engagement is a challenging task for educators in internet-enabled technology-enhanced learning platforms. This chapter investigates the role of various SNS platform to ensure sustainable learning. Quantitative data were collected (n = 285) using an online survey technique with the students from a recognized university in China. All the proposed hypotheses were supported. The findings indicated that constructs such as affective engagement (AE) and social engagement (SE) are significant forecasters of social interaction (SI) that may lead to achieve authentic learning task (ALTask) post COVID-19. Further, lack of attention (LAN) was found to significantly moderate social interaction and authentic learning tasks post COVID-19.

DOI: 10.4018/978-1-6684-5027-7.ch004

1. INTRODUCTION

The ultimate purpose of student engagement during the post COVID-19 is sustainable academic success. Academic success has become a threat and educational organizations expect ubiquitous learning platforms to boost the learning through effective engagement of the students. The earlier supremacy of emerging technological advancement has contributed to the academic field as being vital learning tool while supporting the students, teachers and learners facilitating the personalized learning process and information access as well as engaging students improve the skills and encourage socializing through social media platform. As a matter of fact, there has been many researchers who stated the great influence of social media and social interaction among learners and e-learning authenticity concerning academic perspective. Barton et al. (2021) has come up with an assessment of social media impacts on student learning and exploration of new sites of education in online platform. The study found that joined students in the online courses have been engaged with social interaction, earned better scores in academic performances and diverse outcome from learning. Hosen et al. (2021) highlights in the research that influence of social media in the education has contributed to knowledge formation and social media introduced many analytics tool to engage the students for obtaining scores in online courses. Student engagement in the online courses demonstrates the participation to fulfil the academic contents and activities by interacting within community. Therefore, student engagement requires the e-learning tool and assistance of social media for learning and achieving higher education Zheng et al. (2021).

This chapter sheds light on university student engagement and learning on a special focus on Post COVID-19 by answering the following research questions:

1. How does student engagement affect the authentic learning task during the post COVID-19?
2. Under what conditions this association will fluctuate when students have low or high lack of attention during the post COVID-19?

2. THEORETICAL BACKGROUND

Learning through social media and exploring the ideas with different sources have intrinsically been increased amongst students. Although the social media platforms have been introduced a many years back, yet after pandemic outbreak of Covid-19, the process of student's engagement of learning have contributed to higher achievement (Lacka et al. 2021). By the studies of researchers, different theories and behaviors for understanding the learning process and application of different educational platforms in authentic practice are explained through a framework which is theory of planned behavior. The behaviors towards social media have been created after being habituated with the program (Rana et al., 2019). Students who have been engaged with social media and platform for the purpose of study and collecting materials, it demonstrates their perceived behavioral facts and social human practice. Forming any decisions by the learners to engage in the study or practice may lead to engaging in that behavior that envisage the social behavioral pattern of that individual. In this research study, the theoretical framework on two theories has been developed to establish the cause and effect relationship among social engagement, perspective, post COVID behavior, learners' intentions and their adoptions towards social media platform for study. The broad framework of TAM by researcher David and TPB by Ajzen have explained the social attitudes and forces which implies human behavior (Ajzen and Fishbein, 1980; Rana et al., 2019).

The modification of broad theory of reasoned action that envisages the perceived behavioral control of the human changed to TPB. TPB by Ajzen is applied in the behavioral model for understanding the student's intention and their learning process. The TRA theory differs from TBP in the term of behavioral control that determines the intentions. Students after pandemic has switched to online education and been using materials to study and practice. The engagement to social media has increased after outbreak in order to reduce the time and make the communication more effective (McCarthy, Kneavel, Ernst, 2021). The TAM demonstrates the model of technological adoptions which enhances the student's adaptability in the online platform, and finds key aspects of student's engagement for academic performance (Mutambara, Bayaga, 2021). Moreover, from the researchers study, it purports that authenticity in learning derives from exploring the new platforms and also, learning process remains continued among students that results from acting in the certain situation (Cheng, 2019). TAM and TPB presents the impacts of social media that engages students and their learning even after pandemic is being controlled. To understand the behavior of students after pandemic, many have been recovered from mental illness and also, the major effects of isolation contributed to the change of behavioral control. There are two acts of control including direct and indirect as well as intentions are stated as correspondence between the parts of behavioral control. The authentic learning process that social media has role in can construct the concepts and new ideas in the learners that are relevant to the project or study. After the COVID pandemic, the e-learning process creates many opportunities for students to use and engage with the material at a slower pace if they feel the necessity (Raza et al. 2020). The indirect behavioral control factor was presented as a way to assess one's feelings about a contextual occurrence that might obstruct a behavior but over which the individual has no direct control. The direct behavioral control aspect was introduced to investigate the amount to which an individual's self-efficacy (confidence in one's own ability) perspectives on completing an activity are held. According to the first theory of Fred Davis (technology acceptance model), the students perceived the enjoyment while learning from social media and perceived ease of using to facilitate the programs for learning easily (Al Rahimi, Othman, Musa, 2013).

The social media in student engagement has different impacts that have been utilized after the pandemic and empirical evidences have been found that supports the framework in the learning theory. The study refers to the framework of TAM that applied to interpret the model where a huge number of diversity been shown.

By the theory of planned behavior established by Ajzen, it describes the human social behavior, perspectives that are different and diverse, and perceived behavioral control which are envisaged to contemplate the behavioral control. This has been emphasized by (De Leeuw et al. 2015) that TPB exemplifies as well felicitous for evaluating the students engagement in higher education, high school and also, in inclusive education in different regions and also, the behavior during Covid-19 (Van Uden et al., 2014). The relationship between student engagement and academic achievement is important because engagement behaviors can be managed to improve educational performance by structuring day-to-day academic experiences, aggregate learning, long-term achievement, and scholastic success (Kahu, 2013; Kahu and Nelson, 2018).

By the further contextual part of the theory, the application of mentioned theories of student engagement and authentic learning to explore and generate new ideas for learning promotes the social media after the pandemic that making effective progress for students.

Social Networking and Authentic Learning during Post Covid-19

Social interaction refers to the relationship between two or more individuals which helps society to build block among the members of the society. It could be any kind of relationship between two individuals. It is an essential aspect of social relationship (Hoppler, Segerer, & Nikitin, 2022). It also refers to build discussion about any subject in the society between two or more person. Long time ago, members in the society prefers to use face to face or written interaction which was the simplest way to communication with each other. However, Covid-19 situation and the developed technologies have changes the common medium of communication and people prefers to use social networking application to interact to each other (Calbi, et al., 2021). Nowadays, students prefer to use social networking sites. During Covid-19 period, students could not go to attend classes physically in the classroom and the classes took place by using social networking sites as well. However, the gaps between the students and the teacher takes place because of the limitations of social interactions at the time of taking classes through social networking sites. Students can learn the authentic learning tasks by attending the classes physically and actual social interaction between the teacher and the students creates by attending the classes in the classroom (Jones & Kessler, 2020). Schools have developed their framework to build effective social interaction between teacher and students where a single style of interaction is followed which refer the knowledge will be supplied from teacher to students.

The key note in here is, the task of the teacher is to provide notes, reading materials, lectures and other materials to their students to support their students to gain knowledge. However, it is essential to measure the capacity of the students and the way students can adopt the knowledge that teachers want to provide to their students. Social interaction plays an important role at this section. It is because, students feedback is essential to know their capacity and the way they reacts on certain movement of the teacher. (Li, Flynn, DeRosier, Weiser, & Austin-King, 2021) agrees that, Social networking sites works to minimize gaps between teacher and students but the gaps is still there. Lack of control from teachers to students and insufficient materials to run the classroom is the reason behind that. In order to develop the authentic learning activities for the students is to help them to become the thinker, good speaker, listener, writer and reader in the classroom and directly supervise their activities (Wut & Xu, 2021).

Our main focus is to identify the way social interaction positively affect the authentic learning task. During the Covid-19 period, the gaps between teachers and students took place because of the online classes (Tackie, 2022). At present, the schools are resuming their activities and the outcomes of the students are increasing at the time of measuring their performance on authentic learning tasks (Lockee, 2021). Therefore, it could be said that, the social interaction between teachers and students increased during face to face classes and it affect positively on students' authentic learning tasks. As a result we hypothesize:

H1: *Affective engagement will positively affect social interaction (during post COVID-19)*
H2: *Social engagement will positively affect social interaction (during post COVID-19)*
H3: *Social interaction will positively affect the authentic learning task(during post COVID-19)*

The Mediating Relationship between Social Interaction, Affective Engagement and Authentic Learning Task during Post Covid-19

Social interaction of a student is the process by which the student interact with the teacher, other students and people that around that student. Affective engagement and authentic learning tasks are two entities and the relationship between these two entities varies because of social interaction during post Covid-19 (Ivanec, 2022). Affective engagement assists the teachers to engage the students towards the authentic learning tasks as greater the interests of the students towards authentic learning provides better result. Students show their keen to know deeply about a subject (Elmer, Mepham, & Stadtfeld, 2020). Hence, social interaction and affective engagement may result the students to develop their authentic learning tasks as it refers to engage the student towards sharing academic challenges and learning from their experiences.

According to (Senior, Bartholomew, Soor, Shepperd, Bartholomew, & Senior, 2018), affective learning enable students to understand their capability of learning and provide freedom on their decision-making process to determine the curriculum, happiness or sadness, like or dislike and value of learning. By looking at the situation, it is important for the teachers to encourage students to choose positive activities at the time of enhance their choice. Affective engagement and authentic learning task practice dropped during Covid-19 pandemic period because of lack of social interaction between students and teachers. Students' interest towards authentic learning increases at the time they involve with social interaction and they get chance to provide their opinion towards their teacher (Koob, Schröpfer, Coenen, Kus, & Schmidt, 2021). As a result, we hypothesize that:

H4: *Social interactions mediate the relationship between affective engagement and authentic learning task*

The Mediating Relationship between Social Interaction, Social Engagement and Authentic Learning Task during Post COVID-19

The COVID-19 pandemic has had an extraordinary and wide-ranging impact on education, affecting practically every student on the planet. As social distancing had to be maintained during the COVID-19 era, social interaction and engagement between students and teachers had become near impossible. As a result, educational systems and institutions around the globe had to ensure education of students remotely (Zhao & Watterston, 2021).

Social interaction plays a beneficial role on online learning efficacy (Baber, 2021). In a pandemic setting, online delivery must actively and explicitly adopt strategies to include social contact in online learning (Finnegan, 2021). When strategically integrated into an online education plan, social media may help students and teachers stay connected when they are away, increase student engagement, and make remote learning less remote (Greenhow & Galvin, 2020). Researchers have found evidence that learners who participate in social interaction outperform their peers (Al-Hasan, 2021).

Authentic learning is a teaching strategy that places learning activities in the context of future application (Herrington, 2014). Student engagement is a mutually beneficial collaborative approach between students and their institutions, where students are involved in administration, instruction, research, and community service activities at their institutions (Peters et. al., 2019). In order to effectively utilize authentic learning, the involvement of student engagement is highly essential. According to Chiu (2021), students' cognitive and emotional involvements were decreased in surroundings that lacked emotional attachment. This emotional attachment can be generated mainly through social interaction.

It is true that during the pandemic era, it was rather troublesome to maintain social interaction in order to increase student-teacher engagement and contribute to the authentic learning task in the process. However, in the post pandemic scenario, as educational institutions are gradually returning to their normal selves, this situation is gradually improving. At present, students are comfortable in utilizing both online and in-person social communication with their peers. Furthermore, during this post pandemic era, the creation of a student partnership culture has been recognized as a technique of working within resource constraints and optimizing educational experiences for both students and staff (Whelehan, 2020). This means that social engagement between students and their peers are impacting positively on authentic learning task through the medium of social interaction. Hence, we hypothesize:

H5: *Social interaction mediates the relationship between social engagement and authentic learning task*

The Moderating Role of Lack of Attention during Post COVID-19

Laidlaw et. al. (2011) stated that simply having the option to engage with others might influence social attention positively. The possibilities of such interaction were limited during the pandemic period due to social-distancing protocols. However, in the post COVID era, the opportunity for social interaction has gradually been returning to its former glory. Consequently, the likelihood of students engaging in authentic learning assignments is increasing.

It is evident from the research of Gurjar (2020) that, social networks can be used to facilitate authentic learning in distance education. Although some might argue that social media is harming the attention span of students, results suggest otherwise. It has been observed that, there is no difference in attention span length between people who frequently use social media and those who do not (Kies, 2018). Generation Z students, or in other words, students are mainly born within 1995 to 1999, typically possess a short attention span during long lectures and a high desire for social interactions (Essop, 2020). It can be perceived from this that, social interaction plays a major role in authentic learning task. However, for authentic learning to be fruitful, the role of attention cannot be denied even to the slightest extent.

In the present post COVID world, attention disorder is gradually turning out to be a major concern. From the research work of Delgado-Alonso et. al. (2022), it was found that COVID-19 patients performed poorly on several measures of attention and executive function. One of the five most common chronic symptoms in patients recovering from COVID-19 is attention disorder (Garg et. al., 2021). According to the studies of Hellmouth et. al. (2021), neurocognitive symptoms related with COVID-19 were detected in young and middle-aged persons, even if they were not hospitalized. This scenario is still prevalent at present post pandemic period.

According to the findings of some researchers, adding interactivity to video lectures increases attention span by more than 20% (Geri et. al., 2017). Therefore, it can also be implied that lack of attention may somehow affect student engagement in authentic learning tasks. Hence, we hypothesize:

H6: *Lack of attention moderate the relationship between social interaction and authentic learning task, such that when a lack of attention is higher, the relationship becomes weaker*

Figure 1. Conceptual Framework

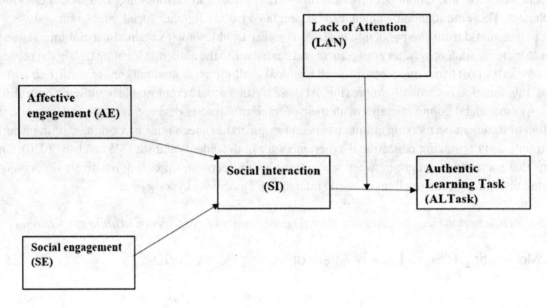

RESEARCH METHODOLOGY

Measurements

A study based on methodology was esteemed most suitable to test the proposed hypotheses. All variables estimated using a five-point Likert-scale moored 1 "Never" to 5 "Very frequently".

Sample and Data Collection

From 586 questionnaires, we get 348 questionnaires in return. After removing the data from the participant that did not use WeChat, we retained 285 completed sets of surveys for the statistical analyses. The final sample consisted of 53.3% of males with a majority 73.7% between 19-25 years old, the majority (61.8%) of participants studying Business/Management, engineering (18%), others (14%). 73% students are undergraduate and 52.3% are in the fourth years of study. Table 1 below represents the differences in sample and data collection where 92% responded positively about virtual class.

Table 1. Reliability, validity and standard loading

Latent variables	Items	Standard Loading	Cronbach's Alpha	Composite reliability (CR)	Average variance extracted (AVE)
Affective engagement	AE1 AE2 AE3 AE4	0.681 0.835 0.761 0.642	0.709	0.822	0.538
Social engagement	SE1 SE2 SE3 SE4	0.812 0.836 0.769 0.606	0.752	0.844	0.579
Social interaction	SI1 SI2 SI3	0.871 0.899 0.877	0.859	0.913	0.779
Lack of attention	LAN1 LAN2 LAN3	0.944 0.840 0.686	0.827	0.867	0.689
Authentic learning task	ALT1 ALT2	0.894 0.904	0.763	0.894	0.809

Table 2. Descriptive statistics and inter-correlations

Constructs	Mean	STD	1	2	3	4	5
1.Affective engagement	3.7693	.60810	**0.734**				
2.Social engagement	3.6737	.62771	0.509**	**0.761**			
3.Social Interaction	3.7754	.77889	0.385**	0.393**	**0.882**		
4.Lack of attention	2.0725	.94001	-0.164**	-0.202**	-0.170**	**0.830**	
5.Authentic learning task	3.3070	.77570	0.403**	0.392**	0.239**	-.094	**0.899**

*Note.*N = 285, *<0.05; **<0.01; the diagonal (bold) values represent the square root of the average variance extracted.

Table 3. Discriminant validity

Constructs	1	2	3	4	5
1.Affective engagement	---				
2.Social engagement	0.701	---			
3.Social Interaction	0.495	0.489	---		
4.Lack of attention	0.208	0.256	0.201	---	
5.Authentic learning task	0.537	0.521	0.295	0.121	---

Hypotheses Testing

Using the structural model, we tested hypotheses H1-H6 by estimating the significance (p value) of the structural paths of the constructs. From the Table 4, it showed that affective engagement had a significant and positive effect on social interaction (path coefficient= 0.255, p< 0.001); thus, H1 was supported. The results also indicated that social engagement positive significantly correlated with social interaction (path coefficient= 0.273, p< 0.001); giving support for H2. Furthermore, giving support for H3, the results showed that social interaction positively affect authentic learning task (path coefficient= 0.228, p< 0.001). H4 and H5, regarding the indirect effect of affective engagement and social engagement on authentic learning task through social interaction was also reflected by the results (path coefficient= 0.058, p< 0.05 for affective engagement, and path coefficient= 0.062, p< 0.05 for social engagement) giving support for both hypotheses. Moreover, Table 4 showed the negative significant results of moderating role of lack of attention in the relationship between social interaction and authentic learning task (path coefficient= -0.140, p< 0.05).

Table 4. Hypothesized structural model

Hypotheses	Coefficients	T value	BC-CIs	Supported
H1: AE ® SI	0.255***	3.648	0.109 and 0.381	Yes
H2: SE ® SI	0.273***	3.779	0.133 and 0.412	Yes
H3: SI ® ALT	0.228***	3.259	0.092 and 0.355	Yes
H4: AE ® SI ® ALT	0.058*	2.446	0.020 and 0.115	Yes
H5: SE ® SI ® ALT	0.062*	1.973	0.017 and 0.132	Yes
H6: SI x LAN ® ALT	-0.140*	1.963	-0.291 and -0.001	Yes

N = 285
*<0.05; **<0.01; ***<0.001

DISCUSSION

The research is all about the relationship between student engagement and authentic learning during the post covid-19 periods from the enhanced perspective of our previous article. Given the factors of promoting students' engagement in times of post covid-19 periods, the results of quantitative data analysis with the help of statistical software Smart PLS 3 indicated that all the 6 hypotheses had been supported. The result elucidates that affective engagement has positive impact on social interaction which in turn leads to authentic learning with availability of efficient online teaching and learning through SNSs platform. A former research article also detected that social networking sites help students to maintain their interaction and communication (Kumari, A., & Verma, J. 2015). Admittedly students have propensity to adhere to online class via a specific platform like WeChat. Loss of internet significantly affects students' education (Onyema, E. M., Eucheria, N. C, 2020). In addition, social engagement along with a specific platform regarding WeChat encourages students to have more social interaction, resulting in authentic learning. On the other hand, lack of attention has a moderating role in between social interaction and authentic learning tasks. Considering the popularity, accessibility, and pervasive use of WeChat while doing online class, there is a possibility to improve the attention of the students. However, there are no differences among the respondents in accordance with the findings of the study, though the maximum number of respondents (63%) was undergraduate students. The result that we had found out has similar effect on students.

THEORETICAL IMPLICATIONS

The research is based on the existing literature of SNSs in educational technology development. In the beginning, the authors had carried out a thorough review of wide spread and well noted literature related to authentic learning tasks and tried with utmost attention to accomplish the rest of the items. Moreover, using TPB as the theoretical background along with imperial analysis, this research measured the effective engagement, lack of attention, social engagement and social interaction that are considered as the antecedents of authentic learning. They disclosed a particular level of variance in authentic learning tasks (80%) with approximately less and more impactful constructs as compared to existing literature. Undoubtedly, this is an authentic learning task with a higher variance. Finally, the data were collected from university students during the post covid-19 periods. It goes without saying that this is the first empirical study that highlighted authentic learning tasks after the covid-19 pandemic. Therefore, this research is creating impediment to the upcoming studies on the similar phenomenon. In addition, keeping the severe consequences of covid-19 and the possibility of upcoming variant in mind, lack of attention as a moderating variable is still deemed to be one of the key reasons of achieving sustainable online learning during the post covid-19 periods. Admittedly, google classroom and zoom can further dominate the authentic learning tasks.

PRACTICAL IMPLICATIONS

The positive effect of authentic learning tasks and other variables in these study makes it clear that the university teachers must have to prepare the course outline following the post covid-19 situation. The teachers and instructors must maintain flexibility and evaluation process for persisting positive attitudes toward learning. Technology-based education along with learning friendly environment is crucial for ensuring proper education. Therefore, the university authority should set up effective and efficient policy for the post pandemic periods so that affecting engagement and social engagement can be expanded with more social interaction. However, the instructors may also consider game-based learning and not to compel students to stay in the class with usual platforms. Students must have been encouraged to have Social Networking Sites (SNSs) such as WeChat as a helpful and efficient tool to spread quality teaching and learning in the post covid-19 outbreak.

LIMITATIONS AND FURTHER RESEARCH

The research has some limitations. The sample size is small, since we were not able to get access to the students of other educational institutions because of strict rules and regulations enforced to mitigate the further risk of covid-19. So, there is a huge change and vast possibility of other researchers to conduct their study on the same phenomenon with bigger sample size including universities and the rest of the educational institutes. Furthermore, future study can be conducted highlighting the most social and suitable networking sites for learning in the post covid-19 period. Finally, this research did not evaluate academic performance. Therefore, it would be helpful, if academic performance is observed in upcoming research that has effective recommendations for coping with any destructive epidemic or even pandemic with less stress.

CONCLUSION

The main aim of the research paper is to find out the relationship between student engagement and authentic learning during the post covid-19 periods. For having so, TPB had been used to develop the study. The moderating role of lack of attention through WeChat was also conducted to evaluate the authentic learning situation during the coid-19 period. The accurate research model indicates some factors that affect student engagement and authentic learning during the post covid-19 period. Following the imperial result, we have provided explanation for educators and educational policy makers.

REFERENCES

Ajzen, I., & Fishbein, M. (1980). Understanding Attitudes and Predicting Social Behavior. *Organizational Behavior and Human Decision Processes*, *50*(2), 179–211. doi:10.1016/0749-5978(91)90020-T

Al-Hasan, A. (2021). Effects of social network information on online language learning performance: A cross-continental experiment. *International Journal of e-Collaboration, 17*(2), 72-87.

Al-Rahimi, W. M., Othman, M. S., & Musa, M. A. (2013). Using TAM model to measure the use of social media for collaborative learning. *International Journal of Engineering Trends and Technology*, *5*(2), 90–95.

Baber, H. (2021). Social interaction and effectiveness of the online learning–A moderating role of maintaining social distance during the pandemic COVID-19. Asian Education and Development Studies. behavior. *University of South Florida, 2007*, 67–98.

Barton, B. A., Adams, K. S., Browne, B. L., & Arrastia-Chisholm, M. C. (2021). The effects of social media usage on attention, motivation, and academic performance. *Active Learning in Higher Education*, *22*(1), 11–22. doi:10.1177/1469787418782817

Calbi, M., Langiulli, N., Ferroni, F., Montalti, M., Kolesnikov, A., & Gallese, V. (2021). *The consequences of COVID-19 on social interactions: An online study on face covering*. Retrieved 04 24, 2022, from Scientific Reports: https://www.nature.com/articles/s41598-021-81780-w

Cheng, E. W. (2019). Choosing between the theory of planned behavior (TPB) and the technology acceptance model (TAM). *Educational Technology Research and Development*, *67*(1), 21–37. doi:10.100711423-018-9598-6

Chiu, T. K. (2021). Student engagement in K-12 online learning amid COVID-19: A qualitative approach from a self-determination theory perspective. *Interactive Learning Environments*, 1–14. doi:10.1080/1 0494820.2021.1926289

Delgado-Alonso, C., Valles-Salgado, M., Delgado-Álvarez, A., Yus, M., Gómez-Ruiz, ·N., Jorquera, M., ... Matías-Guiu, J. A. (2022). Cognitive dysfunction associated with COVID-19: A comprehensive neuropsychological study. *Journal of Psychiatric Research*.

Dhume, S. M., Pattanshetti, M. Y., Kamble, S. S., & Prasad, T. (2012, January). Adoption of social media by business education students: Application of Technology Acceptance Model (TAM). In *2012 IEEE International Conference on Technology Enhanced Education (ICTEE)* (pp. 1-10). IEEE. 10.1109/ ICTEE.2012.6208609

Elmer, T., Mepham, K., & Stadtfeld, C. (2020). *Students under lockdown: Comparisons of students' social networks and mental health before and during the COVID-19 crisis in Switzerland. Plos One, 7.*

Essop, M. F. (2020). Implementation of an authentic learning exercise in a postgraduate physiology classroom setting. *Advances in Physiology Education*, *44*(3), 496–500. doi:10.1152/advan.00083.2020 PMID:32795121

Finnegan, M. (2021). The Impact on Student Performance and Experience of the Move from Face-to-face to Online Delivery in Response to COVID-19: A Case Study in an Irish Higher Education Institute. *All Ireland Journal of Higher Education*.

Garg, M., Maralakunte, M., Garg, S., Dhooria, S., Sehgal, I., Bhalla, A. S., Vijayvergiya, R., Grover, S., Bhatia, V., Jagia, P., Bhalla, A., Suri, V., Goyal, M., Agarwal, R., Puri, G. D., & Sandhu, M. S. (2021). The conundrum of 'long-COVID-19: A narrative review. *International Journal of General Medicine*, *14*, 2491–2506. doi:10.2147/IJGM.S316708 PMID:34163217

Geri, N., Winer, A., & Zaks, B. (2017). Challenging the six-minute myth of online video lectures: Can interactivity expand the attention span of learners? *Online Journal of Applied Knowledge Management*, *5*(1), 101–111. doi:10.36965/OJAKM.2017.5(1)101-111

Greenhow, C., & Galvin, S. (2020). *Teaching with social media: Evidence-based strategies for making remote higher education less remote.* Information and Learning Sciences.

Gurjar, N. (2020). Leveraging social networks for authentic learning in distance learning teacher education. *TechTrends*, *64*(4), 666–677. doi:10.100711528-020-00510-7

Hellmuth, J., Barnett, T. A., Asken, B. M., Kelly, J. D., Torres, L., Stephens, M. L., Greenhouse, B., Martin, J. N., Chow, F. C., Deeks, S. G., Greene, M., Miller, B. L., Annan, W., Henrich, T. J., & Peluso, M. J. (2021). Persistent COVID-19-associated neurocognitive symptoms in non-hospitalized patients. *Journal of Neurovirology*, *27*(1), 191–195. doi:10.100713365-021-00954-4 PMID:33528824

Herrington, J., Reeves, T. C., & Oliver, R. (2014). Authentic learning environments. Handbook of research on educational communications and technology, 401-412. doi:10.1007/978-1-4614-3185-5_32

Hoppler, S. S., Segerer, R., & Nikitin, J. (2022). The Six Components of Social Interactions: Actor, Partner, Relation, Activities, Context, and Evaluation. *Front Phychol, 6.*

Hosen, M., Ogbeibu, S., Giridharan, B., Cham, T. H., Lim, W. M., & Paul, J. (2021). Individual motivation and social media influence on student knowledge sharing and learning performance: Evidence from an emerging economy. *Computers & Education*, *172*, 104262. doi:10.1016/j.compedu.2021.104262

Ivanec, T. P. (2022). The Lack of Academic Social Interactions and Students' Learning Difficulties during COVID-19 Faculty Lockdowns in Croatia: The Mediating Role of the Perceived Sense of Life Disruption Caused by the Pandemic and the Adjustment to Online Studying. *Social Sciences*.

Jones, A., & Kessler, M. (2020). Teachers' Emotion and Identity Work During a Pandemic. *Conceptual Analysis*.

Kahu, E. R. (2013). Framing student engagement in higher education. *Studies in Higher Education*, *38*(5), 758–773. doi:10.1080/03075079.2011.598505

Kies, S. C. (2018). Social media impact on attention span. *Journal of Management & Engineering Integration*, *11*(1), 20–27.

Koob, C., Schröpfer, K., Coenen, M., Kus, S., & Schmidt, N. (2021). Factors influencing study engagement during the COVID-19 pandemic: A cross-sectional study among health and social professions students. *PLoS One*, *16*(7), e0255191. doi:10.1371/journal.pone.0255191 PMID:34314450

Kumari, A., & Verma, J. (2015). Impact of social networking sites on social interaction-a study of college students. *Journal of the Humanities and Social Sciences*, *4*(2), 55–62.

Lacka, E., Wong, T. C., & Haddoud, M. Y. (2021). Can digital technologies improve students' efficiency? Exploring the role of Virtual Learning Environment and Social Media use in Higher Education. *Computers & Education*, *163*, 104099. doi:10.1016/j.compedu.2020.104099

Laidlaw, K. E., Foulsham, T., Kuhn, G., & Kingstone, A. (2011). Potential social interactions are important to social attention. *Proceedings of the National Academy of Sciences of the United States of America*, *108*(14), 5548–5553. doi:10.1073/pnas.1017022108 PMID:21436052

Li, L., Flynn, K. S., DeRosier, M. E., Weiser, G., & Austin-King, K. (2021). Social-Emotional Learning Amidst COVID-19 School Closures: Positive Findings from an Efficacy Study of Adventures Aboard the S.S. GRIN Program. *Frontiers in Education*.

Lockee, B. (2021). Online education in the post-COVID era. *Nature Electronics*, *4*(1), 5–6. doi:10.103841928-020-00534-0

McCarthy, K. S., Kneavel, M., & Ernst, W. (2021). Psychometric properties of concussion knowledge and cognitive mediators of reporting measures. *Brain Injury*, *35*(10), 1210–1217. doi:10.1080/026990 52.2021.1959064 PMID:34347541

Mutambara, D., & Bayaga, A. (2021). Determinants of mobile learning acceptance for STEM education in rural areas. *Computers & Education*, *160*, 104010. doi:10.1016/j.compedu.2020.104010

Onyema, E. M., Eucheria, N. C., Obafemi, F. A., Sen, S., Atonye, F. G., Sharma, A., & Alsayed, A. O. (2020). Impact of Coronavirus pandemic on education. *Journal of Education and Practice*, *11*(13), 108–121.

Peters, H., Zdravkovic, M., João Costa, M., Celenza, A., Ghias, K., Klamen, D., Mossop, L., Rieder, M., Devi Nadarajah, V., Wangsaturaka, D., Wohlin, M., & Weggemans, M. (2019). Twelve tips for enhancing student engagement. *Medical Teacher*, *41*(6), 632–637. doi:10.1080/0142159X.2018.1459530 PMID:29683024

Rana, N. P., Slade, E., Kitching, S., & Dwivedi, Y. K. (2019). The IT way of loafing in class: Extending the theory of planned behavior (TPB) to understand students' cyberslacking intentions. *Computers in Human Behavior*, *101*, 114–123. doi:10.1016/j.chb.2019.07.022

Raza, S. A., Qazi, W., Shah, N., Qureshi, M. A., Qaiser, S., & Ali, R. (2020). Drivers of intensive Facebook usage among university students: An implications of U&G and TPB theories. *Technology in Society*, *62*, 101331. doi:10.1016/j.techsoc.2020.101331

Senior, R. M., Bartholomew, P., Soor, A., Shepperd, D., Bartholomew, N., & Senior, C. (2018). The Rules of Engagement: Student Engagement and Motivation to Improve the Quality of Undergraduate Learning. *Frontiers in Education*.

Tackie, H. (2022). *(Dis)Connected: Establishing Social Presence and Intimacy in Teacher–Student Relationships During Emergency Remote Learning*. SAGE Journals.

Whelehan, D. F. (2020). Students as Partners: A model to promote student engagement in post-COVID-19 teaching and learning. *All Ireland Journal of Higher Education, 12*(3).

Wut, T.-m., & Xu, J. (2021). Person-to-person interactions in online classroom settings under the impact of COVID-19: a social presence theory perspective. *Asia Pacific Education Review*, 371–383.

Zhao, Y., & Watterston, J. (2021). The changes we need: Education post COVID-19. *Journal of Educational Change*, *22*(1), 3–12. doi:10.100710833-021-09417-3

Zheng, W., Yu, F., & Wu, Y. J. (2021). Social media on blended learning: The effect of rapport and motivation. *Behaviour & Information Technology*, 1–11. doi:10.1080/0144929X.2021.1909140

Chapter 5
Redefining Teachers' Interactions and Role Awareness:
From a Learning Perspective to a Focus on Knowledge Management

Salvatore Nizzolino

iD https://orcid.org/0000-0002-3008-2890

Sapienza University of Rome, Italy

ABSTRACT

This chapter's goal is to identify the teacher mental framework oriented to knowledge management (KM) and compatible to the ubiquitous Nonaka's model, regarding the sharing and collaboration practices found in the EU platform eTwinning. The pilot-study shows that when information and communication technology (ICT) skills become standardized, teachers' behavioral attitudes related to sharing and collaboration should be observed from a more holistic perspective. The first part provides a general description of Nonaka's model in connection with the education sector. The second part offers a bird's eye view of the European context framed by EU Acts and frameworks of reference to identify the roots of an emerging teaching profile linked to the awareness of knowledge flow. The third part presents a pilot research involving the idea of innovation related to the growing attitudes of digital collaboration and sharing. Within the eTwinning practice-context, this chapter proposes to switch the general approach from a teacher learning perspective to a teacher "knowledge management" standpoint.

DOI: 10.4018/978-1-6684-5027-7.ch005

INTRODUCTION

Conceptual Frame and Focus

The need of redefining teachers as professionals deeply involved in innovation has been a matter of widespread and increasing interest over the past decades (Avalos, 2011; Cheng 2012, 2013, 2018; Cheng, Wu, & Hu., 2017; Cheng & Chu, 2018; Cochran-Smith & Lytle, 1999; Fox & Wilson, 2015; Harris & Jones, 2018; Lin, F., Lin, S., & Huang, 2008; Periotto & Wessellenns, 2018; Rismark & Sølvberg, 2011; Vuorikari, Punie, Gomez, & Van den Brande, 2016; Zhao & Ordóñez de Pablos, 2009; Zhao, 2010), and this topic is expected to receive even more attention in the future because of the covid-19 pandemic. Nonetheless, previous research literature has not investigated the conditions needed to promote a common awareness and self-awareness for innovation amongst teachers. In fact, according to recent developments in psychological investigations, the level of self-awareness individuals have directly impacts how those individuals involve themselves in the cause of events leading to either success or failure (Silvia & Duval, 2001). Conversely, investigations around the topic of innovation in education constantly explores the link between educational innovation and digital technologies, recognizing information and communication technology (ICT) as the growing dimension that opens up a new mentality and to new strategies that may enable educational communities to discover knowledge and develop cross-domain competences (Mioara, 2012). On the other hand, there is a common consensus recognizing sharing and collaboration as elements of a cross-sectorial awareness that can lead to innovation, especially when they are associated with digital patterns and ICT skills within the lifelong learning frame (Avalos, 2011; Boisot & Child, 1999; Bollinger & Smith, 2001; Bucher & Helmond, 2018; Cheng 2012; 2013; 2018; Cheng et al., 2017; Cheng & Chu, 2018; Cochran-Smith & Lytle, 1999; Fox & Wilson, 2015; Harris & Jones, 2018; Periotto & Wessellenns, 2018; Rismark & Sølvberg, 2011; Von Krogh, 2012; Vuorikari et al., 2016; Zhao & Ordóñez de Pablos, 2009; Zhao, 2010).

Numerous investigations into the social dilemmas of knowledge sharing have found that a sense of group identity can positively influence contributions for the public good; especially once a group perceives that they have a common identity (Cabrera & Cabrera; 2002). Communities of practice generate transformations at all levels when teachers, acting as change agents, are networked and well established (Kools & Stoll, 2016). Many researchers show how the positive interactions of educational social networks, and the active participation of all school stakeholders can positively affect the flow of information in educational establishments, and how they can improve the work engagement (Cheng, 2012, 2013, 2018; Cheng, et al., 2017; Lin et al., 2008; Song, Kim, Chai & Bae, 2014; Parlar, Polatcan, & Cansoy, 2019; Zhao & Ordóñez de Pablos, 2009; Zhao, 2010).

On the other hand, every national school system (which is constantly in transition) should deal with the topic of additional workload and paperwork, especially at certain times of the school year, when teachers' schedules are strictly set by administrators. An excessive bureaucratic workload can turn off motivation, and "feeling overwhelmed can make teachers less receptive to new information and insights" (Collinson and Cook, 2001, p. 8).

There is a growing interest around education environments within the perspective of knowledge management (KM) due to the fact that schools and universities are precisely the first places where individuals (teachers and students) deal with structured information, data, and knowledge, in their two recognized forms: *tacit* and *explicit* (Bollinger & Smith, 2001; Cheng, 2018; 2019; Engeström, 1999; Farnese, Barbieri, Chirumbolo, & Patriotta, 2019; Garavelli, Gorgoglione, & Scozzi., 2002; Geeraerts,

Vanhoof & Van den Bossche, 2016; Hoe, 2006; Ihrig, Canals, Boisot, Nordberg, 2012; F. Lin, S. Lin, & Huang, 2008; McAdam & McCreedy, 1999; Pons, Pérez, Stiven, & Quintero, 2014; Ngulube, 2003; Nonaka & Konno, 1998; Quintas, Lefrere & Jones, 1997; Song et. al, 2014; Swart & Kinnie, 2003; Zhao & Ordóñez de Pablos, 2009; Zhao, 2010).

Explicit knowledge is the most basic form of knowledge, referring to what we are aware of and capable of codifying and transferring through formal language. Examples of *explicit knowledge* in organizations are institutional communications (e.g., newsletters), practices based on formal meetings (e.g., conferences, training courses), or knowledge products such as websites, databases, manuals, and patents (Farnese et al., 2019; Zhao & Ordóñez de Pablos, 2009). It is data that is easy to transfer, is usually documented, recorded, stored, available, accessible, and retrievable. Every time data is refined, processed, organized, and structured; the final result is *explicit knowledge*. Conversely, *implicit knowledge* is unconscious (Farnese et al., 2019; Zhao & Ordóñez de Pablos, 2009), related to the inner world of individuals and implies the practical application of *explicit knowledge*. *Implicit knowledge* emerges in routine, work patterns, and professional habits, and does not involve intelligible interactions, explanations, or clarifications. In other words, *implicit knowledge* is *explicit knowledge* 'internalized.'

KM in the field of education "does not necessarily imply using knowledge for invention-innovation processes that are crucial in the contemporary times in which the innovative business and innovative society prevail" (Mulej, 2008, p. 2). Nevertheless, a KM approach in a school environment should develop acquisition, accumulation, sharing, diffusion, innovation, and facilitation of teachers' teaching and learning (Zhao, 2010). Within the context of any educational environment it is common to recognize practices of KM, which are already used intuitively and unsystematically or consciously applied by the school managers (Periotto & Wesselleness, 2018). One of the purposes of this paper is to highlight some of these hidden dynamics. The *tacit/explicit* knowledge flow circulates continuously in any educational setting, but it is difficult to trace since many passages occur in teachers' inner worlds and it is not easy to record the flow accurately (Lin et al., 2008). As a result of this condition, the shift from one to another mode of knowledge creation "is assumed to happen naturally and remain ignored" (Lin et al., 2008, p. 752).

Interpersonal and interactive knowledge sharing is one of the major knowledge strategies emerging in this context, and schools are expected to develop human capital for the Knowledge Society (Cheng, 2012). Consequently, it is possible to recognize an emerging consensus at any latitude prioritizing the fact that learning exceeds the traditional notion of individuals acquiring knowledge, because of the consequence of the increasing needs to have high-skilled citizens. Thus, the strategic focus on the diverse dimensions related to knowledge includes creation and co-creation as well as assimilation (Avalos, 2011; Boisot & Child, 1999; Bollinger & Smith, 2001; Bucher & Helmond, 2018; Cheng 2012; 2013; 2018; Cochran-Smith & Lytle, 1999; Harris & Jones, 2018; Mansour, Askenas & Ghazawneh, 2013; Rismark & Sølvberg, 2011; Von Krogh, 2012; Vuorikari et al., 2016; Zhao & Ordóñez de Pablos, 2009; Zhao, 2010). The impression is that the current debate and research frame is more weighted towards the ICT side and less to the psychological dimension. The current common mindset assumes that ICT professional patterns inherent in our digital society can reveal, by their own nature, a sufficient evidence of group-awareness and self-awareness.

The KM concept mentioned in this paper refers to the Nonaka model, widely accepted as the most effective to represent the *tacit-explicit* knowledge flow and transformation. The relevant literature around KM processes in public and private organizations regularly makes reference to this model and to the related concepts (Bollinger & Smith, 2001; Cheng, 2019; Engeström, 1999; Farnese et al., 2019; Garavelli et al., 2002; Hoe, 2006; Lin et al., 2008; McAdam & McCreedy, 1999; Ngulube, 2003; Nonaka

& Konno, 1998; Pons et al., 2014; Quintas et al., 1997; Song et. Al., 2014; Zhao & Ordóñez de Pablos, 2009; Zhao, 2010).

Figure 1. Nonaka's model of "knowledge management," showing the knowledge flow through the tacit-explicit dimensions

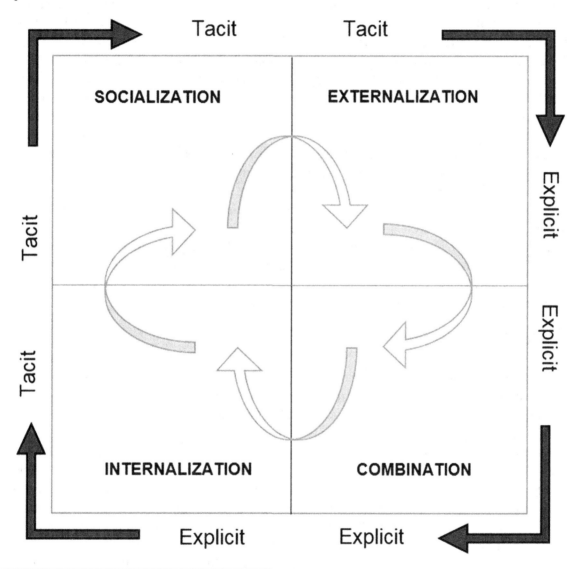

Tacit to Tacit (Socialization) is the dimension rooted in social interactions and implies tacit-to-tacit knowledge transfer, sharing tacit knowledge in teams, groups, or through socially-based work experiences. *Tacit to Explicit* (Externalization) happens between tacit and explicit knowledge through externalization, such as writing, publishing, disseminating outputs, and developing plans, which require the notions of the tacit knowledge to enable its communication. *Explicit to Explicit* (Combination) takes place through the combination of multiple elements that integrate knowledge, which combines different types of explicit knowledge, for example building up a project-plan. Explicit to Tacit (Internalization) is achieved by internalizing norms, generally by an individual applying instructions or learning by doing. Thus, once *explicit knowledge* becomes part of an individual's inner knowledge, it turns again into *tacit*.

KM is related to the concept of Knowledge Intensive Organization (KIO), originally born into international corporations, particularly those with a distinct vocation for research and development. Most of all, this perspective marks a passage from a value-culture of tangible assets as facilities, tools, and machinery, to intangible as skills, knowledge, and expertise (Amaya & Grueso, 2017; Boisot & Child, 1999; Bollinger & Smith, 2001; Cabrera & Cabrera, 2002; Mansour et al. 2013; Pons et al., 2014; Von Krogh, 2012). Thus, we are currently witnessing a rapid transshipment of this focus from the production world (secondary sector) to the service segment (tertiary). It was only a matter of time before the KM-oriented perspective started to also touch the educational sector, and the authors believe that the next unavoidable step is the massive entry of KM-oriented frameworks into the educational public sector worldwide. This transition is taking place thanks to the growing awareness that in the Knowledge Society the educational environment is a context in cognitive relationship with all the other forms of social capital. Thus, any form of digital inequality should be investigated in order to understand the implications of digital skills for engaging social capital-enhancing activities online (Hsieh, 2012).

In this paper, schools are treated as homogeneous environments within a general perspective of collective behavioral environments orientated towards the exchange of good practices, through a more diverse ICT repertoire and communication multiplexity (Hsieh, 2012). The range of relevant skills is analyzed within the frame of the digital educational networking and educational platforms in the context of the EU. Indeed, all the aforementioned research makes reference to digital networking dynamics as one of the prominent aspects fostering innovative professional patterns.

Education is a Social Priority

The UNESCO report titled *Learning: The treasure within* (Delors et al., 1996), established the popular four pillars of education: *learning to know*; *learning to do*; *learning to live together*; *learning to be*. The prevailing perspective is a society-centered focus, rather than on individuals. All the efforts to create the conditions for smart, sustainable, and inclusive growth are now entering a new critical stage due to the unexpected COVID-19 pandemic, and the fact that the programming period of the European 2020 Strategy has ended (European Commission, 2010). The education sector has undergone a "digital shock," especially in those countries with a less pervasive digitalization. The continuous renewal in education revealed its limits and, henceforth, every definition of teachers' role should exceed the function of professionals implementing other's ideas. The need to redefine teachers as 'professionals deeply involved in innovation' is becoming a matter of widespread and increasing interest (Avalos, 2011; Cheng 2012; 2013; 2018; Cochran-Smith & Lytle, 1999; Collinson & Cook, 2001; Fox & Wilson, 2015; Harris & Jones, 2018; Lin et al., 2008; Rismark & Sølvberg, 2011; Song et al., 2014; Vuorikari et al., 2016; Zhao & Ordóñez de Pablos, 2009; Zhao, 2010), and this topic is expected to receive further considerable attention. The pervasive expansion of KM approaches is influencing also the educational sector, even at lower grades. Although this effect is not yet declared and visible at the same manner in all countries, the nature of teaching is, worldwide, increasingly less routine, and more prone to knowledge sharing, collaborative re-contextualization, and experimentation (Cheng, 2013; 2018; Zhao & Ordóñez de Pablos, 2009; Zhao, 2010). There is extensive literature spreading the general recognition of the complexity of teacher training and how professional development is a continuous process that can benefit co-learning and knowledge sharing (Avalos, 2010; Cheng 2013, 2018; Cochran-Smith & Lytle, 1999; Rismark & Sølvberg, 2011; Vuorikari et al., 2016; Zhao & Ordóñez de Pablos, 2009; Zhao, 2010). There are multiple contexts where it is possible to highlight this professional transformation, clearly promoted by institutional regulations, national or international policies, or emerging as innovative impulses justified by the new skills required for global citizenships. In order to better focus on this collective process, it is appropriate to mention some relevant acts, frameworks, and other institutional outputs inside and outside the European Union.

Considering the concerns of the EU members stated in the *Declaration of Rome* (Declaration, 2017), the objectives stated in *Project Europe 2030* (González, 2010) and in the *Memorandum on Lifelong Learning* (Commission of the European Community, 2000), it is the duty of each educational institution in Europe to create an environment that can offer students new ways of learning, more flexible training, and education to meet the standards required by the European society, which is mainly mobile, technical, and digital. Nonetheless, as the report *Project Europe 2030* states, there are social and cultural gaps in European society still unresolved, for which schools can provide a vital contribution:

Urgent action is needed to address this situation, including providing teachers with the professional recognition they deserve; developing flexible and open curricula capable of nurturing curiosity and creativity among children; and strengthening links between public education systems, business, and society. (González, 2010, p. 22)

On the other hand, EU has always considered education a lifelong journey. Indeed, at the beginning of the new millennium, the EU had already framed the early stages of school education into the vision of a Lifelong Learning perspective:

High quality basic education for all, from a child's youngest days forward, is the essential foundation. Basic education followed by initial vocational education and training, should equip all young people with the new basic skills required in a knowledge-based economy. It should also ensure that they have 'learnt to learn' and that they have a positive attitude towards learning. (Commission of the EC, 2000, p. 7)

The *WISE survey 'School in 2030,'* conducted in 2014, showed that education systems are predicted to undergo major changes. Schools will become interactive environments where innovations in technology and *curricula* will fundamentally change the role of teachers and reshape the landscape of learning; thus, schools will evolve to become learning networks. Online resources and technologies will support peer-to-peer networking, dialog, and exchange, facilitating a move towards collaborative learning. The most robust attempt to enlighten the digital path for the future of school is the promotion of computational thinking, using the subject of *coding* in computer lab activities. In many EU countries, the Ministries of Education (and other national authorities) are fostering the STEM projects (Science, Technology, Engineering and Math), which allow primary and low-secondary schools to organize courses for students ages five to 14, using humanoid robots, mbots, neuron kits, and 3-D printers. The low secondary school grades have been increasing the use of *gamification* through digital tools, such as Kahoot, Quizzlet, Voki, Padlet, Class Dojo, and dozens of other popular software. Currently, teachers are committed to gaining new skills in the eLearning field, according to the *European Framework for Digital Competence-DigComp* (Vuorikari et al., 2016). There are teachers with coordination responsibility in this area and 'internal innovation teams' promoting these ubiquitous improvements. These approaches may vary according to the national educational policies of each Member State of the Union, but the sharing and innovation context is the indispensable factor that must lead to collaboratively innovating pedagogic practices (Redecker, 2017). Scholars, authors and researchers, directly or indirectly agree that Sharing leads to Innovation on condition that the sharing process follows an established frame or a model (Avalos, 2012; Cheng, 2012; 2017; 2018; Kools & Stoll, 2016; Rismark & Sølvberg, 2011; Vourikari et al., 2016; Zhao & Ordóñez de Pablos, 2009; Zhao, 2010).

But this is not all; indeed, schools should also assume major responsibilities related more specifically to the labor market. According to the report by the European Commission: *Rethinking Education: Investing in skills for better socio-economic outcomes* (2012), attention should be particularly focused on the development of entrepreneurial skills, because they not only contribute to new business creation, but also to the employability of young people. To address this complex and vast range of targets, the European Commission published policy guidance to support improvements in the quality and prevalence of entrepreneurship education across the EU. All of the member states should foster entrepreneurial skills through new and creative ways of teaching and learning from primary school onwards, in addition to a focus from secondary schools to higher education on the opportunity of business creation as a career destination. Real world experience, through problem-based learning and enterprise links, should be embedded across all disciplines and tailored to all levels of education. A collective school evolution can take advantage of the European networks to benchmark approaches and teaching mindsets against the European need for skills and abilities. The Erasmus Plus program, especially the *Key Action 2[1]*, for the exchange of good practices among schools, is one of the most powerful ways to develop such experiences.

All of the educational perspectives and priorities mentioned thus far are interconnected, and their main objective is to foster the best Europe-oriented practices in each school and turn them into points of contact. School networking currently focuses on investigating how different education systems are dealing with curricular methodologies, compulsory subjects, and their integration with Formal, Non-Formal, and Informal skills, according to European guidelines. This collective change can benefit from the education social networking, increasingly widespread through educational social media and education platforms. As Mulej (2008) highlights, an educational holistic approach to KM should replace the traditional discipline-based curriculum.

Current quantities of available knowledge and sources of knowledge are by far too large for anybody to absorb all of them. Thus, a narrow specialization of knowledge is unavoidable, but so is also the requisite holism of observation, perception, decision making, and action, requiring the requisite holism of knowledge. The latter requires interdisciplinary creative co-operation, because an individual transdisciplinary knowledge with a requisite depth is impossible. (Mulej, 2008, p. 10)

Nowadays, in every education space, the concept of sharing should evoke not only a local or national exchange, but also an international horizon. The benefits of international networking are already at hand in every school environment, thanks to ICT and, in particular, to eTwinning, the huge European platform for school networking and educational projects (Nizzolino & Canals, 2021). This would mean that schools are not just more organizations adapting themselves only to local complexities (Boisot & Child, 1999), but they are going to significantly adapt some internal skills to match the complexity of international networking environments.

The report, *A New Skills Agenda for Europe* (European Commission, 2016), indicates to all the stakeholders the most appropriate strategies and actions required to provide a skill set for EU citizens, in particular those transversal competencies that are appropriate to increase occupability, competitivity, and growth, in order to better address personal skills towards those challenges that the EU is facing. The agenda recommends also that this set of skills should be attainable and reachable for everyone from the earliest age. In the context of the *Lisbon Convention*—ratified through the Bologna process—and launched in March 2000, school education is involved in order to match the younger generations' expectations, thus school and vocational education, in particular, should cope with the task to provide the best opportunities for young learners to acquire those skills useful to face a global market.

PILOT RESEARCH, METHODOLOGY, AND RESULTS: TEACHERS AND INNOVATION

The level of implementation of the previously mentioned frameworks is not consistent within the EU. One issue the authors would like to draw attention to is related to the level of relevance given to teachers as "Intellectual Capital," since this is not equal everywhere. Indeed, one can note how these two factors are interdependent and symbiotic. Countries with a higher awareness of teachers as Intellectual Capital (and valuable Social Capital) are beginning to implement models based on KM in schools. Outside EU, it is no coincidence that China, which tops the list of the world teachers' ranking status (Dolton, Marcenaro, Vries, & She, 2018), is currently the international pathfinder in the implementation of KM systems in the education sector, while in Europe one could note Finland and Norway for the same reasons.

The main issue in many European school systems seems to be the teachers' lack of perception of their potential to generate innovation. Despite the collective endeavor to spread eTwinning popularity and implementation, like any other knowledgment-related-tool, it may have reached its saturation point unless "some kind of artificial intervention, such as the use of organizational development programs, is required" (Rismark and Sølvberg, 2011). Despite the struggle to make eTwinning a tool used on daily basis, the authors can represent the current self-awareness of teachers as agents of innovation through the following pilot survey completed by 142 teachers from 7 EU countries, where all respondents were reached through a partnership-network of public schools involved in an Erasmus Plus project[2].

The eTwinning platform is an online community of schools in Europe. It is a digital space offering a great range of activities, exchange opportunities, and professional development. According to the real-time detection of the platform, the current number of members exceeds 800,000 individual users and more than 200,000 schools involved in more than 100,000 active projects[3]. The platform contents are available in 28 languages, and it periodically disseminates newsletters and reports. It is possible to access as a registered member on the condition that personal details are associated with a public school (or recognized as equivalent) in the European Union. Therefore, users are all teachers, head teachers, and librarians, and through their projects more than four million students experienced digital exchange and online activities, both on the national and international level. The eTwinning platform was created to detect and manage the relational complexity of a very specific segment: School Education in the European Union. Despite the great amount of reports available, the usual focus highlights the accomplishments or the experiences related to specific projects, the sharing of contents, and teachers' professional development. Instead, in this paper, the authors aim to explore the presence of a mental framework oriented to KM within this web-space. The 142 pilot study respondents were all full-time, established teachers from different grades, with teaching experiences ranging from 2 to 34 years. All of the participants were active eTwinning users who were involved in various projects and networks through the platform. The survey excluded temporary and supply teachers as well as administrative staff. The selection of the seven countries included: Greece, Finland, Italy, Lithuania, Poland, Romania, and Spain, in order to have a cluster of school systems according to determined indicators.

Romania joined the EU in 2007, and Lithuania in 2004, so later than the others. There was a high interest to understand how their National Education Systems have been internalizing the European priorities during the last decades, and how they matched the *2020 European Benchmark* related to Reading, Math, and the Sciences, according to the charts available in the European statistics platform[4]. Foreign Language Learning in secondary education is another factor that drove the selection of partners. Romania, Poland, and Lithuania reached far better results than Italy, according to the official EU charts[5]. Finland reached one of the highest positions in official performances; thus, it was desirable to explore their mindset and methodology. Overall, the cluster of partners offers a representative sample of wide differences among EU member states, and also variegated geopolitical peculiarities.

All partners had various grades of distance from the *2020 EU Benchmarks* at the moment of the survey, so the authors wanted to review the different factors that might be the cause of these differences and to also verify those educational environments that were obtaining better results. Partners were found through the eTwinning platform in the Erasmus Plus Forum. Every participant school had experience in previous European projects and collaborations so their teams knew how to deal with related organizational aspects linked to the networking features offered by eTwinning.

The first objective of the survey was to check the association between the teaching profession and the idea of innovation, as teachers themselves may convey it. The second objective was to detect similarities between the perception teachers have of the knowledge flow (during their daily routine) and Nonaka's model. The third objective was to have the participating teachers define eTwinning from their point of view, and see if the individual definitions could be linked to the previous findings.

Table 1. Countries of the 142 surveyed teachers

1) What country do you work in?	
Country	**% of Participants**
Spain	34.8
Italy	34.8
Lithuania	8.7
Greece	8.7
Finland	4.3
Poland	4,3
Romania	4,3

Table 2. School levels of the 142 surveyed teachers

2) According to your National School System what grade level do you teach?	
Grade	%
Early Childhood Education and Care	0
Primary Education	47.8
Lower Secondary Education	39.1
Upper Secondary General Education	8.7
Upper Secondary VET	4.4

Table 3. Perception of the Knowledge Society concept by the 142 surveyed teachers

3) When I think of the concept of Knowledge Society…	
	%
I perfectly know what this expression means and I can explain it to other people.	8.7
I know the concept in general terms.	34.8
I have met this concept several times and I am willing to know more about it.	17.4
I need to look more deeply into the topic.	34.8
I have never heard of it.	4.3

Only 8.7% declared to perfectly know the concept of Knowledge Society, while 34.8% affirmed that they did not know the topic at all (actually the third and fourth options may be seen as similar periphrasis to avoid the impact of "I do not know.").

Table 4. Link between teachers' role and knowledge dimensions. Only one response was allowed

4) Which definition better associate teachers' role to knowledge	
	Num. (%)
Teachers retrieve/recover knowledge	5 (3,52)
Teachers promote knowledge	21 (14,79)
Teachers transfer knowledge	14 (9,86)
Teachers share knowledge	19 (13,38)
Teachers process/elaborate knowledge	10 (7,04)
Teachers simplify knowledge	11 (7,75)
Teachers codify knowledge	6 (4,23)
Teachers evaluate knowledge	10 (7,04)
Teachers build up new knowledge	13 (9,15)
Teachers innovate knowledge	10 (7,04)
Teachers may contribute to k. innovation	9 (6,34)
Teachers may create opportunity to research/develop new knowledge	14 (9,86)

The authors decided to process these specific results collecting the definitions which received from a minimum of 11 feedbacks, to the maximum (21+14+19+11+13+14) for a total of 92 respondents. This sample represents the 64.7% of the total users, and gives back a 'logic sequence,' which can potentially match the Nonaka's KM model based on the four knowledge modes (Figure 1).

Table 5. Equivalence relation between teachers' associations to knowledge and Nonaka's Knowledge Management cycle (see figure 1)

Higher % of Responses	Four Modes of Nonaka's Knowledge Conversion
Promote 14.79% Share 13.38%	SOCIALIZATION
Transfer 9.86%	EXTERNALIZATION
Create opportunities to develop/research 9.86% Build up 9.15%	COMBINATION
Simplify 7.75%	INTERNALIZATION

This exploratory survey made it possible to discover that a low number of teachers perceive their role linked to the innovation paradigm; but conversely it reveals some hidden patterns that offer an opportunity to go beyond what is perceived as daily routine. What is remarkable here is the fact that this survey neither mentions anything about KM models nor did respondents know this topic, which does not belong to ordinary school environments. The highest number of responses concentrated on the definitions linked to *promotion* and *sharing* of knowledge, while the lowest ranking was given to the ideas of *codification* and *innovation*. The *evaluation* paradigm seems to be in the group of low raking responses, but it is not a surprise if one considers that many school systems are moving away from the XX century concept of performance assessment. In short, those who responded to the survey despite neglecting the link between teachers and innovation, revealed hidden patterns suitable to the notorious Nonaka's model (Figure 1). Indeed, eTwinning itself can be seen as a space where teachers are driven to manage knowledge through the sharing of experiences, information, and best practices, with the result of improving both individual and collective values. There is clearly a co-relation here when one highlights that the majority of respondents were, indeed, eTwinning active users. One should not forget that the situated learning framework (Lave & Wenger, 2006) emerges today as a digital space, and teachers' communities of practices cannot be studied outside the *infosphere* where they take shape.

The fifth answer of this pilot survey required a short description as feedback after asking the question, *"Can you briefly describe the role of eTwinning in your teaching activity?"* The authors extracted the 142 feedback comments from the questions, which asked participants to define, with a short comment, the role of *eTwinning* in teachers' jobs. The 142 commentaries ranged from the shortest of only three words, "a useful tool," to the largest of 27 words, "It is a platform that helps me to exchange experiences with foreign teachers and change my teaching habits. Students can improve both their digital and language skills." The authors adopted the software T-LAB, which analyzes texts and extracts co-occurrences and word associations. The 142 comments were listed as a whole segmented text and processed as a T-LAB file project. The first seven co-occurrences that were both verbs and nouns were selected (Adverbs and prepositions were excluded.).

Figure 2. T-LAB co-occurrences chart

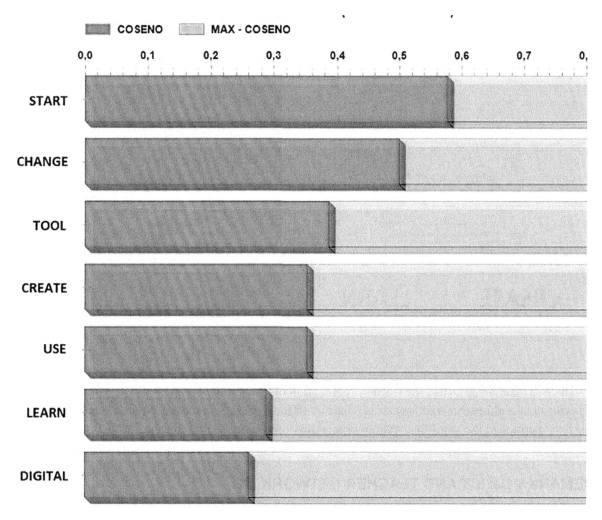

A psycholinguist approach can identify concepts strongly related to personal motivation and a change of paradigm; teachers' perspectives describe converged steps to trigger developments.

Figure 3. T-LAB co-occurrences hierarchically related to the objective (change) and the practice (tool)

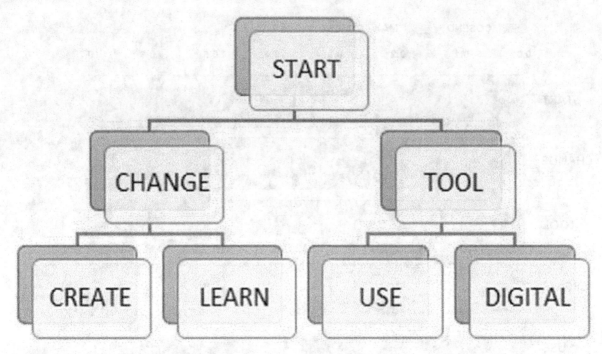

The two main areas reflect the teachers' perception of eTwinning simply as a *digital tool* capable of *bringing change* through a *creative process* that entails the *learning dimension*. None of the 142 surveyed teachers mentioned the word 'innovation' or any direct reference to this concept.

REMARKS ON ICT AND TEACHER NETWORKING

In the last report about eTwinning, impact on teachers' practice, the authors discovered that the respondents (belonging in variable percentage to all member countries) were also asked if they were participating in any other online or onsite training apart from eTwinning. The vast majority (74%) responded positively (Pateraki, 2018). This data showed that eTwinning active users (as those who agreed to fully engage the proposed surveys) are individuals motivated to continuously improve their skills and knowledge. The Pateraki report proposed a methodology named the MeTP 2.0 Framework (MENTEP-Mentoring Technology-Enhanced Pedagogy). The self-evaluation path included a pre-questionnaire with some demographic questions, an assessment results' page, a feedback page, and a post-questionnaire. This process was particularly useful to detect the improvement of collaborative competences.

(…) this is the competence in which the biggest increase/improvement was noted. Twenty-one percent of the respondents who initially obtained a medium score, obtained a high score in the post-questionnaire, meaning that the initial 45% of high scoring teachers became 66%. Exceeding this threshold (from medium to high scores) shows that the collaborative competence had the biggest potential in terms of improvement (starting from quite low) and the fact that this is where teachers had the highest increase

probably demonstrates that most teachers felt more confident after having taken part in eTwinning activities, most of which deal with collaboration. (Pateraki, 2018, p. 25)

The interaction among eTwinning, the Erasmus Plus Program, and the National Education Agencies in every European country can guarantee a network of tailored self-education opportunities to develop teachers' competencies. One of the most relevant aspects of this open source ecosystem is the fact that everything falls within the scope of Non-Formal Training, and most commonly these training events are picked up as voluntary initiatives. The aspect of collaborative skills also represents one of the upgrades from the first version of the *DigComp* framework to the *DigComp 2.0* (Vourikari, 2016). In the version 1.0, *Communication* was a stand-alone skill, while in the version 2.0, it became *Communication and collaboration*.

Not all EU member states have been adopting EU frameworks at the same level. Concerning *Dig-Comp 2.0* (Vuorikari et al., 2016), only few countries adopted it explicitly to support teachers' professional development: Lithuania, Norway, and Spain (which are included in the pilot survey), Portugal and Croatia; while other countries are applying the framework more specifically for students' assessments, employability, or policy support. Through the systematic observation of all the efforts performed by the national school systems of the Union members, it is not temerarious to affirm that only a few countries have been reaching the expected results in their public education systems. The worldwide reference report, TALIS (OECD, 2020), reveals the most salient features linked to teaching and learning from 48 countries. A specific section of this report relates the 48 countries ranked according to the percentage of head teachers complaining about ICT inadequacies in their schools. In the eTwinning frame, a good deployment of ICTs is essential to allow teachers and students to use the platform on a regular basis. Table 5 summarizes the 22 countries out of 48, which are part of the eTwinning community. Five of the seven countries involved in the previous surveys also took part in the TALIS data collection. Surprisingly, Finland (among the top performers of *2020 EU Benchmark*[6]) seems to struggle with ICT issues similar to those of other EU countries. This simple data suggests that high education performances are not linked only to high ICT efficiency; digital tools are a medium and not an end. Similarly, the previously mentioned five countries applying *DigComp 2.0* to develop teachers' skills belong to very different stages of digital deployment in schools.

Table 6. Countries selected in the TALIS analysis for being part of the eTwinning network (Personal elaboration from TALIS data)

N°	Country	% of Headteachers complaining about ICT inadequacies
1	Slovenia	4
2	Malta	6
3	Sweden	10
4	Norway	11
5	Estonia	12
6	Denmark	13
7	UK	15
8	Belgium (Flanders)	16
9	Netherlands	16
10	Finland	20
11	Spain	21
12	Turkey	22
13	Chec. Republic	24
14	Bulgaria	26
15	Georgia	29
16	France	30
17	Lithuania	30
18	Italy	31
19	Hungary	36
20	Latvia	41
21	Romania	50
22	Portugal	55

The next comparisons in this paper may suggest that there is no direct link between the national level of digital implementation in schools and innovating educational patterns. Conversely, the strategy focused on teachers' professional development also derives from a combination of other elements.

Usually, some domestic policies tend to relate the scarce ICT performances to a need to upskill and reskill a professional category. Indeed, if we compare the previous table to some public data offered by the EU educational platform eTwinning, we discover that it is not always possible to find a direct correlation between ICT issues and a low attitude to educational networking.

Table 7. Countries selected in the TALIS analysis for being part of the eTwinning network and eTwinning real data per analyzed country (Available online data on 01/06/2020)

Country	Project created	Schools	Teachers	Conversion rate projects: *schools*	Conversion rate projects: *teachers*
FINLAND	4071	2422	8089	1,680	0,503
GREECE	16893	8652	28322	1,952	0,596
ITALY	29630	11093	84826	2,668	0,349
LITHUANIA	7877	1795	9326	4,388	0,844
POLAND	32761	18382	70972	1,782	0,461
ROMANIA	20385	9438	30786	2,159	0,662
SPAIN	26610	15427	68005	1,754	0,391

This simple conversion-rate-view provides the relationship between the number of online projects created on the platform and their ratio to the total number of teachers who subscribed the platform. Lithuania (nr. 17 in Table 6) reaches the highest performances despite the very small number of schools present on the platform, thanks to the highest project/teacher ratio. It is not far from the one-project-per-teacher-ratio. The values refer only to those teachers 'who started a new project'; the platform statistics do not include teachers who joined the project afterwards. Romania, where the authors found the highest percentage of head teachers complaining due to ICT inadequacies (position 21 in Table 6) presents a project to teacher ratio, which doubles that of Italy. As stated, not all EU member states have been adopting EU frameworks in the same way, and concerning DigComp 2.0 (Vuorikari et al., 2016), Lithuania is the only country (among the seven in this pilot-research) that adopted it to support teachers' continuous development. What these data suggest is that specific frameworks based on 'sharing and collaboration through ICT' can establish a continuous motivation for teachers, which is quite different from just having the most advanced ICT technology available in the classroom to improve the teacher-student experience. Of course, hi-tech tools help and foster the willingness to experiment, but there is much more behind a Digital Whiteboard or an ICT lab. There are profound dimensions, such as human motivation, group identity, and the awareness of social roles.

CONCLUSION

Educational networking provides teachers with opportunities to experience KM modes, even unknowingly. This is why the focus should move from the teacher-learning perspective to the teacher-knowledge-management perspective. Indeed, when reading reports issued by the *European eTwinning Unit*, one can still recognize a strong focus on surveys and data intended to offer a review on the relationship between the platform and teachers' continuous learning. On the other hand, collaborations may arise naturally, as an inner attitude of a teacher's personality, out of the problems and circumstances that teachers experience in common. Notwithstanding the overall positive spirit, it should be remembered that, frequently, schools can be stressful environments, so teachers may also appear "contrived, inauthentic, grafted on, perched precariously (and often temporarily) on the margins of real work" (Little, 1990, p. 510).

Despite the shared EU frameworks, national policies may vary widely concerning the way to deal with the psychological wellness of teachers, hence, this topic deserves a different focus. The EU frameworks generally focus on causal conditions and do not suggest or develop individual strategies or group strategies to promote an innovation paradigm. These are sets of variables, which should be managed locally, in every specific education establishment.

The main areas that require further investigations, not frequently mentioned in the examined literature, are summarized as:

1   School establishments in the EU are environments implicitly conducive to the Nonaka's Knowledge Management model. The pilot-survey reveals a favorable teachers' mindset in relation to the knowledge flow in their working routines.
2   ICT deployment and teachers' digital skills are generally considered essentials, but they can obfuscate other complementary dimensions, such as behavioral attitudes and psychological conditions. Especially those skills required to create and develop professional networks that embody a set of articulated social and interpersonal abilities, which adopt ICT tools merely to express themselves. This focus involves a more holistic perspective when teachers' continuous development is at stake.
3   Innovation in education, at the present stage, is a matter of advanced social competencies in the frame of digital skills. Thus, every national education policy should start considering establishing a more integrated behavioristic approach (or even a psychological framework) besides the notorious and recognized digital policies for education.
4   Concepts such as 'Innovation' and 'Knowledge Society' are not yet part of most teachers' vision and perceptions, thus, the role of the digital cognitive interaction between educators and the other Social Capitals is not yet rooted in the awareness of the school sector.

REFERENCES

Amaya, N. Y., & Grueso, M. P. (2017). Factores distintivos de las organizaciones intensivas en conocimiento. *Podium (São Paulo)*, *32*, 75–87. doi:10.31095/podium.2017.32.6

Avalos, B. (2011). Teacher professional development in teaching and teacher education over ten years. *Teaching and Teacher Education*, *27*(1), 10–20. doi:10.1016/j.tate.2010.08.007

Boisot, M., & Child, J. (1999). Organizations as adaptive systems in complex environments: The case of China. *Organization Science*, *10*(3), 237–252. doi:10.1287/orsc.10.3.237

Bollinger, A. S., & Smith, R. D. (2001). Managing organizational knowledge as a strategic asset. *Journal of Knowledge Management*, *5*(1), 8–18. doi:10.1108/13673270110384365

Brown, M. E., & Hocutt, D. L. (2015). Learning to use, useful for learning: A usability study of Google apps for education. *Journal of Usability Studies*, *10*(4), 160.

Bucher, T., & Helmond, A. (2018). The affordance of social media platforms. The SAGE handbook of social media, 233–253.

Cabrera, A., & Cabrera, E. F. (2002). Knowledge-sharing dilemmas. *Organization Studies, 23*(5), 687–710. doi:10.1177/0170840602235001

Cheng, E. C. K. (2012). Knowledge strategies for enhancing school learning capacity. *International Journal of Educational Management, 26*(6), 577–592. doi:10.1108/09513541211251406

Cheng, E. C. K. (2013). Applying knowledge management for school strategic planning. *KEDI Journal of Educational Policy, 10*(2), 339–356.

Cheng, E. C. K. (2018). Managing records and archives in a Hong Kong school: A case study. *Records Management Journal, 28*(2), 204–216. Advance online publication. doi:10.1108/RMJ-02-2017-0004

Cheng, E. C. K. (2019). Knowledge management strategies for sustaining Lesson Study. *International Journal for Lesson and Learning Studies, 9*(2), 167–178. doi:10.1108/IJLLS-10-2019-0070

Cheng, E. C. K., & Chu, C. K. W. (2018). A Normative Knowledge Management Model for School Development. *International Journal of Learning and Teaching, 4*(1), 76–82. Advance online publication. doi:10.18178/ijlt.4.1.76-82

Cheng, E. C. K., Wu, S. W., & Hu, J. (2017). Knowledge management implementation in the school context: Case studies on knowledge leadership, storytelling, and taxonomy. *Educational Research for Policy and Practice, 16*(2), 177–188. doi:10.100710671-016-9200-0

Cochran-Smith, M., & Lytle, S. (1999). Relationships of knowledge and practice: Teacher learning community. *Review of Research in Education, 24*, 249–305.

Collinson, V., & Cook, T. F. (2001). I don't have enough time - Teachers' interpretations of time as a key to learning and school change. *Journal of Educational Administration, 39*(3), 266–281. doi:10.1108/09578230110392884

Commission of the European Community. (2000). *A Memorandum on Lifelong Learning.* SEC.

Council of the European Union. (2017). *The Rome Declaration. Declaration of the leaders of 27 member states and of the European Council, the European Parliament and the European Commission.* Author.

Delors, J., Mufti, I. A., Amagi, I., Carneiro, R., Chung, F., & Geremek, B. (1996). International Commission on Education for the Twenty-first Century. *Learning: The Treasure Within.*

Dolton, P., Marcenaro, O., Vries, R. D., & She, P. W. (2018). *The Global Teacher Status Index 2018.* The Varkey Foundation.

Engeström, Y. (1999). Innovative learning in work teams: analyzing cycles of knowledge 8 creation in practice. *Perspectives on Activity Theory, 377*, 404.

European Commission. (2010). *A strategy for smart, sustainable and inclusive growth.* COM.

European Commission. (2016). *A New Skills Agenda for Europe: Working together to strengthen human capital, employability and competitiveness.* Author.

Farnese, M. L., Barbieri, B., Chirumbolo, A., & Patriotta, G. (2019). Managing Knowledge in Organizations: A Nonaka's SECI Model Operationalization. *Frontiers in Psychology*, *10*, 2730. doi:10.3389/fpsyg.2019.02730 PMID:31920792

Fox, A. R., & Wilson, E. G. (2015). Networking and the development of professionals: Beginning teachers building social capital. *Teaching and Teacher Education*, *47*, 93–107. doi:10.1016/j.tate.2014.12.004

Garavelli, A. C., Gorgoglione, M., & Scozzi, B. (2002). Managing knowledge transfer by knowledge technologies. *Technovation*, *22*(5), 269–279. doi:10.1016/S0166-4972(01)00009-8

Geeraerts, K., Vanhoof, J., & Van den Bossche, P. (2016). Teachers' perceptions of intergenerational knowledge flows. *Teaching and Teacher Education, 56,* 150–161. .2016.01.024 doi:10.1016/j.tate

González, F. (2010). *Project Europe 2030: Challenges and Opportunities* (A report to the European Council by the Reflection Group on the Future of the EU 2030), May 2010). The González Report.

Granovetter, M. S. (2001). The strength of Weak Ties. In *Social networks* (pp. 347–367). Academic Press.

Harris, A., & Jones, M. (2018). Leading schools as learning organizations. *School Leadership & Management*, *38*(4), 351–354. doi:10.1080/13632434.2018.1483553

Hoe, S. L. (2006). Tacit knowledge, Nonaka and Takeuchi SECI model and informal knowledge processes. *International Journal of Organization Theory and Behavior*, *9*(4), 490–502. doi:10.1108/IJOTB-09-04-2006-B002

Hsieh, Y. P. (2012). Online social networking skills: The social affordances approach to digital inequality. *First Monday*, *17*(4). Advance online publication. doi:10.5210/fm.v17i4.3893

Ihrig, M., Canals, A., Boisot, M. H., & Nordberg, M. (2012). Mapping critical knowledge assets in the ATLAS Collaboration at CERN: An I-Space approach. *OLKC 2012-International Conference on Organizational Learning, Knowledge and Capabilities*.

Kools, M., & Stoll, L. (2016). *What Makes a School a Learning Organisation?* doi:10.1787/19939019

Lave, J., & Wenger, E. (2006). *Situated learning. From observation to active participation in social contexts*. Erickson Editions.

Lin, F., Lin, S., & Huang, T. (2008). Knowledge sharing and creation in a teachers' professional virtual community. *Computers & Education*, *50*(3), 742–756. doi:10.1016/j.compedu.2006.07.009

Little, J. W. (1990). The persistence of privacy: Autonomy and initiative in teachers' professional relations. *Teachers College Record*, *91*(4), 509–536. doi:10.1177/016146819009100403

Mansour, O., Askenas, L., & Ghazawneh, A. (2013). *Social media and organizing–An empirical analysis of the role of wiki affordances in organizing practices*. Academic Press.

McAdam, R., & McCreedy, S. (1999). A critical review of knowledge management models. *The Learning Organization*, *6*(3), 91–100. doi:10.1108/09696479910270416

Mioara, M. S. (2012). The impact of technological and communication innovation in the knowledge-based society. *Procedia: Social and Behavioral Sciences*, *51*, 263–267. doi:10.1016/j.sbspro.2012.08.156

Mulej, M. (2008). The Contemporary School and Knowledge Management. *Journal on Efficiency and Responsibility in Education and Science, 1*(1), 1–19.

Ngulube, P. (2003). Using the SECI knowledge management model and other tools to communicate and manage tacit indigenous knowledge. *Innovation, 27*(1), 21–30.

Nizzolino, S., & Canals, A. (2021). Social Network Sites as Community Building Tools in Educational Networking. *International Journal of e-Collaboration (IJeC), 17*(4), 132-167. doi:10.4018/IJeC.2021100110

Nonaka, I., & Konno, N. (1998). The Concept of "Ba": Building a foundation for knowledge creation. *California Management Review, 40*(3), 40–54. doi:10.2307/41165942

OECD. (2020). TALIS 2018 Results (Volume II): Teachers and school leaders as valued professionals. OECD Publishing. doi:10.1787/19cf08df-en

Parlar, H., Polatcan, M., & Cansoy, R. (2019). The relationship between social capital and innovativeness climate in schools. The intermediary role of professional learning communities. *International Journal of Educational Management, 34*(2), 232–244. doi:10.1108/IJEM-10-2018-0322

Pateraki, I. (2018). Measuring the impact of eTwinning activities on teachers' practice and competence development - Monitoring eTwinning Practice Framework. Central Support Service of eTwinning, European Schoolnet.

Periotto, T. R. C., & Wessellenns, J. L. (2018). The School Manager and the Use of Knowledge Management Practices for Structuring Organizational Processes. *International Journal of Learning, Teaching and Educational Research, 17*(10), 43–54. doi:10.26803/ijlter.17.10.3

Pons, N. L., Pérez, Y. P., Stiven, E. R., & Quintero, L. P. (2014). Design of a Knowledge Management model to improve the development of IT project teams (Diseño de un modelo de Gestión del Conocimiento para mejorar el desarrollo de equipos de proyectos informáticos). *Spanish Journal of Scientific Documentation, 37*(2), 44. doi:10.3989/redc.2014.2.1036

Quintas, P., Lefrere, P., & Jones, G. (1997). Knowledge management: A strategic agenda. *Journal of Long Range Planning, 30*(3), 385–391. doi:10.1016/S0024-6301(97)90252-1

Redecker, C. (2017). *European framework for the digital competence of educators: DigCompEdu* (No. JRC107466). Joint Research Centre (Seville site). ,jrc107466 doi:10.2760/159770

Rismark, M., & Sølvberg, A. M. (2011). Knowledge Sharing in Schools: A Key to Developing Professional Learning Communities. *World Journal of Education, 1*(2), 150–160. doi:10.5430/wje.v1n2p150

Silvia, P. J., & Duval, T. S. (2001). Objective self-awareness theory: Recent progress and enduring problems. *Personality and Social Psychology Review, 5*(3), 230–241. doi:10.1207/S15327957PSPR0503_4

Song, J. H., Kim, W., Chai, D. S., & Bae, S. H. (2014). The impact of an innovative school climate on teachers' knowledge creation activities in Korean schools: The mediating role of teachers' knowledge sharing and work engagement. *KEDI Journal of Educational Policy, 11*(2).

Swart, J., & Kinnie, N. (2003). Sharing knowledge in knowledge-intensive firm. *Human Resource Management Journal, 13*(2), 60–75. doi:10.1111/j.1748-8583.2003.tb00091.x

Von Krogh, G. (2012). How does social software change knowledge management? Toward a strategic research agenda. *The Journal of Strategic Information Systems*, *21*(2), 154–164. doi:10.1016/j.jsis.2012.04.003

Vuorikari, R., Punie, Y., Carretero Gomez S., & Van den Brande, G. (2016). *DigComp 2.0: The digital competence framework for citizens. Update phase 1: The conceptual reference model* (No. JRC101254). Joint Research Centre (Seville site). doi:10.2791/11517

Zhao, J. (2010). School knowledge management framework and strategies: The new perspective on teacher professional development. *Computers in Human Behavior*, *26*(2), 168–175. doi:10.1016/j.chb.2009.10.009

Zhao, J., & Ordóñez de Pablos, P. (2009). School innovative management model and strategies: The perspective of organizational learning. *Information Systems Management*, *26*(3), 241–251. doi:10.1080/10580530903017781

ENDNOTES

1 Erasmus Plus programme guide 2020 version available at: https://ec.europa.eu/programmes/erasmus-plus/resources/documents/erasmus-programme-guide-2020_en

2 The Erasmus+ was titled *News-New Skills New Schools, Common Standards and Skills in Education*. Project identification code 2017-1-IT02-KA219-036511_1.

3 eTwinning.net (24-05-2020)

4 http://ec.europa.eu (statistics sections).

5 https://ec.europa.eu/eurostat/statistics-explained/images/c/c2/Foreign_language_learning_in_general_upper_secondary_education%2C_by_country_Fig_6.P

6 See note 4.

Chapter 6
The Impact of COVID–19 on the Indian Economy and a Future Distaster Preparedness System Using Web Scraping

E. D. Kanmani Ruby

Vel Tech Rangarajan Dr. Sakunthala R&D Institute of Science and Technology, India

G. AloyAnuja Mary

Vel Tech Rangarajan Dr. Sakunthala R&D Institute of Science and Technology, India

B. Sathya Sri

Vel Tech Rangarajan Dr. Sakunthala R&D Institute of Science and Technology, India

K. S. Vinod

Vel Tech Rangarajan Dr. Sakunthala R&D Institute of Science and Technology, India

S. Vishnu Kumar

Vel Tech Rangarajan Dr. Sakunthala R&D Institute of Science and Technology, India

Janani P.

Vel Tech Rangarajan Dr. Sakunthala R&D Institute of Science and Technology, India

ABSTRACT

The COVID-19 pandemic has affected countries economically due to lack of documented guidance; it has also resulted in increased spread and mortality rate. This motivated the authors to design a disaster preparedness system to enable countries to plan strategically and strengthen their efforts in future events. Web-scraping technique is used for crowdsourcing both past and current information such as government policies, associated cost, the spreading and mortality rate, and the medicines used; the results are stored in a database. The framework aims to enable the government bodies and other stakeholders to detect, prevent, and respond to future novel pandemics. Thus, the proposed model aids as a reference tool and can be used for predictive analysis. This information collectively helps countries to acknowledge their strength, weakness, opportunity, and threat (SWOT) ranking and allows them in their national capacities to improve their strategies, infrastructure, and to draft plans in line with the most updated guidance.

DOI: 10.4018/978-1-6684-5027-7.ch006

I. INTRODUCTION

The outbreak of COVID-19 has impacted nations throughout, notably the nationwide lockdowns that have brought social and economic life to a standstill as per studied (Nicola, M., et al, 2020). Ever since the spread of COVID-19 virus, economic activities in both manufacturing and services sectors have delayed; hospitality, tours and travels, healthcare, retail, banks, hotels, property, education, health, Information Technology, recreation as discussed (Kumar, S. U et al, 2020). The economic stress has started to grow rapidly, analysts and consultants worldwide have projected larger and greater economic troubles for the world economy. A joint report from the World Health Organization (WHO) and the International Bank for Reconstruction and Development (IBRD) have projected the economic slowdown to range between 2.2% to 4.8%. The Primary Sectors of Republic of India, which encompasses industries related to extraction and production of raw materials alone provides employment to 43.21% of the total population and also contributes to 16.1% of the Indian gross domestic productions, has affected badly. This also has affected the secondary industries which gets their raw materials from primary sector. The impact of COVID-19 in primary and secondary sector has affected the basic requirements of human life.

This is believed to be outcome of non-documented pre-historic detailed data, to assist governments and other stake holders in handling such situations. The outbreak of COVID-19 has urged the scientific community to take measures to find methods to deal with such situations in current and future. It is stated that one is to design a disaster preparedness system, which includes an early prediction feature as demonstrated (Chamberlian, S.D (2020)). An Artificial Intelligence (AI) based prediction feature requires abundance of data to train itself. A COVID-19 database, which can collect past and future data through crowd sourcing, is the need of the hour.

Web-scraping seems to be a promising technology to collect necessary present and past data for the development of database. Through web-scraping information like age, gender, climatic condition, medical severity, mortality rate and survival rate etc. can be collected. The vaccines used, the implementation cost, method of public distribution, after effects of vaccination etc. can also be collected. To make web-scraping more effective, different e-mediums like social media, blog post, e-journals, e-magazines and e-NEWS-papers are highly concentrated.

Thus, the target of this work is to develop a self-updating database that collects COVID-19 related information and stores them. The template of the database is designed in such a way to help Deep Learning Algorithms (DLA) to uses this information to train themselves. Through this an early indication of a future pandemic possibility can be understood and this can lend an idea for stack-holders to handle the situation. The database is designed in such a way, redundancy of information is handled using data-normalization techniques. It can process text, image and META-Data.

II. IMPACT OF COVID-19 ON INDIAN ECONOMY

COVID-19 has become a world-changing event and isn't solely a humanitarian crisis however conjointly economic and social crisis as stated (Nicola, M., et al, 2020). It is stated that the continuous, dramatic and ubiquitous corona virus epidemic has deformed the India's blooming economy in a fickle and obscure manner as discussed (Chaudhary, M et al (2020)).COVID-19, set foot on Republic of India in 2020 and is heading for a second wave as on March-2021. Its impact on the business atmosphere is worldwide and the worsening situation as it appears is completely different from the slowdowns of the past that has affected the economic order. During first wave the severity of the same was less compared to the second wave, but still the government and other stakeholders are struggling to plan a proper execution plan to eradicate the same and recover the economy. Because of the speedy unfold of COVID-19 virus, many industries that drives growth are guaranteed to limit their business operations resulting in disruption of economic activities as discussed (Nicola, M., et al, 2020). The happening that's being encountered by the various sectors of the economy square is highlighted below.

III. FOOD AND AGRICULTURE

The Indian economy being upto 70-percentage agriculture based, this sector was one of the few sectors not to suffer a lot. The schemes announced by central government to allow transportation of Agri and Agri related products inter-state made the impact to be less. Individual state level local monitoring bodies also allowed the district-wise transportation which actually boomed the sector. Sales through online platforms rose to a newer height; peoples involved directly (IT infrastructure) and in-directly (sales executives, delivery executives and banking sector) saw a stable economic growth. But still due to local and micro-containment zones the Agri-related logistics sector suffered a small impact. Road side vendors and daily whole-sale mandis also suffered a small loss. A clear over-view of this sector was missing in place to plan and implement schemes to boost this sector in particular; covering bottom level farmers and mandi-dealers, small cargo transporters. Shielding the countryside food production areas future, will hold the answer for macro-level impact in Indian food sector due to COVID-19 virus spread.

IV. AVIATION AND TOURISM

India being a diversified cultural and natural resource country attracts a huge crowd each year as tourist. This was the first sector to feel the heat of COVID-19 virus. According to Federation of Indian Chambers of Commerce & Industry (FICCI), the industry jointly contributes about 2.4% and 9.2% of the total Gross Domestic Product (GDP) of the country. In the 2018-2019 financial year alone, the industry served approximately 43 million people and generated USD 247.3 billion. Indian tourism is mainly dominated by domestic travelers than international people. Due to the announcement of union government's travel and tourism ban, the industry has suffered from cash flow and maintenance has become a great problem. The industries expect an all-time high lay-off of 38 million peoples in near future, to manage the expected losses of about 85 billion Rupees according to Indian Association of Tour Operators (IATO). Apart from this, the industry has also innovated different ways to proceed with contact less boarding and travelling, which shows a positive sign and can expect to result in a better growth strategy for the industry.

IV.1 Telecom

Pre-dated to COVID-19 spread in India, the telecom sector saw a major break-through in terms of technology. The Voice over IP (VoIP) and data tariff made many Indians to subscribe new connections ("NRF | Coronavirus leads to more use of contactless credit cards and mobile payments despite cost and security concerns," n.d.) Post COVID-19 spread, Work from Home (WFH) became the new normal of corporate culture. India, being the country of hosting most of the worldwide IT and its allied companies saw a surge in data users. 2019 saw more than one billion active connections, contributing to 6.5-percent of total GDP of the country and made sure India's four million people's employability was not affected. The WFH demanded an increased broadband usage of almost 10-percentage hikes, which directly imparted pressure on the network. This affected the service providers; they braced a sharp dropping in adding new customers.

IV.2 Pharmaceuticals

India boasts, holding the world top Pharmaceuticals. Ever since the out-break of COVID-19, the pharmaceutical sector has been on the rise. With a market size of $55 billion during the beginning of 2020, it has been surging in India. The prices of raw material sky-rocketed due to Import and Export restrictions. India being specialized in Generic drugs, was the most impacted country because of her heavy reliance on imports, in addition the disrupted supply-chain, and labor unavailability also stressed the industry. The union government's restriction on exporting drugs and kits to other countries to ensure sufficient quantities for internal use also has put the industries under pressure.

IV.3 Oil and Gas

The world's third largest consumer of Oil and Gas, Indian publics are the worst hit by the COVID-19 in this category. India contributes to 5.2 percentage of the global oil demand, but its demand fell down 2/3rd due to complete lockdown and curfew. This resulted in very less demand for transport fuels and to make up the loss occurred the union government increased the excise and special taxes on the crude oil import. Even though the crude oil market priced dipped the public's were not in a position to enjoy the benefits due to increased taxes.

IV.4 Small and Medium Enterprises

It is suggested that an important phase of the Indian economy, Micro, Small & Medium Enterprises (MSME) sectors have arisen, creating a serious contribution to the creativity, export, production and especially economic development of the country as stated (Card Flight Small Business Report, 2020). The COVID-19 crisis is considered as a resilience test for start-ups in Republic of India. These MSMEs have created over 70% of the job-roles in Republic of India, employing over 114 million individuals and contributing 30% of the GDP. Several of these MSMEs have loan obligations and Equated Monthly Installment (EMIs) to pay. In addition to that, movement of decayable product is hindered due to transport restrictions in state levels; so these businesses stare at vast losses. Social distancing and migration of skilled workers are another important factor that affects theses industries.

IV.5 Education Sector

The Government of India has taken selection of preventive measures to prevent outbreak of COVID-19 virus; declared lock-down of all academic establishments on March 21, 2020. CBSE delayed all examinations of secondary and higher secondary faculties on March 18, 2020 throughout India. CBSE planned to conduct examinations by maintaining a distance of a minimum of one meter between the students, taking the exam with a constraint of not having more than 24 students in a room. If the examination center is small, then the students should be divided into different rooms consequently. Indian government has established the nationwide curfew on March 22. Government of India has been extending curfew periods from time to time, adopting different methods to fight with the pandemic. However instructional establishments stayed closed incessantly and On-line learning became the simplest answer throughout COVID-19 pandemic situation. This forced the faculty community to shift teaching using traditional board and chalk to online mode. Initially many felt difficult, later got adapted with increased user-friendly platforms like Microsoft Teams, Zoom, Google meet, WhatsApp, Telegram, YouTube live, Facebook live etc. This has provided an opportunity for faculties to develop new and competent instructional content, which has resulted in new economical and productive methodologies. Ministry of Human Resource Development (MHRD), Government of India on its part has also created arrangements along with on-line portals and academic channels to prompt Direct to Home, TV and Radios channels to continue learning.

IV.6 Migrant Labor

The International Labor Organization in its report defines the corona virus pandemic as the worst world crisis since world-war II. Four hundred million people, working within the Republic of India are at a risk of falling deeper into economic crisis, as half of them are low-paid, low-skilled jobs; it's a loss of 195 million regular jobs. Republic of India is a diversified country with abundant opportunities. Skilled labors transit from rural areas to urban, semi urban areas in search of jobs. The major relocation corridors in Republic of India are Uttar-Pradesh, Bihar, Madhya Pradesh, Rajasthan and Gujarat towards states like Maharashtra, Tamil Nadu, Kerala, Karnataka and Delhi. These migrant employees are utilized within the construction sector, domestic work, textile, brick work, transportation, mining and agriculture. Throughout the curfew, 93% of these laborers have lost one to four weeks of labor. A survey of 3196 migrant employees across northern and central Republic of India, between 27 March and 29 March, reveals that 80% of migrant employees feared that they're going to run out of food before curfew ends. The survey disclosed that 55% of employees get a daily wage between 200 and 400, and 39% of the employees are paid between 400 and 600. Only 3-5 percentage of the employees get 600 and above. In general, these employees are debt ridden and have very little savings of their own. About 49.2% of the surveyed employees didn't had rations and 39.4% of them had ration which might last up to two weeks only.

V. WEB SCRAPING AND DEEP LEARNING TECHNIQUES

Web-scraping is a technique used by individuals and companies alike to access information from web pages. Using web scrapping one can fetch e-contents of interest from web. A subset of AI is deep-learning which requires a greater number of samples to train itself. In the following section a clear understanding of both the technologies are discoursed and its adaptability to the proposed method is also conversed.

V.1 Web Scraping

Web scraping at, its core, is collecting publicly available information from the internet for a specific purpose as discussed (Mufid, M. R., et al, 2020). It is a technique; using computer scripted languages to create a code to access web pages and crawl data of interest. The data of interest is crawled and stored in a separate file which can be later modified in accordance with what is desired by the model. Web scraping applications (also called intelligent agents, automatic agents, or autonomous agents) only focus on obtaining data through data retrieval and extraction with varying data sets and sizes. The two parts of web scraping are the scraper and the crawler. The crawler is an artificial intelligence function that surfs the web to search the particular data required by following the links across the internet. The scraper is an explicit tool created to extract the data from the website. The design of the scraper helps quickly and accurately to extract the data. They, are called by different name like,

- Spiders
- Crawlers
- Bots

Data scientists often need hundreds of thousands of data points in order to build, train, and test machine learning models. In some cases, this data is already pre-packaged and ready for consumption. Most of the time, the scientist would need to venture out on their own and build a custom dataset. This is often done by building a web scraper to collect raw data from various sources of interest, and refining it so it can be processed later on. These web scrapers also need to periodically collect fresh data to update their predictive models with the most relevant information. Web Scraping is a spontaneous method to acquire huge repository of data from websites as discussed (Mufid, M. R., et al, 2020). Most of this data is amorphous data in an HTML format which is then converted into structured data in a spreadsheet or a database so that it can be used in various applications. The various methods to do web scraping to get data from websites which includes online services, API's or even creating your code for web scraping from scratch. Many big websites like Yahoo, Bing, Twitter, Facebook, StackOverflow, Google, etc. have API's which give access to their data in structured form as discussed (Das, A et al, 2016). Web scraping is a best method that will allow to scrape the websites that do allow to access large amount of data in structured form.

Figure 1. Web scraping technology overview

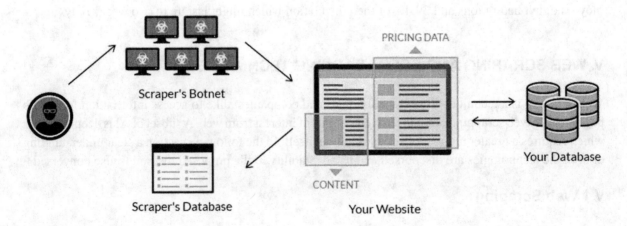

V.2 Deep Learning

Deep learning (DL) is a technique that imitates the functioning of the human brain as to how the brain processes the given data and creates patterns which is used in decision making. It is a subset of Machine Learning (ML) in AI. They have networks capable of unsupervised learning from the unstructured or unlabeled information. These networks are also called Deep Neural Networks (DNN) or Deep Neural Learning. DL has grown over time along with the digital revolution and this has brought about an explosion of data of all forms, from different parts of the globe. This data is termed as big data and is collected from different sources like Internet, Social medias like Facebook, Twitter, E-commerce platforms, Internet Search Engines and online movies among others.

Traditional ML-Flat Algorithms like Support Vector Machines (SVMs), Decision Trees (DTs), Logistic Regression (LR) and Naive Bayes classifiers cannot be directly applied on raw data such as text, image, numeric data, csv file, etc. These algorithms need an extra extraction step, which is a pre-processing step. The classic ML algorithms use the result of this extraction process to represent the given raw data to perform a task like classification or categorization. The process of extraction requires a thorough knowledge of the domain and is quite complicated for humans. For getting optimal results this preprocessing layer must be adapted, tested and refined over many iterations. Normally unstructured data is very vast that it could take long time for humans to grasp it and extract knowledge from the data, thus the use of DL could come in handy. Deep learning does not require this extraction step. The DL learns on their own from raw data; directly by DNN and produces more compressed and abstract representation of raw data over several layers. This representation of compressed and abstract raw data is used to produce the desired result. Deep learning model requires little or no human intervention to optimize and perform the feature extraction step, because during the neural network training process itself the network is optimized to produce possibly the best abstract representation of the input raw data.

Let us take an example of the problem of object classification, for example we take an image and want to check if it has a car or not. If we want to use machine learning then we need to feed the features that are specific to car like shape, color, size, presence of wheels etc. as input to the ML algorithm, then the algorithm will identify whether the car is present in the image or not. The ML algorithm would perform image classification by this method. The programmer must intervene with the algorithm directly for the ML algorithm to decide on the classification. The DL algorithm does not need preprocessing step of feature extraction. The model itself would identify the distinct characteristics of a car and can-do perfect prediction. Thus, the main advantage of deep learning is that the preprocessing step of feature extraction is not necessary for classification. We input the raw data to the DNN model and the rest is taken care by the deep learning algorithm.

Figure 2. Difference between ML and DL algorithms

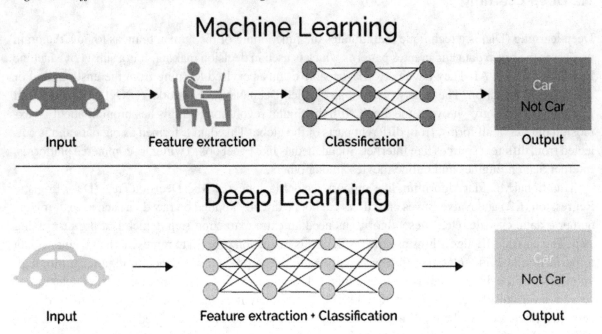

VI. DISASTER PREPAREDNESS SYSTEM

In general disaster preparedness are the activities implanted with risk lessening measures that can prevent disaster situations. If a disaster did occur, the measures to be taken to mitigate, resulting in saving maximum lives and livelihoods is also considered as disaster preparedness. Disaster preparedness provides a platform to design effective and realistic planning in reduction of efforts and to increases overall effectiveness. The economic seriousness of COVID-19 could be understood from the chapter two; thus, a disaster preparedness system is the need of the hour to help in future happenings. A database to support and train DL algorithms is proposed. As DL algorithms can vary, but the data set to train is of importance.

Infodemics, as an information set of information with true, false, rumors, conspiracy theories and stigma; is one of the key factors to be considered while creating an automated database updating tool, specially when its designed using web-scraping. (M, N., et al, 2020) Suggests that Infodemics, are common during the COVID-19 pandemics. Because of this, there is a tendency of COVID-19 related conspiracy theories, stigma, rumors and other false information currently on online media, together with fact finding agencies and websites the data crawling tool has to be incorporated to avoid storing false information.

(M, N., et al, 2020) is stated that the primary cross-sectional knowledge on actual level of psychological impact among Indian community; and the way psychological state of individuals is affected throughout a virulent disease of this nature. On-line surveys (or self-administered questionnaires) are found as a good approach of assessing issues associated with psychological state and this becomes a prudent technique of conducting analysis within the amount of imprisonment. Since these findings pertain to the initial amount of pandemic in Republic of India, a bigger longitudinal study ought to be conducted within the current time to guide policy manufacturers in understanding the psychological impact.

COVID-19 related information, includes parameters like age group, Climate condition, gender, survival rate, vaccine after effects, economy rate, unemployment and so on are extracted using web scraping technique, and are updated into a database. Meanwhile the collected information is to be checked for redundancy to fine grain the data. Thus, the database consists of fine-grained past and present data, which can be used to train the DL algorithms.

VII. COVID-19 RELATED DATA COLLECTION

In this section, the design of disaster preparedness system proposes discussed. The Figure 3 shows the block diagram of our automated database updating system. The system design consists of the following modules namely, web scraping module, crowd sourcing module and other connected devices. The data collected is stored in a database in a format; that can be later used for training DL algorithms to detect a possible outbreak in future or to handle the outbreak in a sensible manner. This database is constantly updated by the intelligent algorithm designed, which can sense the changes related to COVID-19 information in E-space and updates database accordingly. While creating a database it is very important that redundant data is not stored in the database. This is taken care by data normalization script written to avoid duplication of data in the covid database.

Figure 3. Block diagram of proposed model

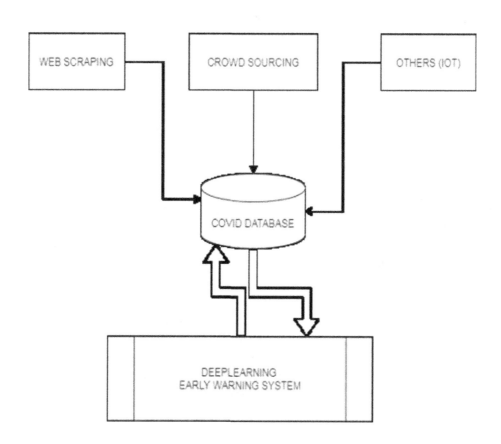

VII.1 Web Scraping Module

The web scraping module of proposed model is designed using computer programming scripting language Python. The tool uses python library packages like beautiful soup, pandas, scrappy etc., which helps to gather data from the internet and web sites. The data collected by this technique is stored in a temporary database-table to be fine-grained. Figure 2 explains the steps involved in a web scraping process.

Figure 4. Steps involved in web scraping

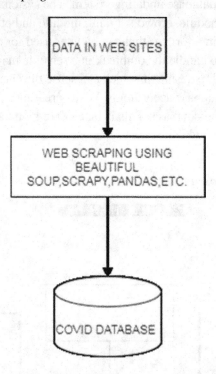

VII.2 Crowd Sourcing and Citizen Science

It is stated that Crowd sourcing is the method of collecting information directly from the field; data collected from citizens and people got affected as demonstrated (Das, A et al, 2016; Poblet, M et al, 2013; Riccardi, M. T., 2016). Crowd sourcing is a way of data gathering in which the people or individual of a particular region provide data about occurrences of certain events for example like spread of corona virus, or number of deaths due to covid etc. This information is collected and stored in a database. A lot of information can be gathered by this method, also the information will be from a diverse set of people. This method need not necessarily be online and existed before the evolution of the internet era. Crowd sourcing has the following advantages namely, speed of data collection will be more, quality is better, and it is also more flexible and scalable. Out sourcing is different from crowd sourcing in that the crowd sourcing is more public, less specific, when compared to out sourcing which is more specific.

Citizen science makes public involve and collaborate in scientific and technical research, this helps improve the technical knowledge of both public and scientific community, using this, the people share and contribute to data collection and monitoring programs. Citizen science is a new concept which helps involve public to participate in scientific research activities, so this uses the strength of both scientific community and the members of the non-technical group to determine the research topics, collect data related to research and also analyze data and interpret it and make further findings and help develop new applications and techniques that helps solve other scientific questions as discussed (Chinese startup Rokid pitches COVID-19 detection glasses, 2021).

Citizen science projects are the best way for people of nonscientific community to get involved in the scientific process. This project recruit volunteers to collect information and answer real world questions for example effect of covid 19 on world economy or effect of deforestation on climate etc. Statistics reveal that when public participate in scientific research, they become more literate in that particular field which they participate. This helps for better understanding of overall scientific process and improves the knowledge in the research domain. The Covid -19 citizen science project by University of California, San Francisco is a new initiative which allows any individual around the globe, above the age of 18 to become citizen.

VII.3 Connected Devices

The internet has reduced the distance between all, in recent years the Internet of Things (IoT) has revolutionized especially healthcare as discussed (M, N., et al, 2020). Using the connected device, more personalized patient's diagnosed data can be collected. Connected device can give inputs like diagnostic data, pre-defined protocols, after patient recovery rate etc. Some examples of the connected device like smart thermometersis is demonstrated (Can thermal imaging take the heat out of the coronavirus crisis, 2021; Chinese startup Rokid pitches COVID-19 detection glasses, 2021; VentureBeat, 2021) can be used to record temperature, and location data. This can be used to predict the regional transmission.

VII.4 Health Data

The data gathered from connected devices can offer predictive diagnoses and useful public health insights. A real time example of the same is, the announcement of Fitbit about building an algorithm to analyze data from their connected health trackers to detect COVID-19 before symptoms as stated (Fitbit Blog, 2021). Documenting these data could help in future prediction similar disease.

VII.5 The Internet of Medical Things (IoMT)

The IoMT is a common term used to describe connected medical devices such as electronic intensive care units (eICUs). The data collected from eICUs can give a more specific insight into patient critical information as studied (M, N., et al, 2020).

VIII. RESULTS AND DISCUSSIONS

The practicability of implementing the proposed model has been proto typed, the results show a promising feasibility status. The Figure 5, shows the Python code snippet used to collect data through web-scraping.

First the importing of beautiful soup; a Python package is used and followed by the content of interest and the source of the data is notified. The script is compiled and run to collect the data of interest.

Figure 5. Python code snippet used for web-scraping

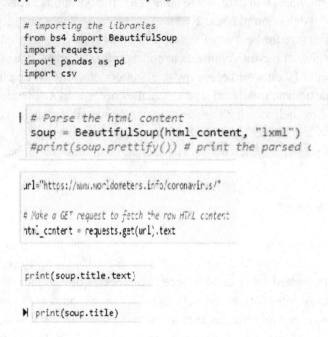

```
# importing the libraries
from bs4 import BeautifulSoup
import requests
import pandas as pd
import csv
```

```
# Parse the html content
soup = BeautifulSoup(html_content, "lxml")
#print(soup.prettify()) # print the parsed (
```

```
url="https://www.worldometers.info/coronavirus/"

# Make a GET request to fetch the raw HTML content
html_content = requests.get(url).text
```

```
print(soup.title.text)
```

```
print(soup.title)
```

The Figure 6a, shows the original web site which host the content of interest and the figure 6b, shows the output of above code snippet. This output can be further formatted to a comma separated value file, for easy integration into database.

Figure 6. Comparison of original data and scraped data

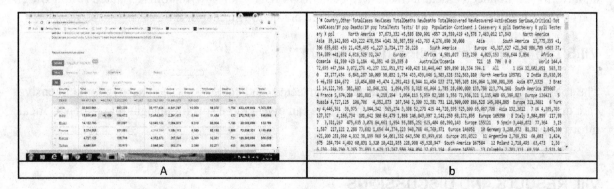

| A | b |

IX. CONCLUSION

The scale of disruption caused by COVID-19 pandemic has evident that the current economic downturn fundamentally different from recessions. But the nation understands the extent of the pandemic and beyond any doubt feels that the need of the hour is to organize for future. The sudden cash crunch and employability loss are results non documented guidance. Adopting new principles web-scraping and database maintenance and utilization of DL algorithms can save human kind from future mishaps. Disaster preparedness system can be used as an early warning tool, as well as help in decision making process; being a knowledge base. DL algorithm can provide useful information to governments and other stake holders in policies making. Also, it can be a useful tool on the disaster mitigation; to reduce the effect on the different sectors which would get affected.

REFERENCES

Can thermal imaging take the heat out of the coronavirus crisis? (n.d.). Retrieved July 16, 2021, from https://www.ifsecglobal.com/global/thermal-imaging-coronavirus-crisis

Card Flight Small Business Report. (2020, Oct. 7). Retrieved July 16, 2021, from https://www.cardflight.com/small-business-impact/report-30

Chamberlian, S. D. (2020). Real-time detection of COVID-19 epicenters within the United States using a network of smart thermoters. https://doi/org/ doi:10.1101/2020.04.06.20039909

Chaudhary, M., Sodani, P. R., & Das, S. (2020). Effect of COVID-19 on Economy in India. *Some Reflections for Policy and Programme, 22*(2), 169–180. doi:10.1177/0972063420935541

Chinese startup Rokid pitches COVID-19 detection glasses in US. (n.d.). Retrieved July 16, 2021, from https://techcrunch.com/2020/04/16/chinese-startup-rokid-pitches-covid-19-detection-glasses-in-u-s

Das, A., Mallik, N., Bandyopadhyay, S., Das Bit, S., & Basak, J. (2016). Interactive information crowdsourcing for disaster management using SMS and Twitter: A research prototype. *IEEE International Conference on Pervasive Computing and Communication Workshops, PerCom Workshops*. doi:10.1109/PERCOMW.2016.7457101

Early Findings from Fitbit COVID-19 Study Suggest Fitbit Devices Can Identify Signs of Disease at Its Earliest Stages. (n.d.). Retrieved July 16, 2021, from https://blog.fitbit.com/early-findings-covid-19-study

Italian airport leads Europe in adopting AR thermal scanning helmets. (n.d.). Retrieved July 16, 2021, from https://venturebeat.com/2020/05/07/italian-airport-leads-europe-in-adopting-ar-thermal-scanning-helmets

Kumar, S. U., Kumar, D. T., Christopher, B. P., & Doss, C. G. P. (2020). The Rise and Impact of COVID-19 in India. *Frontiers in Medicine, 7*, 250. doi:10.3389/fmed.2020.00250 PMID:32574338

M, N., S, P., RM, P., M, D., M, V., & HR, A. (2020). Internet of Things for Current COVID-19 and Future Pandemics: an Exploratory Study. *Journal of Healthcare Informatics Research, 4*(4), 325–364. doi:10.1007/s41666-020-00080-6

Mufid, M. R., Basofi, A., Mawaddah, S., Khotimah, K., & Fuad, N. (2020). Risk diagnosis and mitigation system of covid-19 using expert system and web scraping. *IES 2020 - International Electronics Symposium: The Role of Autonomous and Intelligent Systems for Human Life and Comfort*, 577–583. 10.1109/IES50839.2020.9231619

Nicola, M., Alsafi, Z., Sohrabi, C., Kerwan, A., Al-Jabir, A., Iosifidis, C., Agha, M., & Agha, R. (2020). The socio-economic implications of the coronavirus pandemic (COVID-19): A review. *International Journal of Surgery (London, England)*, 78, 185–193. doi:10.1016/j.ijsu.2020.04.018 PMID:32305533

NRF. (n.d.). *Coronavirus leads to more use of contactless credit cards and mobile payments despite cost and security concerns*. Retrieved July 16, 2021, from https://nrf.com/media-center/press-releases/coronavirus-leads-more-use-contactless-credit-cards-and-mobile-payments

Poblet, M., García-Cuesta, E., & Casanovas, P. (2013). *Crowdsourcing Tools for Disaster Management: A Review of Platforms and Methods*. doi:10.1007/978-3-662-45960-7_19

Riccardi, M. T. (2016). The power of crowd sourcing in disaster response operations. *International Journal of Disaster Risk Reduction*, 20, 123–128. doi:10.1016/j.ijdrr.2016.11.001

Chapter 7
Progression of E–Publishing Capacity Building in Nigeria

Emmanuel Ifeduba

https://orcid.org/0000-0002-7121-3279

Redeemer's University, Canada

ABSTRACT

The variety of opportunities offered by the internet makes it attractive for publishing, especially for developing nations previously unable to distribute publications on a global scale. However, Nigerian publishers striving to seize the moment are grossly under-reported in literature, notwithstanding that their innovations could create opportunities globally. This study, therefore, describes the progression of e-publishing in Nigeria with emphasis on e-publishing capacity building, collaboration, and outsourcing. Data were collected from publishers and their websites by means of in-depth interviews, website observation, and survey, and findings indicate that publishers are building e-publishing capacity by launching websites, e-book clubs, online bookshops, and e-libraries in schools and by collaborating with foreign e-book distribution firms. This study, therefore, provides updated information on an emerging market with huge investment and collaboration potential.

INTRODUCTION

Digital capability refers to the skills and practices that publishers and their organisations need to acquire in order to thrive in today's world. And though some of the skills and practices have been long acquired by Nigerian publishers, digital publishing was almost non-existent in Nigeria by 2002 despite the fact that local publishers were aware of its potentials and seemed to be interested in the benefits it offers. Thus, the few publishers who spearheaded digital innovation adoption saw the need to mobilise the local publishing industry to brace up to the realities of digital publishing (Mohammed, 2011; Okojie, 2014; Tiamiyu, 2005; Echebiri, 2005; Nwankwo, 2005). However, by 2020, the situation had changed significantly, and studies indicate that a fairly reasonable measure of digital publishing is currently taking place ((Worldinternetstatistics.com, 2020; Ifeduba, 2020; Okojie, 2014).

DOI: 10.4018/978-1-6684-5027-7.ch007

Notwithstanding, sections of the local publishing community seem to be stuck with inhibiting perceptions such as perceived inadequacy of infrastructure, high cost of content creation and poor demand for digital contents. To clear these perceptions and situate e-publishing in its rightful historical perspective, a clear description of the progression of digital publishing and e-collaboration in the country is hereby undertaken with a view to clarifying the strides made in digital innovations, types of businesses trending online, the role of local innovation champions and global online distributors as well as emerging business models.

In digital capacity building, some capabilities are fundamental. These are information, media and data literacy capabilities, digital creation capabilities, problem solving and innovation capabilities, collaboration capabilities, communication and participation capabilities, digital learning and development capabilities and digital identity and wellbeing (Jisc, 2021).

BACKGROUND: E-PUBLISHING AND COLLABORATION TRENDS

E-collaboration among firms, individuals or groups engaged in a common publishing task, or related tasks using electronic technologies, is evolving. And publishers engage in e-collaboration in several ways, including the use of blogs, wikis, portals, groupware, calendar sharing, discussion boards, document synchronization, cloud storage, video conferencing, white boards and instant messaging. These online collaboration tools help publishers to collectively author, edit, and review materials in a group work space irrespective of distance or location, while supporting easy management of projects and exchange of workflows in the haste to meet deadlines (Malik, 2021). Publishers are also increasingly deploying easy-to-use solutions such as IBM Workplace, Slack or Box Asana and Atlassian Confluence, thereby allowing organizations to maximize employee productivity by offering either a complete or a customized collaboration platform (Genius Project.com, 2022).

E-collaboration tools and applications are increasingly becoming important in all walks of life including collaborative and distributive publishing research (International Resources Management Association, 2018; Juan, A.A. et al., 2012) crisis management communication (Zhao, 2022) and to gain competitive advantage in challenging times such as the world has seen since 2019 (Zhao, 2021). E-publishers, therefore, have numerous reasons (including content creation, content supplies and new product development) to seek e-collaboration solutions for (Hall, 2020). Studies suggest that publishers and their intermediaries collaboratively aggregate supply and demand in ways that streamline the market for providers and consumers (O'Leary, 2014) implying that the scope of e-collaboration is gradually getting wider with respect to publishing. E-collaboration has also been deployed for entrepreneurship training and capacity building as well as in adapting, implementing and pilot-testing of co-innovation platforms, and for the facilitating of venture capital for start-ups (Osmani et al, 2020).

There is a relationship between internet access and e-collaboration, and global internet access records indicate that over 50% of the world's population had access to the internet by 2018, and that people are increasing the amount of time they spend online consuming digital media. For instance, a study indicates that by 2017 Americans spent about 5.9 hours a day, and there is a growth from 20 minutes to 3.3 hours a day in their use of mobile devices alone (Monojoy, 2018). Other factors driving publishers to e-collaboration include online learning whose demand skyrocketed following the challenges arising from the COVID-19 pandemic lockdowns (Monojoy, 2018; WIPO, 2020). Similarly, consumers in African countries are increasing their demand for digital products even though readers are generally only willing to spend less on digital products (Watson, 2018).

Lack of collaboration could affect innovation adoption and capacity building, and the Internet facilitates both, having evolved as a tool for cross–cultural collaboration. Thus, it has been argued that adoption of collaborative practices often appear to be fashionable as soon as industry peers identify such practices as being modern, central to improved performance or relevant to mainstream social evolution (Silva, 2012; Moreno and Suriñach, 2014). Hence the world of digital publishing largely depends on collaboration, which often takes the form of industry forums on the Internet, seminars, conferences and exchange of hyperlinks. This is on the understanding that an organization has greater chances of accessing new ideas and information when it is in a collaborative relationship with another. But Ifeduba (2021) observed that the local publishing industry was badly inhibited by excessive inter-company jealousies and competition that had prevented them from taking advantage of collaborative opportunities that abound in all areas of publishing, including Internet co-publishing (Jewell, 2013).

Collaborative platforms available to local publishers include the African Publishers Network (APNET) the African Books Collective (ABC) the Nigerian Publishers Association (NPA) and the International Publishers' Association (IPA). Curiously, local publishers collaborate with these bodies slack in aligning with some other local organisations. For instance, it has been claimed that the National Information Technology Development Agency, NITDA, has a virtual library at its Information Resource Centre with 14 million books and periodicals including audio books but had challenges securing collaborators from local university presses (Kemabonta, 2011). In contrast, Whithey et al (2011) found that university presses in some other countries were broadening intra-university press and library and inter-university as well as inter-press collaborative engagement to accommodate digital editions and titles. Similarly, publishers and technology firms in South Africa collaborate on digital innovations (Radinku, 2014).

In the case of Nigeria, the factors driving authors and publishers to e-publishing option are different and incidental (Yaya, Achonna and Osisanwo, 2013; Ifeduba, 2018). These include censorship, which is often political. Thus Fabre (2014) argues that each system of dictatorship evolves its own method of information control, and where the control fosters an unsustainable publishing environment, inhospitable to the flourishing of a self-sustaining industry, publishers would naturally look outwards for collaborators and partners, and may resort to outsourcing (Akpokodje and Ukwuoma, 2016).

Outsourcing, however, comes with obvious disadvantages including loss of important instructions in translation when handing out remote work via email or telephone and denying the staff or a talented local agency crucial work or development opportunities. While these disadvantages could cost serious time, money and hassles, the outsourcing firm may not grow in all vital directions and may not be contributing to the growth of the immediate community (Riggins, 2017).

From a theoretical point of view, it has been argued that the existence of change agents or innovation champions could be crucial to innovation adoption (Abukhzam, and Lee, 2010; Boston University School of Public Health, 2013). In Nigeria, innovation champions, that is, self-appointed advocates of emerging e-publishing processes seem to play key roles in e-publishing innovation adoption and diffusion by taking the risk of trying new technologies (Gogan, Conboy and Weiss, 2020). They acquire new skillsets in order to benefit from new and emergent technologies designed to align different sets of stakeholders in networks of open innovation (Bartlett, 2017) and collaborative convergence (Yang, Steensma and Ren, 2021).

PURPOSE OF THE STUDY AND METHODS EMPLOYED

The purpose of this paper is to draw update information on the creative and innovative ways in which Nigerian publishers build capacity, to describe the roles of innovators and leading online distributors in the emerging business models. In-depth interviews, website observation and survey methods were employed in data collection in order to achieve these objectives. Data were collected from 91 purposively selected publishing firms, 82 available publishing websites with the aid of a website observation guide. Additional data were collected by means of in-depth interviews and analysed using frequency tables, text and charts.

CAPACITY BUILDING INNOVATIONS AND STRATEGIES

The findings indicate that local innovation leaders have established about 82 book publishing websites. Although five websites were established between 1998 and 2000, according to the responses, website observation indicates that the earliest websites were established about 2002. Since then, there has been a gradual increase in the number with 2012 and 2017 witnessing the establishment of more websites than other years.

Another discernible strategy is the establishment of online book clubs. The findings indicate that Rainbow Book Club established in 2005 is the oldest online book club in Nigeria. At the time of this study, there were 11 online book clubs established between 2005 and 2019. The book clubs are: Rainbow, Aimee's Kids Book Club, Lagos Book Club, Ònkàwé Book Club, Childpreneur Book Camp, Bookworms Arise Book Club, Medina Book Club, Channels Book Club, Booklify and Page Book Connoisseurs. Details on year of establishment are presented in Table 1:

Table 1. Online book clubs and establishment dates

Online Book Clubs	Date Established
1. Rainbow Book Club *www.rainbowbookclub*.org	2005
2. Aimee's Kids Book Club *www.aimees*library.com	2011
3. Lagos Book Club www.lagosbookclob.org	2014
4. Ònkàwé Book Club www.onkawebookclubib.wordpress.com	2017
5. Childpreneur Book Camp www.thereadinggymng.com	2017
6. Bookworms Arise Book Clubs www.bookwormsarise.wordpress.com	2017
7. The Lagos October Book Club www.lagosoctoberbookclub.com	2017
8. Medina Book Club www.medinabookclub.com	2017
9. Channels Book Club www.channelstv.com	2018
10. Booklify, www.booklify.ng	2018
11. Page Book Connoisseurs www.pagebookstore.com/	2018
12. Liam &Noel's Book Club	NA
13. Lagos International Book Club	NA
14. Thinkers Pool Book Club	2016
15. Lukandi Book club	NA
16. Channels Book club	2014
17. Anambra Book Club	NA
18. Oshogbo Book Club, https://osogbobookclub.wordpress.com	2014

From Field Data

Online Bookshops

Most of the online sellers are offshoots of conventional bookshops that have existed long before the launch of the Internet however their online presence was established between 2000 and 2018. Bible wonderland limited, Jumia Books and Iwe Bookstore are among the thriving shops; they also sell books on their websites. There is also a set of bookshops that are not in business to sell only books online. Such bookshops undertake online bookselling as part of bigger businesses as is the case with Amazon. Books sold in the online shops range from fiction, religious, educational to motivational and self-help, family, lifestyle, business, finance, science and technology titles. Details of the various types of online bookshops are presented in Table 2:

Table 2. Online bookshops and establishment dates

Online bookshops	Date Established
2. Taebiyah book plus www.*tarbiyahbooksplus*.com	2012
3. CSS bookshop limited www.*cssbookshopslimited*.com	2014
4. Sunshine bookshops www.*sunshinebooks*.com.au	2015
5. Laterna Books limited www.*laternabooks*.com	2016
6. The Bookseller limited www.*thebookseller*.com	2017
7. Havilah www.avilahBookshop.com	2017
8. Gvribook www.vibuk.com	2017
9. Dominion bookstore www.domionline*store*.org	2017
10. Schoolstore.Ng www.schoolstore.ng	2010
11. Jasper books Nigeria limited www.*jasperbooks*.com	2013
12. Book to my door www.*bookstomydoor*.com	2013
13. Mixsie fun books www.*mixsie.site*	2017
14. www.biblewonderland.com	2012

From Field Data

Businesses Common on the Websites of Print Publishers

Over 61% of the publishers favour the establishment of websites for the purpose of promoting print titles and digital titles, where digital titles have been produced. The second business commonly transacted on the websites is customer enquiries/feedback which featured in 38.5% of the sites. It must be noted that increased enquiry is usually interpreted as a logical response to successful promotion. It may also lead to actual sales; and actual sale of print titles is the third trendy activity on the sites. This trend suggests that the publishers set up websites not only to promote and sell print titles but also to take a cautious step into the largely unknown digital environment. Other activities on the websites include manuscript transfer, sale of digital content, use of site as corporate showroom, socialisation platform and collaboration venue.

The digital devices through which published contents could be accessed by consumers include Ipad, kindle, smart phones, dedicated devices, laptop computer and desktop computer. This suggests that there is an obvious mismatch and possible disconnect between consumers' choice of devices and publishers' choice of devices. It is clear that smart phones and tablets are the popular devices, notwithstanding, the majority of publishers hardly prioritize digital delivery to mobile devices in a market with about 170 million mobile subscriptions and about 25 million users of smartphones (O'Dea, 2020).

Diffusion of e-Books in Schools

Some of the start-up e-publishers, having observed the gap in digital delivery, are resorting to direct community delivery to elite schools, sometimes in collaboration with state governments, government agencies or Non-Governmental Organisations (NGOs). A survey in search of evidence of use of e-books in schools indicated that e-books are used in 15 states and Abuja. And secondary schools in Lagos State are leading in this collaborative adoption and use of e-books. However, there is no evidence of adoption in 21 states. Details are presented in Table 3:

Table 3. Diffusion of e-books in secondary schools (States and Abuja)

SN	States	Frequency	Percent
1.	Abia	2 schools	5.2
2.	Akwa Ibom	1 schools	2.6
3.	Anambra	3 schools	7.8
4.	Benue	1 schools	2.6
5.	Edo	2 schools	5.2
6.	Enugu	1 schools	2.6
7.	Imo	1 schools	2.6
8.	Jigawa	1 schools	2.6
9.	Kaduna	3 schools	7.8
10.	Kogi	1 schools	2.6
11.	Lagos	10 schools	26.3
12.	Ogun	3 schools	8.8
13.	Ondo	1 schools	2.6
14.	Osun	1 schools	2.6
15.	Oyo	1 schools	2.6
16.	Abuja	2 schools	5.2
17.	Uncategorised	4 schools	10.5
		Total = 38	**100**

From Field Data

Diffusion of e-Libraries

In 2002, the Nigeria Virtual Library Project was approved by the Federal Executive Council thereby authorising Nigerian universities and other institutions to launch e-libraries. In pursuit of that mandate, over 115 universities have launched e-libraries, but the website observation indicates that their library holding capacities are low and often limited to e-journals, question paper banks, online databases and a few other publications. However, there is evidence of e-collaboration with multinational organizations and international organizations/agencies.

The online library of the National Open University of Nigeria, named The Information Gateway, provides a gateway to a wide range of free information resources for round the clock download. Through e-collaboration, it has built a sizable collection of tertiary education textbook holding. Details of the Open Educational Resources (OER) textbook holdings are presented in Table 4:

Table 4. OER text books accessible through NOUN virtual library

SN	OER Texts	Available Subject Areas
1	Free Technology Books	Computer Science, Engineering and Programming
2	OER Commons	Applied Science, Arts and Humanities, Business and Communication, Career and Technical Education, Education, English Language Arts, History, Law, Life Science, Mathematics, Physical Science, Social Science
3	Gutenberg	Multidisciplinary
4	Khan academy	Science and Engineering, Arts and Humanities, Economics and Finance, Computing (with Video options)
5	Open Stax College	Maths, Science, Social Science, Humanities
6	Open Text Books Library	Accounting and Finance; Business, Human Resources, Management, Marketing; Computer Science and Information Systems; Economics; Education; Engineering; Humanities (Arts, History, Linguistics, Literature, Rhetoric and Writing, Philosophy, Journalism, Media Studies and Communications); Law; Mathematics (Applied and Pure); Medicine; Natural Sciences (Biology, Chemistry, Physics) Psychology, Sociology
7	College Open Text Books	Applied Science (Computer & Information Sc., Engineering & Electronics, Health and Nursing Business (Accounting and Finance, General Business)Humanities (Education, English and Composition, Fine Arts, History, Languages and Communication, Literature, Philosophy) Natural Sciences (Biology and Genetics, Chemistry, General Sciences, Mathematics, Physics, Statistics and Probability) Social Science (Anthropology and Archaeology, Economics, Law, Political Science, Psychology, Sociology)
8	Open Culture	Art History, Biology, Business and Management, Chemistry, Classics, Computer Science and Information Systems, Earth Science, Economics and Finance, Education, Electrical Engineering, Engineering, History, Languages, Law, Linguistics, Mathematics, Music, Philosophy, Physics, Political Science, Psychology, Sociology, System Theory

Adapted from Open Access Data on NOUN Website

ROLE OF START-UP PUBLISHERS IN CAPACITY BUILDING

To help young and new writers showcase their writing skills and share their works with readers, Naijastories was launched in March, 2010 by a bibliophilic author/publisher. Positioned as a literary critique and social networking site, it connects writers and readers in a literary community of over 10,000 members with over 15,000 works authored by 924 writers. Naijastories is credited with pioneering an online-first publishing model in which successful digital titles are given long tails by transforming them to print. By 2018, it had published print versions of over 15 successful titles in several genres, including science fiction, short story, drama, comedy, horror, fantasy fiction, poetry, flash fiction, romance fiction, adventure fiction and non-fiction titles. For distribution, they collaborate with Createspace on paperbacks, Amazon on Kindle and print, Barnes and Noble on Nook and Smashwords on other e-book formats. It also collaborates with Nairaland blog on promotion and delivers PDF formats by email to Nigerian readers only.

Okadabooks, as a reading and publishing platform with a vision to improve literacy across the country, collaborates with Teach-for-Nigeria, an organization that trains and sends teachers across Nigeria, to educate children in low-income communities. It also collaborates with Samsung, Wattpad and Google on distribution and promotion. The Okadabooks website runs on a free EPUB reader-friendly application and many of its 27,000 titles (print and digital) have been offered free of charge since 2018. Over 4000 registered participants and other readers have made over 500,000 downloads since 2012. One of its major strategies is to allow all genres of literary works to be published on the site without restrictions, and this has led to the publishing of over 1009 titles in e-book format. Though it set out with a focus on Africa, it has since broadened its business focus to include global favourites such as *Oliver Twist* and other popular novels. In terms of supply, it stocks books from a broad base of conventional publishers including Bahati Books, Cassava Republic, Learn Africa plc., Love Africa, Parressia and many more; a strategy which makes it a change agent in local collaboration, which had been hitherto reported as a major factor inhibiting innovation adoption in Nigeria.

Digital collaboration received a boost in 2013 when an educational publisher produced the first major dedicated digital tablet for state-wide adoption in Osun State public schools. First Veritas Publishers, which customized the tablet for the state government, departed from the no-collaboration tradition for which Nigerian publishing had suffered setback in the past, by collaborating with Evans Publishers and several other leading organisations. This collaborative effort led to the distribution of 25, 477 devices with free pre-loaded textbooks and curriculum-based contents to final year students and teachers in senior secondary schools. Since then, steps have been taken in Lagos, Anambra, Ogun, Edo and a number of other states to introduce e-books in both public and private schools.

At the tertiary level, the National Open University of Nigeria launched a growing e-courseware repository with nearly 2500 PDF textbooks and hundreds of other digital resources and made all of them freely available to its students and the general public. To pursue the ambitious goal of ultimately enrolling half a million students, its library e-book collection is expected to grow to 100,000 volumes by 2025. Employing e-collaboration as a major tool, the university provides students with an information gateway linked to the sites of leading providers of educational contents such as the British Library for Development Studies (Europe's largest research collection on economic and social change in developing countries), Sage, Law Pavilion, Project Muse journals, AGORA, Bibliomania, Bioline International. The National Open University gateway is also linked to Chemistry Central, Bridge Development and Gender and Directory of Open Access Journals, which provides access to 2,565 quality controlled scientific and scholarly journals. EBSCO collaborates with the institution to distribute full text for more than 2,300 journals while HINARI, JSTOR and many others provide thousands of titles and documents.

Emergence of Internet-Driven Publishing Models

Available data indicates that six distinct models of innovative publishing are beginning to emerge in the environment under study, and a number of them leverage on collaborative opportunities. They are: Prints-only model, sold offline but promoted online; sale of prints offline with a few digital titles online; sale of prints offline and sale of digital offline by subscription through dedicated apps; Born-digital online-only for either free downloads or subscription supported with site advertisement revenue. Others are free digital contents sponsored by government, whether online or offline and born-digital online and sold online only until transformed to print, income supported with site advertisement revenue. Details are presented in Table 5:

Table 5. Emerging publishing revenue models

SN	Emerging Business Models
1	Producing prints only, selling it offline but promoting online
2	Primarily selling prints offline while marketing a few digital titles online
3	Selling a combination of prints and digital offline.(digital sold by subscription through dedicated apps only).
4	Born-digital titles for free downloads or subscription, supported with site advertisement revenue
5	Born-digital and sold online and later transformed to print
6	Free digital contents sponsored by government, whether online or offline.

From Field Data

Outsourcing to International Distributors

Collaborating with other publishers, as digital publishing often requires, could play a role in technology adoption and capacity building. But responses from nearly 50% of conventional publishers indicate that there is very little collaboration among the local publishers, suggesting that they hardly engage in shared assignments necessary in digital capacity building, while less than 26% indicated that some degree of collaboration takes place among local publishers. In the same vein, nearly 47% indicated that the publishers hardly use joint publication to drive their businesses. As a result, the majority of them are yet to develop online distribution skills and channels due to the novelty and perceived technicalities of the digital environment. They rather rely heavily on Amazon, Banes and Noble, Okadabooks, African Books Collective and other international platforms for digital distribution. Other collaborators include Naija Stories, I-tunes and Worldreader.org.

The tendency to look outward became so strong that by 2019, there were 578 Nigerian titles on Amazon platform alone, though this number includes print titles. Leading foreign collaborators include CreateSpace, Amazon's self-publishing platform, LAP LAMBERT academic publishing, Monarch Books and African Books Collective (ABC). Findings also indicate that self-publishing is on the rise as over 50% of the digital titles were self-published through Createspace, wattpad and other platforms. Wattpad platform was patronized by 334 authors, especially self-publishing authors; Amazon, 224; Barnes and Noble, 148 and ABC, 55.

Publishers' membership of local professional bodies is an indication that local collaboration may not be ruled out in the long run. Thus, the finding that over 76% of the respondents belong to at least one professional body, suggests that a change in the current collaboration behaviour may be in sight. The professional associations providing platforms for collaboration include Nigerian Publisher Association (NPA) African Publishers Network, ABC, and Association of Nigerian Authors (ANA). Others are Christian Booksellers Association of Nigeria (CBAN) Law Publishers Association (LPA) Nigerian Bar Association (NBA) Nigerian Book Fair Trust (NBFT) United Bible Societies as well as Nigerian Booksellers Association, Afro-Asian Book Council, Chartered Institute of Professional Printers of Nigeria (CIPPON).

DISCUSSION OF FINDINGS

Findings of this study indicate that the publishers, at the initial stage of innovation adoption, only cautiously launched websites to register their presence on the web, promote their print products and attend to enquiries. This strategy of approaching e-publishing adoption with cautious optimism accords with findings of previous studies indicating that publishers often establish websites as a logical first step to e-publishing (Hashim, 2012). And this pattern is also not unconnected with their perception of website launch as a cost-effective avenue to promote their print titles. This perspective seems to be common among textbook publishers who generally indicated that their textbook customers would rather buy recommended texts through schools and bookshops than go online to purchase digital editions.

The findings also show that the e-book market is developing in three directions: the first is in the direction of print publishers diversifying cautiously to e-publishing. The second involves technology savvy start-ups spearheading the development of local digital capacity mainly with titles born digital. These include NaijaStories, Okadabooks, First Veritas and the National Open University of Nigeria (NOUN) which thrive on digital formats. The third direction is the direction of dedicated tablets for a large community, as in the case of *Opon Imo* tablets and other school-based devices.

The quest to develop the much-needed digital publishing capacity in an infrastructure-challenged environment has made collaboration with global giants compelling. Thus, agreements have been signed with Samsung Corporation to upload 7500 of Okadabook titles on Samsung application. Naijastories, which publishes and distributes mainly short stories online, stated that collaboration with writers, reviewers, readers and publishers is inevitable. Similarly, the NOUN is partnering with over twenty major international organisations and institutions to provide digital contents for students. In the same vein, the UNESCO has expressed interest in collaborating with the publishers of the *Opon Imo* community e-book.

In terms of financial sustainability, some sell their prints-only titles offline but promote online whereas government institutions generally provide free contents leveraging on public subventions and tertiary education fund. In between these two extremes are models championed by start-ups striving to carve online niches for themselves. Though Naijastories creates and gives out so much content for free online, it depends heavily on online revenue from sales and advertisements, diversifying to print formats for only titles that have succeeded online. Similarly, Okadabooks depends heavily on online sales and solicits donations for its literacy development campaigns. The First Veritas model seems to pursue a balance of digital offline and print.

Outsourcing distribution to international platforms has given a long tail to 805 locally produced titles distributed through Amazon, Wattpad and Barnes and Noble. The implication is that pricing may have been taken out of the control of local publishers due to author-centric policies pursued by Amazon and some others. However, since the majority of the authors collaborating with Wattpad, Naijastories and Amazon's Createspace are authors critically challenged by censorship in the North (Ifeduba, 2018) and those spurred by a long spate of manuscript rejection in the south they seem to have little choice. On the whole, making reasonable sales online is difficult without seeking collaboration and without taking advantage of outsourcing opportunities. For such firms, outsourcing, as a business practice in which aspects of the functions or services of an organisation are farmed out to a third party, lower costs due to economies of scale or lower labour rates, increases efficiency and provides additional capacity, thereby helping to build overall capacity. It offers increased focus on strategy and core competencies, it gives access to skills and resources, increases operational flexibility to meet changing business and commercial conditions while accelerating time to market (Overby, 2017).

However, disadvantages of outsourcing could be grave for developing economies. Riggins (2017) stated that loss of control, hidden costs, security risks, reduction of quality control, sharing the financial burdens of another firm, risking public backlash, shifting time frames, loss of focus, translation challenges and moral dilemmas are some of the major disadvantages of outsourcing. Furthermore, it is argued that when outsourcing to overseas third parties, local firms create jobs for other economies rather than their home economies whereas insourcing brings new employees into the local organisation (Indeed Editorial Team, 2021).

FUTURE RESEARCH DIRECTIONS

This study explored the progression of e-publishing capacity building, e-collaboration and outsourcing in Nigeria without investigating the factors facilitating or inhibiting the progression. Therefore, another study to investigate the factors inhibiting e-collaboration as well as the determinants of e-collaboration in publishing, e-publishing capacity building and outsourcing in the studied setting and in similar environments would be illuminating. It may also be enlightening to undertake a qualitative research investigation into the e-commerce and e-content creation activities of those authors migrating online and collaborating online without collaborating offline. Such research has the potential to reveal underlying needs, challenges and experiences needed to advance not only scholarship but also sustainable publishing.

The findings of this study, on the one hand, show that e-collaboration and outsourcing centre mainly on trade books. On the other hand, the publishing industry is dominated by educational print publishers as previous studies indicate (Amadi, 2011). The situation, thus, creates a gap regarding ways of deepening e-publishing adoption and diffusion in the educational publishing sub-sector. Therefore, to increase collaboration on the production and distribution of educational books, it might be necessary to adapt from the innovative practices introduced by the National Open University of Nigeria and provide a collaborative digital highway for the distribution of textbooks since this would be cheaper in the long run for all the parties. To accomplish this objective, there is need to design studies focused on the following recommendations:

RECOMMENDATIONS

Recommended Research Direction1: Exploration of E-collaboration Trends in Textbook Distribution, E-Learning and Computer-Based Examinations in Nigeria

There is evidence showing that in 2022 use of e-book was reported in schools across15 states by both private and public schools. Whereas it may be difficult to mobilise the private schools for community adoption and distribution of e-books, the Osun state model seems to have provided a template which could guide other states and Local Government Councils in collectively providing digital distribution highways for public schools. An e-publishing collaboration grant from the Federal Government to states or the leading innovators identified in this study would be needed to accomplish this goal. Having created several reading and literacy programmes, the Federal Government could do so under its various reading promotion programmes. The innovative activities of the start-up publishers seem to position them better than others publishers in leading the campaign for deepening content creation, global distribution and local e-reading capacity.

Recommended Research Direction 2: The Role of E-collaboration and Government Funding in Reading Promotion and E-content Creation

With the gradual diffusion of e-books to schools across the 36 states of Nigeria, the need to collect and analyse data on user experiences, challenges and prospects has become urgent. Therefore, a third research direction is recommended thus:

Recommended Research Direction 3: Student and Teacher E-book User Experiences in Nigerian Private and Public Schools

Since digital publishing is still evolving, a longitudinal study of this topic is recommended. Such a study should include variables to interrogate digital distribution challenges and advantages. The role of governments in the digital book adoption process should be examined in yet another study.

CONCLUSION

This study establishes that e-publishing is diffusing steadily into Nigerian publishing industry, schools, and that this is made possible with a strategy involving innovative market development, e-collaboration and outsourcing on the part of publishers. On the part of line and trade, distributors, retailers and not-for-profit organisations are actively establishing online bookshops and online book clubs to increase digital engagement for the purpose of content consumption. In the forefront are a few start-up organisations collaborating with local content creators to create over 50,000 titles distributed through their own websites, while others collaborated with global leaders such as Wattpad and Amazon's Createspace. Thus, it could be rightly stated that e-publishing awareness is high, business interest on the rise and that market size is increasing with bright prospects for investment and more collaboration

REFERENCES

Aboelmaged, M. G. (2010). Predicting e-procurement adoption in a developing country: An empirical integration of technology acceptance model and theory of planned behaviour. *Industrial Management & Data Systems, 110*(3), 392–414. doi:10.1108/02635571011030042

Abukhzam, M., & Lee, A. (2010). Workforce attitude on technology adoption and diffusion *The Built & Human. Environmental Reviews, 3*, 60–72.

Abulude, F.O. (2014). Digital publishing: how far in Nigeria? *Continental J. Information Technology, 8*(1), 18 – 23. doi:.23 doi:10.5707/cjit.2014.8.1.18

Adesanoye, F. A. (2007). Rebuilding the publishing industry, rebranding the NPA. *The Publisher, 14*, 3–13.

Akpokodje, V.N., & Ukwuoma, S.C. (2016). *Evaluating the impact of eBook on reading motivation of students of higher learning in Nigerian universities*. Academic Press.

Amadi, M. N. (2011). Supporting Learning in the Digital Age: E-learning Strategies for National Open University of Nigeria. *US-China Education Review*, *B7*, 975–981.

Bartlett, D. (2017). Champions of local authority innovation revisited. *Local Government Studies, 43*(2), 142-149. doi:10.1080/03003930.2016.1245184

Boston University School of Public Health. (2013). *Diffusion of Innovations Theory*. https://sphweb. bumc.bu.edu/otlt/MPH-Modules/SB/SB721

Christopher, N.M. (2010). Applying marketing concepts to book publishing in Nigeria. *The Journal of International Social Research, 3*(11), 207-212.

Conford, R. (2011). Digital publishing in West Africa: what works, what doesn't and why. *Transcripts from the information for change workshop*. htt://publishingperspetives.com/08/ditialpublishing-West Africa

Echebiri, A. (2005). Book production in Nigeria' in the new millennium. In F. A. Adesanoye & A. Ojeniyi (Eds.), *Issues in Book Publishing in Nigeria* (pp. 197–218). Heinemann Educational Publishers.

Eyitayo, S. A. (2011). Book, technology and infrastructural development: what the future holds for the book industry in Nigeria. In *Book Industry Technology and the Global Economic Trend*. Nigerian Book Fair Trust.

Gogan, J., Conboy, K., & Weiss, J. (2020). Dangerous Champions of IT Innovation. *ScholarSpace*. http://hdl.handle.net/10125/64494

Hall, F. (2020). *Creative Digital Collaboration in Publishing: How do digital collaborative partnerships work and how might publishing companies adapt to facilitate them?* [Doctoral thesis]. University College London. https://discovery.ucl.ac.uk/id/eprint/10110283/

Hashim, N. A. (2012). E-*commerce Adoption by Malaysian SMEs* [Doctoral thesis]. University of Sheffield. https://etheses.whiterose.ac.uk/14590/1/574600.pdf

Hovav, A., & Gray, P. (2001). *Managing academic electronic publishing six case studies*. Paper presented at the 9th European conference an information systems, Bled, Slovenia.

Ifeduba, E. (2018). Book Censorship in Nigeria: A study of Origin, Methods and Motivations. *Library Philosophy and Practice,* 1954. https://digitalcommons.unl.edu/libphilpr

Ifeduba, E. (2020). Digital Publishing Readiness in Nigeria's Print Book Market, *Global Knowledge. Memory and Communication, 69*(6/7), 427–442. doi:10.1108/GKMC-04-2019-0047

Ifeduba, E. (2021). Predictors of E-Publishing Adoption in Environments of Uncertainty. *Global Knowledge, Memory and Communication, 70*. https://www.emerald.com/insight/content/doi/10.1108/GKMC-11-2020-0164/full/html doi:10.1108/GKMC-11-2020-0164

Indeed Editorial Team. (2021). *Outsourcing: Advantages and Disadvantages*. https://www.indeed.com/career-advice/career-development/outsourcing-benefits

Information Resources Management Association. (2018). *E-Planning and Collaboration: Concepts, Methodologies, Tools, and Applications* (3 Volumes). https://www.igi-global.com/book/collaborative-distributed-research/58272 doi:10.4018/978-1-5225-5646-6

JISC. (2021). *What is digital capability?* https://www.digitalcapability.jisc.ac.uk/what-is-digital-capability/

Juan, A. A. (2012). *Collaborative and Distributed E-Research: Innovations in Technologies, Strategies and Applications.* https://www.igi-global.com/book/collaborative-distributed-research/58272 doi:10.4018/978-1-4666-0125-3

Lemo, T. (2004). *Publishing in a difficult economic environment.* Academic Press.

Mohammed, A. M. (2011). *Publishing education and the global economic trend. In Book Industry, Technology and the Global Economic Trend.* Nigerian Book Fair Trust.

Monojoy, B. (2018). Digital Publishing Trends: Mary Meeker's 2018 Report. *What's New in Publishing.* https://whatsnewinpublishing.com/key-insights-for-publishers-from-mary-meekers-internet-trends-2018-report/

Nwankwo, V. (2005). Print-On-Demand: an African publisher's experience. In F. A. Adesanoye & A. Ojeniyi (Eds.), *Issues in Book Publishing in Nigeria* (pp. 173–183). Heinemann Educ. Books.

O'Dea, S. (2020). *Number of smartphone users in Nigeria from 2014 to 2025.* https://www.statista.com/statistics/467187/forecast-of-smartphone-users-in-nigeria/

O'Leary, B. (2014). An architecture of collaboration. *Publishing Research Quarterly, 30*(3). www.researchgate.net

Obidiegwu, D. (2009). *The book chain and national development. In Chain and National Development.* NBFT.

Obidiegwu, O. (2006). Enhancing productivity in the publishing industry. *The Publisher, 13*(1), 3–10.

Obiwuru, T. C., Oluwalaiye, O. B., & Okwu, A. T. (2011). External and internal environments of business in Nigeria: An appraisal. *International Bulletin of Business Administration., 12*, 15–23. www.googlescholar.com

Okojie, V. (2014). *Emergence of e-book and the survival of the physical book in Africa.* Paper presented at the Nigerian international book fair, University of Lagos.

Osmani, M. W., Haddadeh, R., Hindi, N., & Weerakkody, V. (2020). The Role of Co-Innovation Platform and E-Collaboration ICTs in Facilitating Entrepreneurial Ventures. *International Journal of E-Entrepreneurship and Innovation, 10*(2), 62–75. Advance online publication. doi:10.4018/IJEEI.2020070104

Overby, S. (2017). *What is outsourcing? Definitions, best practices, challenges and advice.* https://www.cio.com/article/272355/outsourcing-outsourcing-definition-and-solutions.html

Rabiu, N., Ojukwu, N. N., & Oladele, P. (2016). Availability and accessibility of e-books in Nigerian libraries: A survey. *Information Impact: Journal of Information and Knowledge Management, 7*(1), 163 – 175. www.researchgate.com

Ridwan, S.M. (2015). *Application of electronic scholarly publishing in digital age: prospects and challenges in Nigerian universities.* Academic Press.

Riggins, N. (2017). 20 Advantages and Disadvantages of Outsourcing from Your Small Business. *Small Business Trends*. https://smallbiztrends.com/2017/02/advantages-and-disadvantages-of-outsourcing.html

Tiamiyu, M. (2005). Prospects of Nigerian book publishing in the electronic age. In F. A. Adesanoye & A. Ojeniyi (Eds.), *Issues in Book Publishing in Nigeria* (pp. 143–157). Heinemann, Nigeria.

Uwalaka, N. M. (2000). *Book publishing performance in the Nigerian Economic Environment* [PhD dissertation]. University of Ibadan, Nigeria.

Venkatesh, V., Thong, J. Y., & Xu, X. (2012). Consumer acceptance and use of information technology: Extending the unified theory of acceptance and use of technology. *Management Information Systems Quarterly*, *36*(1), 157–178. doi:10.2307/41410412

Warren, J. (2010). The Progression of Digital Publishing. *International Journal of the Book, 7*(4). www.googlescholar.com

Watson, A. (2018). *U.S. Digital Publishing Industry - Statistics & Facts*. Statista. https://www.statista.com/topics/1453/digital-publishing/

WIPO. (2020). *The Global Publishing Industry in 2018*. Geneva: World Intellectual Property Organization. Retrieved from https://www.wipo.int/edocs/pubdocs/en/wipo_pub_1064_2019.pdf

Yang, H., Steensma, H. K., & Ren, T. (2021). State ownership, firm innovation and the moderating role of private-sector competition: The case of China. *Competitiveness Review*, *31*(4), 729–746. doi:10.1108/CR-02-2019-0024

Zhao, J., & Kumar, V. (2022). Technologies and Systems for E-Collaboration during Global Crises. *Pages*, *335*. Advance online publication. doi:10.4018/978-1-7998-9640-1

Zhao, J., & Richards, J. (2021). E-Collaboration Technologies and Strategies for Competitive Advantage amid Challenging Times. *Pages*, *346*. Advance online publication. doi:10.4018/978-1-7998-7764-6

ADDITIONAL READING

Yang, H., Steensma, H. K., & Ren, T. (2021). State ownership, firm innovation and the moderating role of private-sector competition: The case of China. *Competitiveness Review*, *31*(4), 729–746. doi:10.1108/CR-02-2019-0024

Zhao, J., & Kumar, V. (2022). Technologies and Systems for E-Collaboration during Global Crises. *Pages*, *335*. Advance online publication. doi:10.4018/978-1-7998-9640-1

Zhao, J., & Richards, J. (2021). E-Collaboration Technologies and Strategies for Competitive Advantage amid Challenging Times. *Pages*, *346*. Advance online publication. doi:10.4018/978-1-7998-7764-6

KEY TERMS AND DEFINITIONS

E-Publishing Capacity Building: Refers to the process of developing and strengthening the skills, instincts, abilities, processes, and resources that publishing firms need to survive, adapt, and thrive in in the information age.

Open Educational Resources (OER): Refers to all teaching, learning and research materials in the public domain, or materials that have been released under an open license, with no restriction or limited restrictions, permitting no-cost access, use, adaptation, and redistribution by others.

Publishing E-Collaboration: Is collaboration, conducted without face-to-face interaction among individuals or members of a virtual publishing team using information and communication technologies.

Chapter 8
Exploring Academic Achievements and Gender Differences in Twitter– Assisted Education

Zhonggen Yu

(iD) https://orcid.org/0000-0002-3873-980X

Department of English Studies, Beijing Language and Culture University, Beijing, China & Faculty of Foreign Studies, Beijing Language and Culture University, Beijing, China

Wei XU

Faculty of Humanities and Social Sciences, City University of Macau, Taipa, Macau

Paisan Sukjairungwattana

Faculty of Liberal Arts, Mahidol University, Nakhon Pathom, Thailand

ABSTRACT

The recent decade has been witnessing an increasing number of studies committed to the use of Twitter in education. It is necessary to determine the effect of Twitter use on education through a meta-analytical review since related meta-analyses are scanty and previous findings are inconsistent. By searching a number of databases, the authors selected 23 publications to examine the effect of the use of Twitter in education. It is concluded that the use of Twitter exerts a significant and positive effect on general education, that the use of Twitter exerts a significant and positive effect on academic achievements in education, and that there are no significant gender differences in the effect of Twitter use in education. Other social media could also be considered in terms of their use in education.

DOI: 10.4018/978-1-6684-5027-7.ch008

INTRODUCTION

Twitter Applied to Education

As a popular social interactive tool, Twitter has become increasingly acceptable since its birth (Hitchcock, & Young, 2016). Besides interpersonal communication, Twitter could be applied to the field of education due to its multiple functions. Online communicative platforms could promote participation, conceptualization, and collaboration through Twitter (Gao et al., 2012). Learners could conveniently and easily communicate with each other through tweets or instant messages. Twitter could transmit voice, pictures, texts, and videos, through which teachers and learners could obtain and transmit enough information and deal with knowledge transfer or acquisition (Chapman, & Marich, 2020). Use of Twitter could improve academic results in General Surgery Residency Programs (Hill, Dore, Em, McLoughlin, et al., 2021). Twitter with learning contents directly in the tweets could improve learning outcomes of radiology (Kauffman, Weisberg, Zember, & Fishman, 2021).

Positive reports have been made regarding the use of Twitter in education. Twitter has gained popularity when applied to the field of education (Hitchcock & Battista, 2013; Young, 2014). Twitter applied to education could improve engagement, cooperation, critical thinking skills, and learning environments (Greenhow & Gleason, 2012). Teachers could supervise students' learning and encourage them to participate in academic activities through Twitter (Chamberlin & Lehmann, 2011; Gao et al., 2012).

Twitter-Assisted Academic Achievements

Recent years have witnessed a great deal of research into Twitter-assisted academic achievements in education. With the rapid development of social media, the educational system has undergone a radical shift toward globalization assisted with social media (Arceneaux, & Dinu, 2018). Facebook has been demonstrated able to globalize and facilitate education although other social media have not been included (Davis et al., 2014). The use of Twitter platform could improve learners' performance in the classroom, leading to better academic achievements in numerous ways (Feezell, 2019). Teachers and students could raise and answer questions by using Twitter conveniently and anonymously, which promotes the effect of learning and improve academic achievements (Young, 2009). Outside the classroom, students could discuss and solve difficult problems through the Twitter platform, share different opinions, increase their interactions, and improve academic achievements (Manzo, 2009). Through tweets out of class, they could conceptualize and memorize psychological issues better than they had done in class (Blessing, Blessing, & Fleck, 2012).

Although there have been a great number of studies committed to the effect of social media on education, very few of them have conducted a meta-analytical review on the effect of Twitter on education. Therefore, the first research objective in this study is to address the effect of Twitter on education in general.

Gender Differences in Twitter-Assisted Learning

A number of researchers have studied the effect of Twitter on gender differences in education. Results of the effect of Twitter on gender differences are inconsistent and diverse. In Twitter-assisted learning of principles of economics courses, male students outperformed females in several specifications such as the final course grade and gap-closing measure (Al-Bahrani, Patel, & Sheridan, 2017). With social media, males uttered more than females and the latter could disregard disadvantages and catch a new opportunity to join the conversation (McConnell, 1997). Females contributed much more than males in online discussions (Davidson-Shivers, Muilenburg, & Tanner, 2001).

There are also significant gender differences in the preferences for the variety of posts in teacher Twitter spaces. Male students tend to upload online resources, advise peers, broaden their popularity on the Twitter platform, and sometimes criticize others they dislike. But, female students tend to post positive comments to encourage chat partners on the platform (Kerr, & Schmeichel, 2018). These different styles may have cultivated different learning strategies. Male students tend to keep open in online learning assisted with social media, while females closed. The open-minded learners may be able to absorb more knowledge but they are subject to distractions. The closed learners may be more absorbed in what they are learning and thus understand the contents more comprehensively.

In the social media-associated cyberspace, the interactions are free of gender but males and females interact in different ways. Males prefer progressive languages while females like defensive ones (Herring, & Stoerger, 2014). The progressive learners may focus more on information outside the learning contents, while the defensive learners tend to concentrate on their own discipline. It is thus not surprising that males are more easily influenced by distractions than females and that males tend to post more on the platform than females.

The new decade has been witnessing an increasing number of both male and female users of social media. US adult women (72%) who use social media such as Twitter have outnumbered adult men (66%) based on a 2017 Pew report (Pew Research Center, 2017). However, Pew Research Center reported that male Twitter users outnumbered females and users of other social media such as Reddit failed to strike a balance between males (71%) and females (29%). Recent research interest has shifted to gender differences in interactions (e.g., Meeks, 2016) on social media platforms especially in education. Gender differences in interactions of Twitter use may lead to different performances and cause gender differences in academic achievements, motivation, satisfaction, and cognition levels. While many studies have been committed to the effect of Twitter on gender differences in education (e.g., Al-Bahrani et al., 2017; Feliz et al., 2013; Kerr & Schmeichel, 2018), very few of them have systematically reviewed the effect. It is thus meaningful to conduct a meta-analysis of the effect of gender differences on education to provide constructive suggestions for learners, teachers, and software developers. In summary, the main research problems and research gaps in previous literature are the generalized effect of Twitter use in education, the summarized effect of Twitter use on academic achievements, and the summarized gender differences in use of Twitter in education.

RESEARCH QUESTIONS AND HYPOTHESES

Based on the literature, there have been many studies focusing on the use of Twitter in education, and the findings are inconsistent and even sometimes contradictory. It is thus meaningful to conduct a meta-analysis to determine the effect of Twitter use in education. We aim to address three research questions in this study, i.e. (1) What is the effect of Twitter use in education? (2) What is the effect of Twitter use on academic achievements in education? (3) What is the effect of Twitter use on gender differences in education? We propose three research hypotheses: (1) Twitter use is significantly more effective than non-twitter use in education; (2) Twitter use can lead to significantly higher academic achievements than non-twitter use in education. (3) There are significant gender differences in Twitter use in education.

THEORETICAL FRAMEWORK

The use of social media could realize connected and seamless learning. Connected learning addresses the gap between pre-class, in-class, after-class, on-campus, and out-of-campus learning activities (Ito, Gutiérrez, Livingstone, Penuel, Rhodes, Salen, & Watkins, 2013). Similar to seamless learning, connected learning associates various sorts of learning approaches such as social media-assisted learning, flipped class-based learning, and mobile learning. It provides learning opportunities whenever and wherever the learners feel convenient, encouraging students to participate in learning activities and improving their academic achievements. Interactions in the formal learning context could share opinions, and resources through social media such as Twitter, Skype, and micro-blogs, while the friendship-based context could strengthen social associations through social media (Nissinen, Vartiainen, Vanninen, & Pollanen, 2019). In this way, social media could strengthen the style of connected learning and thus enhance learning interest and improve learning outcomes.

Social media brings about both benefits and challenges to education. Learners who have weak self-regulation may be indulged in the digital gaming world rather than the learning atmosphere. However, we cannot deny that social media-assisted education can lead to positive learning outcomes of many kinds. Knowledge acquisition is a connected process (Piaget, 1971), which needs to be socially constructed (Vygotsky, 1978). Knowledge becomes hard to be absorbed without social connections. When learning a language, learners are trying to construct meaning by interpreting symbols and signs (Vygotsky, 1978). Social media can realize this connection and interpretation in association with social units. By improving collaboration, social media can enhance learning awareness and facilitate the transfer of knowledge. In the connected collaboration, individual learners tend to be influenced by group efforts and experiences, which can improve their learning effectiveness (Freire, 1998). Twitter can help learners to exchange ideas, symbols, signs, experiences, contents, and efforts, which forms a connected world, benefits learners, and enhances educational effectiveness. In this information technology-driven world, it is essential for learners to be familiar with the use of social media, blogs, videos, and mobile apps, which has become either a big challenge or a fair opportunity for both teachers and students (Leu, Kinzer, Coiro, & Cammack, 2004).

RESEARCH METHODS

Literature Search

We obtained 217 results in EBSCOhost by searching Academic Search Premier via Boolean phrases, i.e. TI Twitter AND TI education ranging from January 1, 2008 to December 31, 2020. By including merely those with full texts, we obtained 101 results. We reduced the results to 62 by limiting them to peer-reviewed journal articles.

We searched Taylor & Francis Online for [[Publication Title: Twitter] OR [Publication Title: tweet*]] AND [[[All: "control group"] AND [All: "experimental group"]] OR [All: "treatment group"]], which led to 8 results. We obtained 7 results by deleting an irrelevant article titled "Populist Twitter Posts in News Stories: Statement Recognition and the Polarizing Effects on Candidate Evaluation and Anti-Immigrant Attitudes" authored by Raffael Heiss and Christian von Sikorski & Jörg Matthes published in Journalism Practice, Volume 13, 2019 - Issue 6.

We obtained 64 results for "Twitter OR tweet" in Title and "education OR learn" anywhere and "mean AND SD OR S.D. OR standard deviation" anywhere in the database Wiley Online Library.

By entering [Abstract education OR learn] And [Title Twitter OR tweet OR hashtag*] And [All control group] into the database Sage, 22 results returned. We finally included 3 of them after perusing the full-texts. The literature search flowchart is shown in Figure 1.

Figure 1. A flowchart of literature inclusion

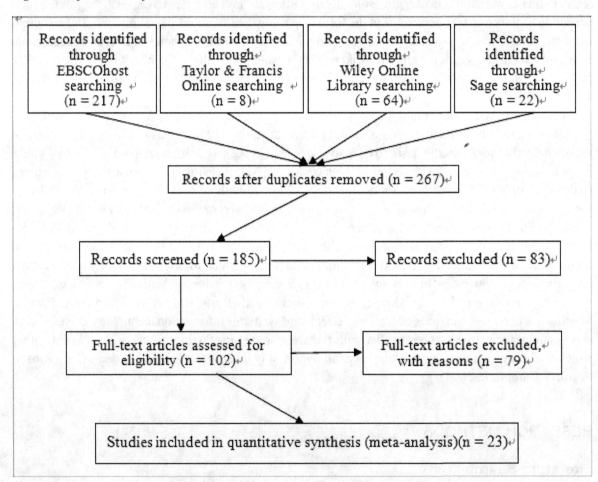

Inclusion and Exclusion Criteria

We established both inclusion and exclusion criteria to obtain high-quality literature. A total of 6 inclusion criteria were established, i.e. (1) The literature should be peer-reviewed journal articles; (2) The literature should be written in English; (3) The literature should be of high quality; (4) The literature should be related to the effect of Twitter on gender differences or academic achievements in education; (5) The included literature should explore the effect of Twitter through both a control and a treatment groups; (6) The literature should report the mean, standard deviation and the total number of participants for each group. If they were not reported, we would try to obtain the information through corresponding with the author.

To refine the results, we set up 4 exclusion criteria, i.e. (1) The study is in itself a review of literature; (2) The literature does not focus on the effect of Twitter use on academic achievements or gender differences in education; (3) The literature does not provide enough information for the meta-analysis and we failed to obtain enough information even though we corresponded with the author; (4) The literature was not written in English. We merely selected the publications written in English due to the limitation of library sources.

Quality Assessment of Obtained Literature

We applied The STARLITE tool (Booth, 2006) to the quality assessment of obtained literature and excluded those of lower quality. We adopted sampling techniques to comprehensively select the studies. We prefer the peer-reviewed journal articles to other types of studies such as conference proceedings, unpublished articles, and dissertations. We searched the literature keying in the terms applicable to different syntactic requirements of online databases. We also tried to expand the limitation of time in order to obtain reliable and comprehensive studies.

After evaluating the quality and excluding those lower-quality literature, we finally included 23 peer-reviewed journal articles. The sample (N=23) is enough for a meta-analysis since previous studies have adopt similar numbers of samples to conduct meta-analyses. For example, 23 studies were included for a meta-analysis of virtual reality training programs for social skill development (Howard & Gutworth, 2020). Tsai & Tsai. (2018) included 26 published studies to meta-analytically explore digital game-based second-language vocabulary learning and conditions of research designs. Fewer studies were included for a meta-analysis. For example, 10 studies were included to examine the effectiveness of entertainment education narratives via a meta-analysis.

Coding of Selected Literature

It is an important step to encode various items in meta-analysis. The study coding includes the following elements: (1) Literature information: author, year of publication, journal title; (2) Research methods: information of participants, sample size, source of data, measurement of reliability coefficient; (3) Measurement indicators: mean, standard deviation and the number of participants; (4) research hypotheses, research questions, or highlights.

RESULTS

The data obtained from the selected literature were entered into Stata/MP 14.0 for meta-analysis.

Calculation of Effect Sizes

Via the Stata/MP 14.0, the standardized mean difference (SMD) or Cohen d is used to measure the effect size. The effect size will be considered very small if $d \approx 0.1$, small if $d \approx 0.2$, medium if $d \approx 0.5$, large if $d \approx 0.8$, very large if $d \approx 1.2$ and huge if $d \approx 2.0$ (Sawilowsky, 2009). the calculation formula of effect size is: $d =$ mean difference between the treatment (with Twitter) and the control (without Twitter) groups/the standard deviation of pooled results (Table 1).

As shown in Table 1, the three subgroups obtained medium ($d = 0.63$), medium ($d = 0.54$) and small ($d = 0.40$) effect sizes respectively through a random-effect model. We also report the research results via forest plots according to the sequence of research questions proposed.

Table 1. Effect sizes (d)

Studies	d
The effect of twitter on academic achievements in education	**0.63**
Al-Bahrani et al., 2017	0.03
Arceneaux & Dinu, 2018	0.00
Attai et al., 2015	3.07
Blessing et al., 2012	0.00
Fouz-González, 2017	0.00
Fouz-González, 2017	-0.47
Hitchcock & Young, 2016	2.27
Hitchcock & Young, 2016	2.53
Hitchcock & Young, 2016	2.68
Hitchcock & Young, 2016	-2.35
Junco et al., 2010	0.50
Junco, 2012	0.28
Katrimpouza et al., 2019	0.42
Kuznekoff et al., 2015	-0.53
Loutou et al., 2018	1.15
Loutou et al., 2018	1.77
Luo & Xie, 2019	-0.02
Luo & Xie, 2019	-0.17
Luo & Xie, 2019	-0.57
Luo & Xie, 2019	-0.20
Webb et al., 2015	2.32
The effect of twitter on gender differences in education	**0.54**
Al-Bahrani et al., 2017	0.46
Feliz et al., 2013	0.54
Kerr & Schmeichel, 2018	0.02
Kerr & Schmeichel, 2018	0.06

Continued on following page

Table 1. Continued

Studies	d
Kerr & Schmeichel, 2018	0.04
Kerr & Schmeichel, 2018	0.02
Kerr & Schmeichel, 2018	-0.06
Kerr & Schmeichel, 2018	0.05
The effect of twitter in education	**0.40**
Al-Bahrani et al., 2017	-0.02
Arceneaux & Dinu, 2018	-0.20
Attai et al., 2015	1.11
Blank, 2016	0.72
Blessing et al., 2012	0.45
Colliander et al., 2015	0.38
Cozma & Hallaq, 2019	-0.61
DeGroot et al., 2015	0.63
Dissanayeke et al., 2016	1.01
Evans, 2014	0.08
Feezell, 2019	0.31
Feliz et al., 2013	0.54
Fouz-González, 2017	-0.27
Hitchcock & Young, 2016	1.60
Junco et al., 2010	0.40
Junco, 2012	0.39
Katrimpouza et al., 2019	0.42
Kerr & Schmeichel, 2018	0.02
Kuznekoff et al., 2015	-0.53
Loutou et al., 2018	1.41
Luo & Xie, 2019	-0.20
Luo & Xie, 2019	-0.57
Luo & Xie, 2019	-0.17
Luo & Xie, 2019	-0.02
Smith & Tirumala, 2012	1.17
Webb et al., 2015	2.32

What is the Effect of Twitter use in Education?

This research question aims to determine the effect of Twitter use on the generic educational field. As shown in Figure 2, the standard mean differences between the experimental (Twitter use) and control (Non-Twitter use) groups source from the analysis results via Stata/MP 14.0. In the forest plot, the horizontal lines indicate the confidence interval. The width of the diamond at the bottom is negatively correlated with the confidence interval. The narrower the diamond is, the stronger reliability of the study will have. The vertical line in the forest plot is referred to as a no-effect line, indicating that if the line or the diamond touches the vertical line or goes through the zero value, the result of the mean differences in both groups will not be statistically significant (p > .05), and vice versa.

Figure 2. A forest plot of the effect of twitter in education

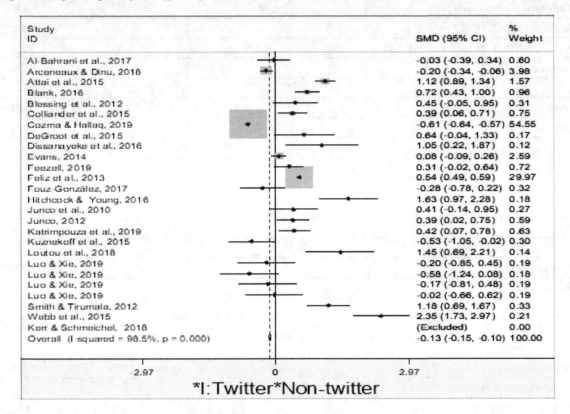

The value of I^2 indicates the extent of percentage of variability effect sizes caused by heterogeneity, ranging from 0% to 100%. On condition that the value is less than 50%, then the between-studies variation will be considered not heterogeneous, and a fixed-effect model can be used in the meta-analytical review. On the other hand, if the value of I^2 is more than 50%, the between-studies variation of selected studies will be deemed heterogeneous, and the data can be meta-analytically investigated via a random-effect model. The value of I^2 in this study is 99% (p < .00001), which is significantly higher than 50%, so we shift to a random-effect model to conduct the meta-analysis.

The weight indicates the influencing power of an individual study against the pooled result as shown in the form of a *diamond*. The amount of weight is positively related to the influencing power. This means that the larger the value of weight is, the more influencing power the individual study will have against the pooled result and vice versa. The study conducted by Dissanayeke et al. (2016) has the lowest weight (0.12%), and thus it has the weakest influencing power against the pooled result. On the contrary, the studies with the highest weight (3.1%) are authored by Cozma & Hallaq (2019) (54.55%) and Feliz et al. (2013) (29.97%). Both results thus have higher influencing power against the pooled result. Similarly, the horizontal line of the studies conducted by Dissanayeke et al. (2016) is the longest, hence the lowest reliability, while the lines of the studies conducted by Cozma & Hallaq (2019) and Feliz et al. (2013) are among the shortest, hence the highest reliability.

Some limitations may exist in the study authored by Dissanayeke et al. (2016). The sample size (N = 13 for either group) may be not large enough to represent the population. Based on constructivism and connected learning theory, knowledge should be systematically constructed through connected learning rather than born in the human brain. The mobile Twitter platform, however, may fail to provide connected learning due to the instability of the platform especially when learners keep in a moving state. They may merely connect a few peers and have access to limited resources of knowledge. The effective number of students who kept connected to the platform was only 7, which greatly influenced the quality of the study result. It is also hard for them to construct an organic system in this fragile connection. It is thus reasonable to find that the study is of lower effect and weight.

Some limitations still exist in the studies whether they are of higher or lower reliability. In the study conducted by Feliz, Ricoy, & Feliz (2013), some participants could have access to a number of tweets created by peers and teachers. Different mobile devices provided different interfaces and functions, which negatively influenced the study's reliability. The sample size was not representative enough and the demographic information of two instructors was not clarified. This might cause a lower weight or reliability.

The study (Cozma, & Hallaq, 2019) merely selected student-run TV stations that won awards from the Broadcast Education Association (BEA). The stations that did not win the award are excluded. This may cause TV station bias. Merely selecting exemplary rather than typical student organizations could also cause sample bias. Data sourcing from typical student organizations may be worthier to be included in the study. Typical student TV stations may apply various learning strategies to social media-based activities. The lower weight of the study may generally come out of the biases of sampling.

To examine the effect of Twitter use in education, we included 23 studies and 26 effect sizes. The pooled result neither touched the no-effect line nor went through the zero value (SMD = -0.13, 95% CI = -0.15, -0.10) (Figure 2). Therefore, the pooled mean of the experimental group is significantly lower than the control group at the *.05* significance level, indicating that Non-Twitter use exerts a significantly ($p < 0.01$) more positive effect than Twitter use in the educational field. We therefore reject the research hypothesis that Twitter use is significantly more effective than non-twitter use in education with a very small effect size ($d = $-0.13). As shown in Figure 3, there is an absence of publication bias (Egger's test coefficient = 3.57, t = 1.85, p = 0.07).

We carried out the sensitivity analysis to calculate the pooled effect size by excluding individual studies. It is shown in Figure 4 that no individual study influenced the overall pooled effect size given a named study is omitted, indicating that the results of this meta-analysis are stable.

Figure 3. A funnel plot of the effect of twitter in education

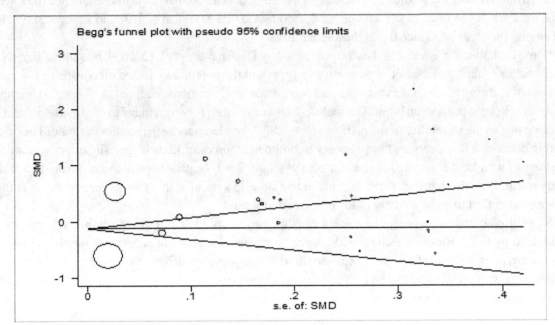

Figure 4. A plot of the random-effect influence analysis in the effect of twitter in education

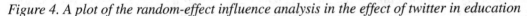
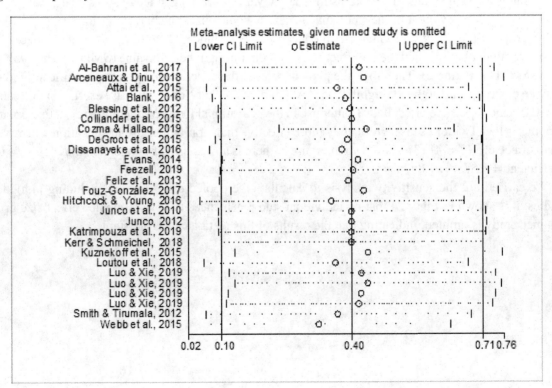

What is the Effect of Twitter use on Academic Achievements in Education?

"The effect of Twitter use on academic achievements" is an important subgroup included in this study. "Academic achievement" is an important dimension to measure the effect of Twitter on educational outcomes. To address the effect of Twitter use on academic achievements in education, we included 13 studies and 26 effect sizes (Figure 5). I^2 is 99%, significantly larger than 50% ($p < .00001$). Thus, the between-studies variation are considered heterogeneous, and a fixed-effect model is not appropriate. We, therefore, adopted a random-effect model for the analysis. The pooled result does not cross the no-effect line and the confidence interval does not (SMD = 0.36, 95% CI = 0.27, 0.45) go through the zero value. Thus the result is statistically significant and the mean in the treatment group is significantly larger than that in the control group. The use of Twitter exerts a significant ($p < 0.01$) and positive effect on academic achievements in education. We therefore accept the research hypothesis that Twitter use can lead to significantly higher academic achievements than non-twitter use in education with a small effect size ($d = 0.36$). No publication bias was revealed through a funnel plot (Figure 6) (Egger's test coefficient = 2.55, t = 1.04, p = 0.311) since the studies are symmetrically distributed along both sides of the middle line.

The sensitivity analysis was also conducted to calculate the pooled effect size by excluding individual studies (Figure 7). No individual study influenced the overall pooled effect size since all the meta-analysis estimates were included between the upper and lower CI limits given a named study was omitted. This indicates that the results of this meta-analysis are reliable and powerful.

Figure 5. A forest plot of the effect of twitter on academic achievements in education

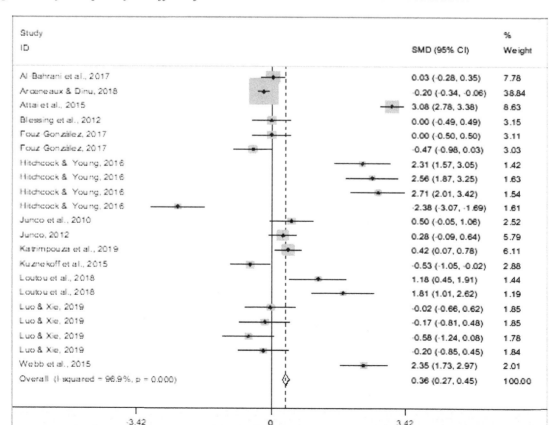

Figure 6. A funnel plot of the effect of twitter on academic achievements in education

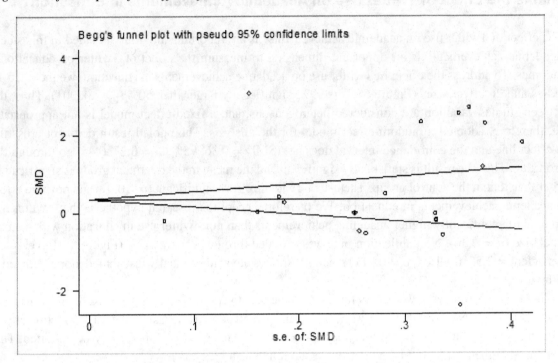

Figure 7. A plot of the random-effect influence analysis in the effect of twitter on academic achievements in education

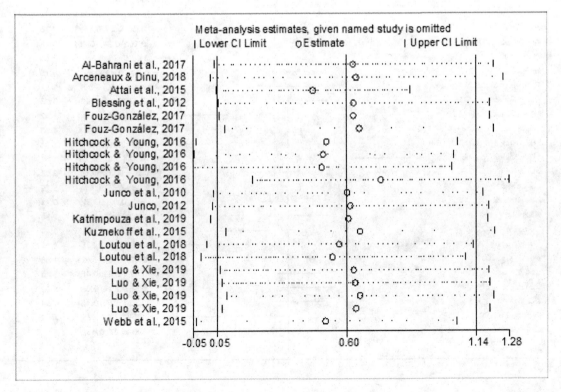

What is the Effect of Twitter use on Gender Differences in Education?

"The effect of Twitter use on gender differences in education" is another important subgroup in this study. Gender differences are an important dimension exerting an influence on the effect of Twitter use in the educational field. There have been several studies committed to gender differences in Twitter use in education. We included three studies and eight effect sizes to summarize the pooled effect (Figure 8). I^2 is 98%, significantly larger than 50% (p < .00001). Thus, the between-studies variation is not homogeneous, and a fixed-effect model is not appropriate. Consequently, we adopted a random-effect model to conduct the meta-analysis. As shown in Figure 8, the pooled result for the mean differences of gender differences does not cross the no-effect line and the confidence interval (SMD = 0.90, 95% CI = 0.86, 0.94) does not go through the zero value. Thus the result is statistically significant and the mean in the treatment group (male) is significantly larger than that in the control group (female). There are significant gender differences (p < 0.01) at the 0.05 significance level in the effect of Twitter use on education. We therefore accept the research hypothesis that there are significant gender differences in Twitter use in education with a huge effect size (d = 0.90).

We also tested the publication bias by drawing a funnel plot (Figure 9). As shown in Figure 9, studies are symmetrically distributed along the middle line (Egger's test coefficient = 28.31, t = 1.70, p = 0.14). We, therefore, conclude that there is no publication bias. A plot of the random-effect influence analysis (Figure 10) indicates that the results of this meta-analysis are stable since all the meta-analysis estimates are positioned between the upper and lower CI limits given the named study was omitted.

Figure 8. A forest plot of the effect of Twitter on gender differences in education

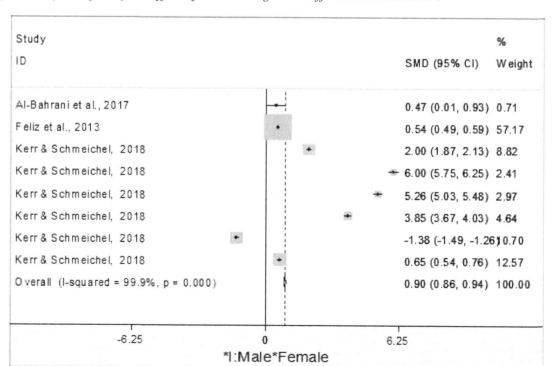

Figure 9. A funnel plot of the effect of Twitter on gender differences in education

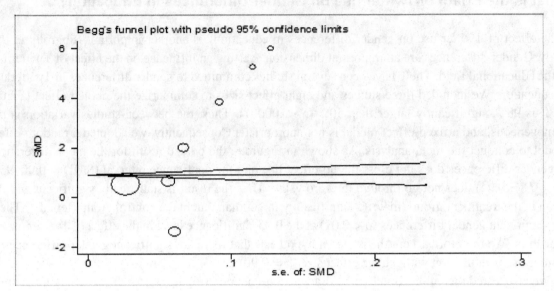

Figure 10. A plot of the random-effect influence analysis in the effect of Twitter on gender differences in education

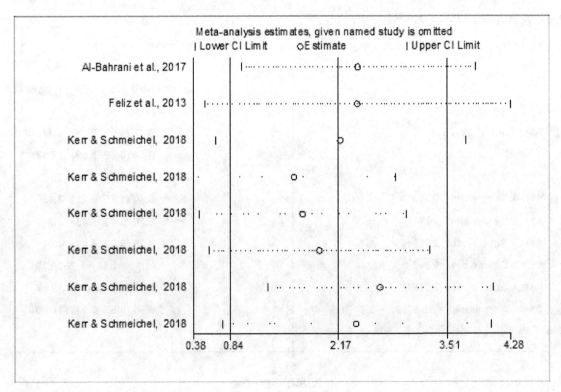

DISCUSSION

The application of Twitter to education could cultivate an interactive and seamless learning environment (Kim et al., 2015). With Twitter on their mobile devices, students could have easy access to learning resources wherever and whenever they feel comfortable and convenient. They could also discuss difficult issues, solve problems, and share opinions with teachers and peers. They could collaborate with peers and teachers and form harmonious learning environments. Students could upload or download a sea of learning resources that they feel beneficial to their learning. Prior to class, teachers could inform students via Twitter of the teaching contents in order for them to preview the contents that they could learn. Students could internalize the contents by learning them according to teachers' guidance. In this way, they could benefit and get ready for the class with the nearly acquired knowledge in their brain. This may greatly promote their learning effectiveness and efficiency. Students could also resort to teachers or peers if they came across any difficult questions through Twitter. Teachers could provide timely feedback to students through the platform of Twitter easily and conveniently. A seamless, connective, and interactive learning environment would be formed and established in the way assisted with Twitter.

The application of Twitter to the field of education could improve the collaborative learning. Collaborative learning could improve knowledge acquisition through the interactions and discussions on the platform of Twitter. Students could find the peers or teachers they felt comfortable with, which could improve their learning effectiveness. A group leader could also lead or push students to engage in learning activities, improving their learning efficiency and effectiveness (Yu, 2019). Twitter could also promote students to complete their assignment under the influence of peers through the platform of Twitter (van Uden-Kraan et al., 2008; Han et al., 2012). With Twitter, teachers could also conveniently know the learning progress and adjust their teaching pace accordingly.

The frequent use of Twitter could improve academic achievements. With Twitter, students could complete their assignment, share their opinions, communicate with peers, or ask for help from teachers. Teachers could transmit knowledge, upload learning resources, and evaluate students' assignment conveniently through the platform of Twitter. Students could spot their shortcomings or incorrect options in their assignment and acquire precious learning experiences with these interactive processes, coupled with improved academic achievements. Teachers could also remind students of the deadline for assignment or homework and raise the completion rates of learning tasks. Students, pushed ahead by teacher, would increase their engagement and completion rates, improving their academic achievements (Yu, & Yi, 2020).

Teachers could also allot assignment or homework to students through the platform of Twitter and keep trace of students' learning behaviors (Paulsen et al., 2015). Students' learning behaviors could be recorded and played through Twitter, through which teachers could reward those who did a good job and punish those who failed to complete learning tasks. Teachers could form a video conference if they felt necessary. Students might be invited to join the conference and answer questions raised by teachers. They could also ask questions and share their own opinions for teachers' feedback. This collaborative learning and teaching process could improve academic achievements.

There were significant gender differences in Twitter-assisted learning outcomes. Although it was argued that Twitter could improve academic achievements and facilitate online learning without bias of genders (Eisenchlas, 2012), male students still outnumbered females significantly in online learning participation, online discussions, and online posts (Herring, 2004). Male students dominated the online learning activities and were significantly more active than females because they tended to hold more intense interest in the use of Twitter than females (Selfe & Meyer, 1991). The Twitter-assisted interactions, similar to face-to-face interactions, could facilitate learning process and decrease the gender differences in Twitter-assisted learning outcomes (Coates, 1993).

CONCLUSION

Future research could focus on how to narrow down or minimize the gender differences in twitter-assisted learning outcomes. Interest is an important teacher for both males and females. Designers could make every effort to arouse students' learning interest in order to reduce gender differences. Designers could attempt to design individual courses to cater to various need of both genders. Developers could carefully take into consideration the convenience and conciseness of the interface of Twitter because it could increase students' engagement in Twitter-assisted learning. They could also be ready to ask question with the concise and easy operations. Future research could also explore the effectiveness of the use of other social media, e.g. What's App, WeChat, Telegram, and Linked-in. Versatility of learning needs and styles might be in need of various learning tools.

ACKNOWLEDGMENT

We would like to extend our gratitude to anonymous reviewers and funding. This work is supported by 2019 MOOC of Beijing Language and Culture University (MOOC201902) (Important) "Introduction to Linguistics"; "Introduction to Linguistics" of online and offline mixed courses in Beijing Language and Culture University in 2020; Special fund of Beijing Co-construction Project-Research and reform of the "Undergraduate Teaching Reform and Innovation Project" of Beijing higher education in 2020-innovative "multilingual +" excellent talent training system (202010032003); The research project of Graduate Students of Beijing Language and Culture University "Xi Jinping: The Governance of China" (SJTS202108).

REFERENCES

Al-Bahrani, A., Patel, D., & Sheridan, B. J. (2017). Evaluating Twitter and its impact on student learning in principles of economics courses. *The Journal of Economic Education*, *48*(4), 243–253. doi:10.1080/00220485.2017.1353934

Arceneaux, P. C., & Dinu, L. F. (2018). The social mediated age of information: Twitter and Instagram as tools for information dissemination in higher education. *New Media & Society*, *20*(11), 4155–4176. doi:10.1177/1461444818768259

Attai, D. J., Cowher, M. S., Al-Hamadani, M., Schoger, J. M., Staley, A. C., & Landercasper, J. (2015). Twitter social media is an effective tool for breast cancer patient education and support: Patient-reported outcomes by survey. *Journal of Medical Internet Research*, *17*(7), e188. doi:10.2196/jmir.4721 PMID:26228234

Blessing, S. B., Blessing, J. S., & Fleck, B. K. B. (2012). Using Twitter to Reinforce Classroom Concepts. *Teaching of Psychology, 39*(4), 268–271. doi:10.1177/0098628312461484

Booth, A. (2006). "Brimful of STARLITE" toward standards for reporting literature searches. *Journal of the Medical Library Association, 94*(4), 421–429. PMID:17082834

Chamberlin, L., & Lehmann, K. (2011). Twitter in higher education. In C. Wankel (Ed.), Educating educators with social media (Cutting-edge technologies in higher education (vol. 1, pp. 375–391). Emerald Group Publishing. doi:10.1108/S2044-9968(2011)0000001021

Chapman, A. L., & Marich, H. (2020). Using Twitter for Civic Education in K-12 Classrooms. *TechTrends*. Advance online publication. doi:10.100711528-020-00542-z

Coates, J. (1993). *Women, men, and language: A sociolinguistic account of gender differences in language*. Longman.

Cozma, R., & Hallaq, T. (2019). Digital Natives as Budding Journalists: College TV Stations' Uses of Twitter. *Journalism & Mass Communication Educator, 74*(3), 306–317. doi:10.1177/1077695818805899

Davidson-Shivers, G. V., Muilenburg, L., & Tanner, E. (2001). How do student participate in synchronous and asynchronous online discussions? *Journal of Educational Computing Research, 25*(4), 351–366. doi:10.2190/6DCH-BEN3-V7CF-QK47

Davis, A. L., Unruh, S. L., & Olynk, W. N. (2014). Assessing students' perceptions of internationalization of course content. *The Global Studies Journal, 6*(2), 1–12. doi:10.18848/1835-4432/CGP/v06i02/40884

Dissanayeke, U., Hewagamage, K. P., Ramberg, R., & Wikramanayake, G. (2016). Developing and testing an m-learning tool to facilitate guided-informal learning in agriculture. *International Journal on Advances in ICT for Emerging Regions, 8*(3), 12. doi:10.4038/icter.v8i3.7165

Eisenchlas, S. A. (2012). Gendered discursive practices online. *Journal of Pragmatics, 44*(4), 335–345. doi:10.1016/j.pragma.2012.02.001

Evans, C. (2014). Twitter for teaching: Can social media be used to enhance the process of learning? *British Journal of Educational Technology, 45*(5), 902–915. doi:10.1111/bjet.12099

Feezell, J. T. (2019). An Experimental Test of Using Digital Media Literacy Education and Twitter to Promote Political Interest and Learning in American Politics Courses. *Journal of Political Science Education*. Advance online publication. doi:10.1080/15512169.2019.1694531

Feliz, T., Ricoy, C., & Feliz, S. (2013). Analysis of the use of Twitter as a learning strategy in master's studies. *Open Learning, 28*(3), 201–215. doi:10.1080/02680513.2013.870029

Freire, P. (1998). *Pedagogy of freedom: Ethics, democracy, and courage*. Rowman & Littlefield Publishers.

Gao, F., Luo, T., & Zhang, K. (2012). Tweeting for learning: A critical analysis of research on microblogging in education published in 2008–2011. *British Journal of Educational Technology, 43*(5), 783–801. doi:10.1111/j.1467-8535.2012.01357.x

Greenhow, C., & Gleason, B. (2012). Twitteracy: Tweeting as a new literacy practice. *The Educational Forum, 76*(4), 464–478. doi:10.1080/00131725.2012.709032

Han, J. Y., Kim, J., Yoon, H. J., Shim, M., McTavish, F. M., & Gustafson, D. H. (2012). Social and psychological determinants of levels of engagement with an online breast cancer support group: Posters, lurkers, and nonusers. *Journal of Health Communication, 17*(3), 356–371. doi:10.1080/10810730.201 1.585696 PMID:22085215

Herring, S. C. (2004). Computer-mediated communication and woman's place. In R. T. Lakoff (Ed.), *Language and woman's place: Text and commentaries* (pp. 216–222). Oxford University Press.

Herring, S. C., & Stoerger, S. (2014). Gender and (a)nonymity in computer-mediated communication. In S. Ehrlich, M. Meyerhoff, & J. Holmes (Eds.), The handbook of language, gender, and sexuality (2nd ed., pp. 567-586). John Wiley & Sons.

Hill, S. S., Dore, F. J., Em, S. T., McLoughlin, R. J., Crawford, A. S., Sturrock, P. R., Maykel, J. A., Alavi, K., & Davids, J. S. (2021). Twitter Use Among Departments of Surgery With General Surgery Residency Programs. *Journal of Surgical Education, 78*(1), 35–42. doi:10.1016/j.jsurg.2020.06.008 PMID:32631768

Hitchcock, L. I., & Battista, A. (2013). Social media for professional practice: Integrating Twitter with social work pedagogy. *The Journal of Baccalaureate Social Work, 18*(Supplement 1), 33–45. doi:10.18084/ basw.18.suppl-1.3751j3g390xx3g56

Hitchcock, L. I., & Young, J. A. (2016). Tweet, Tweet!: Using Live Twitter Chats in Social Work Education. *Social Work Education, 35*(4), 457–468. doi:10.1080/02615479.2015.1136273

Howard, M. C., & Gutworth, M. B. (2020). A meta-analysis of virtual reality training programs for social skill development. *Computers & Education, 144*, 103707. doi:10.1016/j.compedu.2019.103707

Ito, M., Gutiérrez, K., Livingstone, S., Penuel, B., Rhodes, J., Salen, K., & Watkins, S. C. (2013). *Connected learning: An agenda for research and design*. Digital Media and Learning Research Hub. Retrieved from https://dmlhub.net/

Kauffman, L., Weisberg, E. M., Zember, W. F., & Fishman, E. K. (2021). #RadEd: How and why to use twitter for online radiology education. *Current Problems in Diagnostic Radiology, 50*(7), 369–373. Advance online publication. doi:10.1067/j.cpradiol.2021.02.002 PMID:33637393

Kerr, S. L., & Schmeichel, M. J. (2018). Teacher Twitter Chats: Gender Differences in Participants' Contributions. *Journal of Research on Technology in Education, 50*(3), 241–252. doi:10.1080/153915 23.2018.1458260

Kim, Y., Jeong, S., Ji, Y., Lee, S., Kwon, K. H., & Jeon, J. W. (2015). Smartphone response system using twitter to enable effective interaction and improve engagement in large classrooms. *IEEE Transactions on Education, 58*(2), 98–103. doi:10.1109/TE.2014.2329651

Leu, D. J., Kinzer, C., Coiro, J., & Cammack, D. (2004). Toward a theory of new literacies emerging from the Internet and other Information and Communication Technologies. In R. Ruddell & N. Unrau (Eds.), *Theoretical models and processes of reading* (5th ed., pp. 1570–1613). International Reading Association.

Manzo, K. K. (2009). Twitter lessons in 140 characters or less. *Education Week, 29*, 1–14.

McConnell, D. (1997). Interaction patterns of mixed sex groups in educational computer conferences. Part I-empirical findings. *Gender and Education, 9*(3), 345–363. doi:10.1080/09540259721303

Meeks, L. (2016). Gendered styles, gendered differences: Candidates' use of personalization and interactivity on Twitter. *Journal of Information Technology & Politics, 13*(4), 295–310. doi:10.1080/19331 681.2016.1160268

Nissinen, S., Vartiainen, H., Vanninen, P., & Pollanen, S. (2019). Connected learning in international learning projects Emergence of a hybrid learning system. *International Journal of Information and Learning Technology, 36*(5), 381–394. doi:10.1108/IJILT-05-2018-0055

Orozco-Olvera, V., Shen, F. Y., & Cluver, L. (2019). The effectiveness of using entertainment education narratives to promote safer sexual behaviors of youth: A meta-analysis, 1985-2017. *PLoS One, 14*(2), e0209969. doi:10.1371/journal.pone.0209969 PMID:30753185

Paulsen, T. H., Anderson, R. G., & Tweeten, J. F. (2015). Concerns Expressed by Agricultural Education Preservice Teachers in a Twitter-Based Electronic Community of Practice. *Journal of Agricultural Education, 56*(3), 210–226. doi:10.5032/jae.2015.03210

Pew Research Center. (2017). *Social media fact sheet.* Retrieved from https://www.pewinternet.org/fact-sheet/social-media/

Piaget, J. (1971). *Psychology and epistemology—Towards a theory of knowledge.* Kingsport Press.

Sawilowsky, S. S. (2009). New effect size rules of thumb. *Journal of Modern Applied Statistical Methods, 8*(2), 597–599. doi:10.22237/jmasm/1257035100

Selfe, C. L., & Meyer, P. (1991). Testing claims for online conferences. *Written Communication, 8*(2), 163–192. doi:10.1177/0741088391008002002

Tsai, Y. L., & Tsai, C. C. (2018). Digital game-based second-language vocabulary learning and conditions of research designs: A meta-analysis study. *Computers & Education, 125,* 345–357. doi:10.1016/j.compedu.2018.06.020

van Uden-Kraan, C. F., Drossaert, C. H., Taal, E., Seydel, E. R., & van de Laar, M. A. (2008). Self-reported differences in empowerment between lurkers and posters in online patient support groups. *Journal of Medical Internet Research, 10*(2), e18. doi:10.2196/jmir.992 PMID:18653442

Vygotsky, L. S. (1978). *Mind in society—The development of higher psychological processes.* Harvard University.

Young, J. (2014). iPolicy: Exploring and evaluating the use of iPads in a social welfare policy course. *Journal of Technology in Human Services, 32*(1-2), 39–53. doi:10.1080/15228835.2013.860366

Young, J. R. (2009). Teaching with twitter: Not for the faint of heart. *The Chronicle of Higher Education, 56,* A1–A11.

Yu, Z. (2019). A Systematic Review on Mobile Technology-Assisted English Learning. *International Journal of e-Collaboration, 15*(4), 71–88. doi:10.4018/IJeC.2019100105

Yu, Z., & Yi, H. (2020). Acceptance and effectiveness of Rain Classroom in linguistics classes. *International Journal of Mobile and Blended Learning, 12*(2), 77–90. doi:10.4018/IJMBL.2020040105

Chapter 9
Computer Programming Practical Works Activities:
From Human to Automatic Scoring

karima Boussaha
https://orcid.org/0000-0003-4622-7625
University of Oum El Bouaghi, Algeria

Amira Hanneche
University of Oum El Bouaghi, Algeria

Zakaria Chaoua
University of Oum El Bouaghi, Algeria

ABSTRACT

The most important cause to the difficulties many freshmen feel to learn programming is their lack of generic problem solving skills and programming debugging skills on their own. On this basis, this chapter introduces a new learner's self-assessment environment as CEHL. The proposed system helps the learner to take full responsibility for learning and completing his work by relying on him to correct his mistakes. CEHL developed so-called S_Onto_ALPPWA in its current second version allowing comparing learners' productions with those elaborated by the teacher. The authors conducted to analyze the effectiveness of two developed versions of an automated assessment scoring tool. Version 1 and Version 2 of this tool are detailed in authors previously published articles by comparing them with the expert scoring. So to achieve this objective, the researchers use a correlational research design to examine the correlations between S_Onto_ALPPWA and expert raters' performances.

INTRODUCTION

Programming is not an easy subject to be studied for learner or to be tough for teacher. There are many reasons behind the difficulty of this particular discipline, including them programming requires cor-

DOI: 10.4018/978-1-6684-5027-7.ch009

rect understanding of abstract concepts. Many students have learning problems due to the nature of the subject. In addition, there are often not enough of resources and students suffer from a lack of personal instruction. Also the student groups are large and heterogeneous and thus it is difficult to design the instruction so that it would be beneficial for everyone., the unavailability of the assistants, the obstruction of learners, and the material is expensive and cannot be duplicated. This often leads to high drop-out rates on programming courses. As a result of the lack of adequate devices and the previously mentioned problems, the practical work in general and especially the practical work of programming languages in computer science in the introductory courses in the first university cycle in the university years is usually accomplished by a group of learners and this learning method negatively influences the objectivity of the learners' assessment operation because when the assessment is given, it is one mark for all the group members and this makes the assessment subjective and does not reflect the true level of each learner belonging to the group, because there are elements of the group that do not work and relies on the active elements. In addition to this problem, practical works in programming languages suffer from a severe and widespread problem, which is the phenomenon of learners' dropout. Knowing that the studies confirm that the rate of failure or abandonment of the programming in the introductory courses in the first university cycle varies from 25 to 80% of the share in the world (Aiouni et al., 2018). This problem of programming failures does not only concern our institution. Several studies on algorithmic / programming learning conducted by different institutions in other countries have converged towards the same conclusion (Boussaha et al.,2015a).

The researchers tried to conduct a periodic follow-up of the students in order to know the reasons behind this failure in studying programming languages practical works activities. This study was covered in detail by the researchers in paragraph 4 of this research chapter, and perhaps the most important reasons the authors have come up with are the classic way in which this type of activity is studied and taught. in addition due to the intrinsic characteristics of the discipline

To resolve these problems, several problem-based learning systems are developed (Tadjer et al., 2018) these systems did solve the hardware problem, but the assessment problem was still not resolved.

The researchers think that the self-assessment, in its formative function, is in the middle of the training considering its regulating function, which is paramount. The construct of self-assessment refers to the degree to which students can regulate aspects of their thinking, motivation, and behavior during learning (Tadjer et al.,2018)(Tadjer, et al.2020).

In the past decades, Self-assessment in the CEHL environment is not addressed enough. Currently, this topic has been addressed by some researchers in several disciplines, but many of them neglected to deal with the self-assessment topic in the programming language practical works activities.

The present work concerns more particularly, the learners' self-assessment in the CEHL (Computing Environment for Human Learning) environments of remote practical works in programming. Our goal is to suggest a self-assessment CEHL environment for thinking about measures of cognitive knowledge, a self-assessment CEHL that will help generate feedbacks, guide future research, and develop learners' efforts.

In speaking to this issue, in this book chapter, the authors aim to prototype the second version of the learner's self-assessment environment as a CEHL system. After they had a first prototype version published in [Boussaha et al .,2015a]. The self-assessment environment developed in its second version so-called S_Onto_ALPPWA(System Based Ontology for Assessing Learner's Programming Practical Works Activities) addressed all the weaknesses of the first version[Boussaha et al.,2015a] and allowed an individual assessment for each learner by comparing learners' productions with those elaborated by the teacher.

As mentioned previously, it is reported that the studies confirm that the rate of failure or abandonment of the programming in the introductory courses in the first university cycle varies from 25 to 80% of the share in the world. So the main research questions the authors can ask are:

- What are the main reasons behind the learners' dropout in the learning programming language practical works activities?
- Does the self-assessment CHEL for learning practical works activities based on a hybrid matching-agent algorithm and ontologies reduce the rate of dropout or abandonment of the programming in the introductory courses in the first university cycle and help learners to improve their learning.
- Does the self-assessment CHEL for learning practical works activities based on a hybrid matching-agent algorithm and ontologies in its second version is better than the first version based on graph matching algorithm published in [Boussaha et al.,2015a?

This book chapter is organized as follows. In the second section, the authors review the various related works about self-assessment that will guide the discussion in subsequent, for each of these works, the researchers try to illustrate its strengths and limitations in section three. In the third section, the authors deal with the reasons behind learners' dropout in programming practical works activities. In the fourth section, the researchers describe the methodology of the self-assessment proposed approach. Five, the researchers discuss in some detail several components of the general architecture of the self-assessment proposed approach, also the proposed hybrid matching-agent algorithm, and the modeling of the practical work with the ontology. In section six the researchers illustrate the developed environment using a concrete case study with some screenshots from the two developed versions. Section seven details the comparison between the two prototype versions of the developed system with an experimental study. In the eighth section, the researchers draw some conclusions about the self-assessment proposed approach, suggest some directions for future research, and raise some issues that merit consideration in the development and evaluation of the self-assessment CEHL.

RELATED WORKS

The construct of self-assessment refers to the degree to which students can regulate aspects of their thinking, motivation, and behavior during learning(Pintrich, and Zusho,2002;Tadjer et al.,2018; Tadjer, et al.2020). According to Sadler (1989), he refers to ''assessment that is specifically intended to generate feedback on performance to improve and accelerate learning''. Such feedback helps students to restructure their understanding/skills and build more powerful ideas and capabilities (Nicoland and Macfarlane,2006; Zimmerman,2008; Pintrich, and Zusho,2002). This kind of self-assessment has been a constant demand in higher education for graduating students to be equipped with the capacity for lifelong learning that helps learners to continually upgrade their skills and knowledge through their self-motivation and learning(Wigfield et al,2011; Zimmerman,2004; Tadjer et al.,2020; Hadadi&Boaarab-dahmani et al.,2018). Its principal goal is to help students take greater responsibility when it comes to managing their learning; this is done by helping them become more strategic learners through self-assessment learning(De Corte et al.,2011). Being equipped with skills such as self-assessment is important because a major function of education is the development of lifelong learning skills(Zimmerman,2004; Tadjer et al.,2020; Deep et al.,2019).

So several works focused on the self-assessment in the broad sense, the authors can cite among others Black and Wiliam(1998), Sadler(2005), Zimmerman(2008,2004), Pintrich(2002), Boud and Falchikov (2007), Tadjer et al.,(2018,2020), Pang et al.,(2019),Indira et al.(2019), Seman et al.(2018)and others.

In what follows, the authors give the literature about the self-assessment in a specific activity, it is the learners' self-assessment in practical works.

The teaching of practical works is fundamental in scientific and technical learning disciplines, in in-class as well as in distance, and meets the learners' needs. Unfortunately, learners are often deprived of this essential instructional teaching opportunity. This is, in fact, due to several problems. The authors cite, among others, the unavailability of the assistants, the obstruction of learners, and the material is expensive and cannot be duplicated. To minimize these problems thus teaching must answer to these needs(Guillaume,2006).

Although learner's self-assessment in practical works represents an important activity during learners' training, it has not been addressed enough. In this context, the authors find some works which focus on practical works that are presented in Bennouna et al. (2008), and Choquet et al. (2011). Other works that deal with learners' assessment in the modeling process(Alonso et al.,2008) and (Mitrovic &Suraweera,2004) have also been proposed.

The authors in Bennouna et al. (2008), proposed a formative assessment method of learners' skills using algorithms of supervised classification. Of course, this work has considerably forwarded the domain by proposing novel strategies for learners' assessment in practical works. However, it does not deal with learning programming languages.

The authors in Choquet et al. (2011), describe a way to identify and model indicators that can be calculated and provided in real-time to teachers when they are involved in synchronous tutoring of practical work. The author based on his work on the collection and the storage of tracks of the learning session participants (learners and teachers).

Alonso(2008), developed a CEHL called Diagram dedicated to the training of OOM (Object-Oriented Modelling) concepts starting from a textual specification. It proposes an automatic method for analyzing learners' diagrams by comparing and matching class diagram components. The proposed method is implemented as an integrated component of the diagram called ACDC (Automatic Class Diagram Comparator). Furthermore, the author only uses matching methods, which are based on simple matchers (i.e., matchers that use only one kind of data). This work treated the problem of learners' assessment in online courses and classrooms, but it does not treat the learners' assessment in the practical works.

The authors in Mitrovic and Suraweera(2004), presented a problem-solving environment for the university level students in which they can practice conceptual database design using the entity-relationship data model. This work presents an intelligent tutor called KERMIT (Knowledge-based Entity-Relationship Modeling IntelligentTutor). It uses CBM(Constraint-Based-Modeling) to model the domain knowledge and generate student models. This work treated the problem of learners' assessment in online courses and classrooms, but it does not treat the learners' assessment in the practical works.

The authors in Hadadi et al.(2019), proposed learner modeling and automated assessment in MOOCs,based on the ODALA approach.

The proposed learner model includes different dimensions: general information, Cognitive state, learning style, preference, and behavior dimensions. The authors in this paper deal with the cognitive state dimension that is updated based on the results of the proposed activities. Inparticular, they proposed an assessment planner where the acquisition of knowledge and skills takes different levels. This planner follows the learner's progress with the transition from a level to another in the pyramid of pedagogical activities. Of course, this work has considerably forwarded the domain by proposing novel strategies for learners' assessment. However, it does not deal with practical works activities.

The authors in Tadjer et al. (2020) proposed a method that aims to improve the soft skills as well as the students' cognitive skills in a problem-based learning environment by taking into account the traces of the students who contribute to the development of a software project. So, the authors in this research paper proposed a method that is based on traces in order to help students to improve their skills. This work treated the problem of learners' soft skills assessment in online courses and classrooms, but it does not treat the learners' assessment in the practical works.

The authors present, in this book chapter, a new environment for learner's self-assessment which extends our published works introduced in previous papers (Author et al.,2015a; Author et al.,2012). In the previous works, the researchers have used graphs as a modeling tool. So, the researchers could only detect syntactic errors in the learner's programs. In the present work, the authors have managed to detect syntactic and semantic errors in the learner's programs by using ontologies as modeling tools.

The main objective of the developed environment is to evaluate learners' practical works about the development of Java object-oriented programs. Among the approaches quoted above, the approach proposed in Alonso(2008), Mitrovic, and Suraweera(2004) consider only the structural aspect of the application (i.e. the dynamic aspect is omitted). Furthermore, only the approach proposed in Alonso(2008) is based on matching techniques. It uses simple matchers during the comparison process between class diagrams. Our approach considers both structural and dynamic aspects of object-oriented programs. It uses a new hybridization strategy between two kinds of ontology matching (static and dynamic matching) and agents to compare, learners' programs, and teacher's one.

THE REASONS BEHIND LEARNERS' DROPOUT IN PROGRAMMING PRACTICAL WORKS ACTIVITIES

Studies confirm that the rate of failure or abandonment of the programming in the introductory courses in the first university cycle varies from 25 to 80% of the share in the world(Guibert,2005; Guittet et al.,2006). To confirm these results A follow-up of the results of the students of the second year in computer science of our university(Larbi Ben Mh'idi university, Oum Elbouaghi, Algeria) is realized after the end of the third semester during 02 successive years (2015-2016; 2016-2017). This monitoring consists of comparing the success rate of students in object-oriented programming with other modules taught during the same years. The result obtained shows a success rate of 09.16% over the two consecutive years concerned by the follow-up. In this study, the evolution of the student level was monitored through their results in object-oriented programming. Then, the scores obtained in the comparators were validated with those obtained in the other units of value for the same semester. Tables 1 and 2 show the obtained results.

Table 1. The learners' success rate in the object-oriented programming language module

Learner's mark	2015-2016	2016-2017
	January	January
<10	91,21%	90,48%
>= 10	08,79/	09.52%

The Method Used to Calculate the Success Rate for Learners

To calculate the success rate for learners the authors applied a follow-up of the results of the students of the second year in computer science of our university (Larbi Ben Mh'idi university, Oum Elbouaghi, Algeria). This follow-up is realized after the end of the third semester during 02 successive years (2015-2016; 2016-2017). This monitoring consists of calculating the number of students who obtained marks greater than or equal to ten 10 among the total of students of the second year in the computer science of our university. By the same method, the researchers calculate the failure rate, so the authors calculate the number of students who obtained marks smaller than ten among the total of students in the module of object-oriented programming language. These results are calculated twice by a scientific program used in our computer science department.

Table 2. Comparisons between the object-oriented programming module success rate and the other modules

year	Learner's mark	LT	ADS	NM	IS	MS	ML	OOP
2015-2016	<10	67, 03%	42,86%	78,03%	61,54%	71,43%	91, 21%	91,21%
	>=10	32,97%	57,14%	21,97%	38, 46%	28,57%	08,79%	08,79%
2016-2017	<10	87,48%	45,24%	90, 48%	30,95%	50%	76,19%	90,48%
	>=10	12,52%	54,76%	09,52%	69,05%	50%	23,81%	09,52%

LT: Language Theory; ADS: Algorithmic and Data Structures; NM: Numerical Methods; IS: Information System; MS: Machine Structure; ML: Mathematical Logic; OOP: Object-Oriented Programming.

This problem of programming failures does not only concern our institution. Several studies on algorithmic / programming learning conducted by different institutions in other countries have converged towards the same conclusion(Guibert,2005; Guittet et al.,2006). Learning algorithmic / programming was always a source of difficulty not only for students but also for teachers too. This is due to the intrinsic characteristics of the discipline and the classic methods of teaching(classic practical works in the classes rooms).

METHODOLOGY OF THE SELF-ASSESSMENT PROPOSED APPROACH

The process of learners' self-assessment the authors proposed consists of two main phases (Figure 1). During the two phases 1 and 2, the teacher's program and the learners' program are treated after they are transformed into two ontologies. The researchers detail what follows the two phases.

Phase One: During this phase, the learner and the teacher have to develop two Java object-oriented programs that undergo an analysis process for generating two ontologies. The first one is generated from the teacher program, it is named reference ontology(RO)and the second one is generated from the learner program it is named learner ontology(LO).

Figure 1. The methodology of the assessment proposed approach

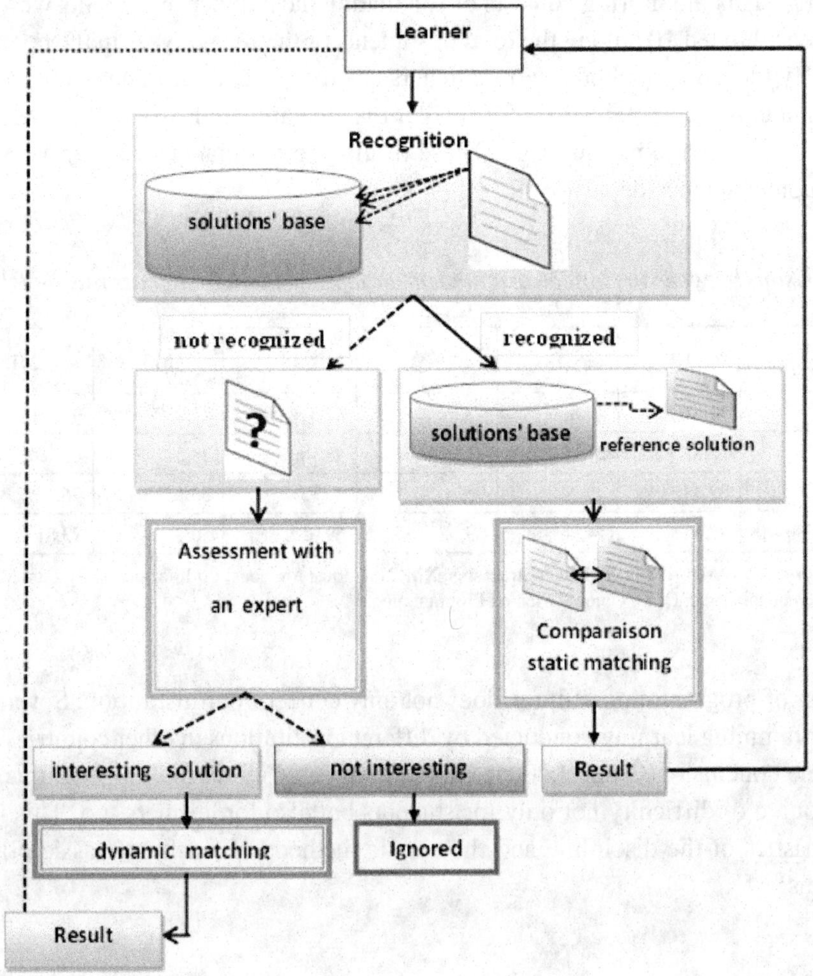

Phase Two: This phase consists of applying the matching technique(Euzenat and Shvaiko,2008; Euzenat et al,2010; Giuseppe and Talia,2010; Zghal,2010), which the authors adopted. It offers two kinds of matching: static matching and dynamic matching. The second step of the assessment process consists of recognizing the reference solution in the solution's base: to compare the proposed solution with the solutions' base, the authors must measure the degree of similarity and retain the solution closest to the solution proposed by the learner. Here the researchers propose an agent named decision agent this agent gives us two possible decisions according to a decision threshold (DT):

- reference ontology found: a found ontology can be presented in two forms: identical or similar.
  - identical ontologies: (LO = RO) here the similarity (Sim) calculated by the decision agent is equal to 1.
  - Similar ontologies: (LO ≈ RO) here the similarity (Sim) calculated by the decision agent is less than 1 and greater than the decision threshold (DT). (DT<Sim <1).

In this case(reference ontology found), the authors apply the static matching between the two ontologies to make the comparison between the learner's program and the teacher's one.

- reference ontology not found: here the similarity (Sim) calculated by the decision agent is less than the decision threshold. (Sim <DT) in which case the intervention of a human expert is necessary. The human expert will begin to assess the learner's solution:

  - if he decides that it is interesting: in this case, it is proposed to generate a dynamic matching between the learner ontology and the ontologies that exist in the solution's base. This matching has for goal to find the correspondences (the semantic relations) between the learner's ontology and the ontologies in the solution's base to diminish the addition of a new ontology in the base.
  - if he decides that it is not interesting: in this case, the solution is rejected.

Let us note that to calculate the similarity between the two ontologies the authors re-use the matching algorithm of Wu-Palmer and Dice(1994), This algorithm is based on ontologies and the similarity calculation between ontology concepts.

Wu-Palmer: *SimwPalmer (C1, C2)* = $\dfrac{2*D}{D1+D2+2*D}$ *(wu-palmer and Dice,1994)*

Dice: *Simc (x, y)* = $\dfrac{2xy}{\|x\|_2^2 + \|y\|_2^2}$ (Palmer&Wu,1994)

The Wu-Palmer measurement: $\text{Sim wPalmer}(C1,C2) = \dfrac{2*D}{D1+D2+2*D}$ (Wu-Palmer and Dice,1994)

The principle for calculating the Wu-Palmer similarity is based on the distances D1 and D2 which separate the concepts C1 and C2 from the concept (the most specific father) (MSF) and the distance D that separates MSF from the root concept.

Distance_WPalmer Calculated
Distance_WPalmer (concept1, concept2)

D¬0; D1¬0; D2¬0 ;

MSF¬seek for father (concept1, concept2) ;

D ¬distance (root,MSF) ;

D1 ¬distance (concept1, MSF) ;

D2 ¬distance (concept2, MSF)

In table 3 below the authors present the results of the similarity calculated:

Table 3. Examples of the obtained results during the assessment of learner's program in the system

Concept 1 (teacher)	Concept 2 (learner)	Results of the calculated similarity between concept 1 and concept 2
Public class person	Public private class person	0.8
Public int end_date ;	Public int end date ;	0.72
public int id_card;	Id_card (without type)	0.64
Void veif(){hotelbooking.exist();}	void verif(){}	0.52

Explanation

The syntax error value is 0.9.

The semantic error value is 0.8.

Example

The similarity between C1 (Void verif () {hotelbooking.exist ();}) and C2 (void verif () {}) is given by:

D: the distance from the root concept.

D1: the distance of the concept of the learner's program.

D2: the distance from the concept of the teacher's program.

SimwPalmer (C1, C2) = (2 * 1) / (0.8 + 1 + 2 * 1) = 0.52

ARCHITECTURE OF THE SELF-ASSESSMENT PROPOSED APPROACH

The architecture of the proposed approach has four levels:

- The resource level: contains resources to be evaluated (learners' programs).
- The ontology level presents the modeling of resources in the form of concepts linked by hierarchical relationships. Each resource is associated with several concepts.
- The interface level: where we find the learner and the three agents (decision agent, ontology agent, and matching agent).

- The expert level helps the matching and ontology agents. After his intervention for assessing the proposed solution: if he decides that it is interesting he sends a positive message to the matching agent and the ontology agent, if he decides that it is not interesting he sends an ignorant message of the solution to the matching and ontology agent.

The Role of Each Agent in the Self-assessment Proposed Architecture

Decision Agent (DA)

it is responsible for looking for the reference solution of the solution proposed by the learner if it is found, it sends a message to the matching agent (MA) to launch the static matching. In this case, the ontology agent does not work. In the case where the decision agent does not find the reference solution. It sends a message to the matching agent to launch a dynamic matching, the matching agent itself sends a message to the ontology agent to create relations (correspondences) between the concepts of the proposed solution ontology and the concepts of the ontologies in the solution's base.

Matching(Alignment) Agent (MA)

it is responsible for launching the two kinds of matching: static and dynamic matching according to the message sent either by the decision agent or by the expert.

Ontology Agent (OA)

it is responsible for creating relations (correspondences) between the concepts of the proposed solution ontology and the concepts of the ontologies in the solution's base in the case where the proposed solution does not find in the solution's base and the human expert he decides that the proposed solution is interesting after his assessment intervention.

Let us note that, this paper is a part of a global project. For this reason, the authors are focusing in this research paper on the design and the development of the ontologies.

The Modeling of the Practical Work with the Ontology

- According to Boaarab-Dahmani et al.(2017), ontology has been defined as a formal representation of knowledge. An ontology is made up of four main elements: concept, instance, relation, and axiom.
- Concepts: are the fundamental elements of an ontology. They represent generic classes or a group of objects, in a domain, which share common properties. The concepts are organized hierarchically or each of them can have several sub-concepts and have one or more parent concepts(Hadadi& Bouaarab-Dahmani,2019)
- An instance: is an occurrence object of concept.
- A relation: used to express the non-taxonomic semantic relation between two concepts in a given domain. Indeed, the so-called "semantic" relations are above all defined between instances. The authors derive from its relations between concepts, with more or less well-defined semantics (Hadadi& Bouaarab-Dahmani,2019).

- The role of an axiom in an ontology is to impose constraints on concepts, their instances, and their relationships.
- The researchers explain the interest of using ontologies in the field of distance learning of practical work, particularly in the learners' assessment in this type of activity.

The Benefits of Using Ontologies in Interactive Environments for Learning Practical Work Activities

- The formal representation of knowledge: ontology provides the basis for a formal encoding of entities, attributes, their relationships.
- Reuse and sharing of educational objects is relevant in the case of systems using educational resources that are already built because building them again can waste time. This is through reusable ontology libraries.
- Identification of educational objects: an ontology can be used as a meta-descriptor to describe the semantic content of educational objects;
- Knowledge acquisition: The use of ontologies increases the speed and reliability of the knowledge acquisition process when building practical work.
- it provides annotation markers that might facilitate the interoperability and exchange of learning resources,

The General Structure of the Practical Work Ontology

In this work, the authors need an ontology to fully understand the structure of practical work, as well as to ensure the correct assessment of learners. To build an ontology, there are several effective and correct methodologies. The designer will carefully choose the most suitable methodology with his objectives so that he does not find a major divergence that sometimes leads to a contradiction. For the construction of our ontology, the researchers relied on the use of the Stanford methodology: it is suitable with the work on E-Learning. The authors used this method because Stanford University itself, which is developing the latter(ontology), is developing an editor called "protégé 2000" to properly show the practical side of ontology. This method goes through the following steps to build an ontology (Konys, 2018).

Step 1: Determine the domain and scope of the ontology

The field of use designed in our ontology is E-Learning. The purpose of using our ontology is to properly structure the practical work offered by the teacher, as well as implicitly ensure an automated task which is the self-assessment task which is the key point in distance training. The authors' ontology will be used by two actors: the learner and the teacher.

Step 2: Reuse of existing ontologies

The authors don't need to reuse an existing ontology, the authors have to build their ontology because the domain is restricted.

Step 3: List the important terms of the ontology

The important terms in our work are practical work, assessment, resource, editor, correction type, learner answer...etc.

Step 4, 5, and 6: Description of the ontology classes, their properties, and the class hierarchy

The authors have summarized these steps as follows: table 4 details each class with its attributes and its designation.

Table 4. The set of classes, attributes of the Practical work ontology

Class	Data Properties	Designation
PW(practical work)		This is the main class of our ontology.
date	Start-date End-date	Every PW has a start date and an end date.
Language	None-language	This class shows the language used by the learner to write his code.
Notion	Content-notion	Each PW has a notion that shows the main goal to be achieved and the work to be done in that practical work.
Example	Content –exple	Each PW presents examples to help learner to understand.
Observation	Observation	This class represents well the observation assigned to a learner after he has passed his assessment (the result of the test).
Question	Num-qst Ennonce-qst Type-qst Num-open-qst- Content-open -qst Num-closed-qst Content-closed-qst	As the precise class for assessing learners, it is presented as an open or closed question. Open question: represents questions for which the answer is open, a learner constructs his practical work freely. Closed question: represents questions whose answer is true or false or by a choice between propositions well defined in advance.
the standard answer	Ennonc-qst Content-Stdans	It represents the answer key to an open question, but it is not a final version as the learner will respond in their style.
Answer	Content -Answ	It shows the answer proposed by the learner concerning the practical work.
Eror	Content-err Num-er Type-er	This is the class that defines the set of errors that the learner makes when responding to an open-ended question. And it contains subclasses: Syntax and lexicon errors. The semantic error represents all the errors of meaning.
Goal	Goal	The objective of the PW was proposed by the teacher.
Author	First name Last name Grade	This class represents the author who writes the resource (reference) provided to the learner.
Editor	First name Last name	This class represents the publisher name of the resource.
Format	Type-format	This class represents the format of the resource.
Language	Language	This class represents the language of the resource.
Type	Type	It shows whether the resource is of type site web, article,....
Title	Title	The title of each PW suggested by the teacher.

To create our ontology the authors used the "protégé 2000" editor. "Protégé 2000" is an authoring system for creating ontologies. It was created at Stanford University and is very popular in the field of the Semantic Web and computer science research. ''Protégé 2000'' is developed in Java. "Protégé 2000" can read and save ontologies in most ontology formats: RDF, RDFS, OWL, etc.

In figure 2, the authors present an OntoGraf generated from the "Protégé 2000" editor to clearly understand the hierarchy of the practical work ontology. Consequently figure 3 shows the creation of the practical work ontology with the "protégé2000" editor.

Figure 2. The OntoGraf of the practical work ontology

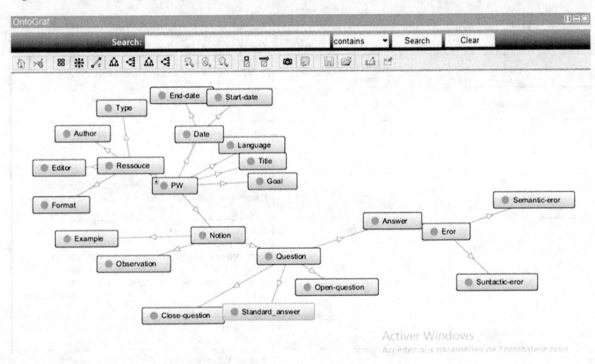

Figure 3. The hierarchy of concepts in the practical work ontology

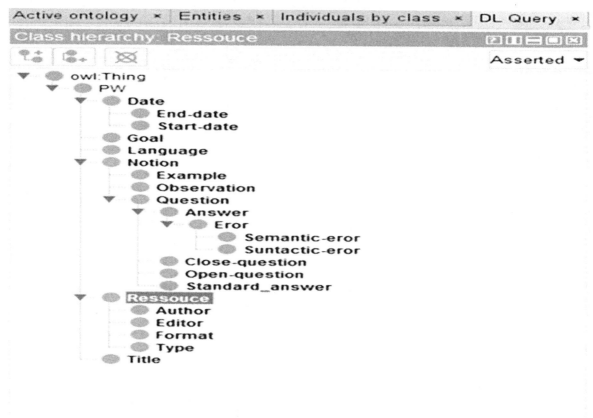

In table 5, the researchers represent the different links between some classes of practical work ontology, in our ontology: there are different types of links which are:

- Generalization/specialization type links: this is "is a" type links: this is known in inheritance links, they are defined in the strict hierarchy of the model.
- The links "is connected of": this type of link defines the semantics between two classes. In our ontology, the authors used generalization/specification type links as well as a set of semantic links between classes.

Table 5. The description of the links between the classes of the practical work ontology

Object Properties	Domains	Ranges	Inverse Of	Comment
attribute	Answer	Observation	is attributed to	Each completed PW has an observation.
Compare with	Answer	Standard _answer	Is compared to	The standard_answer is compared by the learner's answer to getting an assessment.
Contain	Notion	Question	Is Expressed A	Each notion of PW contains questions.
Is a	Error	Syntactic_eror Semantique_eror	/	Each PW has errors and these can be syntactic or semantic.
May be	Question	Close_question Open_question	/	Each PW has closed or opens questions.
Publish in	PW	Start-date	Is Date In	a PW has a publication date.
Must have	Question	Standar_answer	Contains	Each question in the PW has a typical standard_anwser.

The Proposed Hybrid Matching-Agent (Alignment) Algorithm Applied in the Self-Assessment Proposed Architecture

Below is the algorithm that describes the general assessment method

[1]:Input : S: solution ; RS: reference solution ; recognized: boolean ;

[2]:Output: assessment solution S, Sim, a set of syntactic and semantic errors, observations ;

[3]: Begin

[4]:S¬modeling the solution S; // with ontology: two ontologies are generated: learner's ontology from the leaner's program and teacher's ontology from the teacher's program

[5]:Recognized¬recognized(S, RS) ;

[6]: if recognized then // the decision is offered by the decision Agent(DA)

[7]: Generated static Matching(S, RS); applying the matching algorithm of Wu-Palmer and Dice(1994).

[8]:Return(résults: feedback(syntactic and semantic errors), observation) ;

[9]:else

[10]: Solution S assessed by a human expert

[11]:if S is interesting then//the decision is offered by a human expert

[12]:Generated dynamic Matching;// To remove the problem of the scalable base's solution

[13]:Return(results: feedback(syntactic and semantic errors), observation) ;

[14]else

[15]:S is rejected

[16]:end

[17]:end

[18]:end

Algorithm Explanation

line [1]: represents *the inputs* of the algorithm:

S: represents the proposed learner's solution

RS: represents the reference solution proposed by the teacher

Recognized: this function has two values: ***true or false***.

line [2]: represents ***the outputs*** of the algorithm

Sim: represents the calculated similarity between the learner's proposed solution and the teacher's solution.

a set of syntactic and semantic errors found in the learner's solution.

Observation: this function has five possibilities (Excellent; Very good, Average Below, Average, Failing) according to the value of the similarity calculated, the system give the observation for the learner:

- if the *sim* ϵ [0.8; 1] the observation will be "Excellent".
- if the *sim* ϵ [0.6; 0.8] the observation will be "Very good".
- if the *sim* ϵ [0.5; 0.6] the observation will be "Average".
- if the *sim* ϵ [0.3; 0.5] the observation will be "Below Average".
- if the *sim* ϵ [0; 0.3] the observation will be "Failing".

line [4]: the function ***modeling*** this function consists in modeling the solution proposed by the learner and the solution proposed by the teacher with an ontology. So two ontologies are generated: learner's ontology from the learner's program and teacher's ontology from the teacher's program.

line [5]: the function ***recognized*** consists in checking in the base solution for the ontologies the ontology similar to the ontology proposed by the learner: if the ontology is founded in the base solution the function ***recognized*** will be ***true***, but if the ontology is not founded, the function ***recognized*** will be ***false***.

line [6]: if the function **recognized** will be **true,** the decision is offered by the decision Agent(DA) like explain in the paragraph of the decision agent (AD)previously.

line [7]: the function ***generate*** consists of generating a static Matching between the learner's solution and the teacher's one (S, RS) by applying the matching algorithm of Wu-Palmer and Dice(1994).

line [8]: the function ***Return*** consists of showing the results for the learner, these results are feedbacks with syntactic and semantic error and observation. The observation has one of the five values possibles (Excellent; Very good, Average, Below Average, Failing).

line [9][10]: if the learner's proposed ontology is not founded in the base solution the function ***recognized*** will be ***false***, in this case, the Solution "S" **assessed** by a ***human expert***. If the human expert decides that the proposed solution is ***interesting***, the system will be generating a dynamic Matching *line [12].* This dynamic matching is to find the ***nearest solution*** in the base solution for the solution proposed by the learner. The authors propose this type of matching to remove the problem of the scalable base's solution. In this case, the system will give the results *line[13]*(with feedback and observation) as it explained previously(line [8]).

line [14]: when the human expert decides that the learner's proposed solution is not interesting the system will reject it (*line[15]*).

ENVIRONMENT PRESENTATION

General Architecture of the Assessment Tool

This work introduces a new learner self-assessment environment called S_Onto_ALPPWA: (System-based Ontology for Assessing Learners' Programming Practical Works Activities), for allowing comparing learners' productions (Java object-oriented programs) with those elaborated by the teacher. The subjacent idea is to proceed to an indirect comparison of two object-oriented programs through their graphic representations described by two ontologies using the matching algorithms as a comparison strategy. S_Onto_ALPPWA is composed of three main components: the Editor Tool, the Generator Tool, and the Errors Tool. The most important component is the Errors tool, which is implemented using the matching developed algorithm that evaluates the learner's solution in terms of similarity values and observations. Its architecture is presented in Figure 4.

Figure 4. The general architecture of the assessment tool

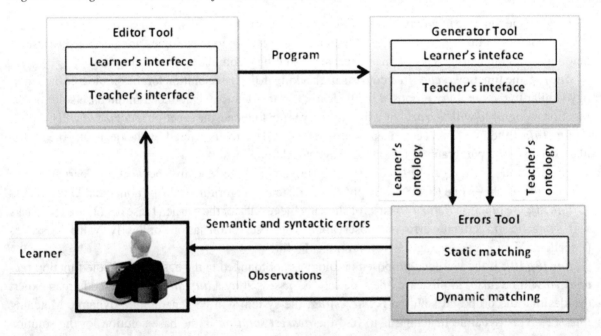

- *Editor Tool:* allows learners and teachers to edit codes and programs.
- *Generator Tool:* allows learners and teachers to generate different ontologies from their codes.
- *Errors Tool:* is The most important component. It is implemented using the developed matching algorithm that evaluates learner's solution in terms of similarity values to compare between learners' programs and the teacher's one and gives an observation to the learner according to the value of similarity calculated like flowing:
  - $[0.8; 1] \Rightarrow$ the observation will be "Excellent".
  - $[0.6; 0.8] \Rightarrow$ the observation will be "Very good".
  - $[0.5; 0.6] \Rightarrow$ the observation will be "Average".

    ◦   [0.3; 0.5] ⇒ the observation will be "Below Average".

    ◦   [0; 0.3] ⇒ the observation will be "Failing".

It offers also to the learners a set of syntactic and semantic errors detected in their programs. Figure 5 presents the screenshot of the three different components of the assessment tool developed(S_Onto_ALP-PWA).

Figure 5. S_Onto_ALPPWA's different components

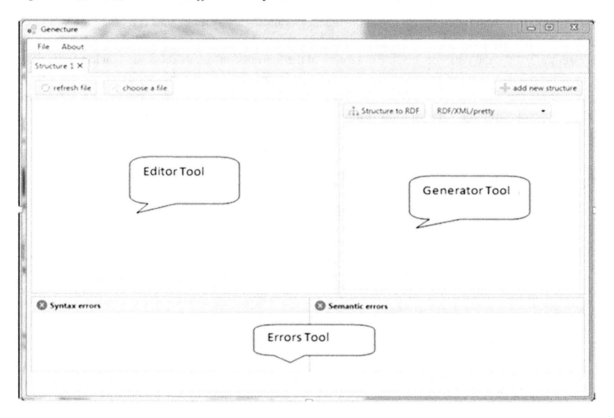

Case Study

The Practical Work Statements

The authors present in what follows the environment using a concrete case study. It is about a simple hotel booking process. When a client arrives at the hotel, he presents his ID card. The hotel receptionist checks the availability of rooms. He proposes to the client the types and the price list of rooms. The client chooses a room and informs the date of departure to hotel receptionist. The latter gives him the number of the reserved room. In this book chapter, the authors don't write Teacher's Program Practical Work (Reference Solution) and Program Fragment of Learner's Solution with Some Errors for the sake of brevity. For more details consult the previously published article[Boussaha et al., 2021].

Some Screenshots from S_Onto_ALPPWA Second Version

Using the developed environment, teachers and learners can write or choose their java object-oriented programs for implementing the hotel booking process. The comparison of the two edited programs is accomplished by comparing their ontological representations. Firstly, the teacher uses the generator tool to generate the ontology from his Java program. This ontology should be stored for later use. After that, the learner must generate the ontology from his Java program. The main objective of the developed environment is to allow learners to auto-evaluate their skills in java object-oriented programming. Figure 7 illustrates the different errors detected and the observations. During the comparison process the authors proposed, the researchers use the teacher's ontologies as references (i.e., they are supposed correct because they are generated from the teacher's correct programs). So, the list of detected errors is essentially different concepts that are not found in the learners' program. Also, several kinds of errors may be detected in learners' programs (see Figures 6.7).In this section from this book chapter, the authors display only the screenshots from the errors tool which is the main component. if like more details for the screenshots from the two rest tools (Editor, generator) you can see the original article published in [Boussaha et al., 2021].

Figure 6. List of detected errors in the case of learner's correct programming practical work

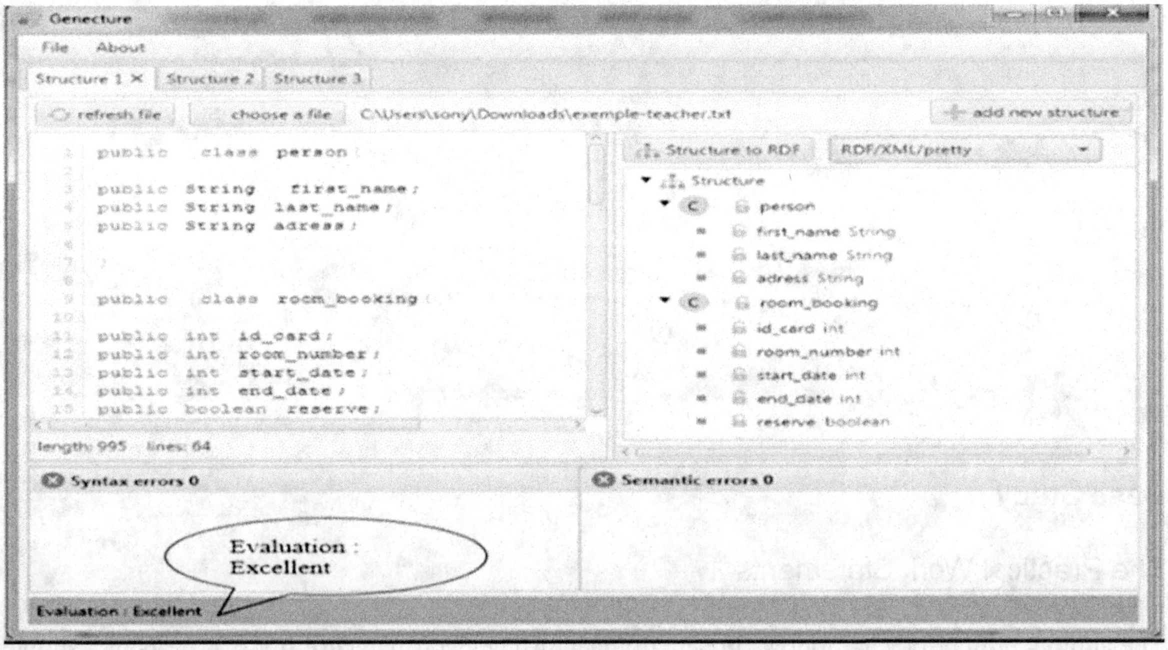

Our tool displays to learners the list of the detected errors in their programs. Figure 7 illustrates the errors detected in learners' programs.

Figure 7. List of detected errors in the case of learner's incorrect programming practical work

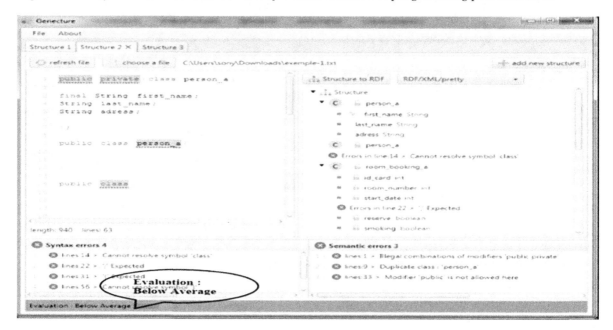

Some Screenshots From S_Onto_ALPPWA First Version

S_Onto_ALPPWA Overview (the First Version Developed) [Boussaha et al.,2015a]

The researchers have proposed the first version of a new learner's self-assessment environment for allowing learners to evaluate and test their skills in Object-Oriented Programming using C++ language. It implements our approach that considers both structural and dynamic aspects of object-oriented programs. The developed environment allows comparing indirectly the learners' programs with the teacher's one through the comparison (syntactic comparison) of their UML graphical descriptions (class and communication diagrams) using two kinds of matchers (hybrid and composite matchers).

The environment provides several tools for both teachers and learners. Initially, it allows the teacher to write his C++ program and generate from it the UML diagrams which are used as reference descriptions during the assessment process. Secondly, it also permits learners to develop their C++ programs, generate from it the UML diagrams, and launch the assessment process. The latter is accomplished by applying the matching techniques (hybrid and composite) the authors proposed and provides scores of similarity and dissimilarity between the learner's program and the teacher's one. like it is shown in figure 8.

Figure 8. Global similarity measure between teacher's and learner's diagrams[Boussaha et al.,2015a]

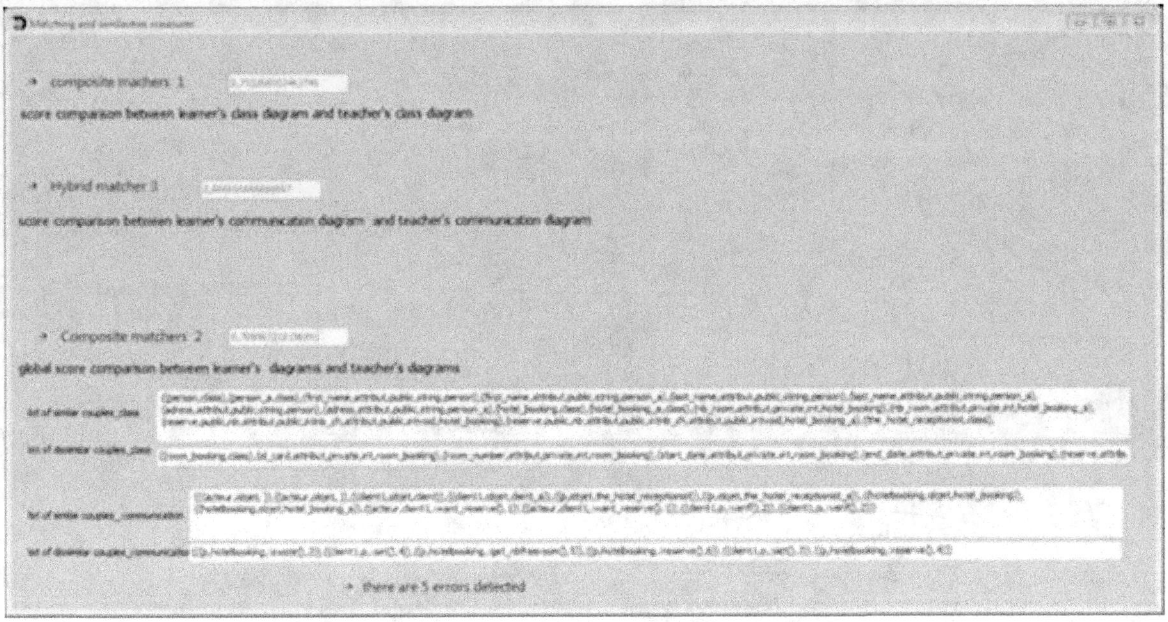

Let us remember that the authors use the same case study it is about a simple hotel booking process (see section practical work statement previously) but in this first version, the learner and the teacher develop C++-oriented object programs. Figure 9 shows the set of detected errors in the learner's program.

Figure 9. List of detected errors in the case of learner's incorrect programming practical work [Boussaha et al.,2015a]

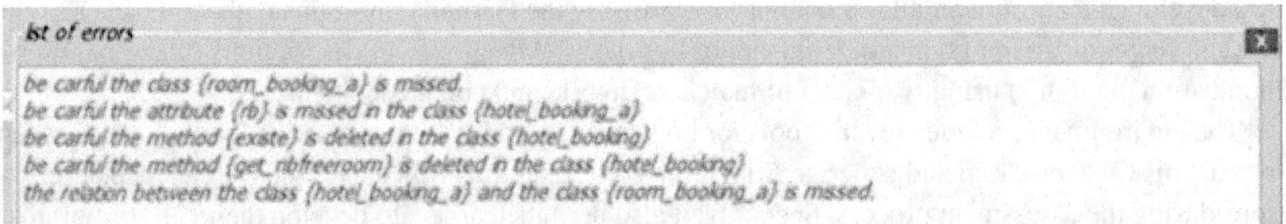

The major limitation of this first version, it takes into account only the syntactic comparison[Boussaha et al.,2015a]. The semantics aspects of C++ programs (semantic comparison) were taken in the second version, which the researchers explained at length in our previously published article[Boussaha et al.,2021].

In the next paragraph, the authors describe an experiment that finally allows us to decide which of the two S_Onto_ALPPWA's versions is better, the first or the second one.

COMPARAISON BETWEEN THE TWO DEVELOPED S_ONTO_ALPPWA VERSIONS: EXPERIMENTAL STUDY

Experimental Procedure

The participants of this study, selected through random sampling, consisted of 12 teachers of computer science from different Algerian universities (see Table 6). They were invited on the purpose of this experiment and were asked to score students' solutions carefully.

The data used in this study represent 68 programs retrieved from the computer science department of the University of Oum el Bouaghi Algeria. These programs have been the answers to two exercises of second-year computer science students. The first exercise (n=33) is a simple exercise about writing an object-oriented program C++ that orders three integer numbers. The purpose of the given exercise is the ability to use conditional structure. The second exercise (n=35) is an exercise about writing a program that seeks the existence of a value in an array. The purpose of this exercise is the ability to manipulate the data structure.

The collected programs (n=68) were printed and scored by the twelve teachers and after that submitted to the two versions of the S_Onto_ALPPWA for automatic scoring.

Results

The Null hypothesis reformulated from the research question following is:

Null hypothesis H0:'' witch the version of the two versions of S_Onto_ALPPWA, based on a hybrid matching algorithm or ontologies-agent algorithm can give near scores to teachers' scores. Spearman's rho statistic can be used to see how well the two versions of S_Onto_ALPPWA rank the students compared to teachers.

Results in table 6 for the Spearman coefficient rho show, a strong positive correlation between the two versions of S_Onto_ALPPWA and the teachers' overall average scores in the two exercises. Also, the authors observe an excellent correspondence between the two versions of S_Onto_ALPPWA and teachers. except for three teachers in the first exercise (Teach 7, Teach 10, Teach 12) and one teacher in the second exercise (Teach 10) where Spearman's rho correlation was not significant.

Table 6. Teachers and the first version of S_Onto_ALPPWA correlations

Teacher	Gender	Exercise 1	Exercise 2
Teach 1	Male	0.63***	0.43**
Teach 2	Male	0.51**	0.42**
Teach 3	Male	0.52**	0.40**
Teach 4	Male	0.62***	0.49**
Teach 5	Female	0.61***	0.56***
Teach 6	Female	0.62***	0.39*
Teach 7	Male	0.24 n.s	0.48**
Teach 8	Female	0.53**	0.27 n.s
Teach 9	Male	0.70***	0.36*
Teach 10	Male	0.29 n.s	0.41*
Teach 11	Female	0.69***	0.55**
Teach 12	Female	0.27n.s	0.52**
Average		0.67***	0.62***

Let us note that the Spearman's rho values in the second version are all lower than the values in the first version of S_Onto_ALPPWA because the second version detects syntactic and semantic errors, so the scores automatically decrease. On the other hand, the first version can detect only syntactic errors that make the scores are high so the researchers can confirm that the second version of S_Onto_ALP-PWA is more precise than the first one as demonstrated in table 7.

Table 7. Teachers and the second version of S_Onto_ALPPWA correlations

Teacher	Gender	Exercise 1	Exercise 2
Teach 1	Male	0.60***	0.42**
Teach 2	Male	0.49**	0.41**
Teach 3	Male	0.50**	0.39*
Teach 4	Male	0.61***	0.47**
Teach 5	Female	0.59***	0.55***
Teach 6	Female	0.60***	0.37*
Teach 7	Male	0.21 n.s	0.47**
Teach 8	Female	0.52**	0.25 n.s
Teach 9	Male	0.69***	0.35*
Teach 10	Male	0.27 n.s	0.40*
Teach 11	Female	0.67***	0.52**
Teach 12	Female	0.24n.s	0.50**
Average		0.64***	0.59***

As the distribution of both S_Onto_ALPPWA and the overall average scores of teachers meet the normality assumption, the Pearson correlation coefficient is calculated and the authors noticed that S_Onto_ALPPWA scores had a significant correlation with teachers' overall average scores not only in the first exercise ($rs = 0.67$, $p < 0.05$ table 1) ($rs = 0.64$, $p < 0.05$ table 7) but also in the second exercise ($rs = 0.62$, $p < 0.05$ table1) ($rs = 0.59$, $p < 0.05$ table 7).

Let us remember, the researchers have already confirmed that the second version of S_Onto_ALPPWA is more precise than the first one.

CONCLUSION AND FUTURE WORK

Due to the outbreak of the coronavirus pandemic and the total confinement imposed on all countries to prevent the spread of the virus, there are different kinds of online systems that have been widely used in recent years and have attracted more attention in educational institutions. The researchers propose a CEHL (Computing Environment for Human Learning) self-assessment environment. This type of self-assessment has been a constant demand in higher education for graduate students to be endowed with the capacity for lifelong learning that helps learners to continuously improve their skills and knowledge through their self-assessment and their learning. The proposed system helps the learner to take full responsibility for learning and completing his work by relying on himself to correct his mistakes because the proposed system is based on the technique of self-assessment and learning by the problem based on feedback provided by the system for each solution proposed by the learner. The developed environment allows comparing indirectly the learners' programs with the teacher's one through the comparison (syntactic and semantic comparison) of their ontologies descriptions using two kinds of matching (static and dynamic matching). The authors deduct that using ontologies plays an important role in instructional design and the development of course content. It helps learners access content in a knowledge-guided way.

The experiment study that the authors carried out intending to compare the first and second S_Onto_ALPPWA versions allowed us to confirm that the second version S_Onto_ALPPWA had the same behavior of teachers' scoring. So the researchers can say that the second version S_Onto_ALPPWA is a promising and ambitious tool for helping in the assessment of students' computer programming practical works activities and it can free teachers from all the disadvantages of traditional students' assessment by shortening time, reducing effort, and granting accurate and objective assessment. The authors believe that the efficiency of the second version S_Onto_ALPPWA can help teachers in scoring large classes with the same precision. This study opened new areas of research, to provide new suggestions and additions in the current work to improve the services provided in the future. For future work, the researchers still need to assess how much this second version S_Onto_ALPPWA can improve students' achievement in programming but in the Moocs context.

REFERENCES

Aiouni, R., Bey, A., & Bensebaa, T. (2018). eALGO: An automated assessment tool of flowchart programs for novices. *International Journal of Innovation and Learning*, *23*(2), 5. doi:10.1504/IJIL.2018.088785

Alonso, M., Auxepaules, L., Lemeunier, T., & Py, D. (2008). Design of Pedagogical Feedbacks in a Learning Environment for Object-Oriented Modeling. *Promoting Software Modeling through Active Education.Educators Symposium of the ACM/IEEE 11th International Conference on Model Driven Engineering Languages and Systems (MoDELS'08),* 39-50.

Andrade, H., & Du, Y. (2007). Student responses to criteria-referenced self-Assessment. *Assessment and Evaluation. Int. Journal of Higher Education (Columbus, Ohio), 32*(2), 159–181.

Arnous, S. (2014). *Conception générique d'un outil de configuration de e-TP EIAH* [Ph.D. dissertation]. INSA, Lyon, France.

Bennouna, M., Delestre, N., Pécuchet, J.-P., & Tanana, M. (2008). Évaluation du savoir-faire en électronique numérique à l'aide d'un algorithme de classification [Paper presentation]. The conférence Technologies de l'Information et de la Communication pour l'Éducation (TICE'08), Paris, France.

Bennouna, M., Delestre, N., Pécuchet, J.-P., & Tanana, M. (2009). Génération d'exemples pour l'évaluation de l'apprenant en électronique numérique à l'aide d'un algorithme de classification [Paper presentation]. The Conférence EIAH, France.

Black, P., & Wiliam, D. (1998). Assessment and classroom learning. *Assessment in Education: Principles, Policy & Practice, 5*(1), 7–74. doi:10.1080/0969595980050102

Bouarab-Dahmani, F., Comparot, C., Si-Mohammed, M., & Charrel, P. J. (2017). Ontology-Based Teaching Domain Knowledge Management for E-Learning by Doing Systems. *Electronic Journal of Knowledge Management, 13*(2), 156-171.

Boussaha, K. (2011). Modélisation d'une situation d'évaluation de l'apprenant avec UML: CAS d'application pour l'apprentissage des langages de programmation [Paper presentation]. the 8eme colloque sur l'optimisation et les systèmes d'information. COSI'2011, Guelma, Algeria.

Boussaha, K. (2016). *l'évaluation de l'apprenant dans les environnements d'apprentissage de TéLé-TPs* [Ph.D. dissertation]. Badji Mokhtar Univ, Annaba, Algeria.

Boussaha,K., & Bensebaa, T.(2009). *Design of an environment of Remote practical works between realities and prospects* [Paper presentation]. The International Conference of Novel Digital Technology.

Boussaha, K., Mokhati, F., & Chaoua, Z. (2015a). Architecture of a specific platform for training practical works: Integration of learners assessment component. *Int. J. of Technology Enhanced Learning, 7*(3). doi:10.1504/IJTEL.2015.072809

Boussaha, K., Mokhati, F., & Chaoua, Z. (2015b). *Using a matching approach to assess learners in their Practical works activity with a specific CEHL* [Paper presentation]. The 2nd International Conference on Multimedia Information processing, CITIM'2015, Mustapha Stambouli University -Faculty of Science and Technology, Mascara, Algeria.

Boussaha, K., Mokhati, F., & Hanneche, A. (2021). System-Based Ontology for Assessing Learner's Programming Practical Works Activities (S_Onto_ALPPWA). *International Journal of Web-Based Learning and Teaching Technologies, 16*(5), 80–107. doi:10.4018/IJWLTT.20210901.oa5

Boussaha, K., Mokhati, F., & Taleb, N. (2012). *A novel learner self-assessment approach – application to practical work* [Paper presentation]. The 4th international conference on computer supported Education, the CSEDU 2012, Porto, Portugal.

Chilowicz, M. (2010). *Recherche de similarité dans du code source* [Ph.D.dissertation]. Paris –Est Univ.

Choquet, C. Després, C., Iksal, S., Jacobi, P., Lekira, A, Py, D., Pham, T., Ngoc, T., & Ngoc, D. (2011). Using indicators during synchronous tutoring of practical work [Paper presentation]. The 11th IEEE International Conference on Advanced LearningTechnologies, ICALT'11.

Cross, V., & Xinran, Y. (2011). *Investigating Ontological Similarity Theoretically with Fuzzy Set Theory, Information Content, and Tversky Similarity and Empirically with the Gene Ontology* [Paper presentation]. the 5th International Conference on Scalable Uncertainty Management, Dayton, OH.

De Corte, E., Mason, L., Depaepe, F., & Verschaffel, L. (2011). Self-regulation of mathematical knowledge and skills. In B. J. Zimmerman & D. H. Schunk (Eds.), Handbook of self-regulation of learning and performance. New York: Routledge.

Deep, S., Salleh, B. M., & Othman, H. (2019). Study on problem-based learning towards improving soft skills of students in effective communication class. *International Journal of Innovation and Learning*, *25*(1), 17–34. doi:10.1504/IJIL.2019.096512

Euzenat, J., DjoufakKengue, J. F., & Valtchev. (2010). The Results of the Ontology Alignment Evaluation Initiative. *Ontology Matching Workshop, International Semantic Web Conference.*

Euzenat, J., & Shvaiko, P. (2008). *Ten Challenges for Ontology Matching* [Paper presentation]. Confederated International Conferences, OTM 2008, Monterrey, Mexico.

Giuseppe, P., & Talia, D. (2010). UFOme: An Ontology Mapping System with Strategy Prediction Capabilities. *Data Knowledge*, *69*(5), 444–471.

Guibert, N. (2006). *Validation d'une approche basée sur l'exemple pour l'initiation à la programmation* [Ph.D. dissertation]. Poitiers univ, France.

Guillaume, D. (2006). *Vers une scénarisation de l'évaluation en EIAH* [Paper presentation]. EIAH.

Guittet, L., Guibert, N., & Girard, P. (2005). A study of the efficiency of an alternative programming paradigm to teach the basics of programming. LISI /ENSMA, 86961 Futuroscope Chasseneuil Cedex, France.

Hadadi, L., & Bouaarab-Dahmani, F. (2018). Multi-level computer-aided learner assessment in massive open online courses. *International Journal of Knowledge and Learning*, *12*(4), 2018.

Hadadi, L., & Bouaarab-Dahmani, F. (2019). Gradual Learners' Assessment in Massive Open Online Courses Based on ODALA Approach. *Journal of Information Technology Research*, *12*(July-September), 2019.

Indira, B., Valarmathi, K., & Devaraj, D. (2019). An approach to enhance packet classification performance of software-defined network using deep learning. *Soft Computing, 23*(18), 8609–8619. 03975-8. doi:10.1007/s00500-019-

Konys, A.(2018). An Ontology-Based Knowledge Modelling for a Sustainability Assessment Domain. *Sustainability, 10*, 300. doi:10.3390/su10020300

Mitrovic, A., & Suraweera, P. (2004). An Intelligent Tutoring System for Entity Relationship Modelling. *International Journal of Artificial Intelligence in Education, 14*(3), 375–417.

Nicoland, D., & Macfarlane-Dick, D. (2006). Formative assessment and self-regulated learning: A model and seven principles of good feedback practice. *Int. Journal of Higher Education, 31*(2), 199–218.

Palmer, M. S., & Wu, Z. (1994). Verb Semantics And Lexical Selection. *32nd Annual Meeting of the Association for Computational Linguistics*, 133-138.

Pang, E., Wong, M., Leung, C. H., & Coombes, J. (2019). Competencies for fresh graduates' success at work: Perspectives of employers. *Industry and Higher Education, 33*(1), 55–65. https://doi.org/10.1177/0950422218792333

Pintrich, P. R., & Zusho, A. (2002). The development of academic self-regulation: The role of cognitive and motivational factors. In Development of achievement motivation. Academic Press.

Sadler, D. R. (1989). Formative assessment and the design of instructional systems. Assessment and Evaluation Research Unit, Department of Education, University of Queensland, StJ~ucia, Queensland4067. *Australia in Instructional Science, 18*(11), 119–144.

Sambell, K. (2016). Assessment and feedback in higher education: Considerable room for improvement? *Student Engagement Int. Journal of Higher Education, 1*(1), 2016.

Seman, L. O., Hausmann, R., & Bezerra, E. A. (2018). On the students' perceptions of the knowledge formation when submitted to a project-based learning environment using web applications. *Computers & Education, 117*, 16–30. https://doi.org/10.1016/j.compedu.2017.10.001

Tadjer, H., Lafifi, Y., & Seridi-Bouchelaghem, H. (2018). A new approach for assessing Learners in an Online problem-based learning environment. *International Journal of Information and Communication Technology Education, 14*(4), 18–33. https://doi.org/10.4018/IJICTE.2018100102

Tadjer, H., Lafifi, Y., Seridi-Bouchelaghem, H., & Gülseçen, S. (2020). Improving soft skills based on students' traces in problem-based learning environments. *Interactive Learning Environments*. Advance online publication. doi:10.1080/10494820.2020.1753215

Tchounikine, P. (2009). *Précis de recherche en ingénierie des eiah*. http ://membresliglab. imag.fr/tchounikine/Precis.html

Wigfield, A., Klauda, S. L., & Cambria, J. (2011). *Influences on the development of academic self-regulatory processes*. Academic Press.

Zghal, S. (2010). *Contributions à l'alignement d'ontologies OWL par agrégation de similarités* [Ph.D. dissertation]. Tunis Univ, Tunisia.

Zimmerman, B. J. (2004). Sociocultural influence and students' development of academic self-regulation: A social-cognitive perspective. Big theories revisited, 139-164.

Zimmerman, B. J. (2008). Investigating self-regulation and motivation: Historical background, methodological developments, and future prospects. *American Educational Research Journal, 45*(1), 166–183.

Zimmerman, B. J., & Schunk, D. H. (Eds.). (2011). *Handbook of self-regulation of learning and performance*. Routledge.

Chapter 10
Building a Distributed Web–Based Research and Innovation Ecosystem for University–Industry Partnership

Samuel O. Oladimeji

https://orcid.org/0000-0002-6243-2787

University of Calabar, Nigeria

Idongesit E. Eteng

University of Calabar, Nigeria

ABSTRACT

This research study aimed at developing a distributed system of web-based collaboration that would create a research and innovation ecosystem for university-industry partnership. Based on in-depth literature review, the focus-group approach to qualitative research was conducted with key stakeholders in university-industry partnership coming together to understand the research problem and system requirements. The requirements gathered at the project initiation stage guided the system design and implementation of a distributed collaborative research and innovation system that runs on three separately located servers: two for two different universities and one for all industry players. The system developed was modeled to describe how it works and to demonstrate how it would meet the identified functional requirements. Recommendations were given to guide further research and development that would improve the impact of this research study.

INTRODUCTION

University-Industry Partnership (UIP) has been considered to be very essential to creating innovation that meets business objectives in developing and commercializing universities (Burbridge and Morrison, 2021). This is largely due to the strategic role of the academia in leading technology creation and transfer,

DOI: 10.4018/978-1-6684-5027-7.ch010

which has led to the increase in collaborations between Universities and Industries (Giones, 2019). These collaborations between Universities and Industries have resulted in an Innovation Ecosystem defined as a community of people and institutions in constant collaboration with policies and resources to promote the translation of new ideas into products, processes and services (Cantu-Ortiz, 2015). Reciprocal communication between the Universities and Industry has been identified as very effective in establishing positive expectations among partners (Bstieler et al., 2017). Building a research and innovation ecosystem becomes very essential as it provides an environment for Universities and Industries to collaborate with the goal of producing mutually desired outcomes. In this vein, national and international research conventions have accepted the fact that multidimensional innovations for the future should significantly rely on distributed research collaborations that consist of sharing and integration of data, resources and knowledge, remote collaborative access to scientific instruments, and pooled human expertise (Hey et al., 2009). Therefore, an improvement in the capacity for research in Universities to drive innovation will enable researchers to compete with other countries in today's global village (Nwakpa, 2015). Unfortunately, knowledge transfer through UIPs has faced significant challenges due to weaknesses in the area of collaboration and communication between universities and industries and therefore promoting effective communication should be emphasized (Marinho et al., 2020; Yusuf, 2012). The "European paradox", which refers to having a strong capacity for research and yet lacking the capacity to translate it into innovative products, perfectly describes this challenge (Ranga et al., 2013).

Research has shown that deploying web-based platforms for collaborative research can significantly support technology creation and transfer activities in academia (Brody, 2017; Eteng and Oladimeji, 2019). This implies that a web-based research and innovation ecosystem will enhance multidisciplinary interaction between lecturers and students, which will translate to increased productivity in research collaboration processes. Distributed computing has transformed the University landscape making collaborative research possible and creating more opportunities for universities to implement systems comprising of new sets of structures that can be accessed through the Internet (Boronenko & Alexandrov, 2009). A distributed computer system has been defined as an assembly of autonomous computing components (van Steen & Tanenbaum, 2016). This chapter is aimed at developing a web-based tool that supports collaborative research involving researchers and industry players to promote innovation using distributed computing. This was done by embarking on requirement gathering from the research arms of selected Universities for appropriate system modelling through an interview; developing a distributed database for University-Industry partnership using MySQL; developing a web-based groupware that supports seamless Academia-Industry partnership and implementing a system testing procedure to validate the collaborative system developed while ensuring that it can be adopted by Universities and Industries to promote research and innovation.

BACKGROUND

The Distributed Web-Based Ecosystem

Qualities of a Web-Based Distributed System

The initial purpose of the Web was to provide geographically dispersed researchers access to shared documents essential for research projects. To make this possible, relevant documents were made to link each other (Berners-Lee et al., 1994). Hence, users were able to view documents with no difference whether the document was stored locally or anywhere else around the world. This provided a foundation for transparency in web-based distributed systems. The Web has transformed the content of documents from being purely static to being dynamically generated (van Steen & Tanenbaum, 2017). A web-based application is usually known to serve as the client-side software that consists of a browser that acts as the user interface. In effect, the Web browser, as a client, enables a user to fetch web pages from the Web server and displays them on the user's screen either for a desktop computer or a smartphone. Another very prominent aspect of web-based systems is the Web server. The Apache server has remained the most popular since 1996. In 2009, it became the first web server software to serve more than 100 million websites (Canepa, 2016)

Web Server Clustering: The demand for internet-based information and services is skyrocketing due to the expansion and pervasive nature of web-based applications (Jader et al., 2019). This rise in the use of web-based applications has significantly increased the need for web servers to process huge amounts of clients' requests and deliver responses within limited periods. This places a lot of pressure on web servers, especially as the demand for effectiveness and efficiency keeps rising. Hence, the load on these web servers keep rising (Kunda et al., 2017). To manage this load on web servers, clustering of servers has been introduced to web-based systems, which leads to distributed web-based systems. This helps to ensure that the systems are more responsive and more efficient (Cruz, and Goyzueta, 2017). Web server clustering provides load balancing techniques that improve the management of traffic, reduces response time and increases the throughput while minimizing the load on servers in the web servers (Handoko et al., 2018). Each web server acts as a node and each node collaborates with the rest such that they perform as one server using the same resources for storage, internet protocols (IP), and other applications. Even when one server is down, the other servers continue to operate in its absence, to ensure that clients continue to enjoy services from the web-based system (Handoko et al., 2018). This is done by replicating a server in a cluster of servers such that the front end of the replicas is based on a pre-arranged mechanism of distribution. This is what web-based distributed systems are known for. Figure 1 demonstrates this.

Figure 1. How a cluster of web servers works in combination with a front end
(Source: van Steen & Tanenbaum, 2017)

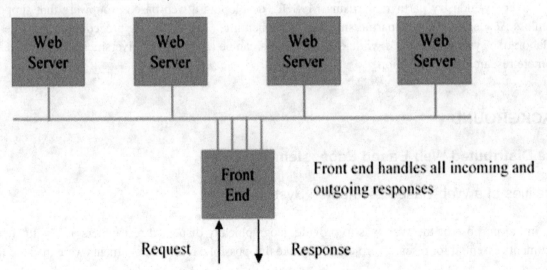

Related Works

Collaborative Innovation Applied in Process Mining

A research study was conducted to leverage the interdependence of enhancing data science skills through joint university courses and collaborative research projects while involving students trained with a collaborative teaching approach (Zandkarimi et al., 2020). The case study of process mining in a successful university-industry partnership for research and teaching was adopted. The study described how the partnership evolved with a focus on the selection of industry and academic partners. Sustainable collaboration was sustainably fostered among partners into maturity. Lessons were identified to project key success factors. A key outcome of the study was the creation of a framework that presented the collaboration dynamics of the partnership to establish new initiatives while serving as a guide for university-industry partnerships in the field of data science. This framework is presented in Figure 2. The research study, however, did not demonstrate how a collaboration platform can be introduced to enhance the collaborative research and innovation processed described.

Figure 2. The agile University-Industry collaboration framework
(Zandkarimi et al., 2020)

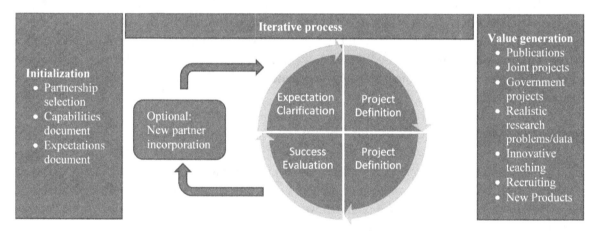

Linking Academic Research with Economic Development

A research study was conducted to examine the major issues concerning the links between academic research and economic development in Ethiopia by considering Addis Ababa University as a case (Kahsay, 2017). The study was conducted on two (2) major premises. First premise is that Universities play vital roles in boosting the economic development and competitiveness of a country through their missions of academic research and the formation of skilled human capital. Second premise is that strong UIP is crucial in enhancing scientific and technological innovation processes and the commercialization of academic research through technology transfer that is necessary for economic development. In this study, Kahsay (2017) admits that a collaborative link connecting Universities and the Industry is necessary to promote technology transfer and the commercialization of academic research. Results of the study showed that the vision of the country is the key driving force for investing in human capital and research-intensive activities for enhancing the knowledge production capabilities of the country. It was also observed that the UIP in the country was generally at its beginning phase. It was concluded that despite the vital role of University research in economic development the UIP regarding research, innovation and technology transfer is very weak in the Ethiopian context.

Grid Computing: A Form of Distributed Computing for Collaborative Research

Murumba and Micheni (2017) conducted a research study to demonstrate how grid computing, a form of distributed computing, could enhance collaborative research in Kenyan Universities as well as Universities in other developing countries. In the study, a collection of computational resources on-demand to match computational needs of research through generic service matchmaking on the Web was referred to as a collaborative research grid. The study further sought to identify the Information Technologies being used for collaborative research systems in Kenyan Universities and to establish the opportunities and benefits grid technologies present for collaborative research systems as well as the challenges of adopting grid technologies in collaborative systems. A literature review served as the methodology employed for this study to explore and understand grid technologies and their potential use in collaborative research systems. At the end of the study, it was concluded that collaborative research systems will be enhanced if Universities in the country are willing to integrate their research systems with grid technologies. It was also concluded that Universities can collaborate in implementing grid infrastructure as a way of saving the initial investment costs that would be incurred during the implementation of the grid-enabled system (Murumba & Micheni, 2017). While this literature reviewed highlighted the need for Universities to collaborate, it did not demonstrate how distributed computing can enable Universities-Industry collaborative research.

Collaborative Web-Based Learning Forum

Eteng and Okoro (2013) conducted a research study that aimed at discovering how an online forum can be used to create a learning environment where enthusiasts are enabled to share knowledge and experiences among themselves. An online platform was developed to make this possible using a database structure that supported a multi-threaded discussion environment. Design artefacts that could serve as reuse components were developed for similar future developments. The study focused on introducing into the application developed user authentication, a moderator to vet messages before posting, a visualization platform for discussion threads, and the relationships among articles. In conclusion, it was observed that the application developed enhanced the learning process in classrooms rather than take the place of the classroom. The collaboration platform presented by this literature only supported the academic learning process and not research processes that include separate autonomous databases.

Interlaced Collaborative Writing (ICW)

Robinson, Dusenberry, & Lawrence (2016) conducted a research study that discussed the case history of how virtual collaborative research could be conducted regularly by a successful, high-productive team. The aim of the study was major to discuss the importance of psychological safety as a key foundation and its benefits if this foundation is established and maintained. In this study, the case presented strategies for teams that produce collaborative work from the early stages of brainstorming and idea generation to the co-production of research projects and paper writing. Interlaced collaborative writing (ICW) was described as an approach to collaborative writing enabled by synchronous virtual tools that reinforces and maintains the psychological safety required for co-constructions of knowledge. The case history discussed is comprised of a multidisciplinary work of four humanities scholars who collaborate virtually as a peer-based research team. This research team through its ICW approach has produced so many forms of deliverables with various accolades. A major challenge this study considered was how distributed collaborative research can be shaped by technology-based tools also known as virtual tools.

Distributed Collaboration for Secure Cloud Computing

Malar and Prabhu (2020) conducted a research study that proposed a distributed collaborative trust service recommender (DTSR) system to address a model for solving the issue of security of cloud computing. This study highlighted how security-related issues have arisen with the increasing popularity of cloud computing as an essential platform for software applications and infrastructural resources (Li et al., 2016). In addressing these issues trust management systems have been researched widely under several domains such as peer-to-peer networks, pervasive computing and grid computing. Having considered the fact that trust service recommender systems employed to deal with cloud computing security issues operate in a distributed and collaborative manner, this study was conducted to address a model that solves these issues. A trust computation model with three modules was proposed. The three modules were called trust engine, finding recommenders, and risk engine respectively. The trust engine decides whether a transaction with an entity in the cloud can take place or not using a particular cloud service provider (CSP). The finding recommenders module predicts the risk of the entities present in the system, while the risk engine computes the weighted average of the trust level so that the observed results are reported to the trust engine. The interaction that takes place in the cloud environment is evaluated and provides updates of the trust levels of entities according to user experience ratings scored by cloud service users (CSUs). The evaluation is computed by the trust engine based on Pearson correlation coefficient (Herlocker et al., 1999). The recommenders determined by the trust engine is combined and aggregated to produce a predicted score, which is used by the risk engine to help the CSU decide which CSP is secure enough for transaction. The success of a distributed collaborative system in solving security issues with cloud computing demonstrated how the collaborative efforts of distributed CSUs help to provide the ratings required by other prospective CSUs. This study has demonstrated the possibility for distributed users to contribute to a specific task being conducted on a web-based platform in a seamless manner. Thereby, laying a foundation for the possibility of developing a distributed collaborative research platform for university-industry partnership.

The Psychology of Collaboration

A research study was conducted by Herman Miller to provide a literature review of various research on the psychological aspect of collaboration spaces (Oseland, 2012). The study highlighted the effect of psychological factors on collaboration and the influence of workspace layout, furniture and design. Emphasis was made particularly on the impact of personality factors and collaborative team member profiles. The study described collaboration as involving two or more individuals working together to achieve a common goal while creating a new product in the form of a solution, idea, or insight, which exceeds what they could have achieved individually. Trust was highlighted as a very important prerequisite for effective collaboration through continuous interaction. A survey conducted by Green (2012) revealed that workers at highly collaborative companies experienced their most collaborative moments during very short events, with 34% taking less than 15 minutes. Three categories of collaboration space were also identified as teamwork-related, service-related and amenity-related, with each of them providing various degrees of functionality (Hua et al., 2010). The study concluded that the most effective collaborations take place in teams with mixed personality groups. Hence, the need to factor different personality types and their communication and interaction preferences into creating collaboration spaces.

METHODOLOGY AND SYSTEM DESIGN

The Software Development Process

Due to the innovative nature of this research study, the adaptive software development (ASD) model was implemented for the software development process. This model was suitable because of its capacity to help in dealing with uncertainties at the point of initiation of the project. With this development model, less rigidity was required in the development process. The ASD model divides the development process into three (3) major sections: speculate, collaborate and learn as shown in Figure 3. Changes made to the requirement specifications in the course of system development were easily introduced in the development process without hampering the development process flow (Highsmith III, 2000)

Figure 3. Adaptive Software Development (ASD) model
(Highsmith 2002)

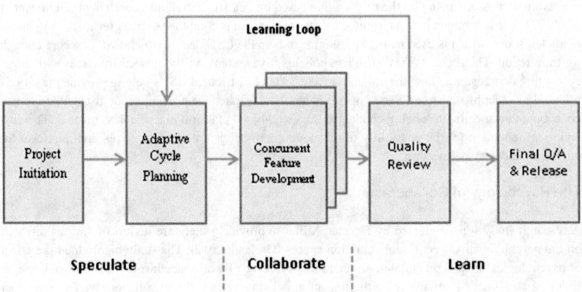

Speculate (Initiation and Planning): At this stage of the development process, there was speculation about the outcome of the system development. All the same, planning was conducted as a necessity with room for flexibility due to the level of uncertainty regarding the possible outcomes of the project

Collaborate (Concurrent Feature Development): This stage of the development included collaborative activities such as focus group interactions, informal and formal interactions with various user levels including students, lecturers, academic administrators, entrepreneurs and prospective consumers. Collaboration and communication tools such as social media platforms were used to facilitate various activities. While collaborating, research and development requirements, as well as the need for rapid decision making, was taken into consideration.

Learn (Quality Review): Due to the uncertain nature of the outcome of this project, it was imperative to learn from mistakes and unexpected outcomes. Quality review in the case of this study was done in the form of system testing after the system was developed. Details of this are indicated in Section "Implementation and Testing".

System Architecture of the Developed Collaboration Tool

The application was designed using the requirements gathered from interviews conducted with lecturers of Calabar (Unical) and Cross River University of Technology (Crutech), representatives of the Directorate of Research in Unical and Crutech, and staff of a selected business outfit. Information from the interviews conducted help to gather expectations and preferences of potential users of the web-based application as well as features to include in the design of this application. This groupware was designed to enrich the content and quality of research outputs; stimulate creativity; foster learning and knowledge retention (Barkley et al., 2014); increase commitment to research project outcomes; engender better understanding among University students.

Organizational Structure

Figure 4 presents a structural model that depicts how research work is conducted in the University and Industry at the moment. In most cases, lecturers along with students take it upon themselves to conduct their research work with little or no support from Industries. Hence, research in the University is almost only directed towards graduation of students and promotion of lecturers and not solving day-to-day problems. This system of operation does not create any space for a research and innovation ecosystem to form as both entities as completely independent of each other.

Figure 4. Current operational architecture for research work in University and Industry

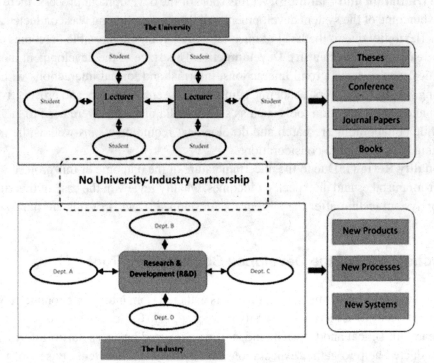

System Architecture of the Developed Application

A system architecture was designed to represent the developed system for the study as shown in Figure 5. It showed how lecturers, students and the admin staff representing the Academia arm of Collaborative Research and how industry players represent the Industry arm of Collaborative Research. The various servers demonstrated that the Academia is made of several Universities with their autonomous, yet interconnected, databases while a separate yet collaborative server for the Industry hosts all industry players subscribed on the collaboration platform. The web-based Collaboration Tool is distributed across the servers for Unical, Crutech and Industry Players. The system was designed to ensure that the breakdown of one server does not affect the continued operation of the collaborative research tool by users stored on other servers. The various services provided by the Distributed Collaborative Research Tool is shown in Figure 5.

Figure 5. System architecture for the distributed collaboration tool

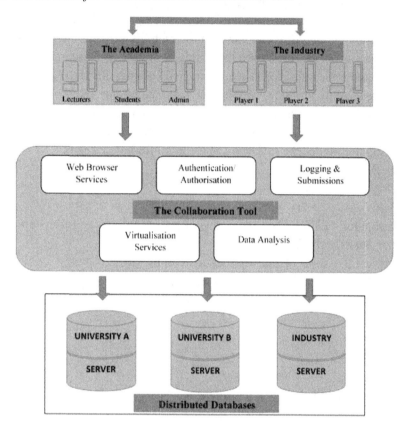

The system architecture in Figure 6 demonstrates how lecturers and students in the Universities can now collaborate with Industry Players in a Research and Innovation Ecosystem that produces innovative research as against the previous system of research in the Industry and University as demonstrated in Figure 4 where there is no form of collaboration or partnership between the two institutions.

System Modelling

The modelling process transformed the business processes into an activity diagram that demonstrated the the activities carried out with adherence to the process of research projects in the University. The activity diagram also demonstrated how the various components of the system relate to one another. The Activity Diagram in Figure 6 shows a summary of the workflow of the user's actions on a step-by-step basis from the beginning till the end.

Functional Requirements

Principal Investigator:

1. The lecturer opens the Academic Research Collaborative Tool (ARCTool) using a URL via a system browser.

2. System asks the lecturer to sign in or sign up.
3. Lecturer signs up with personal and academic details or signs in with email address and password.
4. The independent server designated for the lecturer's University saves the lecturer's account.
5. The ARCTool presents the lecturer with the option of creating a Research Project.
6. Lecturer creates the Research Project as a Principal Investigator by filling in the Project Title, Industry, Statement of the Problem, and Project Timeline on the ARCTool and submits.
7. The ARCTool creates the Research Project and saves it in the designated University's server.
8. The ARCTool presents the Principal Investigator with an option to invite Team Members.
9. Principal Investigator invites the following to form the Research Team:
   a. Research Partners (lecturer)
   b. Research Mentees (student)
   c. Industry Players (industry worker)
10. Principal Investigator's University server saves Team Members and transfers to the designated servers of other Team Members.
11. Principal Investigator assigns responsibilities to team members.
12. Principal Investigator makes submissions on the documentation pane of the ARCTool.
13. The ARCTool saves submissions in Principal Investigator's University server and transfers them to other designated servers.

Research Partner:

1. The lecturer opens the ARCTool using a URL via a system browser.
2. System asks the lecturer to sign in or sign up.
3. Lecturer signs up with personal and academic details or signs in with email address and password.
4. The independent server designated for the lecturer's University saves the lecturer's account.
5. The lecturer accepts an invitation from Principal Investigator to become Research Partner.
6. Research Partner makes academic, intellectual, and technical submissions to the documentation pane including attaching files.
7. ARCTool saves submissions in Principal Investigator's University server and transfers them to other designated servers.

Research Mentee:

1. The student opens the ARCTool using a URL via a system browser.
2. System asks the lecturer to sign in or sign up.
3. Student signs up with personal and academic details or signs in with email address and password.
4. The independent server designated for the student's University saves the student's account.
5. The student accepts an invitation from Principal Investigator to become Research Mentee.
6. Research Mentee makes academic, intellectual, and technical submissions to the documentation pane including attaching files.
7. ARCTool saves submissions in Principal Investigator's University server and transfers them to other designated servers.

Admin:

1. University staff opens the ARCTool using a URL via a system browser.
2. University staff creates an admin account on the ARCTool.
3. The independent server designated for the Admin's University saves the account.
4. Admin signs in with username and password.
5. Admin views collaborative research activities without the ability to make any contribution as a team member.
6. Admin accesses the University's server to conduct oversight duties.
7. Admin contacts users via email where necessary.

Industry Player:

1. Industry worker opens the ARCTool using a URL via a system browser.
2. System asks the industry worker to sign in or sign up.
3. Industry worker signs up with personal and academic details or signs in with email address and password.
4. The independent server designated for Industry Players saves the Admin's account.
5. Industry worker accepts an invitation from Principal Investigator to become Industry Player.
6. Industry Player provides the research team with technical information and relevant data on the collaboration tool.
7. ARCTool saves submissions in Principal Investigator's University server and transfers them to other designated servers.

Activity Diagram (Figure 6)

Figure 6. Activity diagram for the user scenario of all users except the admin

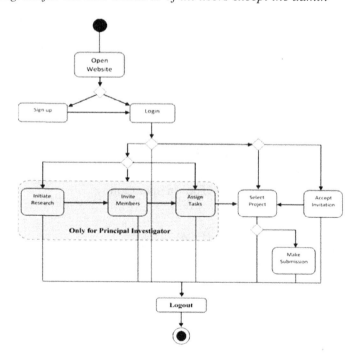

Server Distribution Algorithm

Here are the pseudocodes that describe how distribution within the three servers took place:

Step 1: User registers on academic or industry server
Step 2: User joins research group
Step 3: Users with lecturer roles can create research team
Step 4: User exchanges messages and files with research team
Step 5: If user (receives invite from another server)
Step 6: User accepts invite(
User data is copied to new server
User interacts with research team on new server
)
Step 7: End if
Server maintains storage of own messages
Server shares relevant data in the background with other servers
Server shows data from other servers
: background data transfer (is: invisible, to: user)
: background data transfer (is: triggered, by: user)
Step 8: User edits data
-do line 14
Step 9: Server admin can [
View => [
'server statistics',
'project completion'
],
Edit => [
'user data',
'server settings'
]
]

SCREENSHOTS OF THE COLLABORATION TOOL

Figure 7 – 15 presents screenshots of the ARCTool in operation.

Figure 7. Homepage of the collaboration tool

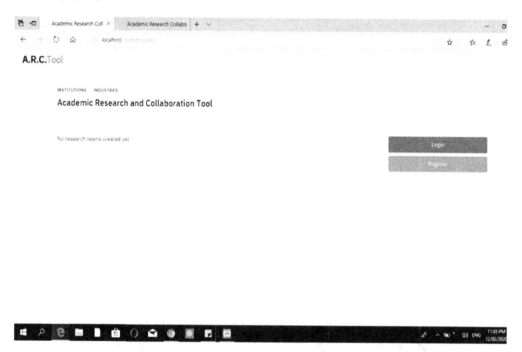

Figure 8. User creates new account

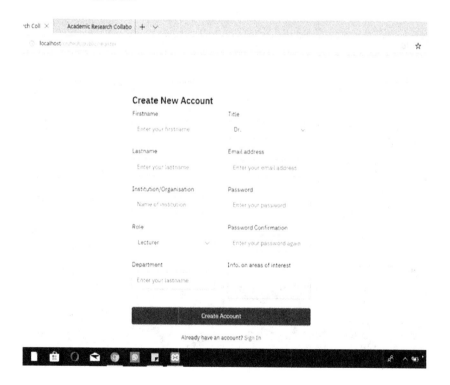

Figure 9. User signs in

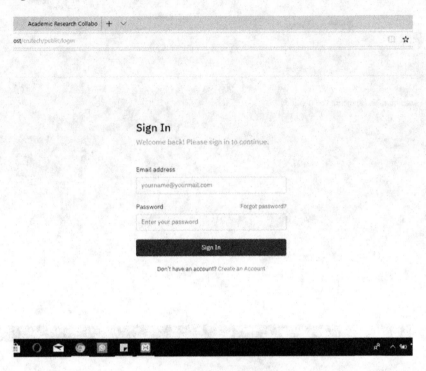

Figure 10. Principal investigator creates new research team

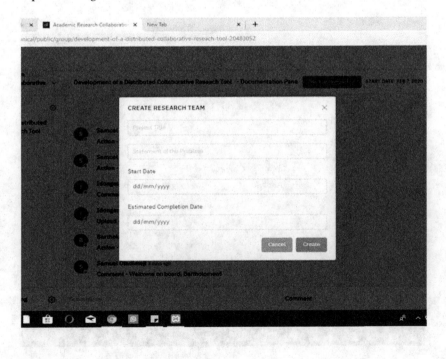

Figure 11. Principal investigator invites team member

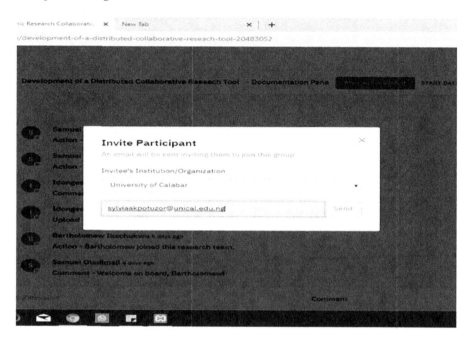

Figure 12. Cost breakdown for research project indicated

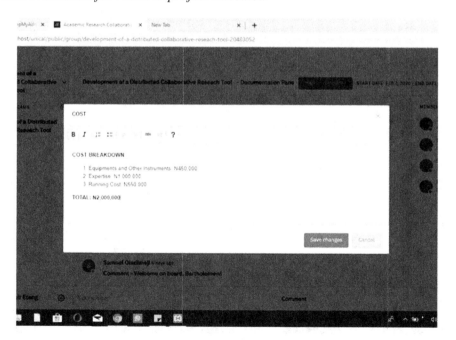

Figure 13. Tasks assigned to team members

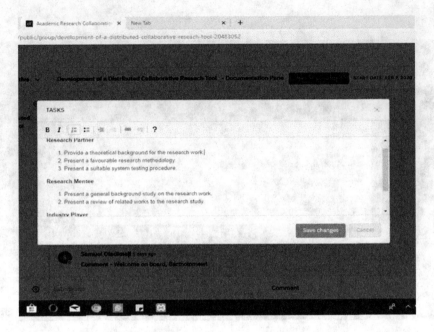

Figure 14. Project timeline determined

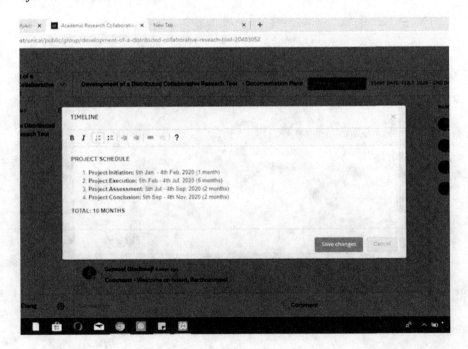

Figure 15. User makes submission into documentation pane

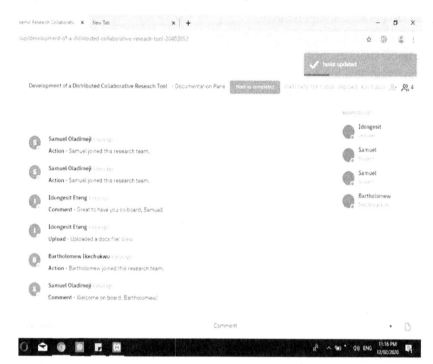

RECOMMENDATIONS

1. The introduction of new digital technologies has significantly contributed to higher productivity in the industry. Introducing a web-based research and innovation ecosystem for University-Industry partnership will help generate digital technologies that are boosting productivity.

2. Despite the key role technological development is playing in sustainable development, it also has the tendency of creating inequalities or perpetuating existing ones as a result of access to these technologies within less privileged groups and countries. To address these challenges, there is the need to localized innovation such that solutions are created based on the peculiar needs of such countries per time while government continues to drive policies that improve the standard of living.

3. The growing ubiquity of collaboration across all human endeavours has placed increasing demand on service providers to connect with several categories of people at the same time. This means that while a lecturer is contributing on a particular collaborative research platform, he could be required to interact with his colleagues in his immediate department on another collaboration platform. As the need for such heterogeneous collaborations as well the frequency increases there will be a need to make it possible to for several heterogeneous collaborative work to take place simultaneously on the same platform to increase productivity.

4. With the increasing demand for University-Industry partnership in global and national innovation, universities are being assessed on their capacity for collaboration. This is because universities that have increased their commitment to and capacity for University-Industry partnership tend to make more impact on their societies. They, therefore should be recognized accordingly. To make this possible and more transparently so, a collaboration index can be developed while a technological

system is created to compute it. This will go a long way in encouraging universities to boost their commitments to collaborative research.

5. To enhance the impact of this study there is a need to further research needs to be conducted to identify and understand the factors that drive University-Industry partnership. This factors can then be focused on when developing new collaborative research tools or improving on the existing ones as a way of advancing the research and innovation ecosystem.

CONCLUSION

This research study has demonstrated how a research and innovation ecosystem can be built with the introduction of a web-based tool that brings Universities and Industries together. With such an ecosystem in place problems in the society can be solved in a more organized, effective and transparent manner.

REFERENCES

Barkley, E., Cross, K., & Major, C. (2014). *Collaborative Learning Techniques: A Handbook for College Faculty* (2nd ed.). John Wiley & Sons.

Berners-Lee, T., Masinter, L., & McCahill, M. (1994). RFC1738: Uniform Resource Locators. RFC Editor.

Boronenko, O., & Alexandrov, V. (2009). Next Generation E-learning based on Grid Technologies and Web 2.0. *Proceedings of ICL 2009*.

Brody, S. (2017). Web-Based Tools for Collaborative Research. *Library High Tech News, 34*.

Bstieler, L., Hermmert, M., & Barczak, G. (2017). The Changing Basis for Mutual Trust Formation in Inter-Organizational Relationships: A Dyadic Study of University-Industry Research Collaborations. *Journal of Business Research*, *74*, 47–54. doi:10.1016/j.jbusres.2017.01.006

Burbridge, M., & Morrison, G. (2021). A Systematic Literature Review of Partnership Development at the University-Industry-Government Nexus. *Sustainability*, *13*(13780), 1–24. doi:10.3390u132413780

Canepa, G. (2016). *Apache HTTP Server Cookbook: Hot Recipes for the Apache Web Server*. Exelixis Media.

Cantú-Ortiz, F. (2015). A Research and Innovation Ecosystem Model for Private Universities. In Private Universities in Latin America: Research and Innovation in the Knowledge Economy (pp. 109-130). MacMillan-Palgrave. doi:10.1057/9781137479389_6

Cruz, J., & Goyzueta, I. (2017). Design of a High Availability System with Proxy and Domain Name Service for Web Services. *Proceedings of 2017 IEEE XXIV International Conference on Electronics, Electrical Engineering and Computing (INTERCON)*. 10.1109/INTERCON.2017.8079712

Eteng, I. E., & Okoro, J. C. (2019). A Collaborative Web-Based Learning Forum. *International Journal of Natural and Applied Sciences*, *8*(1&2), 48–55.

Eteng, I. E., & Oladimeji, S. O. (2019). Development of an Online Collaboration Tool for Research and Innovation in the University. *Journal of Management Science and Business Intelligence*, *4*(1), 25–31.

Giones, F. (2019). University-Industry Collaborations: An Industry Perspective. *Management Decision*, *57*(12), 3258–3279. doi:10.1108/MD-11-2018-1182

Green, B. (2012). *What it Takes to Collaobrate*. Herman Miller Inc.

Handoko, H., & Isa, S., SI, S., & Kom, M. (2018). High Availability Analysis with Database Cluster, Load Balancer and Virtual Router Redundancy Protocol. *Proceedings of the 3rd Internal Conference on Computer and Communication Systems (ICCCS 2018)*.

Herlocker, J., Konstan, J., Borchers, A., & Riedl, J. (1999). An Algorithmic Framework for Performing Collaborative Filtering. In *Proceedings of the 22nd Annual International ACM SIGIR Conference on Research and Development in Information Retrieval*. New York, NY: Association for Computing Machinery. 10.1145/312624.312682

Hey, T., Tansley, S., & Tolle, K. (2009). *The Fourth Paradigm: Data-Intensive Discovery*. Microsoft Research.

Highsmith, J. III. (2000). *Adaptive Software Development: A Collaborative Approach to Managing Complex Systems*. Dorsel House Publishing Co.

Highsmith, J. (2002). *Agile Software Development Ecosystem*. Addison-Wesley Longman Publishing.

Hua, Y., Loftness, V., Kraur, R., & Powell, K. (2010). Workplace Collaborative Space Layout Typology and Occupant of Collaboration Environment. *Environment and Planning. B, Planning & Design*, *37*(3), 429–448. doi:10.1068/b35011

Jader, O., Zeebaree, S., & Zebari, R. (2019). A State of Art Survey for Web Server Performance Measurement and Load Balancing Mechanisms. *International Journal of Scientific & Technology Research*, *8*(8), 535–543.

Kahsay, M. (2017). The Links Between Academic Research and Economic Development in Ethiopia: The Case of Addis Abba University. *European Journal of STEM Education*, *2*(2), 1–10. doi:10.20897/ejsteme.201705

Kunda, D., Chihana, S., & Muwanei, S. (2017). Web Server Performance of Apache and Niginx: A Systematic Literature Review. *Computer Engineering and Intelligent System*, *8*(2), 43–52.

Li, X., He, J., Zhao, B., Fang, J., Zhang, Y., & Liang, H. (2016). A Method for Trust Quantification in Cloud Computing Environments. *International Journal of Distributed Sensor Networks*, *12*(2), 5052614. doi:10.1155/2016/5052614

Malar, M., & Prabhu, J. (2020). A Distributed Collaborative Trust Service Recommender System for Secure Cloud Computing. *Transactions on Emerging Telecommunications Technologies*, *31*.

Marinho, A., Silva, R., & Santos, G. (2020). Why Most University-Industry Partnerships Fail to Endure and How to Create Value and Gain Competitive Advantage through Collaborations: A Systematic Review. *Quality Innovation Prosperity*, *24*(2), 34–50. doi:10.12776/qip.v24i2.1389

Murumba, J., & Micheni, E. (2017). Grid Computing for Collaborative Research Systems in Kenyan Universities. *The International Journal of Engineering and Science*, 6(4), 24–31. doi:10.9790/1813-0604022431

Nwakpa, P. (2015). Research in Tertiary Institutions in Nigeria: Issues, Challenges and Prospects: Implication for Educational Managers. *IOSR Journal of Humanities and Social Science, 20*(6), 45-49.

Oseland, N. (2012). *The Psychology of Collaboration Space*. Herman Miller.

Ranga, M., Hoareaux, C., Durrazi, N., Etzkowitz, H., Marcucci, P., & Usher, A. (2013). Study on University-Business Cooperation in the US. London School of Economics (LSE) Limited.

Robinson, J., Dusenberry, L., & Lawrence, H. (2016). Collaborative Strategies for Distributed Teams: Innovation through Interlaced Collaborative Writing. In *IEEE International Professional Communication Conference (IPCC 2016)*. IEEE. 10.1109/IPCC.2016.7740489

Van Steen, M., & Tanenbaum, A. S. (2016). A Brief Introduction to Distributed Systems Computing. In Proceedings of Very Large Digital Library (VLDL 2009). Springer. doi:10.100700607-016-0508-7

Van Steen, M., & Tanenbaum, S. (2017). Distributed Systems (3rd ed.). Distributed-sys.net

Yusuf, A. (2012). An Appraisal of Research in Nigeria's University Sector. *Journal of Research in National Development*, 10(2), 321–330.

Zandkarimi, F., Nakladad, J., Vieten, J., & Geyer-Klingberg, J. (2020). Co-Innovation in a University-Industry Partnership. A Case Study in the Field of Process Mining. *Proceedings of the 32nd International Conference on Advanced Information Systems (ICAIS 2020)*.

Chapter 11
An Empirical Analysis of Code Smelling and Code Restructuring in Python

Rohit Vashisht

ABES Engineering College, Ghaziabad, India

ABSTRACT

Code smellings are not bugs or errors; rather, they are a fundamental deviation in software design that lowers code quality. Code smells don't always mean the software won't work; it will still provide a result, but it can slow down processing, increase the risk of failure and errors, and make the programme more vulnerable to future flaws. The conceptual theory behind code smell and its various kinds are discussed in this chapter. Identifying and eradicating code smells is a time-consuming and endless process with no guarantee that the software will be smell-free. Also, because it's very hard to uncover and eliminate all smells by hand, adopting automated code review techniques that can detect smells becomes essential. Code refactoring is one method of restructuring written code to reduce the effects of bad code smell on generated software code. A novel three-phase code refactoring framework has been proposed in this study. The effectiveness of Python code smell detection using Pysmell tool and refactoring using the rope automation tool are also studied in this chapter.

A. INTRODUCTION

With forthcoming changes in market trends, technological aspects, and the fundamental way of software development's process, software development is constantly increasing these days. In this age of digitization and technological growth, we rely on a variety of software and services to carry out our daily tasks. As a result, in order to reduce the losses caused by poor software specifications and design, software development companies must focus on delivering high-quality end products. From the perspective of needed quality production in the implementation of the Software Development Life Cycle (SDLC), software design and implementation should be monitored from early phases of SDLC. Code Smells aren't a sign of a program's flaws. A software programme might run fine even if it has code smells. They are

DOI: 10.4018/978-1-6684-5027-7.ch011

either inaccurate or do not prevent the programme from working. They simply indicate a design flaw and may raise the likelihood of errors and programme failure in the future. Hence, to enhance the quality of software code, it is mandatory to properly cross-check the created code and use automated techniques to find bad-smelling code fragments at the appropriate time. Code restructuring is done to come up with a design that executes the similar job as the input software program but with better quality. Generally, code restructuring techniques apply boolean algebra to model logic behind the programme and then apply a set of transformation directives to generate reformed logic. The purpose is to get spaghetti-bowl coding and come up with a procedural designing method that follows the structured programming philosophy (Ngetich et al., 2019). Manual code structure necessitated extensive expertise on the side of the code analyzer, making it difficult to uncover all possible problematic code smells within the time and other available resources.

As a result, the focus of this study is on the literature surrounding code smells, their types, and the various methods for addressing them. It also assesses the utility of a number of automated code restructuring technologies. Automated tools refactor source code more accurately and with a lower failure rate. To retain the internal behaviour of the system and code alterations, the preconditions required before refactoring must be met (Kaya et al., 2018). In this study, Rope, an automated tool for restructuring Python code, was used. Early detection of poor code smells has been shown to result in significant reductions in software development and maintenance effort and cost. Figure 1 depicts the concept of bad smell through a variety of examples.

Figure 1. Examples of bad code smells

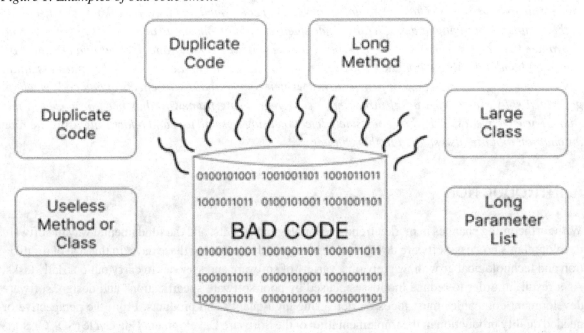

The structural outline of this paper is as follows. Section B discuss the literature review related to code smell and refactoring, section C explains some related terminologies, a novel three phase code refactoring framework has been proposed in section D, section E deals with code smelling and refactoring tools case studies and finally, the major findings with future directions have been concluded in section F.

B. LITERATURE STUDY

R.L. Glass (1998) makes an ad hoc correlation between bad smells and re-factorings. To explicitly identify and detect these bad smells, Mens and Tourwe' utilise a semi-automated technique grounded on logic meta programming, and to provide refactoring opportunities that delete these bad smells (Tourwe and Mens, 2003).

Object-oriented metrics are used by Simon et al. to recognize problematic smells and offer appropriate refactorings (Simon et al., 2001). They offer Move method/attribute and extract/inline class refactorings based on use relationships. The distance-based cohesiveness characteristic, which evaluates the extent to which a class's methods and variables related to each other, is the important underlying notion.

Another pragmatic, but little more formal, method is to use a weaker definition of behaviour preservation, which is not sufficient to ensure the full preservation of programme semantics technically, but which peforms well in many real cases. For example, we can create a notion of call preservation, which ensures that the refactoring preserves all method callings (Mens et al., 2002). In the existence of a type system, a refactoring can be shown to retain type correctness (Tip et al., 2003).

Demeyer (2002) explored the impact of refactorings that substitute conditional logic with polymorphism in the case of object-oriented programming. He finds that following the restructuring, programme performance improves due to the efficient manner in which current compiler technology optimizes polymorphic functions.

Arcelli et al. (2015) offered a work in a fuzzy situation where only the bottom and upper boundaries of threshold values may be identified. The identification task generated a list of performance anti-patterns and their probability of occurrence in the system based on this information. To eliminate each performance anti-pattern, several refactoring options may be available. Their method included a prediction of how beneficial each replacement could be in view of performance gains. The findings showed that a combined study of anti-pattern likelihood and refactoring advantages motivates designers to seek out alternatives that significantly upgrade software performance.

Liu et al. (2019) proposed a deep learning-based method to detect code smells. The major breakthrough was that deep neural networks and advanced deep learning algorithms could automatically choose source code attributes for code smell identification and generate the intricate mapping between those attributes and forecastings. To this goal, the authors presented an automated method for creating labeled training data for a neural network-grounded classifier that did not need human participation. As a first test, the methodology was applied to four well-known code smells: feature envy, long methods, huge classes, and misplaced classes. The proposed approach greatly enhances the state-of-the-art, according to experimental results on open-source apps.

V. Alizadeh and M. Kessentini (2018) presented an interactive solution for reducing the developer's engagement effort when reworking systems, integrating the usage of multi-objective and unsupervised way of learning. They produced multiple feasible refactoring strategies using multi-objective search in the first phase by locating a trade-off between several competing quality indicators. The developers were then guided in identifying their region of interest and reducing the amount of refactoring choices to examine using an unsupervised learning algorithm that clustered the diversed trade-off solutions. They used 14 active developers to test the tool's efficiency on five open source projects and one industrial system by hand. The participants discovered their desired refactorings performed quicker and were more accurately than the existing state of the art, according to the findings.

Wang et al. (2017) presented a system-level multiple refactoring approach that involves merging and dividing related categories to achieve the best functionality distribution at the system level. The "bad smells" generated by cohesion and coupling concerns can be eradicated from both the non-inheritance and inheritance hierarchies using a set of pretreatment processes and preconditions without affecting the code behaviour. The experimental results demonstrated that the given approach operated well in diverse systems and was helpful from the context of the original developers, based on comparative analysis with related research and evaluating the refactoring results using quality attributes and empirical estimation.

Terra et al. (2016) suggested a tool-supported and lightweight structural similarity-based re-modularization technique. The approach was based on the discovery that sequential projects of Move Class, Move Method, and Extract Method refactorings could result in the re-modularization of a software system. They tested the method using a modified version of open-source software and found that it had 100% recall and 50% precision, respectively. The suggested process's design decisions like the usage of structural similarity, the lack of preconditions, and the demand-wise recognition of the target entity, were also assessed in order to get end outcomes.

The suggested approach by Kumar et al. (2018) estimates twenty-five various source code attributes at the method level and uses them as attributes in an ML framework. An freely available source dataset containing five different software applications was used to conduct a series of tests in order to evaluate the suggested approach's effectiveness. To tackle the problem of class imbalance, the proposed method with Synthetic Minority Over-Sampling TEchnique (SMOTE) is being used. The best performance was achieved by the Radial Basis Field (RBF) kernel employing SMOTE, according to the results.

As an expansion of a past presented event-driven service-oriented architecture, Ortiz et al. (2019) provided a scalable framework to deliver real-time context-aware actions based on predictive streaming data processing. They created and deployed a microservices-based architecture for this purpose, which allowed real-time context-aware actions based on predictive streaming data processing. As a consequences, their framework was improved in two ways. On the other hand, it has been refactored to follow a microservice architecture style, which greatly improves its upkeep and evolution. An air quality case study was used to assess the architecture's performance.

Hsieh et al. (2017) attempted to identify exception handling code smells that can happen in a JavaScript application on either the client side or the server side, building on our prior study on exception handling code smells in Java. Each smell's impact on software quality was proven using examples. Refactorings related to the identified smells were proposed, and their consequences on the system were demonstrated, including the amount of robustness attained and other benefits acquired. The goal of the project was to provide a guide to help JavaScript developers and to ignore or detect exception handling code smells.

C. RELATED TERMINOLOGIES

a) Code Smell

Code smells are nothing more than a departure from standard coding conventions that lowers the quality of generated software code while leaving its original functionality and behaviour intact. Coding is about optimizing your entire software so that it performs better, lasts longer, and is more visible. According to the design principles established by an organization, code smell varies from project to project and developer to developer. Code smells indicate that your code needs to be re-factored to better extendability, supportability and readability. Even in code produced by skilled programmers, code smells can exist. It can shorten the software's lifespan and make it more difficult to maintain. When there are smelly codes existing, expanding the software's functionality becomes challenging as well. A lot of the time, code smells go undiscovered.

b) Types of Code Smell

According to the state-of-the-arts, code smells can be classified into five types. From the aspect of the software development, Figure 2 displays the five primary classifications of code smells.

Figure 2. Categories of bad code smell

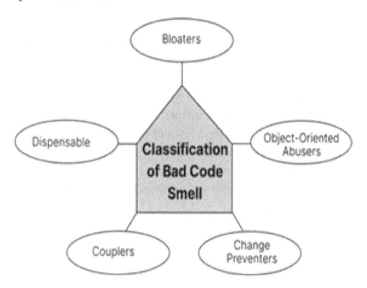

- *Bloaters:* - Bloaters are code, classes, and methods that have grown to such size that they are difficult to deal with. These smells usually do not appear straight away, but rather develop over time as the software program enhances (and especially when no one bothers to remove them). Data clump is very common example of bloater code smell.
- *Object-Oriented Abusers:* - Object-Oriented Designing Strategy (OODS) is widely used in today's software development sectors to conform to real-world examples. Object Oriented Abusers (OOA) is a type of code smell that relates to the implementation of OO concepts that is wrong or inadequate. In OODS, using a Switch-Case statement instead of polymorphism is a common example of OOA.
- *Change Preventers:* - These smells indicate that if the software programmer needs to modify something in one part of the code, he/she will have to update a lot of other parts as well. As a result, programme development becomes substantially more complicated and costly. When the

developer makes modifications to a class, one often find himself/herself having to alter a lot of unrelated methods. One example of this category is the parallel inheritance hierarchy. Move Method or Move Field approaches can be used to solve this problem.

- *Dispensable:* - Dispensable are termed as the noise adders to the existing code. The code is considerably clearer and easier to understand without them. For example, rather than inserting long comments to explain identifiers requirement in coding the logic, take appropriate or related identifiers and name them accordingly.

- *Couplers:* - Coupler smells describe the excessive attraction behaviour of two classes of people. The way the code is written has a role in the excessive coupling between classes. Also, when disproportionate delegation occurs from one class to another, the smell may appear. Coupling smell is an example of inappropriate intimacy in which one class accesses the internal data and methods of another class. Low coupling leads to higher-quality software system development in general.

c) Resolving Plan to handle Bad Code Smell

The process of code review begins once all types of smells have been identified. To manually discover such smells, two or more developers might employ the primary method, the ad-hoc code review process. Many smells are impossible to detect through manual inspection, hence automated code review methods are utilised to detect them. Code smells are injected into the source code, either consciously or unknowingly, and can even arise when fixing other smells. Most smells are purposefully discarded by developers because they appear to have a minor influence or are simply too difficult to explain. Manually detecting bad code smells necessitates a high level of programming knowledge and competence on the part of the code analyst. Manual code smell detection is ineffective due to the human factor. As a result, automated code smelling technologies are required. CodeGrip is a popular automatic code smell detection tool that analyses your code repositories and detects a wide range of smells. Figure 3 displays the bad code smell tackling strategy in detail.

Figure 3. Resolving plan for bad code smell

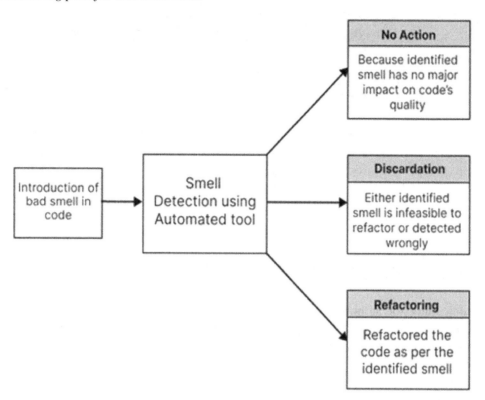

D. PROPOSED FRAMEWORK FOR CODE REFACTORING

The three-phased novel framework for code refactoring is depicted in Figure 4. The identification of bad smell code sections in original source code is done utilizing automated methods in the first phase i.e. the detection phase. Following identification, the stinky instances are captured and extracted from the initial pool of cases.

The Impact Factor (IF) for each recognized smell is evaluated in the second step. It is calculated based on the interaction of the smelly class with other classes. IF of a smelly class is derived by dividing the number of classes to which it is related to the total number of possible couplings. Following the IF estimation, the found smelly cases are ranked in decreasing order of their predicted IF, so that highly ranked cases can be catered on first priority.

Finally, code refactoring is carried out to address the problem of bad code smells. After completing code refactoring, evaluate the impact on software quality factors such as understandability, complexity, and maintainability. The consistency of refactored code and other software artifacts should also be maintained (design document, workflow diagram and other documentations etc.). Finally, a consistent and qualitative re-factored code is generated as an output.

Figure 4. Three phase code refactoring framework

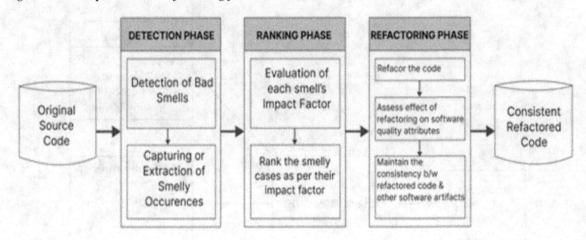

E. CASE STUDY AND DISCUSSION

In this research study, the authors have studied Pysmell, an automated code smell identification tool used for python code. The major eleven types of bad code smells observed in Python code are listed in Table 1, with five generic and six additional code smells (Chen et al., 2016)

Table 1. Categories of code smell

S.No.	Name of Code Smell	Description
1.	Large Class (LC)	Class that has expanded too large with data and methods.
2.	Long Parameter List (LPL)	Method or function with long lists of parameters.
3.	Long Method (LM)	Method or Function with larger size.
4.	Long Message Chain (LMC)	Accessing an object using long chain of attributes or methods by dot operator.
5.	Long Scope Chaining (LSC)	Multiply nested method or function
6.	Long Base Class List (LBCL)	A class definition with too many base classes.
7.	Useless Exception Handling (UEH)	Careless or unnecessary dealing of exceptions
8.	Long Lambda Function (LLF)	A lambda function definition with exceptionally long number of characters.
9.	Complex List Comprehension (CLC)	With complex lists definitions and its comprehension.
10.	Long Element Chain (LEC)	Accessing an object using a long chain of elements.
11.	Long Ternary Conditional Expression (LTCE)	A overly long ternary conditional expression.

Pysmell detects Python smells using metric-based criteria based on predefined thresholds or limits on various software parameters. The authors also discussed about ROPE, an automated tool, to restructure the python code in order to demonstrate the notion of code refactoring. It's a Python refactoring library that's free source. Code completion, locating definitions and their occurrences, checking up docstrings, and arranging imports are all its useful IDE-oriented capabilities. Project is called root object in ROPE which includes all files and directories code to be manipulated. The following are the major steps of refactoring a Python code using ROPE.

- **Step 1.** *Create a project*
  from rope.base.project import Project
  project = Project ('project_dir')
- **Step 2.** *Manage preferences*
  Prefs is a container for numerous settings and preferences that looks like a dictionary. They are stored in a file named as .ropeproject at the project root's directory.
  for p in project.prefs.prefs:
  print (project.pref.get(p))
- **Step 3.** *Get resources*
  Resources are nothing but they are files and directories containing python code to be refactored.
  server = project.get_resource('traad/server.py')
  print(server.name, server.path, server.is_folder())
- **Step 4.** *Create refactoring object*
  from rope.refactor.rename import Rename
  ren = Rename(project, project.get_resource('traad/state.py'), offset = 42)
  This step fails if ROPE can't perform the refactoring in given code using available resources.
- **Step 5.** *Calculate actual changes*
  changes = ren.get_changes('TacoCopter')
  print(changes.description)
  print(changes.get_changed_resources())
- **Step 6.** *Execute the changes*
  project.do(changes)
  After execution of this step, changes are actually implemented in the specified project.

Figure 5. Code Refactoring Procedure Using ROPE

```
from rope.base.project import Project
from rope.refactor.rename import Rename

# Create the project
proj = Project('.')

# Create the partially-bound refactoring
ren = Rename(project,
             project.get_resource('traad/state.py'),
             offset=42)

# Calculate the changes for a fully-specified renaming
change = ren.get_changes('TacoCopter')

# Perform the changes
project.do.changes()
```

In ROPE, there is a history object called *Project.history* that keeps track of the modifications made by the programmer through the code refactoring process. It also maintains account of undone changes and dependencies between them. The undoing of the changes can be done in either of the ways:-

- *Undo the most recent change*
  project.history.undo()
- *Undo the selected changes from history*
  change = project.history.undo_list[3]
  project.history.undo(change)

Figure 6 lists all of the common forms of code refactoring goals that can be accomplished in Python code using the ROPE library.

Figure 6. Goals of Code Refactoring using ROPE

Remove Unneeded Comments	Assign Constants to Variables	Bug Fixing or Adding New Code
Modifying Keys in a Dictionary	**MAIN GOALS OF CODE REFACTORING USING ROPE**	Eliminate Unnecessary Code State
Transforming Duplicate Code into Decorators		Document the Code
Put in Type Hints	Code Hoisting	Update the Test Suit

F. CONCLUSION AND FUTURE WORKS

Detecting code smells is critical for increasing the quality of a software system, optimizing its evolution, and, as a result, lowering total development and maintenance costs and efforts. The authors of this paper explain the concept of code smell, its types, and a method for resolving it. A novel three-phase framework for code restructuring is also provided, which is independent of the programming language and the underlying software design techniques. The paper uses Pysmell as a Python smelling tool and ROPE as a Python code restructuring tool as a case study, with thorough explanations of implementation processes. In the future, these tools can be used to detect Python smells in multiple Python code repositories, and the tool's effectiveness can be compared to manual smell detection. Second, Pysmell uses metric-based thresholds and limits, as previously stated. Instead of using the state-of-the-arts, one interesting direction in this subject is to estimate these threshold values for effective code restructuring.

REFERENCES

Alizadeh, V., & Kessentini, M. (2018). Reducing interactive refactoring effort via clustering-based multi-objective search. *Proceedings of the 33rd ACM/IEEE International Conference on Automated Software Engineering*, 464–474.

Arcelli, D., Cortellessa, V., & Trubiani, C. (2015). Performance-based software model refactoring in fuzzy contexts. *International Conference on Fundamental Approaches to Software Engineering*, 149–164.

Chen, Z., Chen, L., Ma, W., & Xu, B. (2016). Detecting Code Smells in Python Programs. *IEEE 2016 International Conference on Software Analysis, Testing and Evolution (SATE)*, 18–23. doi:10.1109ate.2016.10

Demeyer, S. (2002). *Maintainability versus Performance: What's the Effect of Introducing Polymorphism? Technical Report, Lab. on Reeng.* Universiteit Antwerpen.

Glass, R. L. (1998). Maintenance: Less Is Not More. *IEEE Software*.

Hsieh, C.-Y., Le My, C., Ho, K. T., & Cheng, Y. C. (2017). Identification and refactoring of exception handling code smells in javascript. *Journal of Internet Technology*, 18(6), 1461–1471.

Kaya, M. (2018). Effective software refactoring process. In *2018 6th International Symposium on Digital Forensic and Security (ISDFS)*. IEEE.

Kumar, L., Satapathy, S. M., & Krishna, A. (2018). Application of smote and lssvm with various kernels for predicting refactoring at method level. *International Conference on Neural Information Processing*, 150–161.

Liu, H., Jin, J., Xu, Z., Bu, Y., Zou, Y., & Zhang, L. (2019). Deep learning based code smell detection. *IEEE Transactions on Software Engineering*.

Mens, T., Demeyer, S., & Janssens, D. (2002). *Formalising Behavior Preserving Program Transformations*. Graph Transformation.

Ngetich, M., Otieno, D., & Kimwele, M. (2019). A Model for Code Restructuring, A Tool for Improving Systems Quality In Compliance With Object Oriented Coding Practice. *International Journal of Computer Applications Technology and Research*, 8(5), 196–200. doi:10.7753/IJCATR0805.1010

Ortiz, Caravaca, Garc´ıa-de Prado, & Boubeta-Puig. (2019). Real-time context-aware microservice architecture for predictive analytics and smart decision-making. *IEEE Access, 7*, 183–194.

Simon, Steinbruckner, & Lewerentz. (2001). Metrics Based Refactoring. *Proc. European Conf. Software Maintenance and Reeng.*, 30-38.

Terra, R., Valente, M. T., & Anquetil, N. (2016). A lightweight remodularization process based on structural similarity. *2016 X Brazilian Symposium on Software Components, Architectures and Reuse (SBCARS)*, 111–120.

Tip, F., Kiezun, A., & Baumer, D. (2003). Refactoring for Generalization Using Type Constraints. *Proc. SIGPLAN Conf. Object-Oriented Programming, Systems, Languages, and Applications*, 13-26.

Tourwe, T., & Mens, T. (2003). Identifying Refactoring Opportunities Using Logic Meta Programming. *Proc. European Conf. Software Maintenance and Reeng.*, 91-100.

Wang, Y., Yu, H., Zhu, Z., Zhang, W., & Zhao, Y. (2017). Automatic software refactoring via weighted clustering in method-level networks. *IEEE Transactions on Software Engineering*, *44*(3), 2017.

Chapter 12
The Roles of Habit and Compatibility in the Continued Use of Short-Form Video Sharing Services:
A Study of TikTok

Igor Alexander Ambalov

iD https://orcid.org/0000-0002-6481-3305

Rajapruk University, Thailand

ABSTRACT

Short-form video sharing services (SVSs), such as TikTok, have rapidly grown in popularity in the recent years. Some evidence suggests that because SVSs allow users to quickly and easily create and consume on-demand content, they are addictive, and they appeal to a wide audience. The available literature attempting to explain this phenomenon remains scant. In order to fill this gap, the current study aims to examine the roles of habit and compatibility on SVS continuance intention and the interaction of these relationships with user experience, using TikTok as a context. To this goal, data collected from 157 university-student TikTok users are analyzed using structural equation modeling to determine whether these factors shape their continuance decisions. The findings show that habit and compatibility positively affect continuance intention while experience does not. This study enhances SVS continuance research by theorizing and empirically confirming that habit and compatibility are important influences in the context of continuing SVS usage.

INTRODUCTION

Online social media (OSM) is one dominant force that has been driving information technology (IT) usage behavior for more than two decades. Friendster, MySpace, and Facebook—launched in 2002, 2003, and 2008, respectively—are arguably the most influential in shaping social networking landscape (Boyd

DOI: 10.4018/978-1-6684-5027-7.ch012

& Ellison, 2007). Online media sharing websites/services such as YouTube and Daily Motion (founded in 2005), and Vevo (founded in 2009) were launched around the same time and quickly became very popular among many different (in terms of socio-demographic characteristics) users in various parts of the word where the Internet was available.

While YouTube is still the leader among online media platforms, new market entrants, such as TikTok (various types of short-form videos), Triller (music-oriented short videos), Snapchat (music, sounds, and video effects videos), and Instagram Reels (short soundtracked video clips) are rapidly becoming a major challenge to YouTube domination in this realm. In this context, the present study is interested in examining key cognitive factors pertinent to TikTok usage because this phenomenon, while relatively new, is becoming increasingly widespread worldwide (Statista reports one billion active users as of 2021 [Statista, 2021a]), including Americas, Europe, Australia, and Asia. In Thailand, in particular, the usage of TikTok has greatly increased in the last few years: from 0.53 million in 20017 to 7.4 million in 2021 (Statista, 2021b)—almost a 15-fold increase in four years.

TikTok is a social media service accessed by a website and/or an app for creating and sharing videos that can run up to 15 seconds; users can also use a variety of creative filters to customize and enhance their videos. People who use TikTok are mostly young individuals—about half of all the users (48%) are aged between 18 and 29 and well over half (64%) are high-school or college/university students (Pew Research Center, 2021). According to some media marketing experts and research studies, TikTok is popular among the younger generation because of its simple design and ease of use (Omnicore, 2021; Weimann & Masri, 2020). In fact, it appears to be well-suited for the individual and social needs, and online behaviors of the younger generation of social media users.

TikTok allows individuals to create soundtracked videos and share them with others. It is a form of micro-entertainment that serves as distraction or emotional escape for a couple of minutes during the day. It apparently is easy to use and it is quick to produce a desired result.

Given such a rapid widespread growth and popularity of TikTok, various businesses will benefit from understanding factors that shape users' intention to continue using this technology. TikTok and similar service providers can utilize such knowledge in order to become more effective in their efforts to increase the number of TikTok users. Consequently, other businesses can reach larger audiences in order to distribute important information about their products and services.

The literature suggests that the initial acceptance of technology, including that of social media, does not assure its continuing usage (Bhattacherjee, 2001; Boyd, 2013). Since discontinuance of a technology can be financially and otherwise damaging for the technology provider, understanding users' motivations and intentions is crucial for the provider's survival and success.

Some popular media and online blogs claim that using TikTok (watching and sharing videos) is addictive (e.g., Deutsche Welle, 2021; Commclub, 2020). This view is consistent with recent research studies finding that users get addicted (for various reasons) to using TikTok (Meral, 2021; Scherr & Wang, 2021; Zhang et al., 2019) and that TikTok usage can become habitual (Bayer et al., 2022). According to Bandura (1999), addictions indicate the failure of self-regulatory functions and some previous studies (e.g., LaRose, 2001) view deficient self-regulation as the mechanism behind Internet addictions. Extending this view, Larose et al., (2001) considered the symptoms of Internet-related addictions being, in fact, indicators of habitual usage arising from ineffective self-regulation. The way habit impacts user behavior is an unresolved issue in IT research. Some researchers argue that habit impacts intention (Lankton et al., 2012; Hsiao et al., 2016; Wilson et al., 2012), some others that it affects behavior directly (Bhattacherjee & Lin, 2015; Kim et al., 2005; Lee, 2014; Limayem et al., 2007), and yet some others hold that habit affects both intention and usage simultaneously (Venkatesh et al., 2012). Hence, considering this inconsistency, habit is added to the research model in order to clarify the mechanism by which habit influences IT behavior in general, and in the case of TikTok in particular.

Drawing from the habit literature, this study includes experience, defined here as the length of exposure to a given technology, as a moderator for the habit–continuance intention relationship. User experience represents individual differences among users, and while evidence exists that experience (the duration and frequency of exposure to a technology) interact with habit's influence on intention (Lankton et al., 2012; Venkatesh et al., 2012), it is important to know if this difference plays a role in the context of TikTok usage.

The current study also adds the construct of compatibility from the Innovation Diffusion Theory (IDT) (Rogers, 1983) because of its demonstrated empirical saliency and sound theoretical support in prior IS research. Compatibility has been examined by a wide range of previous studies and demonstrated consistency in predicting innovation adoption (Davis, 1989; Tornatzky and Klein, 1982). While this consistency is referring to technology adoption, more recent empirical evidence on technology continuance shows that compatibility is also an important predictor of IT continuance intention in various domains, including information communication technology (Chang et al., 2020; Hernandez-Ortega et al., 2014), online blogs (Ifinedo, 2018), mobile services (Wang et al., 2020), and e-learning (Chang et al., 2020). A recent study (Luthen & Soelaiman, 2022) also found that compatibility is an important predictor of social media (TikTok) usage.

In the light of the above exposition, this research is interested in examining factors that influence TikTok continuance intention including habit and compatibility. To this end, the current study employs the expectation-confirmation model (ECM) (Bhattacherjee, 2001) as the base theory of IT continuance and extends this model with the constructs of habit and compatibility to formulate a research model of TikTok continuance. The extended ECM is expected to better explain continuance intention to use TikTok by focusing on the constructs of perceived usefulness, satisfaction, confirmation of expectations (the original ECM), in addition to habit and compatibility (the theoretical extensions).

This study contributes to the literature by testing the validity of ECM in the context of an SVS such as TikTok, evaluating the significance and strength of the model relationships, and examining the role of habit and compatibility, moderated by user experience, as direct predictors of SVS continuance intention.

RELATED LITERATURE AND THEORETICAL BACKGROUND

This study adopts the expectation-confirmation model (ECM) of IT continuance as the theoretical foundation for the research model of SVS continuance. The model is appropriate for the current context because it was specifically formulated to explain post-adoption behavior (continuance) which is different from behaviors dealing with technology adoption (acceptance). The remainder of this section will describe the theories and constructs used in formulating the theoretical research model for this study.

IT Continuance Model

The ECM model (see Figure 1) is an adaptation of the expectation-disconfirmation theory (EDT) (Oliver, 1980), also referred to as expectation-confirmation theory (ECT) in marketing literature and consumer behavior research. In adapting ECT to the context of IS, Bhattacherjee (2001) proposed several theoretical extensions to the original theory. However, the underlying conception of ECT—that users' pre-consumption and post-consumption beliefs about utility of a product may substantially differ—remained unchanged. The ECM model posits that continuance intention is directly predicted by perceptions about usefulness of future IS usage and the extent of satisfaction with prior IS usage. In turn, both of these predictors are determined by confirmation of one's expectations from prior IT usage (Bhattacherjee, 2001). This approach differs from that of technology acceptance models in that it relies on constructs reflecting one's experience with a given IT – a factor that is irrelevant to technology acceptance. Given these characteristics, ECM is appropriate for studying continuance intention. In addition, a meta-analysis of ECM revealed that the model is stable across technologies and usage contexts (Ambalov, 2018).

Of note, the ECM is not the main focus of this study, instead it is used as the theoretical framework to examine the role of habit and compatibility SVS post-adoption decisions. Nevertheless, by extending ECM with the constructs of interest this study also contributes to IT continuance research as a whole.

Figure 1. Expectation-confirmation model
(Bhattacherjee, 2001)

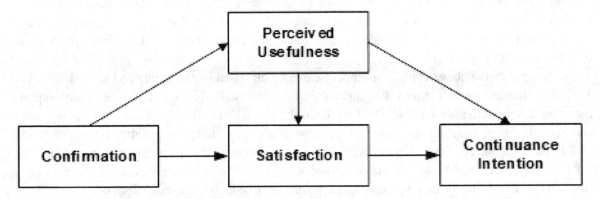

Habit

Some researchers maintain that habit can explain behavior beyond intention (e.g., Ajzen 2002; Ajzen & Fishbein, 2000). In the IT context, this is supported both theoretically and empirically (Bhattacherjee & Lin, 2015; Hu et al., 2018; Lankton et al. 2012; Ortiz de Guinea & Markus, 2009; Venkatesh et al., 2012; Wilson et al., 2010). A popular belief that old habits die hard appears to be true in the context of IT usage as well. Once a habit is formed, it likely continues to lead the behavior regardless of the initial motives. Given that many users to use SVSs on a daily basis, it is likely that they use it out of habit, among other reasons. This especially pertains to the younger generation who appear to be the most avid users of SVSs such as TikTok (Choi et al., 2021; Huang, 2021).

The literature provides two different habit perspectives that were used by previous studies to explain continuance intention and/or behavior. Their approaches to the mechanism by which habit affects behavior are fundamentally different from one another. The habit automaticity perspective or HAP proposes that behavior is activated automatically without conscious intervention, that is, outside of one's awareness (Ortiz de Guinea & Markus, 2009). The instant activation perspective or IAP (also called stored intention) posits that habitual use is an expedited form of cognitive processing – a function of evaluations and intentions, and as such, is a reasoned action (Ajzen, 2002).

Both perspectives have been examined empirically and found partial support; the results obtained by different studies in similar contexts are mixed. For example, while some studies found that habit positively influences users' intentions to continue using online shopping and media services (Barnes, 2011; Barnes & Bohringer, 2011; Hsiao et al., 2016; Mirkovski et al., 2019; Mouakket, 2015), others found that habit inhibits the predictive power of intention on continued internet usage (Kim, et al. 2005; Limayem & Cheung, 2008; Limayem et al., 2007), and yet others (Tamilmani et al., 2018; Venkatesh et al., 2012; Wilson et al., 2010) found that habit directly and positively influences both the intention and the actual behavior to use technology, including internet applications. In addition, in some studies, hypothesized effects of habit received no support. For example, Wilson and Lankton (2010) found both the effect of habit on continuing use of internet applications and its moderating effect on the intention–usage relationship nonsignificant, as also did Gwebu et al., (2014), who reported a nonsignificant effect of habit on intention to continue using an online social network (OSN).

Given the diversity of theoretical explanations and mixed empirical results, further investigation of the role of habit in predicting IT behavior, including SVS usage, is needed to clarify the theoretical nature and the salience of this construct. Hence, habit (the IAP perspective) was added to the research model as an alternative explanation of one's decisions to continue using TikTok.

Compatibility

Compatibility with innovation is one key construct in the IDT, and it has been consistently related to technology adoption behavior (Agrawal & Prasad, 1997). Compatibility is the degree to which the technology is aligned with the potential user's existing values, previous experience and current needs (Rogers, 1983). The reasoning behind its positive influence on the adoption of innovation is that the more compatible an innovation or technology is, the less uncertainty one has to use it for specific tasks. Arguably, if one is uncertain or doubtful that a given innovation provides a good fit for a task, one will likely seek a different technology to accomplish the task, or may suppress the intention to perform the behavior.

According to the intentions and innovations literature, compatibility is a factor that influence adoption decisions in general and IT usage in particular (Rogers, 1983; Moore & Benbasat, 1996). Previous studies found that compatibility has a positive effect on attitude toward using computer-based communication technologies (Van Slyke et al., 2007) and intention to use mobile shopping (Islam et al., 2013; Lu & Su, 2009); and that it positively affects intention to continue e-learning (Chen, 2011). In addition, Karahanna et al., (1999) found that this construct was important to both adopters and continuance users of (Windows) software; however, in the research studies by Taylor and Todd, (1995), and Venkatesh et al., (2003) compatibility was not a significant influence on intention to use technology. Nonetheless, considering the empirical evidence and a solid theoretical foundation, compatibility is added to the research model as an antecedent of continuance intention in order to clarify its importance in a modern IT setting.

Habit and Experience: Moderation Effect

Building on the habit literature, this study includes experience as a moderator for the habit–continuance intention relationship. User experience represents individual differences among users, and while evidence exists that the duration and frequency of exposure to a technology interact with habit's influence on intention (Lankton et al., 2012; Venkatesh et al., 2012), it is important to know if this difference also plays a role in more recent contexts such as OSN usage.

The literature suggests that because of feedback that experience provides to users of a technology, the beliefs about its usage may change overtime (Ajzen, 2002). As proposed by Lankton et al. (2012) the explanation of the moderating effect comes from dual-process theories (e.g., Shiffrin & Schneider, 1997; Smith & DeCoster, 2000) positing that, habitual behavior based on automatic processing becomes stronger with experience and that significant and consistent experience is necessary for automatic processes to develop. In addition, the association between a stimulus and behavior that is necessary to produce habitual behavior grows stronger with experience. It follows that when user experience is low, habit will be weak hence having weaker influence on continuance intention. The opposite should also be true because high experience implies more satisfactory outcomes and, according to IAP, more stable intention to perform the behavior. Thus, habit will have stronger effect on continuance intention for users with more experience, and weaker effect—for users with less experience.

Based on the theoretical and empirical evidence presented above, this study models experience as a moderator of the relation between habit and continuance intention.

Compatibility and Experience: Moderation Effect

Another IDT-based relationship that experience may interact with is between compatibility and intention. As follows from the definition of this construct, the degree of compatibility with a given technology is dependent on how certain one is that the technology aligns with one's objectives, tasks, and usage behavior. Acquiring experience with a system, defined here as the length and frequency of exposure to a given technology, implies obtaining knowledge and expertise with regard to leveraging that system, which in turn implies that the more experience a person has with the system, the more confident the person likely feels about using that system. In the social construction of technology (Orlikowski, 1992; Orlikowski and Gash, 1994) various features of a technology are tried and possibly adopted by individual users in order to fulfil their needs and complete certain tasks. As the usage continues, the users tend to adapt certain features to accomplish some other tasks for which the technology was not intended by design. After the initial adoption phase, users begin to more deeply learn various features and uses of a technology that they become more aware about as their use experience grows. This awareness includes users' knowledge about the system's features that with experience allow for more sophisticated uses of the system. It stands to reason that more sophisticated users have less uncertainty and more confidence about the system's ability to perform tasks that meet (compatible with) their needs, than early or intermediate users.

The empirical support for this interaction effect in the literature is scant. However, a previous study on mobile social network site adoption for learning (Leong et al., 2018) found that the effect of users' perception of task-technology fit—a construct conceptually similar to compatibility in this study— on use intention was statistically significant and practically meaningful. Also, Carlson and Zmud (1999) found that as users gain more experience with a technology, its influence on their perceptions of the appropriateness of the technology to perform certain tasks increases. Furthermore, the result of Thompson el al.'s (1994) investigation of the moderating effect of experience on the relationship between task-fit and usage behavior confirmed this influence.

Thus, given the above argumentation, experience is added to the research model as a moderator of the compatibility and continuance intention relationship.

RESEARCH MODEL AND HYPOTHESIS DEVELOPMENT

This section describes the hypotheses development, which is based on the review of the literature presented above. Since the ECM-based relationships have been thoroughly examined and validated by prior research, the following discussion focus more attention on those dealing with habit and compatibility.

ECM-Based Hypotheses

These four hypotheses are drawn directly from the ECM model, which posits that perceived usefulness—defined as expectations of benefits from future usage—impacts users' decisions to continue using the system. This is because users will likely continue using a technology if they believe that it can enhance their performance in completing certain tasks. This influence has been empirically tested and found support across different settings and with different populations of users (Gao & Bai, 2014; Lin et al., 2017; Sledgianowski & Kulviwat, 2009; Yoon & Rolland, 2015). Hence, the first hypothesis is proposed:

H1. *Perceived usefulness will have a positive effect on usage continuance intention*

Satisfaction is an affect representing one's feelings about a technology based on prior usage experience. In ECM, satisfaction is a key predictor of continuance intention. It is likely that satisfied users will continue using a given technology, and dissatisfied users will do the opposite. This relationship has been examined and found support in previous studies in the context of an OSN (Gao & Bai, 2014; Magro et al., 2013; Yoon & Rolland, 2015). Hence, the second hypothesis is proposed:

H2: *Satisfaction will have a positive effect on usage continuance intention*

In the IT continuance context, confirmation is an important predictor of both perceived usefulness and satisfaction. In the ECM model, it is the extent to which users believe that their expectations of IT use (in terms of user benefits) are realized during actual usage. Confirmation positively influences satisfaction with IT usage because if the users believe that the benefits, they anticipated prior to using the IT have been obtained, it gives them a reason to be satisfied.

Confirmation also has a positive impact on perceived usefulness because when users realize that their initial expectations of benefits are confirmed, it increases their expectations of benefits from future usage. Previous studies that examined and confirmed these relationships in the context of OSM sites (Kim, 2011; Magro et al., 2013; Mirkovski et al., 2018; Yoon & Rolland, 2015). Hence, the third and fourth hypotheses are proposed:

H3: *Confirmation will have a positive effect on perceived usefulness*
H4: *Confirmation will have a positive effect on satisfaction*

It is noted that the original ECM (Bhattacherjee, 2001) also proposed a relationship between perceived usefulness and satisfaction. However, in two consequent revisions of the model (Bhattacherjee et al., 2008; Bhattacherjee & Lin, 2015) this relationship was dropped due to its theoretical ambiguity and lack of empirical support.

Impact of Habit

Based on the earlier discussion about habitual use of technology, habit is defined as a stored intention toward continuing use of IT. This definition is consistent with the IAP perspective of routinized behavior, which explains the intention-behavior relationship based on reasoned action (Ajzen 2002), thereby suggesting a causal path from habit to continuous intention. The empirical support for this effect comes from previous research on habit in the online context, including e-commerce, virtual worlds, mobile internet, microblogging, and social networking (Barnes, 2011; Barnes et al., 2003; Venkatesh et al., 2012; Lankton & McKnight, 2012). Hence, the fifth hypothesis is proposed:

H5: *Habit will have a positive effect on usage continuance intention*

Impact of Compatibility

As described in the literature review above, compatibility is an important factor in the innovations research that has shown consistent association with technology adoption and use.

While Rogers (1983) intended this construct to predict adoption of innovation, other studies showed that compatibility can also predict intention in post-adoption IT usage situations. According to Lucas (2003), if a general theory (e.g., IDT) is true in one context, it implies that the theory is also true in many other contexts, including settings and populations. In addition, the available evidence suggests that compatibility positively affects continuance usage of OSM sites (Ifinedo, 2018; Zolkepli & Kamarulzaman, 2014). Thus, the sixth hypothesis is proposed:

H6: *Compatibility will have a positive effect on usage continuance intention*

Impact of Habit Moderated by Experience

The earlier discussion about habit establishes theoretical and empirical support for the influence of habit on intention to continue usage. In addition to this influence, this study posits that the effect of habit on continuance intention is moderated by experience. That is, the prior user experience with an OSN influences the strength of this relationship such that for users with lower experience the impact of habit on continuance intention is weaker than for users with higher experience. The justification for this interaction is given earlier in section 6.4. In sum, there is ample evidence both theoretical and empirical supporting the importance of usage experience in habit's influence on IT use continuance, including OSM sites and applications. Thus, this study puts forward the seventh hypothesis:

H7: *Experience will moderate the relationship between habit and usage continuance intention, such that with high experience, habit will have a larger positive influence on usage continuance intention than with low experience.*

Impact of Compatibility Moderated by Experience

Following the prior argumentation in section 6.5 about the interaction of technology experience with the impact of compatibility on continuance intention, this study models experience as a moderator of this relationship so that compatibility is more influential for the experienced, that for the inexperienced OSN users. The empirical research discussed earlier supports the presence of this moderating effect in different situations, including an online context. Thus, the eighths and final hypothesis is proposed:

H8: *Experience will moderate the relationship between compatibility and usage continuance intention, such that with high experience, compatibility will have a larger positive influence on usage continuance intention than with low experience.*

RESEARCH MODEL

The hypotheses presented above are shown in the research model in Figure 2. This theoretical model represents an extended expectation-confirmation (ECM-based) research model of SVS continuance and was formulated following a comprehensive literature review on IT adoption and usage.

Figure 2. Theoretical research model

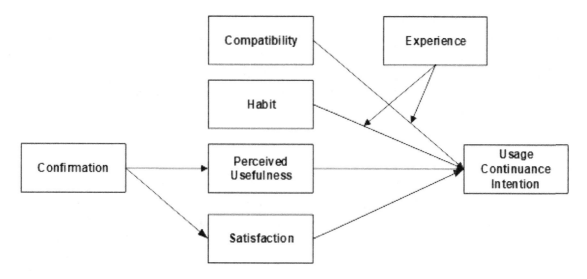

In this model, habit and compatibility are specified as the direct predictors of usage continuance intention (for brevity, continuance intention); both of these relationships are moderated by user experience with an SVS. Satisfaction and perceived usefulness are also specified as direct predictors of usage continuance intention, while confirmation is modeled as a direct predictor of each of these constructs. There is no path drawn from perceived usefulness to satisfaction as was noted earlier.

METHODOLOGY

Study Sample

The sample for this study is comprised of junior and senior students from a private university in Thailand with prior experience using TikTok. This is intentional because students represent a more homogenous population compared to the general public, and since the main focus of this study is testing theoretical predictions, such homogeneity is desired. This is so because "heterogeneity of participants reduces the likelihood of identifying violations of a theory when it is false" (Lynch, 1983). In addition, this is an appropriate sample because the majority of students actively and continuously use SVSs including TikTok.

Scales and Questionnaire

All of the measurement scales were adapted from prior research in order to ensure validity and reliability of the measures. With regard to user experience, however, while the items were borrowed from Lankton et al. (2012), user experience here was modeled as a latent variable with two formative indicators measuring: **(a)** usage frequency per week, *(1) once or less a day to (3) many times a day*; and **(b)** usage length in years, *(1) less than 1 year to (3) more than 2 years*. There was no need to combine the items to form a total score because SmartPLS 3 allows for a moderator to be a latent variable.

The questionnaire was developed in both English and Thai languages. The English version questionnaire items were translated into Thai by a university lecturer native to the language. A pilot test was then used to refine the scales. Both versions were reviewed by two separate groups of students from the target population – Thai-speaking and English-speaking – with ten people in each group. Based on the reviewers' recommendations, several minor corrections were made in both questionnaires. Pilot test data were analyzed using principal component factor analysis. All items loaded on their respective factors as expected, and the Cronbach's alphas were all above 0.7 as recommended by Kline (2016). The measurement items are included in Appendix A.

Data Collection

The data was collected using a self-administered online questionnaire consisting of 27 items including gender and age. The questionnaire was placed online using a free web survey service and a link to it was distributed among students through an instant messaging application. Because this study uses PLS-SEM as the analysis technique, no particular target for the sample size is set; PLS-SEM works well with small sample sizes (Hair et al., 2019). The demographic profile of the respondents in the sample is described in Table 1.

Table 1. Demographic profile of the respondents

Category	Characteristic	Count	Percentage
Gender	Male Female	62 95	39.5 60.5
Age	18–21 22–25 26–29	100 41 16	63.7 26.1 10.2
Usage length (years)	< 1 1–2 > 2	51 79 27	32.5 50.3 17.2
Usage frequency (times per week)	once a few many	35 59 63	22.3 37.6 40.1

DATA ANALYSIS AND RESULTS

Measurement Model Analysis

In order to access the validity of the constructs, the measurement model was analyzed first. Construct validity of the measures was assessed in two ways: (1) a preliminary exploratory factor analysis of all the indicators using principal components method in SPSS; and (2) a confirmatory factor analysis of the hypothesized scales using SmartPLS.

The initial factor analysis for six factors (latent variables) showed a satisfactory result for construct validity based on the criteria by Straub et al. (2004) except for two indicators: PU1 (perceived usefulness); and CMP2 (compatibility) that significantly cross-loaded on other than intended factors. Consequently, these indicators were dropped from further analysis.

Next, the confirmatory factor analysis was performed keeping in mind the recent guidelines for the PLS-SEM method by Hair et al. (2019). The convergent validity was established by examining factor loadings and average variance extracted (AVE) for each construct (see Table 2). The results confirmed the convergent validity of the model constructs: all the factor loadings were significant; they exceeded the recommended minimum of 0.70; and each construct explained more that 50 percent of the variance of its respective indicators.

Table 2. Factor loadings and reliabilities

Factor	Item	Standardized loadings	Mean	Standard deviation	AVE	Composite reliability	Cronbach α
Compatibility	CMP1	0.91	3.94	0.65	0.81	0.93	0.88
	CMP3	0.90	4.04	0.58			
	CMP4	0.89	3.86	0.68			
Confirmation	CON1	0.88	4.00	0.70	0.79	0.94	0.91
	CON2	0.92	3.89	0.69			
	CON3	0.87	3.93	0.71			
	CON4	0.89	3.87	0.70			
Habit	HAB1	0.94	3.48	1.02	0.90	0.97	0.96
	HAB2	0.95	3.67	0.94			
	HAB3	0.94	3.49	1.01			
	HAB4	0.95	3.64	1.06			
Continuance Intention	INT1	0.91	3.96	0.70	0.85	0.94	0.91
	INT2	0.92	3.86	0.71			
	INT3	0.93	3.92	0.73			
Perceived Usefulness	PU2	0.94	3.89	0.71	0.87	0.95	0.93
	PU3	0.92	3.87	0.69			
	PU4	0.94	3.83	0.70			
Satisfaction	SAT1	0.94	3.98	0.70	0.89	0.96	0.94
	SAT2	0.95	4.00	0.71			
	SAT3	0.94	3.90	0.77			

Note: All factor loadings are significant at $p < 0.001$ (2-tailed).

In order to access the discriminant validity, the square root of AVE for each construct (the bolded diagonal elements in Table 3) was compared with the correlations of that construct with every other construct in the model. As seen from the Table 3, the AVE squares for all the constructs were larger than the corresponding inter-construct correlations, supporting discriminant validity of the observed measures.

Table 3. Construct correlations

Construct	1	2	3	4	5	6
1. Compatibility	**0.900**					
2. Confirmation	0.735	**0.891**				
3. Habit	0.613	0.613	**0.946**			
4. Continuance Intention	0.698	0.738	0.655	**0.920**		
5. Perceived Usefulness	0.731	0.745	0.688	0.741	**0.933**	
6. Satisfaction	0.663	0.730	0.573	0.700	0.674	**0.941**

Note: The diagonal bolded elements are the square roots of AVE for that construct

In addition, the heterotrait-monotrait ratio (HTMT) value for every construct was below the recommended conservative minimum of 0.85 thereby further affirming the discriminant validity of the model factors.

A test for multicollinearity revealed that the VIFs for the latent factors ranged from 1.00 to 2.93—which are below the suggested value of 5.00 (Hair et al., 2014)—indicating that multicollinearity is not an issue in this data. Next, a common method bias test using a method suggested by Kock (2015)—this method is based on full collinearity assessment—showed that VIFs for all the variables in the model were below the threshold value of 3.3, indicating that the model is free from bias.

Lastly, the internal consistency reliabilities of the construct measures were accessed and all the constructs demonstrated adequate reliability. As seen from Table 2 the Cronbach alphas (0.88 to 0.96); and the composite reliabilities (0.93 to 0.97) all exceed the recommended minimum of 0.70 (Hair et al., 2019).

Structural Model Analysis

The hypothesized relationships in the research model were tested next. In order to estimate the path coefficients and their statistical significance, the bootstrapping method with 5000 subsamples was used.

Figure 3 displays the results of the SEM analysis of the research model using SmartPLS. The notation *, **, or *** is used with unstandardized effects to indicate statistical significance (two-tailed) at a level of 0.05, 0.01, or 0.001, respectively.

As seen in Figure 3, all the direct effects in the research model are positive and statistically significant ($p < 0.05$), lending support for H1–H6. More specifically, perceived usefulness, satisfaction, habit, and compatibility predict continuance intention; the effect magnitudes for these paths are 0.29; 0.27; 0.18; and 0.19, respectively. Perceived usefulness and satisfaction are in turn predicted by confirmation, and the effect magnitudes for these paths are 0.73 and 0.75, respectively. In addition, the indirect effect of confirmation on continuance intention is significant ($p < 0.001$) and of a considerable magnitude (0.42). The model explains a substantial proportion of variance (R^2) in continuance intention (0.66); perceived usefulness (0.56); and satisfaction (0.53).

Figure 3. SEM analysis of the theoretical research model

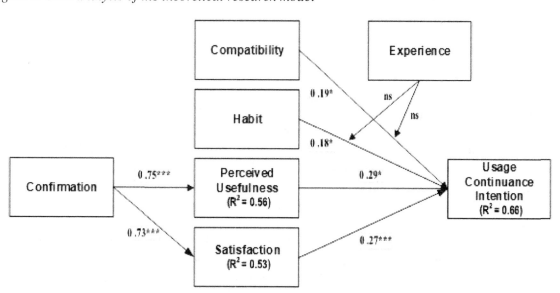

Note: Paths show standardized estimates; parenthesis indicate R^2 values; p. * < .05; ** < .01; *** < .001.

With respect to the moderation effects, the hypotheses positing the moderating influence of experience on the relationships between habit and continuance intention, and compatibility and continuance intention received no support. The interaction effect of experience on each of these paths was statistically nonsignificant regardless of the level of user experience thus indicating that experience is not a moderator in this study. Table 4 describes the result of the structural model analysis including standardized effects, *t*-values, and the statistical significance of unstandardized effects (not shown in the table).

Table 4. Hypotheses test results

No	Hypotheses	*t*-stats	Effect	Sig.	Support
H1	Perceived Usefulness → Continuance Intention	2.50	0.29	$p < 0.05$	Yes
H2	Satisfaction → Continuance Intention.	3.60	0.27	$p < 0.001$	Yes
H3	Confirmation → Perceived Usefulness	16.83	0.73	$p < 0.001$	Yes
H4	Confirmation → Satisfaction	17.50	0.75	$p < 0.001$	Yes
H5	Habit → Continuance Intention	1.98	0.18	$p < 0.05$	Yes
H6	Compatibility → Continuance Intention	2.02	0.19	$p < 0.05$	Yes
H7	Experience x Habit → Continuance Intention	0.53	-0.04	ns	No
H8	Experience x Compatibility → Continuance Intention	0.42	-0.03	ns	No

Note: ns = not statistically significant; x = moderation; continuance intention = usage continuance intention.

DISCUSSION

The focus of this research is to examine the influence of habit and compatibility on users' intentions to continue using SVSs such as TikTok. The SVS phenomenon is fairly new and thus arguably requires more attention from IT and non-IT researchers. As previously mentioned, much of prior habit and compatibility research was conducted in contexts other than SVS and hence the research on this particular technology adoption and usage is scant.

Findings and Contributions

This paper contributes to IT continuance research in general and SVS research in particular in several ways. First, it examines the impact of habit on intention to continue TikTok usage. The findings suggest that users' continuance intentions are positively influenced by habit. In other words, TikTok usage is habitual, among other reasons. In some previous studies, discussed earlier, the effect of habit on intention was nonsignificant, and in some others, habit influenced actual behaviors but not intentions. This study confirms that IAP perspective, which contends that habit affects actual behavior through intention, is a valid mechanism of habit influence on actual behavior thus contributing to habit research empirically. This evidence, however, does not imply that habit has no impact on use behavior directly. Previous studies found a causal link between habit and actual usage in various contexts, including work systems (Bhattacherjee and Lin, 2015), online social networks (Lee, 2014), self-service technologies (Wang, 2013), mobile internet (Venkatesh et al., 2012), university internet applications (Wilson et al., 2010), www (Limayem et al., 2007), and e-commerce (Gefen, 2003). These previous findings and the findings obtained in the current study suggest that future research should examine the impact of habit on actual behavior in the context of continuing use of SVSs.

The study adds to the continuance literature by theorizing and empirically confirming the effect of compatibility on users' intention to continue using an SVS such as TikTok. This is an important contribution because while previous studies provided evidence that compatibility is an important influence on IT adoption and post-adoption intentions, no study to date examined the role of compatibility in SVC users' considerations about the future use of such a system. This study fills this gap empirically. Also, while many other compatibility studies examined the role of this construct in the context of technology adoption and use of more traditional technologies such as e-commerce, work systems, social networking, and so on, the current study extends this role into continued use of the SVS technology.

In this study, compatibility has a positive effect on continuance intention. In practical terms it means that the more one believes that TikTok fits one's social and personal lifestyle, needs, and objectives, and assists in social sharing activities, the more one is willing to continue using this service. Giving that TikTok is a technology that the respondents use quite often, the effect of compatibility on intention is rather modest. It is possible that some users believe that TikTok lacks certain functionality for all of their intended tasks and purposes.

Altogether, this study demonstrates that compatibility plays an important role in users' decisions regarding using TikTok continuously. Future research should examine whether compatibility influences intention to use other SVSs such as Instagram Reels, YouTube Shorts, Triller, and similar others. These types of findings will provide a more complete understanding of the role of compatibility in individual considerations to use online social media in general, and the SVC technology in particular.

Somewhat unexpected but hypotheses H7 and H8 received no empirical support. While experience was hypothesized to have a moderating effect on the influence of habit and the influence of compatibility on usage continuance intention, both moderating effects are nonsignificant. In the current context, it may be that TikTok habits form very fast, or prior to using TikTok students already have experience using social media and other online technologies. In addition, since TikTok is allegedly user friendly, it probably takes little time for younger individuals, such as students, to learn how to use it. Future research should examine the moderating role of experience in different situations, including technologies and populations.

This study also contributes by evaluating the ECM model in an SVS context. The original model relationships concerning confirmation, perceived usefulness, satisfaction, and continuance intention are significant and of medium to high magnitudes (Cohen, 1992). Overall, the research model explained a considerable amount of variance in usage continuance intention, satisfaction, and perceived usefulness: $R^2 = 0.66$; 0.53; and 0.56, respectively. These findings are consistent with previous research that found that these constructs are important in various technology contexts, including e-commerce, social media and now SVSs.

Limitations

The current study has several limitations. First, because the sample is rather small it may not fully represent the population under study. A larger sample size should address this concern. The sample composition is another limitation. University students are a fairly homogenous—in terms of social-demographic characteristics and lifestyles—group of people, and thus IT usage behavior of these individuals may differ from that of other public groups. As reported by King and He, (2006), students can be used as proxies for professional users, but not for general users. Future research should address this limitation by using different sample compositions. Doing so will add to the validity of the findings obtained here and in other similar studies.

The next limitation is the age of the participants. Age may be a potential moderator at the study level. In support of that, several studies found that age moderates certain user motivations, including perceptions of usefulness (e.g., Morris and Venkatesh, 2010; Venkatesh et al., 2012). Future research should study users of different ages to better understand SVS continuance considerations.

Another limitation is that this study examines intention and not the actual behavior. While researchers often model intention as the final outcome variable, still, actual usage is the ultimate goal in understanding technology acceptance and continuance and thus should be of most interest to IT researchers. In addition, some evidence exists that intention does not always accurately and reliably predict behavior (Bhattacherjee and Lin, 2015). In light of this limitation, future research should examine the impact of habit and that of compatibility on SVS usage continuance and compare the results with the current findings.

The last limitation is that the current study includes only users of TikTok. While TikTok appears to be a popular SVS worldwide, there are other similar technologies that may influence research findings and thus should be considered in future studies.

Practical Implications

TikTok providers should be aware that habit and compatibility shape users' decisions to continue using the technology. This suggests that in order to increase users' involvement with TikTok and other similar technologies these applications should have features and functions that are compatible with users' social and personal values, needs, and lifestyles. For example, short-form video sharing activities may be more appealing to busy individuals such as students and professionals because it is a quick and easy way to consume information. As such, the application functions that facilitate such usage should be a focus of future development efforts. It is also important to know which application functions are used more often because frequent usage leads to the development of habit. And, as the study results show, habit is an important influence on continuing TikTok usage.

The findings also show that satisfaction and perceived usefulness each have a significant impact on continuance intention. It implies that TikTok providers should explore more ways to keep existing users satisfied by providing useful and enjoyable online user experience; and it would benefit both sides if this experience is in line with users' personal values and lifestyles.

CONCLUSION

The primary purpose of this study was to examine the roles of compatibility and habit in TikTok usage continuance. In addition, this study hypothesized that these influences were moderated by user experience with TikTok. The data collected from university-student TikTok users show that both constructs are important in shaping users' intentions to continue using the technology. However, in this study, usage experience did not moderate the effect of compatibility and the effect of habit on usage continuance intention. Given that experience-related interactions with compatibility and habit are theoretically plausible—as this study contends—more research is needed to examine if this holds true empirically.

While not the main focus in this study, the ECM-based constructs, perceived usefulness and satisfaction, demonstrated strong influence on TikTok users' continuance intention. This affirms that these constructs are important in the context of using TikTok and possibly other SVSs. However, more empirical evidence is required to support the latter conjecture. In all, the results show that ECM is applicable in an SVS context and can be used to effectively predict intentions of users to continue using this technology. This is also an important outcome because it adds to the model's overall validity and robustness in the information technology domain.

In conclusion, this research contributes by a better understanding of the influences that compatibility and habit have on usage of an important information technology such as SVS; and in addition, it adds to the validity of the IT continuance model (ECM) in this fairly novel context.

ACKNOWLEDGMENT

This research was supported by the Center for Research and Innovation Promotion at Rajapruk University, Thailand (Ref No: 014/2564).

REFERENCES

Agarwal, R., & Prasad, J. (1997). The role of innovation characteristics and perceived voluntariness in the acceptance of information technologies. *Decision Sciences*, *28*(3), 557–582. doi:10.1111/j.1540-5915.1997. tb01322.x

Ajzen, I. (2002). Residual effects of past on later behavior: Habituation and reasoned action perspectives. *Personality and Social Psychology Review*, *6*(2), 107–122. doi:10.1207/S15327957PSPR0602_02

Ajzen, I., & Fishbein, M. (2000). Attitudes and the attitude-behavior relation: Reasoned and automatic processes. *European Review of Social Psychology*, *11*(1), 1–33. doi:10.1080/14792779943000116

Ambalov, I. A. (2018). A meta-analysis of IT continuance: An evaluation of the expectation-confirmation model. *Telematics and Informatics*, *35*(6), 1561–1571. doi:10.1016/j.tele.2018.03.016

Bandura, A. (1999). Social cognitive theory: An agentic perspective. *Asian Journal of Social Psychology*, *2*(1), 21–41. doi:10.1111/1467-839X.00024

Barnes, S. J. (2011). Understanding use continuance in virtual worlds: Empirical test of a research model. *Information & Management*, *48*(8), 313–319. doi:10.1016/j.im.2011.08.004

Barnes, S. J., & Bohringer, M. (2011). Modeling use continuance behavior in micro-blogging services: The case of Twitter. *Journal of Computer Information Systems*, *51*(4), 1–10.

Bayer, J. B., Anderson, I. A., & Tokunaga, R. (2022). Building and breaking social media habits. *Current Opinion in Psychology*, *45*, 279–288. doi:10.1016/j.copsyc.2022.101303 PMID:35255413

Bhattacherjee, A. (2001). Understanding information systems continuance: An expectation-confirmation model. *Management Information Systems Quarterly*, *25*(3), 351–370. doi:10.2307/3250921

Bhattacherjee, A., & Lin, C. P. (2015). A unified model of IT continuance: Three complementary perspectives and crossover effects. *European Journal of Information Systems*, 24(4), 364–373. doi:10.1057/ejis.2013.36

Bhattacherjee, A., & Lin, C. P. (2015). A unified model of IT continuance: Three complementary perspectives and crossover effects. *European Journal of Information Systems*, 24(4), 364–373. doi:10.1057/ejis.2013.36

Boyd, D. (2013). White flight in networked publics: How race and class shaped American teen engagement with MySpace and Facebook. In *Race after the Internet* (pp. 209–228). Routledge.

Boyd, D., & Ellison, N. (2007). Social network sites: Definition, history, and scholarship. *Journal of Computer-Mediated Communication*, 13(1), 210–230. doi:10.1111/j.1083-6101.2007.00393.x

Carlson, J. R., & Zmud, R. W. (1999). Channel expansion theory and the experiential nature of media richness perceptions. *Academy of Management Journal*, 42(2), 153–170.

Chang, C. C., Liang, C., & Chiu, Y. C. (2020). Direct or indirect effects from "perceived characteristic of innovation" to "intention to pay": Mediation of continuance intention to use e-learning. *Journal of Computers in Education*, 7(4), 511–530. doi:10.100740692-020-00165-6

Chang, C. C., Liang, C., & Chiu, Y. C. (2020). Direct or indirect effects from "perceived characteristic of innovation" to "intention to pay": Mediation of continuance intention to use e-learning. *Journal of Computers in Education*, 7(4), 511–530. doi:10.100740692-020-00165-6

Chen, J. L. (2011). The effects of education compatibility and technological expectancy on e-learning acceptance. *Computers & Education*, 57(2), 1501–1511. doi:10.1016/j.compedu.2011.02.009

Choi, Y., Wen, H., Chen, M., & Yang, F. (2021). Sustainable Determinants Influencing Habit Formation among Mobile Short-Video Platform Users. *Sustainability*, 13(6), 3216. doi:10.3390u13063216

Cohen, J. (1992). A power primer. *Psychological Bulletin*, 112(1), 155–159. doi:10.1037/0033-2909.112.1.155 PMID:19565683

Commclub. (2020). *Why TikTok is addicting? (It's not the reason you might think)*. Available at: https://www.nyucommclub.com/content/2020/12/14/why-tiktok-is-addicting-its-not-the-reason-you-might-think

Davis, F. D. (1989). Perceived usefulness, perceived ease of use, and user acceptance of information technology. *Management Information Systems Quarterly*, 13(3), 319–340. doi:10.2307/249008

Davis, F. D. (1989). Perceived usefulness, perceived ease of use, and user acceptance of information technology. *Management Information Systems Quarterly*, 13(3), 319–340. doi:10.2307/249008

Deutsche Welle. (2021). *Why is TikTok so addictive?* Available at: https://www.dw.com/en/why-is-tiktok-so-addictive/av-58852826

Gao, L., & Bai, X. (2014). An empirical study on continuance intention of mobile social networking services: Integrating the IS success model, network externalities and flow theory. *Asia Pacific Journal of Marketing and Logistics*, 26(2), 168–189. doi:10.1108/APJML-07-2013-0086

Gefen, D. (2003). TAM or just plain habit: A look at experienced online shoppers. *Journal of Organizational and End User Computing*, *15*(3), 1–13. doi:10.4018/joeuc.2003070101

George, D., & Mallery, P. (2003). *SPSS for windows step by step: A simple guide and reference. 11.0 update*. Allyn and Bacon.

Gwebu, K. L., Wang, J., & Guo, L. (2014). Continued usage intention of multifunctional friend networking services: A test of a dual-process model using Facebook. *Decision Support Systems*, *67*, 66–77. doi:10.1016/j.dss.2014.08.004

Hair, J. F., Anderson, R. E., Babin, B. J., & Black, W. C. (2014). *Multivariate data analysis* (7th ed.). Pearson Education.

Hair, J. F., Risher, J. J., Sarstedt, M., & Ringle, C. M. (2019). When to use and how to report the results of PLS-SEM. *European Business Review*, *31*(1), 2–24. doi:10.1108/EBR-11-2018-0203

Hernandez-Ortega, B., Serrano-Cinca, C., & Gomez-Meneses, F. (2014). The firm's continuance intentions to use inter-organizational ICTs: The influence of contingency factors and perceptions. *Information & Management*, *51*(6), 747–761. doi:10.1016/j.im.2014.06.003

Hsiao, C. H., Chang, J. J., & Tang, K. Y. (2016). Exploring the influential factors in continuance usage of mobile social Apps: Satisfaction, habit, and customer value perspectives. *Telematics and Informatics*, *33*(2), 342–355. doi:10.1016/j.tele.2015.08.014

Hsu, C. L., Yu, C. C., & Wu, C. C. (2014). Exploring the continuance intention of social networking websites: Empirical research. *Information Systems and e-Business Management*, *12*(2), 139–163. doi:10.100710257-013-0214-3

Hu, T., Stafford, T. F., Kettinger, W. J., Zhang, X. P., & Dai, H. (2018). Formation and effect of social media usage habit. *Journal of Computer Information Systems*, *58*(4), 334–343. doi:10.1080/08874417.2016.1261378

Huang, B. (2021, March). The Reasons for Douyin's Success from the Perspective of Business Model, Algorithm and Functions. In *6th International Conference on Financial Innovation and Economic Development (ICFIED 2021)* (pp. 320-325). Atlantis Press. 10.2991/aebmr.k.210319.058

Ifinedo, P. (2018). Determinants of students' continuance intention to use blogs to learn: An empirical investigation. *Behaviour & Information Technology*, *37*(4), 381–392. doi:10.1080/0144929X.2018.1436594

Islam, Z., Low, P. K. C., & Hasan, I. (2013). Intention to use advanced mobile phone services (AMPS). *Management Decision*, *51*(4), 824–838. doi:10.1108/00251741311326590

Karahanna, E., Straub, D. W., & Chervany, N. L. (1999). Information technology adoption across time: A cross-sectional comparison of pre-adoption and post-adoption beliefs. *Management Information Systems Quarterly*, *23*(2), 183–213. doi:10.2307/249751

Kim, B. (2011). Understanding antecedents of continuance intention in social-networking services. *Cyberpsychology, Behavior, and Social Networking*, *14*(4), 199–205. doi:10.1089/cyber.2010.0009 PMID:21192764

Kim, S. S., Malhotra, N. K., & Narasimhan, S. (2005). Two competing perspectives on automatic use: A theoretical and empirical comparison. *Information Systems Research*, *16*(4), 418–432. doi:10.1287/isre.1050.0070

Kline, R. B. (2016). *Principles and practice of structural equation modeling* (4th ed.). Guilford Press.

Kock, N. (2015). Common method bias in PLS-SEM: A full collinearity assessment approach. *International Journal of e-Collaboration*, *11*(4), 1–10. doi:10.4018/ijec.2015100101

Lankton, N. K., McKnight, D. H., & Thatcher, J. B. (2012). The moderating effects of privacy restrictiveness and experience on trusting beliefs and habit: An empirical test of intention to continue using a social networking website. *IEEE Transactions on Engineering Management*, *59*(4), 654–665. doi:10.1109/TEM.2011.2179048

LaRose, R. (2001). On the negative effects of e-commerce: A social-cognitive exploration of unregulated on-line buying. *Journal of Computer-Mediated Communication*, *6*(3).

Lee, W. K. (2014). The temporal relationships among habit, intention and IS uses. *Computers in Human Behavior*, *32*, 54–60. doi:10.1016/j.chb.2013.11.010

Leong, L. W., Ibrahim, O., Dalvi-Esfahani, M., Shahbazi, H., & Nilashi, M. (2018). The moderating effect of experience on the intention to adopt mobile social network sites for pedagogical purposes: An extension of the technology acceptance model. *Education and Information Technologies*, *23*(6), 2477–2498. doi:10.100710639-018-9726-2

Leong, L. W., Ibrahim, O., Dalvi-Esfahani, M., Shahbazi, H., & Nilashi, M. (2018). The moderating effect of experience on the intention to adopt mobile social network sites for pedagogical purposes: An extension of the technology acceptance model. *Education and Information Technologies*, *23*(6), 2477–2498. doi:10.100710639-018-9726-2

Limayem, M., & Cheung, C. M. K. (2008). Understanding information systems continuance: The case of Internet-based learning technologies. *Information & Management*, *45*(4), 227–232. doi:10.1016/j.im.2008.02.005

Limayem, M., Hirt, S. G., & Cheung, C. M. (2007). How habit limits the predictive power of intention: The case of information systems continuance. *Management Information Systems Quarterly*, *31*(4), 705–737. doi:10.2307/25148817

Lin, X., Featherman, M., & Sarker, S. (2017). Understanding factors affecting users' social networking site continuance: A gender difference perspective. *Information & Management*, *54*(3), 383–395. doi:10.1016/j.im.2016.09.004

Lu, H. P., & Su, P. Y. J. (2009). Factors affecting purchase intention on mobile shopping web sites. *Internet Research*, *19*(4), 442–458. doi:10.1108/10662240910981399

Luthen, M. D., & Soelaiman, L. (2022, April). Factors Affecting the Use of Social-Media TikTok to Improve SME Performance. *3rd Tarumanagara International Conference on the Applications of Social Sciences and Humanities*. Atlantis Press. 10.2991/assehr.k.220404.033

Lynch, J. G. Jr. (1982). On the external validity of experiments in consumer research. *The Journal of Consumer Research*, *9*(3), 225–239. doi:10.1086/208919

Magro, M. J., Ryan, S. D., & Prybutok, V. R. (2013). The social network application post-adoptive use model (SNAPUM): A model examining social capital and other critical factors affecting the post-adoptive use of Facebook. *Informing Science: the International Journal of an Emerging Transdiscipline*, *16*, 37–70. doi:10.28945/1777

Meral, K. Z. (2021). Social Media Short Video-Sharing TikTok Application and Ethics: Data Privacy and Addiction Issues. In Multidisciplinary Approaches to Ethics in the Digital Era (pp. 147-165). IGI Global.

Mirkovski, K., Jia, Y., Liu, L., & Chen, K. (2018). Understanding microblogging continuance intention: The directed social network perspective. *Information Technology & People*, *31*(1), 215–238. doi:10.1108/ITP-07-2015-0168

Moore, G. C., & Benbasat, I. (1996). Integrating diffusion of innovations and theory of reasoned action models to predict utilization of information technology by end-users. In *Diffusion and adoption of information technology* (pp. 132–146). Springer. doi:10.1007/978-0-387-34982-4_10

Morris, M. G., & Venkatesh, V. (2000). Age differences in technology adoption decisions: Implications for a changing work force. *Personnel Psychology*, *53*(2), 375–403. doi:10.1111/j.1744-6570.2000.tb00206.x

Mouakket, S. (2015). Factors influencing continuance intention to use social network sites: The Facebook case. *Computers in Human Behavior*, *53*, 102–110. doi:10.1016/j.chb.2015.06.045

Oliver, R. L. (1980). A cognitive model for the antecedents and consequences of satisfaction. *JMR, Journal of Marketing Research*, *17*(4), 460–469. doi:10.1177/002224378001700405

Omnicore. (2020). *TikTok by the numbers: Stats, demographics & fun facts*. Available at: https://www.omnicoreagency.com/tiktok-statistics

Orlikowski, W. J. (1992). The duality of technology: Rethinking the concept of technology in organizations. *Organization Science*, *3*(3), 398–427. doi:10.1287/orsc.3.3.398

Orlikowski, W. J., & Gash, D. C. (1994). Technological frames: Making sense of information technology in organizations. *ACM Transactions on Information Systems*, *12*(2), 174–207. doi:10.1145/196734.196745

Ortiz de Guinea, A., & Markus, M. L. (2009). Why break the habit of a lifetime? Rethinking the roles of intention, habit, and emotion in continuing information technology use. *Management Information Systems Quarterly*, *33*(3), 433–444. doi:10.2307/20650303

Pew Research Center. (2021). *Social Media Use in 2021*. Available at: https://www.pewresearch.org/internet/2021/04/07/social-media-use-in-2021

Rogers, E. M. (1983). *Diffusion of innovations* (3rd ed.). Macmillan Publishing.

Scherr, S., & Wang, K. (2021). Explaining the success of social media with gratification niches: Motivations behind daytime, nighttime, and active use of TikTok in China. *Computers in Human Behavior*, *124*, 106893. doi:10.1016/j.chb.2021.106893

Shiffrin, R. M., & Schneider, W. (1977). Controlled and automatic human information processing: II. Perceptual learning, automatic attending and a general theory. *Psychological Review, 84*(2), 127–190. doi:10.1037/0033-295X.84.2.127

Sledgianowski, D., & Kulviwat, S. (2009). Using social network sites: The effects of playfulness, critical mass and trust in a hedonic context. *Journal of Computer Information Systems, 49*(4), 74–83.

Smith, E. R., & DeCoster, J. (2000). Dual-process models in social and cognitive psychology: Conceptual integration and links to underlying memory systems. *Personality and Social Psychology Review, 4*(2), 108–131. doi:10.1207/S15327957PSPR0402_01

Statista. (2021a). *TikTok global monthly active users 2018-2021*. Available at: https://www.statista.com/statistics/1267892/tiktok-global-mau

Statista. (2021b). *TikTok users in Thailand 2017-2025*. Available at: https://www.statista.com/forecasts/1142641/tiktok-users-in-thailand

Straub, D., Boudreau, M. C., & Gefen, D. (2004). Validation Guidelines for IS Positivist Research. *Communications of the Association for Information Systems, 13*(1), 24.

Tamilmani, K., Rana, N. P., & Dwivedi, Y. K. (2018, June). Use of 'habit" is not a habit in understanding individual technology adoption: a review of UTAUT2 based empirical studies. In *International Working Conference on Transfer and Diffusion of IT* (pp. 277-294). Springer.

Taylor, S., & Todd, P. A. (1995). Understanding information technology usage: A Test of competing models. *Information Systems Research, 6*(2), 144–176. doi:10.1287/isre.6.2.144

Thompson, R. L., Higgins, C. A., & Howell, J. M. (1994). Influence of experience on personal computer utilization: Testing a conceptual model. *Journal of Management Information Systems, 11*(1), 167–187. doi:10.1080/07421222.1994.11518035

Tornatzky, L. G., & Klein, K. J. (1982). Innovation characteristics and innovation adoption-implementation: A meta-analysis of findings. *IEEE Transactions on Engineering Management, EM-29*(1), 28–45. doi:10.1109/TEM.1982.6447463

Van Slyke, C., Ilie, V., Lou, H., & Stafford, T. (2007). Perceived critical mass and the adoption of a communication technology. *European Journal of Information Systems, 16*(3), 270–283. doi:10.1057/palgrave.ejis.3000680

Venkatesh, V., Morris, M. G., Davis, G. B., & Davis, F. D. (2003). User acceptance of information technology: Toward a unified view. *Management Information Systems Quarterly, 27*(3), 425–478. doi:10.2307/30036540

Venkatesh, V., Thong, J. Y., & Xu, X. (2012). Consumer acceptance and use of information technology: Extending the unified theory of acceptance and use of technology. *Management Information Systems Quarterly, 36*(1), 157–17. doi:10.2307/41410412

Venkatesh, V., Thong, J. Y. L., & Xu, X. (2012). Consumer a acceptance and use of information technology: Extending the unified theory. *Management Information Systems Quarterly, 36*(1), 157–178. doi:10.2307/41410412

Wang, C., Harris, J., & Patterson, P. (2013). The roles of habit, self-efficacy, and satisfaction in driving continued use of self-service technologies: A longitudinal study. *Journal of Service Research, 16*(3), 400–414. doi:10.1177/1094670512473200

Wang, C., Teo, T. S., & Liu, L. (2020). Perceived value and continuance intention in mobile government service in China. *Telematics and Informatics, 48*, 101348. doi:10.1016/j.tele.2020.101348

Weimann, G., & Masri, N. (2020). Research note: spreading hate on TikTok. *Studies in Conflict & Terrorism*, 1-14.

Wilson, E. V., & Lankton, N. K. (2010). An integrative model of IT continuance: Applying measures of intention, prior IT use, and habit strength across conditions of sporadic and frequent IT use. DIGIT 2010 Proceedings.

Wilson, E. V., Mao, E., & Lankton, N. K. (2010). The distinct roles of prior IT use and habit strength in predicting continued sporadic use of IT. *Communications of the Association for Information Systems, 27*(12), 185–206. doi:10.17705/1CAIS.02712

Yoon, C., & Rolland, E. (2015). Understanding continuance use in social networking services. *Journal of Computer Information Systems, 55*(2), 1–8. doi:10.1080/08874417.2015.11645751

Zhang, X., Wu, Y., & Liu, S. (2019). Exploring short-form video application addiction: Socio-technical and attachment perspectives. *Telematics and Informatics, 42*, 101243. doi:10.1016/j.tele.2019.101243

Zolkepli, I. A., & Kamarulzaman, Y. (2015). Social media adoption: The role of media needs and innovation characteristics. *Computers in Human Behavior, 43*, 189–209. doi:10.1016/j.chb.2014.10.050

Compilation of References

Aboelmaged, M. G. (2010). Predicting e-procurement adoption in a developing country: An empirical integration of technology acceptance model and theory of planned behaviour. *Industrial Management & Data Systems, 110*(3), 392–414. doi:10.1108/02635571011030042

Abukhzam, M., & Lee, A. (2010). Workforce attitude on technology adoption and diffusion *The Built & Human. Environmental Reviews, 3*, 60–72.

Abulude, F.O. (2014). Digital publishing: how far in Nigeria? *Continental J. Information Technology, 8*(1), 18 – 23. doi:.23 doi:10.5707/cjit.2014.8.1.18

Adesanoye, F. A. (2007). Rebuilding the publishing industry, rebranding the NPA. *The Publisher, 14*, 3–13.

Agarwal, R., & Prasad, J. (1997). The role of innovation characteristics and perceived voluntariness in the acceptance of information technologies. *Decision Sciences, 28*(3), 557–582. doi:10.1111/j.1540-5915.1997.tb01322.x

Aggarwal, S., Srivastava, M. K., & Bharadwaj, S. S. (2020). Towards a definition and concept of collaborative resilience in supply chain: A study of 5 Indian supply chain cases. *International Journal of Information Systems and Supply Chain Management, 13*(1), 98–117. doi:10.4018/IJISSCM.2020010105

Aiouni, R., Bey, A., & Bensebaa, T. (2018). eALGO: An automated assessment tool of flowchart programs for novices. *International Journal of Innovation and Learning, 23*(2), 5. doi:10.1504/IJIL.2018.088785

Ajzen, I. (2002). Residual effects of past on later behavior: Habituation and reasoned action perspectives. *Personality and Social Psychology Review, 6*(2), 107–122. doi:10.1207/S15327957PSPR0602_02

Ajzen, I., & Fishbein, M. (1980). Understanding Attitudes and Predicting Social Behavior. *Organizational Behavior and Human Decision Processes, 50*(2), 179–211. doi:10.1016/0749-5978(91)90020-T

Ajzen, I., & Fishbein, M. (2000). Attitudes and the attitude-behavior relation: Reasoned and automatic processes. *European Review of Social Psychology, 11*(1), 1–33. doi:10.1080/14792779943000116

Akinsola, S., & Munepapa, J. (2021). Utilisation of e-collaboration tools for effective decision-making: A developing country public-sector perspective. *South African Journal of Information Management, 23*(1), 1–7. doi:10.4102ajim.v23i1.1099

Akpokodje, V.N., & Ukwuoma, S.C. (2016). *Evaluating the impact of eBook on reading motivation of students of higher learning in Nigerian universities*. Academic Press.

Al Omoush, K. S. (2018). Web-Based Collaborative Systems and Harvesting the Collective Intelligence in Business Organizations. *International Journal on Semantic Web and Information Systems, 14*(3), 31–52. doi:10.4018/IJSWIS.2018070102

Al-Bahrani, A., Patel, D., & Sheridan, B. J. (2017). Evaluating Twitter and its impact on student learning in principles of economics courses. *The Journal of Economic Education*, *48*(4), 243–253. doi:10.1080/00220485.2017.1353934

Al-Hasan, A. (2021). Effects of social network information on online language learning performance: A cross-continental experiment. *International Journal of e-Collaboration*, *17*(2), 72-87.

Alizadeh, V., & Kessentini, M. (2018). Reducing interactive refactoring effort via clustering-based multi-objective search. *Proceedings of the 33rd ACM/IEEE International Conference on Automated Software Engineering*, 464–474.

Alonso, M., Auxepaules, L., Lemeunier, T., & Py, D. (2008). Design of Pedagogical Feedbacks in a Learning Environment for Object-Oriented Modeling. *Promoting Software Modeling through Active Education.Educators Symposium of the ACM/IEEE 11th International Conference on Model Driven Engineering Languages and Systems (MoDELS'08)*, 39-50.

Al-Rahimi, W. M., Othman, M. S., & Musa, M. A. (2013). Using TAM model to measure the use of social media for collaborative learning. *International Journal of Engineering Trends and Technology*, *5*(2), 90–95.

Amadi, M. N. (2011). Supporting Learning in the Digital Age: E-learning Strategies for National Open University of Nigeria. *US-China Education Review*, *B7*, 975–981.

Amaya, N. Y., & Grueso, M. P. (2017). Factores distintivos de las organizaciones intensivas en conocimiento. *Podium (São Paulo)*, *32*, 75–87. doi:10.31095/podium.2017.32.6

Ambalov, I. A. (2018). A meta-analysis of IT continuance: An evaluation of the expectation-confirmation model. *Telematics and Informatics*, *35*(6), 1561–1571. doi:10.1016/j.tele.2018.03.016

Andrade, H., & Du, Y. (2007). Student responses to criteria-referenced self-Assessment. *Assessment and Evaluation. Int. Journal of Higher Education (Columbus, Ohio)*, *32*(2), 159–181.

Arcelli, D., Cortellessa, V., & Trubiani, C. (2015). Performance-based software model refactoring in fuzzy contexts. *International Conference on Fundamental Approaches to Software Engineering*, 149–164.

Arceneaux, P. C., & Dinu, L. F. (2018). The social mediated age of information: Twitter and Instagram as tools for information dissemination in higher education. *New Media & Society*, *20*(11), 4155–4176. doi:10.1177/1461444818768259

Arnous, S. (2014). *Conception générique d'un outil de configuration de e-TP EIAH* [Ph.D. dissertation]. INSA, Lyon, France.

Attai, D. J., Cowher, M. S., Al-Hamadani, M., Schoger, J. M., Staley, A. C., & Landercasper, J. (2015). Twitter social media is an effective tool for breast cancer patient education and support: Patient-reported outcomes by survey. *Journal of Medical Internet Research*, *17*(7), e188. doi:10.2196/jmir.4721 PMID:26228234

Avalos, B. (2011). Teacher professional development in teaching and teacher education over ten years. *Teaching and Teacher Education*, *27*(1), 10–20. doi:10.1016/j.tate.2010.08.007

Avizienis, A., Laprie, J. C., Randell, B., & Landwehr, C. (2004). Basic concepts and taxonomy of dependable and secure computing. *IEEE Transactions on Dependable and Secure Computing*, *1*(1), 11–33. doi:10.1109/TDSC.2004.2

Baber, H. (2021). Social interaction and effectiveness of the online learning–A moderating role of maintaining social distance during the pandemic COVID-19. Asian Education and Development Studies. behavior. *University of South Florida*, *2007*, 67–98.

Bandura, A. (1999). Social cognitive theory: An agentic perspective. *Asian Journal of Social Psychology*, *2*(1), 21–41. doi:10.1111/1467-839X.00024

Barhoun, R. (2021a). Reliable Collaboration in a Distributed Collaborative Environment: Modeling and Computing. International Review on Computers and Software.

Barhoun, R. (2021b). A Trust and Activity Based Access Control Model for Preserving Privacy and Sensitive Data in a Distributed and Collaborative System: Application to a Healthcare System. International Review on Computers and Software.

Barhoun, R., Ed-Daibouni, M., & Namir, A. (2019). An Extended Attribute-Based Access Control (ABAC) Model for Distributed Collaborative Healthcare System. *International Journal of Service Science, Management, Engineering, and Technology*, *10*(4), 81–94. doi:10.4018/IJSSMET.2019100105

Barkley, E., Cross, K., & Major, C. (2014). *Collaborative Learning Techniques: A Handbook for College Faculty* (2nd ed.). John Wiley & Sons.

Barnes, S. J. (2011). Understanding use continuance in virtual worlds: Empirical test of a research model. *Information & Management*, *48*(8), 313–319. doi:10.1016/j.im.2011.08.004

Barnes, S. J., & Bohringer, M. (2011). Modeling use continuance behavior in micro-blogging services: The case of Twitter. *Journal of Computer Information Systems*, *51*(4), 1–10.

Bartlett, D. (2017). Champions of local authority innovation revisited. *Local Government Studies, 43*(2), 142-149. doi:10.1080/03003930.2016.1245184

Barton, B. A., Adams, K. S., Browne, B. L., & Arrastia-Chisholm, M. C. (2021). The effects of social media usage on attention, motivation, and academic performance. *Active Learning in Higher Education*, *22*(1), 11–22. doi:10.1177/1469787418782817

Bayer, J. B., Anderson, I. A., & Tokunaga, R. (2022). Building and breaking social media habits. *Current Opinion in Psychology*, *45*, 279–288. doi:10.1016/j.copsyc.2022.101303 PMID:35255413

Belkadi, F., Bonjour, E., Camargo, M., Troussier, N., & Eynard, B. (2013). A Situation Model to Support Awareness in Collaborative Design. *International Journal of Human-Computer Studies*, *71*(1), 110–129. doi:10.1016/j.ijhcs.2012.03.002

Bennouna, M., Delestre, N., Pécuchet, J.-P., & Tanana, M. (2008). Évaluation du savoir-faire en électronique numérique à l'aide d'un algorithme de classification [Paper presentation]. The conférence Technologies de l'Information et de la Communication pour l'Éducation (TICE'08), Paris, France.

Bennouna, M., Delestre, N., Pécuchet, J.-P., & Tanana, M. (2009). Génération d'exemples pour l'évaluation de l'apprenant en électronique numérique à l'aide d'un algorithme de classification [Paper presentation]. The Conférence EIAH, France.

Berners-Lee, T., Masinter, L., & McCahill, M. (1994). RFC1738: Uniform Resource Locators. RFC Editor.

Bhasin, N. K., & Gulati, K. (2021). A Study of the Readiness of Indian Banks to Absorb COVID-19`s Impact Through New Emerging Technologies and Strategies for Competitive Advantage. In J. Zhao & J. Richards (Eds.), *E-Collaboration Technologies and Strategies for Competitive Advantage Amid Challenging Times* (pp. 50–75). IGI Global. doi:10.4018/978-1-7998-7764-6.ch003

Bhasin, N. K., & Gulati, K. (2021). Challenges of COVID-19 During 2020 and Opportunities for FinTech in 2021 for Digital Transformation of Business and Financial Institutions in India. In J. Zhao & J. Richards (Eds.), *E-Collaboration Technologies and Strategies for Competitive Advantage Amid Challenging Times* (pp. 282–299). IGI Global. doi:10.4018/978-1-7998-7764-6.ch011

Bhasin, N. K., & Rajesh, A. (2021). Impact of E-Collaboration Between Indian Banks and Fintech Companies for Digital Banking and New Emerging Technologies. *International Journal of e-Collaboration*, *17*(1), 15–35. doi:10.4018/IJeC.2021010102

Bhasin, N. K., & Rajesh, A. (2022). The Role of Emerging Banking Technologies for Risk Management and Mitigation to Reduce Non-Performing Assets and Bank Frauds in the Indian Banking System. *International Journal of e-Collaboration*, *18*(1), 1–25. doi:10.4018/IJeC.290293

Bhattacherjee, A. (2001). Understanding information systems continuance: An expectation-confirmation model. *Management Information Systems Quarterly*, *25*(3), 351–370. doi:10.2307/3250921

Bhattacherjee, A., & Lin, C. P. (2015). A unified model of IT continuance: Three complementary perspectives and crossover effects. *European Journal of Information Systems*, *24*(4), 364–373. doi:10.1057/ejis.2013.36

Bhorayal, R. (2021). Study: Indian AI Start Up in 2021. *Analytics India Magazine*. https://analyticsindiamag.com/study-indian-ai-startup-funding-in-2021/

Bibbo, Giandini, & Pons. (2016). Sistemas Colaborativos Con Awareness: Requisitos Para Su Modelado. *XLV Jornadas Argentinas de Informática e Investigación Operativa (45 JAIIO) - Simposio Argentino de Ingeniería de Software (ASSE 2016)*, 111–22.

Black, P., & Wiliam, D. (1998). Assessment and classroom learning. *Assessment in Education: Principles, Policy & Practice*, *5*(1), 7–74. doi:10.1080/0969595980050102

Blascovich, J. (2002). Social Influence within Immersive Virtual Environments. In R. Schroeder (Ed.), *The Social Life of Avatars: Presence and Interaction in Shared Virtual Environments* (pp. 127–145). Springer. doi:10.1007/978-1-4471-0277-9_8

Blessing, S. B., Blessing, J. S., & Fleck, B. K. B. (2012). Using Twitter to Reinforce Classroom Concepts. *Teaching of Psychology*, *39*(4), 268–271. doi:10.1177/0098628312461484

Boisot, M., & Child, J. (1999). Organizations as adaptive systems in complex environments: The case of China. *Organization Science*, *10*(3), 237–252. doi:10.1287/orsc.10.3.237

Bollinger, A. S., & Smith, R. D. (2001). Managing organizational knowledge as a strategic asset. *Journal of Knowledge Management*, *5*(1), 8–18. doi:10.1108/13673270110384365

Booth, A. (2006). "Brimful of STARLITE" toward standards for reporting literature searches. *Journal of the Medical Library Association*, *94*(4), 421–429. PMID:17082834

Boronenko, O., & Alexandrov, V. (2009). Next Generation E-learning based on Grid Technologies and Web 2.0. *Proceedings of ICL 2009*.

Boston University School of Public Health. (2013). *Diffusion of Innovations Theory*. https://sphweb.bumc.bu.edu/otlt/MPH-Modules/SB/SB721

Bouarab-Dahmani, F., Comparot, C., Si-Mohammed, M., & Charrel, P. J. (2017). Ontology-Based Teaching Domain Knowledge Management for E-Learning by Doing Systems. *Electronic Journal of Knowledge Management, 13*(2), 156-171.

Boussaha, K. (2011). Modélisation d'une situation d'évaluation de l'apprenant avec UML: CAS d'application pour l'apprentissage des langages de programmation [Paper presentation]. the 8eme colloque sur l'optimisation et les systèmes d'information. COSI'2011, Guelma, Algeria.

Boussaha, K. (2016). *l'évaluation de l'apprenant dans les environnements d'apprentissage de TéLé-TPs* [Ph.D. dissertation]. Badji Mokhtar Univ, Annaba, Algeria.

Boussaha, K., Mokhati, F., & Chaoua, Z. (2015b). *Using a matching approach to assess learners in their Practical works activity with a specific CEHL* [Paper presentation]. The 2nd International Conference on Multimedia Information processing, CITIM'2015, Mustapha Stambouli University -Faculty of Science and Technology, Mascara, Algeria.

Boussaha, K., Mokhati, F., & Taleb, N. (2012). *A novel learner self-assessment approach – application to practical work* [Paper presentation]. The 4th international conference on computer supported Education, the CSEDU 2012, Porto, Portugal.

Boussaha,K., & Bensebaa, T.(2009). *Design of an environment of Remote practical works between realities and prospects* [Paper presentation]. The International Conference of Novel Digital Technology.

Boussaha, K., Mokhati, F., & Chaoua, Z. (2015a). Architecture of a specific platform for training practical works: Integration of learners assessment component. *Int. J. of Technology Enhanced Learning*, *7*(3). doi:10.1504/IJTEL.2015.072809

Boussaha, K., Mokhati, F., & Hanneche, A. (2021). System-Based Ontology for Assessing Learner's Programming Practical Works Activities (S_Onto_ALPPWA). *International Journal of Web-Based Learning and Teaching Technologies*, *16*(5), 80–107. doi:10.4018/IJWLTT.20210901.oa5

Boyd, D. (2013). White flight in networked publics: How race and class shaped American teen engagement with MySpace and Facebook. In *Race after the Internet* (pp. 209–228). Routledge.

Boyd, D., & Ellison, N. (2007). Social network sites: Definition, history, and scholarship. *Journal of Computer-Mediated Communication*, *13*(1), 210–230. doi:10.1111/j.1083-6101.2007.00393.x

Brambilla, M., Cabot, J., & Wimmer, M. (2012). Model-Driven Software Engineering in Practice. *Synthesis Lectures on Software Engineering*, *1*(1), 1–182. doi:10.2200/S00441ED1V01Y201208SWE001

Briggs, de Vreede, & Kolfschoten. (2007). *ThinkLets for E-Collaboration*. IGI Global.

Brody, S. (2017). Web-Based Tools for Collaborative Research. *Library High Tech News, 34*.

Brown, M. E., & Hocutt, D. L. (2015). Learning to use, useful for learning: A usability study of Google apps for education. *Journal of Usability Studies*, *10*(4), 160.

Bstieler, L., Hermmert, M., & Barczak, G. (2017). The Changing Basis for Mutual Trust Formation in Inter-Organizational Relationships: A Dyadic Study of University-Industry Research Collaborations. *Journal of Business Research*, *74*, 47–54. doi:10.1016/j.jbusres.2017.01.006

Bucher, T., & Helmond, A. (2018). The affordance of social media platforms. The SAGE handbook of social media, 233–253.

Burbridge, M., & Morrison, G. (2021). A Systematic Literature Review of Partnership Development at the University-Industry-Government Nexus. *Sustainability*, *13*(13780), 1–24. doi:10.3390u132413780

Cabrera, A., & Cabrera, E. F. (2002). Knowledge-sharing dilemmas. *Organization Studies*, *23*(5), 687–710. doi:10.1177/0170840602235001

Calbi, M., Langiulli, N., Ferroni, F., Montalti, M., Kolesnikov, A., & Gallese, V. (2021). *The consequences of COVID-19 on social interactions: An online study on face covering*. Retrieved 04 24, 2022, from Scientific Reports: https://www.nature.com/articles/s41598-021-81780-w

Can thermal imaging take the heat out of the coronavirus crisis? (n.d.). Retrieved July 16, 2021, from https://www.ifsecglobal.com/global/thermal-imaging-coronavirus-crisis

Canepa, G. (2016). *Apache HTTP Server Cookbook: Hot Recipes for the Apache Web Server*. Exelixis Media.

Cantú-Ortiz, F. (2015). A Research and Innovation Ecosystem Model for Private Universities. In Private Universities in Latin America: Research and Innovation in the Knowledge Economy (pp. 109-130). MacMillan-Palgrave. doi:10.1057/9781137479389_6

Card Flight Small Business Report. (2020, Oct. 7). Retrieved July 16, 2021, from https://www.cardflight.com/small-business-impact/report-30

Carlson, J. R., & Zmud, R. W. (1999). Channel expansion theory and the experiential nature of media richness perceptions. *Academy of Management Journal*, *42*(2), 153–170.

Cassivi, L., Lefebvre, É., Lefebvre, L. A., & Majorique Léger, P. (2004). The Impact of E-collaboration Tools on Firms' Performance. *International Journal of Logistics Management*, *15*(1), 91–110. doi:10.1108/09574090410700257

Chamberlian, S. D. (2020). Real-time detection of COVID-19 epicenters within the United States using a network of smart thermoters. https://doi/org/ doi:10.1101/2020.04.06.20039909

Chamberlin, L., & Lehmann, K. (2011). Twitter in higher education. In C. Wankel (Ed.), Educating educators with social media (Cutting-edge technologies in higher education (vol. 1, pp. 375–391). Emerald Group Publishing. doi:10.1108/S2044-9968(2011)0000001021

Chang, C. C., Liang, C., & Chiu, Y. C. (2020). Direct or indirect effects from "perceived characteristic of innovation" to "intention to pay": Mediation of continuance intention to use e-learning. *Journal of Computers in Education*, *7*(4), 511–530. doi:10.100740692-020-00165-6

Chapman, A. L., & Marich, H. (2020). Using Twitter for Civic Education in K-12 Classrooms. *TechTrends*. Advance online publication. doi:10.100711528-020-00542-z

Chaudhary, M., Sodani, P. R., & Das, S. (2020). Effect of COVID-19 on Economy in India. *Some Reflections for Policy and Programme*, *22*(2), 169–180. doi:10.1177/0972063420935541

Chawla, V. (2020). *Top Credit Scoring StartUps that use AI*. StartUps. https://analyticsindiamag.com/top-credit-scoring-startups-in-india-that-use-ai/

Chen, B., Hatada, K., Okabayashi, K., Kuromiya, H., Hidaka, I., Yamamoto, Y., & Togami, K. (2019, November). Group Activity Recognition to Support Collaboration in Creative Digital Space. In Conference Companion Publication of the 2019 on Computer Supported Cooperative Work and Social Computing (pp. 175-179). doi:10.1145/3311957.3359471

Chen, Z., Chen, L., Ma, W., & Xu, B. (2016). Detecting Code Smells in Python Programs. *IEEE 2016 International Conference on Software Analysis, Testing and Evolution (SATE)*, 18–23. doi:10.1109ate.2016.10

Cheng, E. C. K. (2012). Knowledge strategies for enhancing school learning capacity. *International Journal of Educational Management*, *26*(6), 577–592. doi:10.1108/09513541211251406

Cheng, E. C. K. (2013). Applying knowledge management for school strategic planning. *KEDI Journal of Educational Policy*, *10*(2), 339–356.

Cheng, E. C. K. (2018). Managing records and archives in a Hong Kong school: A case study. *Records Management Journal*, *28*(2), 204–216. Advance online publication. doi:10.1108/RMJ-02-2017-0004

Cheng, E. C. K. (2019). Knowledge management strategies for sustaining Lesson Study. *International Journal for Lesson and Learning Studies*, *9*(2), 167–178. doi:10.1108/IJLLS-10-2019-0070

Cheng, E. C. K., & Chu, C. K. W. (2018). A Normative Knowledge Management Model for School Development. *International Journal of Learning and Teaching*, 4(1), 76–82. Advance online publication. doi:10.18178/ijlt.4.1.76-82

Cheng, E. C. K., Wu, S. W., & Hu, J. (2017). Knowledge management implementation in the school context: Case studies on knowledge leadership, storytelling, and taxonomy. *Educational Research for Policy and Practice*, 16(2), 177–188. doi:10.100710671-016-9200-0

Cheng, E. W. (2019). Choosing between the theory of planned behavior (TPB) and the technology acceptance model (TAM). *Educational Technology Research and Development*, 67(1), 21–37. doi:10.100711423-018-9598-6

Chen, J. L. (2011). The effects of education compatibility and technological expectancy on e-learning acceptance. *Computers & Education*, 57(2), 1501–1511. doi:10.1016/j.compedu.2011.02.009

Chilowicz, M. (2010). *Recherche de similarité dans du code source* [Ph.D.dissertation]. Paris –Est Univ.

Chinese startup Rokid pitches COVID-19 detection glasses in US. (n.d.). Retrieved July 16, 2021, from https://techcrunch.com/2020/04/16/chinese-startup-rokid-pitches-covid-19-detection-glasses-in-u-s

Chiu, T. K. (2021). Student engagement in K-12 online learning amid COVID-19: A qualitative approach from a self-determination theory perspective. *Interactive Learning Environments*, 1–14. doi:10.1080/10494820.2021.1926289

Choi, Y., Wen, H., Chen, M., & Yang, F. (2021). Sustainable Determinants Influencing Habit Formation among Mobile Short-Video Platform Users. *Sustainability*, 13(6), 3216. doi:10.3390u13063216

Choquet, C. Després, C., Iksal, S., Jacobi, P., Lekira, A, Py, D., Pham, T., Ngoc, T., & Ngoc, D. (2011). Using indicators during synchronous tutoring of practical work [Paper presentation]. The 11th IEEE International Conference on Advanced LearningTechnologies, ICALT'11.

Christopher, N.M. (2010). Applying marketing concepts to book publishing in Nigeria. *The Journal of International Social Research, 3*(11), 207-212.

Coates, J. (1993). *Women, men, and language: A sociolinguistic account of gender differences in language.* Longman.

Cochran-Smith, M., & Lytle, S. (1999). Relationships of knowledge and practice: Teacher learning community. *Review of Research in Education*, 24, 249–305.

Cohen, J. (1992). A power primer. *Psychological Bulletin*, *112*(1), 155–159. doi:10.1037/0033-2909.112.1.155 PMID:19565683

Collazos, C. A., Gutiérrez, F. L., Gallardo, J., Ortega, M., Fardoun, H. M., & Molina, A. I. (2019). Descriptive Theory of Awareness for Groupware Development. *Journal of Ambient Intelligence and Humanized Computing*, 10(12), 4789–4818. doi:10.100712652-018-1165-9

Collinson, V., & Cook, T. F. (2001). I don't have enough time - Teachers' interpretations of time as a key to learning and school change. *Journal of Educational Administration*, 39(3), 266–281. doi:10.1108/09578230110392884

Commclub. (2020). *Why TikTok is addicting? (It's not the reason you might think).* Available at: https://www.nyucommclub.com/content/2020/12/14/why-tiktok-is-addicting-its-not-the-reason-you-might-think

Commission of the European Community. (2000). *A Memorandum on Lifelong Learning.* SEC.

Conford, R. (2011). Digital publishing in West Africa: what works, what doesn't and why. *Transcripts from the information for change workshop.* htt://publishingperspetives.com/08/ditialpublishing-West Africa

Council of the European Union. (2017). *The Rome Declaration. Declaration of the leaders of 27 member states and of the European Council, the European Parliament and the European Commission.* Author.

Cozma, R., & Hallaq, T. (2019). Digital Natives as Budding Journalists: College TV Stations' Uses of Twitter. *Journalism & Mass Communication Educator, 74*(3), 306–317. doi:10.1177/1077695818805899

Cross, V., & Xinran, Y. (2011). *Investigating Ontological Similarity Theoretically with Fuzzy Set Theory, Information Content, and Tversky Similarity and Empirically with the Gene Ontology* [Paper presentation]. the 5th International Conference on Scalable Uncertainty Management, Dayton, OH.

Cruz, J., & Goyzueta, I. (2017). Design of a High Availability System with Proxy and Domain Name Service for Web Services. *Proceedings of 2017 IEEE XXIV International Conference on Electronics, Electrical Engineering and Computing (INTERCON).* 10.1109/INTERCON.2017.8079712

Das, A., Mallik, N., Bandyopadhyay, S., Das Bit, S., & Basak, J. (2016). Interactive information crowdsourcing for disaster management using SMS and Twitter: A research prototype. *IEEE International Conference on Pervasive Computing and Communication Workshops, PerCom Workshops.* doi:10.1109/PERCOMW.2016.7457101

Davidson-Shivers, G. V., Muilenburg, L., & Tanner, E. (2001). How do student participate in synchronous and asynchronous online discussions? *Journal of Educational Computing Research, 25*(4), 351–366. doi:10.2190/6DCH-BEN3-V7CF-QK47

Davis, A. L., Unruh, S. L., & Olynk, W. N. (2014). Assessing students' perceptions of internationalization of course content. *The Global Studies Journal, 6*(2), 1–12. doi:10.18848/1835-4432/CGP/v06i02/40884

Davis, F. D. (1989). Perceived usefulness, perceived ease of use, and user acceptance of information technology. *Management Information Systems Quarterly, 13*(3), 319–340. doi:10.2307/249008

De Corte, E., Mason, L., Depaepe, F., & Verschaffel, L. (2011). Self-regulation of mathematical knowledge and skills. In B. J. Zimmerman & D. H. Schunk (Eds.), Handbook of self-regulation of learning and performance. New York: Routledge.

de Vreede, G. J., Antunes, P., Vassileva, J., Gerosa, M. A., & Wu, K. (2016). Collaboration technology in teams and organizations: Introduction to the special issue. *Information Systems Frontiers, 18*(1), 1–6. doi:10.100710796-016-9632-3

Deep, S., Salleh, B. M., & Othman, H. (2019). Study on problem-based learning towards improving soft skills of students in effective communication class. *International Journal of Innovation and Learning, 25*(1), 17–34. doi:10.1504/IJIL.2019.096512

Delgado-Alonso, C., Valles-Salgado, M., Delgado-Álvarez, A., Yus, M., Gómez-Ruiz, N., Jorquera, M., ... Matías-Guiu, J. A. (2022). Cognitive dysfunction associated with COVID-19: A comprehensive neuropsychological study. *Journal of Psychiatric Research.*

Delors, J., Mufti, I. A., Amagi, I., Carneiro, R., Chung, F., & Geremek, B. (1996). International Commission on Education for the Twenty-first Century. *Learning: The Treasure Within.*

Demeyer, S. (2002). *Maintainability versus Performance: What's the Effect of Introducing Polymorphism? Technical Report, Lab. on Reeng.* Universiteit Antwerpen.

Deutsche Welle. (2021). *Why is TikTok so addictive?* Available at: https://www.dw.com/en/why-is-tiktok-so-addictive/av-58852826

Dewan, P. (1999). Architectures for collaborative applications. *Computer Supported Cooperative Work, 7,* 169–193.

Dhume, S. M., Pattanshetti, M. Y., Kamble, S. S., & Prasad, T. (2012, January). Adoption of social media by business education students: Application of Technology Acceptance Model (TAM). In *2012 IEEE International Conference on Technology Enhanced Education (ICTEE)* (pp. 1-10). IEEE. 10.1109/ICTEE.2012.6208609

Dissanayeke, U., Hewagamage, K. P., Ramberg, R., & Wikramanayake, G. (2016). Developing and testing an m-learning tool to facilitate guided-informal learning in agriculture. *International Journal on Advances in ICT for Emerging Regions*, *8*(3), 12. doi:10.4038/icter.v8i3.7165

Dolton, P., Marcenaro, O., Vries, R. D., & She, P. W. (2018). *The Global Teacher Status Index 2018*. The Varkey Foundation.

Dourish & Bly. (1992). *Portholes: Supporting Awareness in a Distributed Work Group.* Dl.Acm.Org.

Dourish, P., & Bellotti, V. (1992). Awareness and Coordination in Shared Workspaces. *Proceedings of the 1992 ACM Conference on Computer-Supported Cooperative Work - CSCW '92*, 107–14.

Duque, R., Rodríguez, M. L., Hurtado, M. V., Bravo, C., & Rodríguez-Domínguez, C. (2012). Integration of collaboration and interaction analysis mechanisms in a concern-based architecture for groupware systems. *Science of Computer Programming*, *77*(1), 29–45. doi:10.1016/j.scico.2010.05.003

Early Findings from Fitbit COVID-19 Study Suggest Fitbit Devices Can Identify Signs of Disease at Its Earliest Stages. (n.d.). Retrieved July 16, 2021, from https://blog.fitbit.com/early-findings-covid-19-study

Echebiri, A. (2005). Book production in Nigeria' in the new millennium. In F. A. Adesanoye & A. Ojeniyi (Eds.), *Issues in Book Publishing in Nigeria* (pp. 197–218). Heinemann Educational Publishers.

Eisenchlas, S. A. (2012). Gendered discursive practices online. *Journal of Pragmatics*, *44*(4), 335–345. doi:10.1016/j.pragma.2012.02.001

Ellis, C. A., Gibbs, S. J., & Rein, G. (1991). Groupware: Some Issues and Experiences. *Communications of the ACM*, *34*(1), 39–58. doi:10.1145/99977.99987

Elmer, T., Mepham, K., & Stadtfeld, C. (2020). *Students under lockdown: Comparisons of students' social networks and mental health before and during the COVID-19 crisis in Switzerland. Plos One, 7.*

Engeström, Y. (1999). Innovative learning in work teams: analyzing cycles of knowledge 8 creation in practice. *Perspectives on Activity Theory, 377*, 404.

Essop, M. F. (2020). Implementation of an authentic learning exercise in a postgraduate physiology classroom setting. *Advances in Physiology Education*, *44*(3), 496–500. doi:10.1152/advan.00083.2020 PMID:32795121

Eteng, I. E., & Okoro, J. C. (2019). A Collaborative Web-Based Learning Forum. *International Journal of Natural and Applied Sciences*, *8*(1&2), 48–55.

Eteng, I. E., & Oladimeji, S. O. (2019). Development of an Online Collaboration Tool for Research and Innovation in the University. *Journal of Management Science and Business Intelligence*, *4*(1), 25–31.

European Commission. (2010). *A strategy for smart, sustainable and inclusive growth.* COM.

European Commission. (2016). *A New Skills Agenda for Europe: Working together to strengthen human capital, employ-ability and competitiveness.* Author.

Euzenat, J., & Shvaiko, P. (2008). *Ten Challenges for Ontology Matching* [Paper presentation]. Confederated International Conferences, OTM 2008, Monterrey, Mexico.

Euzenat, J., DjoufakKengue, J. F., & Valtchev. (2010). The Results of the Ontology Alignment Evaluation Initiative. *Ontology Matching Workshop, International Semantic Web Conference.*

Evans, C. (2014). Twitter for teaching: Can social media be used to enhance the process of learning? *British Journal of Educational Technology, 45*(5), 902–915. doi:10.1111/bjet.12099

Eyitayo, S. A. (2011). Book, technology and infrastructural development: what the future holds for the book industry in Nigeria. In *Book Industry Technology and the Global Economic Trend.* Nigerian Book Fair Trust.

Farnese, M. L., Barbieri, B., Chirumbolo, A., & Patriotta, G. (2019). Managing Knowledge in Organizations: A Nonaka's SECI Model Operationalization. *Frontiers in Psychology, 10*, 2730. doi:10.3389/fpsyg.2019.02730 PMID:31920792

Feezell, J. T. (2019). An Experimental Test of Using Digital Media Literacy Education and Twitter to Promote Political Interest and Learning in American Politics Courses. *Journal of Political Science Education.* Advance online publication. doi:10.1080/15512169.2019.1694531

Feliz, T., Ricoy, C., & Feliz, S. (2013). Analysis of the use of Twitter as a learning strategy in master's studies. *Open Learning, 28*(3), 201–215. doi:10.1080/02680513.2013.870029

Finnegan, M. (2021). The Impact on Student Performance and Experience of the Move from Face-to-face to Online Delivery in Response to COVID-19: A Case Study in an Irish Higher Education Institute. *All Ireland Journal of Higher Education.*

Fox, A. R., & Wilson, E. G. (2015). Networking and the development of professionals: Beginning teachers building social capital. *Teaching and Teacher Education, 47*, 93–107. doi:10.1016/j.tate.2014.12.004

Freire, P. (1998). *Pedagogy of freedom: Ethics, democracy, and courage.* Rowman & Littlefield Publishers.

Fuentes, L., & Vallecillo, A. (2004). *An Introduction to UML Profiles.* Cepis.Org/Upgrade

Gallardo, J., Molina, A. I., Bravo, C., Redondo, M. A., & Collazos, C. A. (2011). An Ontological Conceptualization Approach for Awareness in Domain-Independent Collaborative Modeling Systems: Application to a Model-Driven Development Method. Expert Systems with Applications. doi:10.1016/j.eswa.2010.05.005

Gallardo, J., Bravo, C., & Redondo, M. A. (2012). A Model-Driven Development Method for Collaborative Modeling Tools. *Journal of Network and Computer Applications, 35*(3), 1086–1105. doi:10.1016/j.jnca.2011.12.009

Gallego, F., Molina, A. I., Gallardo, J., & Bravo, C. (2011). A Conceptual Framework for Modeling Awareness Mechanisms in Collaborative Systems. Lecture Notes in Computer Science (including subseries Lecture Notes in Artificial Intelligence and Lecture Notes in Bioinformatics), 6949. doi:10.1007/978-3-642-23768-3_56

Gao, F., Luo, T., & Zhang, K. (2012). Tweeting for learning: A critical analysis of research on microblogging in education published in 2008–2011. *British Journal of Educational Technology, 43*(5), 783–801. doi:10.1111/j.1467-8535.2012.01357.x

Gao, L., & Bai, X. (2014). An empirical study on continuance intention of mobile social networking services: Integrating the IS success model, network externalities and flow theory. *Asia Pacific Journal of Marketing and Logistics, 26*(2), 168–189. doi:10.1108/APJML-07-2013-0086

Garavelli, A. C., Gorgoglione, M., & Scozzi, B. (2002). Managing knowledge transfer by knowledge technologies. *Technovation, 22*(5), 269–279. doi:10.1016/S0166-4972(01)00009-8

Garg, M., Maralakunte, M., Garg, S., Dhooria, S., Sehgal, I., Bhalla, A. S., Vijayvergiya, R., Grover, S., Bhatia, V., Jagia, P., Bhalla, A., Suri, V., Goyal, M., Agarwal, R., Puri, G. D., & Sandhu, M. S. (2021). The conundrum of 'long-COVID-19: A narrative review. *International Journal of General Medicine, 14,* 2491–2506. doi:10.2147/IJGM.S316708 PMID:34163217

Garrigos-Simon, F. J., Lapiedra Alcamí, R., & Barberá Ribera, T. (2012). Social networks and web 3.0: Their impact on the management and marketing of organizations. *Management Decision, 50*(10), 1880–1890. doi:10.1108/00251741211279657

Geeraerts, K., Vanhoof, J., & Van den Bossche, P. (2016). Teachers' perceptions of intergenerational knowledge flows. *Teaching and Teacher Education, 56,* 150–161. .2016.01.024 doi:10.1016/j.tate

Gefen, D. (2003). TAM or just plain habit: A look at experienced online shoppers. *Journal of Organizational and End User Computing, 15*(3), 1–13. doi:10.4018/joeuc.2003070101

George, D., & Mallery, P. (2003). *SPSS for windows step by step: A simple guide and reference. 11.0 update.* Allyn and Bacon.

Geri, N., Winer, A., & Zaks, B. (2017). Challenging the six-minute myth of online video lectures: Can interactivity expand the attention span of learners? *Online Journal of Applied Knowledge Management, 5*(1), 101–111. doi:10.36965/OJAKM.2017.5(1)101-111

Giones, F. (2019). University-Industry Collaborations: An Industry Perspective. *Management Decision, 57*(12), 3258–3279. doi:10.1108/MD-11-2018-1182

Giuseppe, P., & Talia, D. (2010). UFOme: An Ontology Mapping System with Strategy Prediction Capabilities. *Data Knowledge, 69*(5), 444–471.

Glass, R. L. (1998). Maintenance: Less Is Not More. *IEEE Software.*

Gogan, J., Conboy, K., & Weiss, J. (2020). Dangerous Champions of IT Innovation. *ScholarSpace.* http://hdl.handle.net/10125/64494

González, F. (2010). *Project Europe 2030: Challenges and Opportunities* (A report to the European Council by the Reflection Group on the Future of the EU 2030), May 2010). The González Report.

Granovetter, M. S. (2001). The strength of Weak Ties. In *Social networks* (pp. 347–367). Academic Press.

Green, B. (2012). *What it Takes to Collaobrate.* Herman Miller Inc.

Greenberg, S., & Gutwin, C. (2016). Implications of We-Awareness to the Design of Distributed Groupware Tools. *Computer Supported Cooperative Work, 25*(4–5).

Greenhow, C., & Galvin, S. (2020). *Teaching with social media: Evidence-based strategies for making remote higher education less remote.* Information and Learning Sciences.

Greenhow, C., & Gleason, B. (2012). Twitteracy: Tweeting as a new literacy practice. *The Educational Forum, 76*(4), 464–478. doi:10.1080/00131725.2012.709032

Grudin, J. (1994). Computer Supported Cooperative Work: History and Focus. *Computer, 27*(5), 19–26. doi:10.1109/2.291294

Grudin, J., & Poltrock, S. E. (1997). Computer-Supported Cooperative Work and Groupware. *Advances in Computers, 45,* 269–320. doi:10.1016/S0065-2458(08)60710-X

Guibert, N. (2006). *Validation d'une approche basée sur l'exemple pour l'initiation à la programmation* [Ph.D. dissertation]. Poitiers univ, France.

Guillaume, D. (2006). *Vers une scénarisation de l'évaluation en EIAH* [Paper presentation]. EIAH.

Guittet, L., Guibert, N., & Girard, P. (2005). A study of the efficiency of an alternative programming paradigm to teach the basics of programming. LISI /ENSMA, 86961 Futuroscope Chasseneuil Cedex, France.

Gurjar, N. (2020). Leveraging social networks for authentic learning in distance learning teacher education. *TechTrends*, *64*(4), 666–677. doi:10.100711528-020-00510-7

Gutwin, C., & Greenberg, S. (2002). A Descriptive Framework of Workspace Awareness for Real-Time Groupware. *Computer Supported Cooperative Work*, *11*(3-4), 411–446. doi:10.1023/A:1021271517844

Gutwin, C., Greenberg, S., & Roseman, M. (1996). Workspace Awareness in Real-Time Distributed Groupware: Framework, Widgets, and Evaluation. *Proceedings of HCI '96*. 10.1007/978-1-4471-3588-3_18

Gwebu, K. L., Wang, J., & Guo, L. (2014). Continued usage intention of multifunctional friend networking services: A test of a dual-process model using Facebook. *Decision Support Systems*, *67*, 66–77. doi:10.1016/j.dss.2014.08.004

Hadadi, L., & Bouaarab-Dahmani, F. (2018). Multi-level computer-aided learner assessment in massive open online courses. *International Journal of Knowledge and Learning*, *12*(4), 2018.

Hadadi, L., & Bouaarab-Dahmani, F. (2019). Gradual Learners' Assessment in Massive Open Online Courses Based on ODALA Approach. *Journal of Information Technology Research*, *12*(July-September), 2019.

Hair, J. F., Anderson, R. E., Babin, B. J., & Black, W. C. (2014). *Multivariate data analysis* (7th ed.). Pearson Education.

Hair, J. F., Risher, J. J., Sarstedt, M., & Ringle, C. M. (2019). When to use and how to report the results of PLS-SEM. *European Business Review*, *31*(1), 2–24. doi:10.1108/EBR-11-2018-0203

Haliloğlu, E. Y. (2021). Efficiency Assessment of University-Industry Collaboration. In University-Industry Collaboration Strategies in the Digital Era (pp. 155-175). IGI Global.

Hall, F. (2020). *Creative Digital Collaboration in Publishing: How do digital collaborative partnerships work and how might publishing companies adapt to facilitate them?* [Doctoral thesis]. University College London. https://discovery.ucl.ac.uk/id/eprint/10110283/

Handoko, H., & Isa, S., SI, S., & Kom, M. (2018). High Availability Analysis with Database Cluster, Load Balancer and Virtual Router Redundancy Protocol. *Proceedings of the 3rd Internal Conference on Computer and Communication Systems (ICCCS 2018)*.

Handzic, M. (2011). Groupware. *Socio-Technical Knowledge Management,* 58–68. https://www.eclipse.org/acceleo/

Han, J. Y., Kim, J., Yoon, H. J., Shim, M., McTavish, F. M., & Gustafson, D. H. (2012). Social and psychological determinants of levels of engagement with an online breast cancer support group: Posters, lurkers, and nonusers. *Journal of Health Communication*, *17*(3), 356–371. doi:10.1080/10810730.2011.585696 PMID:22085215

Harris, A., & Jones, M. (2018). Leading schools as learning organizations. *School Leadership & Management*, *38*(4), 351–354. doi:10.1080/13632434.2018.1483553

Hashim, N. A. (2012). E-*commerce Adoption by Malaysian SMEs* [Doctoral thesis]. University of Sheffield. https://etheses.whiterose.ac.uk/14590/1/574600.pdf

Hellmuth, J., Barnett, T. A., Asken, B. M., Kelly, J. D., Torres, L., Stephens, M. L., Greenhouse, B., Martin, J. N., Chow, F. C., Deeks, S. G., Greene, M., Miller, B. L., Annan, W., Henrich, T. J., & Peluso, M. J. (2021). Persistent COVID-19-associated neurocognitive symptoms in non-hospitalized patients. *Journal of Neurovirology*, *27*(1), 191–195. doi:10.100713365-021-00954-4 PMID:33528824

Herlocker, J., Konstan, J., Borchers, A., & Riedl, J. (1999). An Algorithmic Framework for Performing Collaborative Filtering. In *Proceedings of the 22nd Annual International ACM SIGIR Conference on Research and Development in Information Retrieval*. New York, NY: Association for Computing Machinery. 10.1145/312624.312682

Hernandez-Ortega, B., Serrano-Cinca, C., & Gomez-Meneses, F. (2014). The firm's continuance intentions to use inter-organizational ICTs: The influence of contingency factors and perceptions. *Information & Management*, *51*(6), 747–761. doi:10.1016/j.im.2014.06.003

Herring, S. C., & Stoerger, S. (2014). Gender and (a)nonymity in computer-mediated communication. In S. Ehrlich, M. Meyerhoff, & J. Holmes (Eds.), The handbook of language, gender, and sexuality (2nd ed., pp. 567-586). John Wiley & Sons.

Herring, S. C. (2004). Computer-mediated communication and woman's place. In R. T. Lakoff (Ed.), *Language and woman's place: Text and commentaries* (pp. 216–222). Oxford University Press.

Herrington, J., Reeves, T. C., & Oliver, R. (2014). Authentic learning environments. Handbook of research on educational communications and technology, 401-412. doi:10.1007/978-1-4614-3185-5_32

Hey, T., Tansley, S., & Tolle, K. (2009). *The Fourth Paradigm: Data-Intensive Discovery*. Microsoft Research.

Highsmith, J. (2002). *Agile Software Development Ecosystem*. Addison-Wesley Longman Publishing.

Highsmith, J. III. (2000). *Adaptive Software Development: A Collaborative Approach to Managing Complex Systems*. Dorsel House Publishing Co.

Hill, S. S., Dore, F. J., Em, S. T., McLoughlin, R. J., Crawford, A. S., Sturrock, P. R., Maykel, J. A., Alavi, K., & Davids, J. S. (2021). Twitter Use Among Departments of Surgery With General Surgery Residency Programs. *Journal of Surgical Education*, *78*(1), 35–42. doi:10.1016/j.jsurg.2020.06.008 PMID:32631768

Hitchcock, L. I., & Battista, A. (2013). Social media for professional practice: Integrating Twitter with social work pedagogy. *The Journal of Baccalaureate Social Work*, *18*(Supplement 1), 33–45. doi:10.18084/basw.18.suppl-1.3751j3g390xx3g56

Hitchcock, L. I., & Young, J. A. (2016). Tweet, Tweet!: Using Live Twitter Chats in Social Work Education. *Social Work Education*, *35*(4), 457–468. doi:10.1080/02615479.2015.1136273

Hoe, S. L. (2006). Tacit knowledge, Nonaka and Takeuchi SECI model and informal knowledge processes. *International Journal of Organization Theory and Behavior*, *9*(4), 490–502. doi:10.1108/IJOTB-09-04-2006-B002

Hoppler, S. S., Segerer, R., & Nikitin, J. (2022). The Six Components of Social Interactions: Actor, Partner, Relation, Activities, Context, and Evaluation. *Front Phychol, 6*.

Hosen, M., Ogbeibu, S., Giridharan, B., Cham, T. H., Lim, W. M., & Paul, J. (2021). Individual motivation and social media influence on student knowledge sharing and learning performance: Evidence from an emerging economy. *Computers & Education*, *172*, 104262. doi:10.1016/j.compedu.2021.104262

Hovav, A., & Gray, P. (2001). *Managing academic electronic publishing six case studies*. Paper presented at the 9th European conference an information systems, Bled, Slovenia.

Howard, M. C., & Gutworth, M. B. (2020). A meta-analysis of virtual reality training programs for social skill development. *Computers & Education*, *144*, 103707. doi:10.1016/j.compedu.2019.103707

Hsiao, C. H., Chang, J. J., & Tang, K. Y. (2016). Exploring the influential factors in continuance usage of mobile social Apps: Satisfaction, habit, and customer value perspectives. *Telematics and Informatics*, *33*(2), 342–355. doi:10.1016/j.tele.2015.08.014

Hsieh, C.-Y., Le My, C., Ho, K. T., & Cheng, Y. C. (2017). Identification and refactoring of exception handling code smells in javascript. *Journal of Internet Technology, 18*(6), 1461–1471.

Hsieh, Y. P. (2012). Online social networking skills: The social affordances approach to digital inequality. *First Monday, 17*(4). Advance online publication. doi:10.5210/fm.v17i4.3893

Hsu, C. L., Yu, C. C., & Wu, C. C. (2014). Exploring the continuance intention of social networking websites: Empirical research. *Information Systems and e-Business Management, 12*(2), 139–163. doi:10.100710257-013-0214-3

Huang, B. (2021, March). The Reasons for Douyin's Success from the Perspective of Business Model, Algorithm and Functions. In *6th International Conference on Financial Innovation and Economic Development (ICFIED 2021)* (pp. 320-325). Atlantis Press. 10.2991/aebmr.k.210319.058

Hua, Y., Loftness, V., Kraur, R., & Powell, K. (2010). Workplace Collaborative Space Layout Typology and Occupant of Collaboration Environment. *Environment and Planning. B, Planning & Design, 37*(3), 429–448. doi:10.1068/b35011

Hu, T., Stafford, T. F., Kettinger, W. J., Zhang, X. P., & Dai, H. (2018). Formation and effect of social media usage habit. *Journal of Computer Information Systems, 58*(4), 334–343. doi:10.1080/08874417.2016.1261378

Ifeduba, E. (2018). Book Censorship in Nigeria: A study of Origin, Methods and Motivations. *Library Philosophy and Practice,* 1954. https://digitalcommons.unl.edu/libphilpr

Ifeduba, E. (2021). Predictors of E-Publishing Adoption in Environments of Uncertainty. *Global Knowledge, Memory and Communication, 70.* https://www.emerald.com/insight/content/doi/10.1108/GKMC-11-2020-0164/full/html doi:10.1108/GKMC-11-2020-0164

Ifeduba, E. (2020). Digital Publishing Readiness in Nigeria's Print Book Market, *Global Knowledge. Memory and Communication, 69*(6/7), 427–442. doi:10.1108/GKMC-04-2019-0047

Ifinedo, P. (2018). Determinants of students' continuance intention to use blogs to learn: An empirical investigation. *Behaviour & Information Technology, 37*(4), 381–392. doi:10.1080/0144929X.2018.1436594

Ihrig, M., Canals, A., Boisot, M. H., & Nordberg, M. (2012). Mapping critical knowledge assets in the ATLAS Collaboration at CERN: An I-Space approach. *OLKC 2012-International Conference on Organizational Learning, Knowledge and Capabilities.*

Indeed Editorial Team. (2021). *Outsourcing: Advantages and Disadvantages.* https://www.indeed.com/career-advice/career-development/outsourcing-benefits

Indira, B., Valarmathi, K., & Devaraj, D. (2019). An approach to enhance packet classification performance of software-defined network using deep learning. *Soft Computing, 23*(18), 8609–8619. 03975-8. doi:10.1007/s00500-019-

Information Resources Management Association. (2018). *E-Planning and Collaboration: Concepts, Methodologies, Tools, and Applications* (3 Volumes). https://www.igi-global.com/book/collaborative-distributed-research/58272 doi:10.4018/978-1-5225-5646-6

Innes, J. E., & Booher, D. E. (2016). Collaborative rationality as a strategy for working with wicked problems. *Landscape and Urban Planning, 154,* 8–10. doi:10.1016/j.landurbplan.2016.03.016

Islam, Z., Low, P. K. C., & Hasan, I. (2013). Intention to use advanced mobile phone services (AMPS). *Management Decision, 51*(4), 824–838. doi:10.1108/00251741311326590

Italian airport leads Europe in adopting AR thermal scanning helmets. (n.d.). Retrieved July 16, 2021, from https://venturebeat.com/2020/05/07/italian-airport-leads-europe-in-adopting-ar-thermal-scanning-helmets

Ito, M., Gutiérrez, K., Livingstone, S., Penuel, B., Rhodes, J., Salen, K., & Watkins, S. C. (2013). *Connected learning: An agenda for research and design*. Digital Media and Learning Research Hub. Retrieved from https://dmlhub.net/

Ivanec, T. P. (2022). The Lack of Academic Social Interactions and Students' Learning Difficulties during COVID-19 Faculty Lockdowns in Croatia: The Mediating Role of the Perceived Sense of Life Disruption Caused by the Pandemic and the Adjustment to Online Studying. *Social Sciences*.

IvyPanda. (2021, February 23). *E-Collaboration: Strategic and Competitive Opportunities*. https://ivypanda.com/essays/e-collaboration-strategic-and-competitive-opportunities/

Jader, O., Zeebaree, S., & Zebari, R. (2019). A State of Art Survey for Web Server Performance Measurement and Load Balancing Mechanisms. *International Journal of Scientific & Technology Research*, 8(8), 535–543.

JISC. (2021). *What is digital capability?* https://www.digitalcapability.jisc.ac.uk/what-is-digital-capability/

Jones, A., & Kessler, M. (2020). Teachers' Emotion and Identity Work During a Pandemic. *Conceptual Analysis*.

Juan, A. A. (2012). *Collaborative and Distributed E-Research: Innovations in Technologies, Strategies and Applications*. https://www.igi-global.com/book/collaborative-distributed-research/58272 doi:10.4018/978-1-4666-0125-3

Kahsay, M. (2017). The Links Between Academic Research and Economic Development in Ethiopia: The Case of Addis Abba University. *European Journal of STEM Education*, 2(2), 1–10. doi:10.20897/ejsteme.201705

Kahu, E. R. (2013). Framing student engagement in higher education. *Studies in Higher Education*, 38(5), 758–773. doi:10.1080/03075079.2011.598505

Kamoun, A., Tazi, S., & Drira, K. (2012). FADYRCOS, a Semantic Interoperability Framework for Collaborative Model-Based Dynamic Reconfiguration of Networked Services. *Computers in Industry*, 63(8), 756–765. doi:10.1016/j.compind.2012.08.007

Karahanna, E., Straub, D. W., & Chervany, N. L. (1999). Information technology adoption across time: A cross-sectional comparison of pre-adoption and post-adoption beliefs. *Management Information Systems Quarterly*, 23(2), 183–213. doi:10.2307/249751

Kauffman, L., Weisberg, E. M., Zember, W. F., & Fishman, E. K. (2021). #RadEd: How and why to use twitter for online radiology education. *Current Problems in Diagnostic Radiology*, 50(7), 369–373. Advance online publication. doi:10.1067/j.cpradiol.2021.02.002 PMID:33637393

Kaya, M. (2018). Effective software refactoring process. In *2018 6th International Symposium on Digital Forensic and Security (ISDFS)*. IEEE.

Kennedy, A., & Carter, K. (2003). *MDA Guide Version 1.0.1*. Object Management Group.

Kerr, S. L., & Schmeichel, M. J. (2018). Teacher Twitter Chats: Gender Differences in Participants' Contributions. *Journal of Research on Technology in Education*, 50(3), 241–252. doi:10.1080/15391523.2018.1458260

Kies, S. C. (2018). Social media impact on attention span. *Journal of Management & Engineering Integration*, 11(1), 20–27.

Kim, B. (2011). Understanding antecedents of continuance intention in social-networking services. *Cyberpsychology, Behavior, and Social Networking*, 14(4), 199–205. doi:10.1089/cyber.2010.0009 PMID:21192764

Kim, S. S., Malhotra, N. K., & Narasimhan, S. (2005). Two competing perspectives on automatic use: A theoretical and empirical comparison. *Information Systems Research*, 16(4), 418–432. doi:10.1287/isre.1050.0070

Kim, Y., Jeong, S., Ji, Y., Lee, S., Kwon, K. H., & Jeon, J. W. (2015). Smartphone response system using twitter to enable effective interaction and improve engagement in large classrooms. *IEEE Transactions on Education*, *58*(2), 98–103. doi:10.1109/TE.2014.2329651

Kleppe, Warmer, & Bast. (2003). The Model Driven Architecture: Practice and Promise. Addison-Wesley.

Kline, R. B. (2016). *Principles and practice of structural equation modeling* (4th ed.). Guilford Press.

Kock, N. (2015). Common method bias in PLS-SEM: A full collinearity assessment approach. *International Journal of e-Collaboration*, *11*(4), 1–10. doi:10.4018/ijec.2015100101

Kock, N., Davison, R., Wazlawick, R., & Ocker, R. (2001). E-collaboration: A look at past research and future challenges. *Journal of Systems and Information Technology*, *5*(1), 1–8. doi:10.1108/13287260180001059

Konys, A.(2018). An Ontology-Based Knowledge Modelling for a Sustainability Assessment Domain. *Sustainability*, *10*, 300. doi:10.3390/su10020300

Koob, C., Schröpfer, K., Coenen, M., Kus, S., & Schmidt, N. (2021). Factors influencing study engagement during the COVID-19 pandemic: A cross-sectional study among health and social professions students. *PLoS One*, *16*(7), e0255191. doi:10.1371/journal.pone.0255191 PMID:34314450

Kools, M., & Stoll, L. (2016). *What Makes a School a Learning Organisation?* doi:10.1787/19939019

Kotsopoulos, D. (2010). When collaborative is not collaborative: Supporting student learning through self-surveillance. *International Journal of Educational Research*, *49*(4-5), 129–140. doi:10.1016/j.ijer.2010.11.002

Kumari, A., & Verma, J. (2015). Impact of social networking sites on social interaction-a study of college students. *Journal of the Humanities and Social Sciences*, *4*(2), 55–62.

Kumar, L., Satapathy, S. M., & Krishna, A. (2018). Application of smote and lssvm with various kernels for predicting refactoring at method level. *International Conference on Neural Information Processing*, 150–161.

Kumar, S. U., Kumar, D. T., Christopher, B. P., & Doss, C. G. P. (2020). The Rise and Impact of COVID-19 in India. *Frontiers in Medicine*, *7*, 250. doi:10.3389/fmed.2020.00250 PMID:32574338

Kunda, D., Chihana, S., & Muwanei, S. (2017). Web Server Performance of Apache and Niginx: A Systematic Literature Review. *Computer Engineering and Intelligent System*, *8*(2), 43–52.

Lacka, E., Wong, T. C., & Haddoud, M. Y. (2021). Can digital technologies improve students' efficiency? Exploring the role of Virtual Learning Environment and Social Media use in Higher Education. *Computers & Education*, *163*, 104099. doi:10.1016/j.compedu.2020.104099

Laidlaw, K. E., Foulsham, T., Kuhn, G., & Kingstone, A. (2011). Potential social interactions are important to social attention. *Proceedings of the National Academy of Sciences of the United States of America*, *108*(14), 5548–5553. doi:10.1073/pnas.1017022108 PMID:21436052

Lankton, N. K., McKnight, D. H., & Thatcher, J. B. (2012). The moderating effects of privacy restrictiveness and experience on trusting beliefs and habit: An empirical test of intention to continue using a social networking website. *IEEE Transactions on Engineering Management*, *59*(4), 654–665. doi:10.1109/TEM.2011.2179048

LaRose, R. (2001). On the negative effects of e-commerce: A social-cognitive exploration of unregulated on-line buying. *Journal of Computer-Mediated Communication*, *6*(3).

Latteier & Pelletier. (2002). *The Zope Book*. Academic Press.

Lave, J., & Wenger, E. (2006). *Situated learning. From observation to active participation in social contexts.* Erickson Editions.

Lee, W. K. (2014). The temporal relationships among habit, intention and IS uses. *Computers in Human Behavior*, *32*, 54–60. doi:10.1016/j.chb.2013.11.010

Lemo, T. (2004). *Publishing in a difficult economic environment.* Academic Press.

Leong, L. W., Ibrahim, O., Dalvi-Esfahani, M., Shahbazi, H., & Nilashi, M. (2018). The moderating effect of experience on the intention to adopt mobile social network sites for pedagogical purposes: An extension of the technology acceptance model. *Education and Information Technologies*, *23*(6), 2477–2498. doi:10.100710639-018-9726-2

Leu, D. J., Kinzer, C., Coiro, J., & Cammack, D. (2004). Toward a theory of new literacies emerging from the Internet and other Information and Communication Technologies. In R. Ruddell & N. Unrau (Eds.), *Theoretical models and processes of reading* (5th ed., pp. 1570–1613). International Reading Association.

Li, L., Flynn, K. S., DeRosier, M. E., Weiser, G., & Austin-King, K. (2021). Social-Emotional Learning Amidst CO-VID-19 School Closures: Positive Findings from an Efficacy Study of Adventures Aboard the S.S. GRIN Program. *Frontiers in Education*.

Limayem, M., & Cheung, C. M. K. (2008). Understanding information systems continuance: The case of Internet-based learning technologies. *Information & Management*, *45*(4), 227–232. doi:10.1016/j.im.2008.02.005

Limayem, M., Hirt, S. G., & Cheung, C. M. (2007). How habit limits the predictive power of intention: The case of information systems continuance. *Management Information Systems Quarterly*, *31*(4), 705–737. doi:10.2307/25148817

Lin, F., Lin, S., & Huang, T. (2008). Knowledge sharing and creation in a teachers' professional virtual community. *Computers & Education*, *50*(3), 742–756. doi:10.1016/j.compedu.2006.07.009

Lin, X., Featherman, M., & Sarker, S. (2017). Understanding factors affecting users' social networking site continuance: A gender difference perspective. *Information & Management*, *54*(3), 383–395. doi:10.1016/j.im.2016.09.004

Little, J. W. (1990). The persistence of privacy: Autonomy and initiative in teachers' professional relations. *Teachers College Record*, *91*(4), 509–536. doi:10.1177/016146819009100403

Liu, H., Jin, J., Xu, Z., Bu, Y., Zou, Y., & Zhang, L. (2019). Deep learning based code smell detection. *IEEE Transactions on Software Engineering*.

Li, X., He, J., Zhao, B., Fang, J., Zhang, Y., & Liang, H. (2016). A Method for Trust Quantification in Cloud Computing Environments. *International Journal of Distributed Sensor Networks*, *12*(2), 5052614. doi:10.1155/2016/5052614

Lockee, B. (2021). Online education in the post-COVID era. *Nature Electronics*, *4*(1), 5–6. doi:10.103841928-020-00534-0

Loda, T., Löffler, T., Erschens, R., Zipfel, S., & Herrmann-Werner, A. (2020). Medical education in times of COVID-19: German students' expectations–A cross-sectional study. *PLoS One*, *15*(11), e0241660. doi:10.1371/journal.pone.0241660 PMID:33206678

Lu, H. P., & Su, P. Y. J. (2009). Factors affecting purchase intention on mobile shopping web sites. *Internet Research*, *19*(4), 442–458. doi:10.1108/10662240910981399

Luthen, M. D., & Soelaiman, L. (2022, April). Factors Affecting the Use of Social-Media TikTok to Improve SME Performance. *3rd Tarumanagara International Conference on the Applications of Social Sciences and Humanities.* Atlantis Press. 10.2991/assehr.k.220404.033

Lynch, J. G. Jr. (1982). On the external validity of experiments in consumer research. *The Journal of Consumer Research, 9*(3), 225–239. doi:10.1086/208919

M, N., S, P., RM, P., M, D., M, V., & HR, A. (2020). Internet of Things for Current COVID-19 and Future Pandemics: an Exploratory Study. *Journal of Healthcare Informatics Research, 4*(4), 325–364. doi:10.1007/s41666-020-00080-6

Magro, M. J., Ryan, S. D., & Prybutok, V. R. (2013). The social network application post-adoptive use model (SNAPUM): A model examining social capital and other critical factors affecting the post-adoptive use of Facebook. *Informing Science: the International Journal of an Emerging Transdiscipline, 16*, 37–70. doi:10.28945/1777

Malar, M., & Prabhu, J. (2020). A Distributed Collaborative Trust Service Recommender System for Secure Cloud Computing. *Transactions on Emerging Telecommunications Technologies, 31*.

Mansour, O., Askenas, L., & Ghazawneh, A. (2013). *Social media and organizing–An empirical analysis of the role of wiki affordances in organizing practices.* Academic Press.

Manzo, K. K. (2009). Twitter lessons in 140 characters or less. *Education Week, 29*, 1–14.

Marinho, A., Silva, R., & Santos, G. (2020). Why Most University-Industry Partnerships Fail to Endure and How to Create Value and Gain Competitive Advantage through Collaborations: A Systematic Review. *Quality Innovation Prosperity, 24*(2), 34–50. doi:10.12776/qip.v24i2.1389

McAdam, R., & McCreedy, S. (1999). A critical review of knowledge management models. *The Learning Organization, 6*(3), 91–100. doi:10.1108/09696479910270416

McCarthy, K. S., Kneavel, M., & Ernst, W. (2021). Psychometric properties of concussion knowledge and cognitive mediators of reporting measures. *Brain Injury, 35*(10), 1210–1217. doi:10.1080/02699052.2021.1959064 PMID:34347541

McConnell, D. (1997). Interaction patterns of mixed sex groups in educational computer conferences. Part I-empirical findings. *Gender and Education, 9*(3), 345–363. doi:10.1080/09540259721303

Meeks, L. (2016). Gendered styles, gendered differences: Candidates' use of personalization and interactivity on Twitter. *Journal of Information Technology & Politics, 13*(4), 295–310. doi:10.1080/19331681.2016.1160268

Mens, T., Demeyer, S., & Janssens, D. (2002). *Formalising Behavior Preserving Program Transformations.* Graph Transformation.

Meral, K. Z. (2021). Social Media Short Video-Sharing TikTok Application and Ethics: Data Privacy and Addiction Issues. In Multidisciplinary Approaches to Ethics in the Digital Era (pp. 147-165). IGI Global.

Mioara, M. S. (2012). The impact of technological and communication innovation in the knowledge-based society. *Procedia: Social and Behavioral Sciences, 51*, 263–267. doi:10.1016/j.sbspro.2012.08.156

Mirkovski, K., Jia, Y., Liu, L., & Chen, K. (2018). Understanding microblogging continuance intention: The directed social network perspective. *Information Technology & People, 31*(1), 215–238. doi:10.1108/ITP-07-2015-0168

Mitrovic, A., & Suraweera, P. (2004). An Intelligent Tutoring System for Entity Relationship Modelling. *International Journal of Artificial Intelligence in Education, 14*(3), 375–417.

Mohammed, A. M. (2011). *Publishing education and the global economic trend. In Book Industry, Technology and the Global Economic Trend.* Nigerian Book Fair Trust.

Molina, A. I., Gallardo, J., Redondo, M. A., Ortega, M., & Giraldo, W. J. (2013). Metamodel-Driven Definition of a Visual Modeling Language for Specifying Interactive Groupware Applications: An Empirical Study. *Journal of Systems and Software, 86*(7), 1772–1789. doi:10.1016/j.jss.2012.07.049

Monojoy, B. (2018). Digital Publishing Trends: Mary Meeker's 2018 Report. *What's New in Publishing.* https://whatsnewinpublishing.com/key-insights-for-publishers-from-mary-meekers-internet-trends-2018-report/

Montebello, A. R. (2003). Beyond Teams: Building the Collaborative Organization. *Personnel Psychology, 56*(4), 1070.

Moore, G. C., & Benbasat, I. (1996). Integrating diffusion of innovations and theory of reasoned action models to predict utilization of information technology by end-users. In *Diffusion and adoption of information technology* (pp. 132–146). Springer. doi:10.1007/978-0-387-34982-4_10

Mora, H., Signes-Pont, M. T., Fuster-Guilló, A., & Pertegal-Felices, M. L. (2020). A collaborative working model for enhancing the learning process of science & engineering students. *Computers in Human Behavior, 103,* 140–150. doi:10.1016/j.chb.2019.09.008

Morris, M. G., & Venkatesh, V. (2000). Age differences in technology adoption decisions: Implications for a changing work force. *Personnel Psychology, 53*(2), 375–403. doi:10.1111/j.1744-6570.2000.tb00206.x

Mouakket, S. (2015). Factors influencing continuance intention to use social network sites: The Facebook case. *Computers in Human Behavior, 53,* 102–110. doi:10.1016/j.chb.2015.06.045

Mufid, M. R., Basofi, A., Mawaddah, S., Khotimah, K., & Fuad, N. (2020). Risk diagnosis and mitigation system of covid-19 using expert system and web scraping. *IES 2020 - International Electronics Symposium: The Role of Autonomous and Intelligent Systems for Human Life and Comfort,* 577–583. 10.1109/IES50839.2020.9231619

Mulej, M. (2008). The Contemporary School and Knowledge Management. *Journal on Efficiency and Responsibility in Education and Science, 1*(1), 1–19.

Murumba, J., & Micheni, E. (2017). Grid Computing for Collaborative Research Systems in Kenyan Universities. *The International Journal of Engineering and Science, 6*(4), 24–31. doi:10.9790/1813-0604022431

Mutambara, D., & Bayaga, A. (2021). Determinants of mobile learning acceptance for STEM education in rural areas. *Computers & Education, 160,* 104010. doi:10.1016/j.compedu.2020.104010

Ngetich, M., Otieno, D., & Kimwele, M. (2019). A Model for Code Restructuring, A Tool for Improving Systems Quality In Compliance With Object Oriented Coding Practice. *International Journal of Computer Applications Technology and Research, 8*(5), 196–200. doi:10.7753/IJCATR0805.1010

Ngulube, P. (2003). Using the SECI knowledge management model and other tools to communicate and manage tacit indigenous knowledge. *Innovation, 27*(1), 21–30.

Nicola, M., Alsafi, Z., Sohrabi, C., Kerwan, A., Al-Jabir, A., Iosifidis, C., Agha, M., & Agha, R. (2020). The socio-economic implications of the coronavirus pandemic (COVID-19): A review. *International Journal of Surgery (London, England), 78,* 185–193. doi:10.1016/j.ijsu.2020.04.018 PMID:32305533

Nicoland, D., & Macfarlane-Dick, D. (2006). Formative assessment and self-regulated learning: A model and seven principles of good feedback practice. *Int. Journal of Higher Education, 31*(2), 199–218.

Nissinen, S., Vartiainen, H., Vanninen, P., & Pollanen, S. (2019). Connected learning in international learning projects Emergence of a hybrid learning system. *International Journal of Information and Learning Technology, 36*(5), 381–394. doi:10.1108/IJILT-05-2018-0055

Nizzolino, S., & Canals, A. (2021). Social Network Sites as Community Building Tools in Educational Networking. *International Journal of e-Collaboration (IJeC), 17*(4), 132-167. doi:10.4018/IJeC.2021100110

Nonaka, I., & Konno, N. (1998). The Concept of "Ba": Building a foundation for knowledge creation. *California Management Review, 40*(3), 40–54. doi:10.2307/41165942

NRF. (n.d.). *Coronavirus leads to more use of contactless credit cards and mobile payments despite cost and security concerns.* Retrieved July 16, 2021, from https://nrf.com/media-center/press-releases/coronavirus-leads-more-use-contactless-credit-cards-and-mobile-payments

Nwakpa, P. (2015). Research in Tertiary Institutions in Nigeria: Issues, Challenges and Prospects: Implication for Educational Managers. *IOSR Journal of Humanities and Social Science, 20*(6), 45-49.

Nwankwo, V. (2005). Print-On-Demand: an African publisher's experience. In F. A. Adesanoye & A. Ojeniyi (Eds.), *Issues in Book Publishing in Nigeria* (pp. 173–183). Heinemann Educ. Books.

O'Dea, S. (2020). *Number of smartphone users in Nigeria from 2014 to 2025.* https://www.statista.com/statistics/467187/forecast-of-smartphone-users-in-nigeria/

O'Leary, B. (2014). An architecture of collaboration. *Publishing Research Quarterly, 30*(3). www.researchgate.net

Obidiegwu, D. (2009). *The book chain and national development. In Chain and National Development.* NBFT.

Obidiegwu, O. (2006). Enhancing productivity in the publishing industry. *The Publisher, 13*(1), 3–10.

Obiwuru, T. C., Oluwalaiye, O. B., & Okwu, A. T. (2011). External and internal environments of business in Nigeria: An appraisal. *International Bulletin of Business Administration., 12*, 15–23. www.googlescholar.com

OECD. (2020). TALIS 2018 Results (Volume II): Teachers and school leaders as valued professionals. OECD Publishing. doi:10.1787/19cf08df-en

Okojie, V. (2014). *Emergence of e-book and the survival of the physical book in Africa.* Paper presented at the Nigerian international book fair, University of Lagos.

Oliver, R. L. (1980). A cognitive model for the antecedents and consequences of satisfaction. *JMR, Journal of Marketing Research, 17*(4), 460–469. doi:10.1177/002224378001700405

Omnicore. (2020). *TikTok by the numbers: Stats, demographics & fun facts.* Available at: https://www.omnicoreagency.com/tiktok-statistics

Onyema, E. M., Eucheria, N. C., Obafemi, F. A., Sen, S., Atonye, F. G., Sharma, A., & Alsayed, A. O. (2020). Impact of Coronavirus pandemic on education. *Journal of Education and Practice, 11*(13), 108–121.

Orlikowski, W. J. (1992). The duality of technology: Rethinking the concept of technology in organizations. *Organization Science, 3*(3), 398–427. doi:10.1287/orsc.3.3.398

Orlikowski, W. J., & Gash, D. C. (1994). Technological frames: Making sense of information technology in organizations. *ACM Transactions on Information Systems, 12*(2), 174–207. doi:10.1145/196734.196745

Orozco-Olvera, V., Shen, F. Y., & Cluver, L. (2019). The effectiveness of using entertainment education narratives to promote safer sexual behaviors of youth: A meta-analysis, 1985-2017. *PLoS One, 14*(2), e0209969. doi:10.1371/journal.pone.0209969 PMID:30753185

Ortiz de Guinea, A., & Markus, M. L. (2009). Why break the habit of a lifetime? Rethinking the roles of intention, habit, and emotion in continuing information technology use. *Management Information Systems Quarterly, 33*(3), 433–444. doi:10.2307/20650303

Ortiz, Caravaca, Garc´ıa-de Prado, & Boubeta-Puig. (2019). Real-time context-aware microservice architecture for predictive analytics and smart decision-making. *IEEE Access, 7*, 183–194.

Oseland, N. (2012). *The Psychology of Collaboration Space*. Herman Miller.

Osmani, M. W., Haddadeh, R., Hindi, N., & Weerakkody, V. (2020). The Role of Co-Innovation Platform and E-Collaboration ICTs in Facilitating Entrepreneurial Ventures. *International Journal of E-Entrepreneurship and Innovation, 10*(2), 62–75. Advance online publication. doi:10.4018/IJEEI.2020070104

Overby, S. (2017). *What is outsourcing? Definitions, best practices, challenges and advice.* https://www.cio.com/article/272355/outsourcing-outsourcing-definition-and-solutions.html

Palmer, M. S., & Wu, Z. (1994). Verb Semantics And Lexical Selection. *32nd Annual Meeting of the Association for Computational Linguistics*, 133-138.

Pang, E., Wong, M., Leung, C. H., & Coombes, J. (2019). Competencies for fresh graduates' success at work: Perspectives of employers. *Industry and Higher Education, 33*(1), 55–65. https://doi.org/10.1177/0950422218792333

Parlar, H., Polatcan, M., & Cansoy, R. (2019). The relationship between social capital and innovativeness climate in schools. The intermediary role of professional learning communities. *International Journal of Educational Management, 34*(2), 232–244. doi:10.1108/IJEM-10-2018-0322

Pateraki, I. (2018). Measuring the impact of eTwinning activities on teachers' practice and competence development - Monitoring eTwinning Practice Framework. Central Support Service of eTwinning, European Schoolnet.

Paulsen, T. H., Anderson, R. G., & Tweeten, J. F. (2015). Concerns Expressed by Agricultural Education Preservice Teachers in a Twitter-Based Electronic Community of Practice. *Journal of Agricultural Education, 56*(3), 210–226. doi:10.5032/jae.2015.03210

Periotto, T. R. C., & Wessellenns, J. L. (2018). The School Manager and the Use of Knowledge Management Practices for Structuring Organizational Processes. *International Journal of Learning, Teaching and Educational Research, 17*(10), 43–54. doi:10.26803/ijlter.17.10.3

Peters, Lang, & Lie. (2011). ITFG. *E-Collaborations and Virtual Organizations, 252*–75.

Peters, H., Zdravkovic, M., João Costa, M., Celenza, A., Ghias, K., Klamen, D., Mossop, L., Rieder, M., Devi Nadarajah, V., Wangsaturaka, D., Wohlin, M., & Weggemans, M. (2019). Twelve tips for enhancing student engagement. *Medical Teacher, 41*(6), 632–637. doi:10.1080/0142159X.2018.1459530 PMID:29683024

Pew Research Center. (2017). *Social media fact sheet.* Retrieved from https://www.pewinternet.org/fact-sheet/social-media/

Pew Research Center. (2021). *Social Media Use in 2021*. Available at: https://www.pewresearch.org/internet/2021/04/07/social-media-use-in-2021

Piaget, J. (1971). *Psychology and epistemology—Towards a theory of knowledge*. Kingsport Press.

Pintrich, P. R., & Zusho, A. (2002). The development of academic self-regulation: The role of cognitive and motivational factors. In Development of achievement motivation. Academic Press.

Poblet, M., García-Cuesta, E., & Casanovas, P. (2013). *Crowdsourcing Tools for Disaster Management: A Review of Platforms and Methods.* doi:10.1007/978-3-662-45960-7_19

Pons, N. L., Pérez, Y. P., Stiven, E. R., & Quintero, L. P. (2014). Design of a Knowledge Management model to improve the development of IT project teams (Diseño de un modelo de Gestión del Conocimiento para mejorar el desarrollo de equipos de proyectos informáticos). *Spanish Journal of Scientific Documentation, 37*(2), 44. doi:10.3989/redc.2014.2.1036

Quintas, P., Lefrere, P., & Jones, G. (1997). Knowledge management: A strategic agenda. *Journal of Long Range Planning, 30*(3), 385–391. doi:10.1016/S0024-6301(97)90252-1

Rabiu, N., Ojukwu, N. N., & Oladele, P. (2016). Availability and accessibility of e-books in Nigerian libraries: A survey. *Information Impact: Journal of Information and Knowledge Management, 7*(1), 163 – 175. www.researchgate.com

Rana, N. P., Slade, E., Kitching, S., & Dwivedi, Y. K. (2019). The IT way of loafing in class: Extending the theory of planned behavior (TPB) to understand students' cyberslacking intentions. *Computers in Human Behavior, 101*, 114–123. doi:10.1016/j.chb.2019.07.022

Ranga, M., Hoareaux, C., Durrazi, N., Etzkowitz, H., Marcucci, P., & Usher, A. (2013). Study on University-Business Cooperation in the US. London School of Economics (LSE) Limited.

Raza, S. A., Qazi, W., Shah, N., Qureshi, M. A., Qaiser, S., & Ali, R. (2020). Drivers of intensive Facebook usage among university students: An implications of U&G and TPB theories. *Technology in Society, 62*, 101331. doi:10.1016/j.techsoc.2020.101331

Redecker, C. (2017). *European framework for the digital competence of educators: DigCompEdu* (No. JRC107466). Joint Research Centre (Seville site). ¸jrc107466 doi:10.2760/159770

Renukdas, R. S. (2021). *Datamatic Blog Minimize NPA with Integrated Loan Prediction for NBFC`s and Banks.* https://blog.datamatics.com/minimize-npas-with-integrated-loan-prediction-in-nbfc-and-banking-apps

Riccardi, M. T. (2016). The power of crowd sourcing in disaster response operations. *International Journal of Disaster Risk Reduction, 20*, 123–128. doi:10.1016/j.ijdrr.2016.11.001

Ridwan, S.M. (2015). *Application of electronic scholarly publishing in digital age: prospects and challenges in Nigerian universities.* Academic Press.

Riggins, N. (2017). 20 Advantages and Disadvantages of Outsourcing from Your Small Business. *Small Business Trends.* https://smallbiztrends.com/2017/02/advantages-and-disadvantages-of-outsourcing.html

Rismark, M., & Sølvberg, A. M. (2011). Knowledge Sharing in Schools: A Key to Developing Professional Learning Communities. *World Journal of Education, 1*(2), 150–160. doi:10.5430/wje.v1n2p150

Robert, S., Gérard, S., Terrier, F., & Lagarde, F. (2009). A Lightweight Approach for Domain-Specific Modeling Languages Design. In *2009 35th Euromicro Conference on Software Engineering and Advanced Applications.* IEEE. 10.1109/SEAA.2009.81

Robinson, J., Dusenberry, L., & Lawrence, H. (2016). Collaborative Strategies for Distributed Teams: Innovation through Interlaced Collaborative Writing. In *IEEE International Professional Communication Conference (IPCC 2016).* IEEE. 10.1109/IPCC.2016.7740489

Rogers, E. M. (1983). *Diffusion of innovations* (3rd ed.). Macmillan Publishing.

Sachdev, N. B. (2021). *The Fintech Way of solving India`s high NPA situation.* The Tech Panda. https://thetechpanda.com/the-fintech-way-of-solving-indias-high-npa-situation/34589/

Sadler, D. R. (1989). Formative assessment and the design of instructional systems. Assessment and Evaluation Research Unit, Department of Education, University of Queensland, StJ~ucia, Queensland4067. *Australia in Instructional Science, 18*(11), 119–144.

Sambell, K. (2016). Assessment and feedback in higher education: Considerable room for improvement? *Student Engagement Int. Journal of Higher Education, 1*(1), 2016.

Sanil, H.S., Singh, D., Raj, K.B., Choubey, S., Bhasin, N.K.K., Yadav, R., & Gulati, K. (2021). Role of machine learning in changing social and business eco-system – a qualitative study to explore the factors contributing to competitive advantage during COVID pandemic. *World Journal of Engineering*. doi:10.1108/WJE-06-2021-0357

Sargent, R. G. (2013). Verification and Validation of Simulation Models. *Journal of Simulation*, *7*(1), 12–24. doi:10.1057/jos.2012.20

Sawilowsky, S. S. (2009). New effect size rules of thumb. *Journal of Modern Applied Statistical Methods*, *8*(2), 597–599. doi:10.22237/jmasm/1257035100

Scherr, S., & Wang, K. (2021). Explaining the success of social media with gratification niches: Motivations behind daytime, nighttime, and active use of TikTok in China. *Computers in Human Behavior*, *124*, 106893. doi:10.1016/j.chb.2021.106893

Selfe, C. L., & Meyer, P. (1991). Testing claims for online conferences. *Written Communication*, *8*(2), 163–192. doi:10.1177/0741088391008002002

Seman, L. O., Hausmann, R., & Bezerra, E. A. (2018). On the students' perceptions of the knowledge formation when submitted to a project-based learning environment using web applications. *Computers & Education*, *117*, 16–30. https://doi.org/10.1016/j.compedu.2017.10.001

Senior, R. M., Bartholomew, P., Soor, A., Shepperd, D., Bartholomew, N., & Senior, C. (2018). The Rules of Engagement: Student Engagement and Motivation to Improve the Quality of Undergraduate Learning. *Frontiers in Education*.

Shannak, R. (2013). The Impact of Using E-collaboration Tools on Company Performance. *European Scientific Journal*, *9*(10), 1–18.

Shiffrin, R. M., & Schneider, W. (1977). Controlled and automatic human information processing: II. Perceptual learning, automatic attending and a general theory. *Psychological Review*, *84*(2), 127–190. doi:10.1037/0033-295X.84.2.127

Silvia, P. J., & Duval, T. S. (2001). Objective self-awareness theory: Recent progress and enduring problems. *Personality and Social Psychology Review*, *5*(3), 230–241. doi:10.1207/S15327957PSPR0503_4

Simon, Steinbruckner, & Lewerentz. (2001). Metrics Based Refactoring. *Proc. European Conf. Software Maintenance and Reeng.*, 30-38.

Sledgianowski, D., & Kulviwat, S. (2009). Using social network sites: The effects of playfulness, critical mass and trust in a hedonic context. *Journal of Computer Information Systems*, *49*(4), 74–83.

Smith, E. R., & DeCoster, J. (2000). Dual-process models in social and cognitive psychology: Conceptual integration and links to underlying memory systems. *Personality and Social Psychology Review*, *4*(2), 108–131. doi:10.1207/S15327957PSPR0402_01

Solano, A., Granollers, T., Collazos, C. A., & Rusu, C. (2014). Proposing Formal Notation for Modeling Collaborative Processes Extending HAMSTERS Notation. In Advances in Intelligent Systems and Computing (Vol. 275). Springer Verlag. doi:10.1007/978-3-319-05951-8_25

Song, J. H., Kim, W., Chai, D. S., & Bae, S. H. (2014). The impact of an innovative school climate on teachers' knowledge creation activities in Korean schools: The mediating role of teachers' knowledge sharing and work engagement. *KEDI Journal of Educational Policy*, *11*(2).

Srikanth, M., & Saravanan, P. (2021). *Bad Bank is Actually a Good Idea*. National Institute of Rural Development and IIM Tiruchirappalli.

Stahl, T., Völter, M., Bettin, J., Haase, A., & Helsen, S. (2006). *Model-Driven Software Development - Technology, Engineering, Management*. Pitman.

Statista. (2021a). *TikTok global monthly active users 2018-2021*. Available at: https://www.statista.com/statistics/1267892/tiktok-global-mau

Statista. (2021b). *TikTok users in Thailand 2017-2025*. Available at: https://www.statista.com/forecasts/1142641/tiktok-users-in-thailand

Straub, D., Boudreau, M. C., & Gefen, D. (2004). Validation Guidelines for IS Positivist Research. *Communications of the Association for Information Systems*, *13*(1), 24.

Swart, J., & Kinnie, N. (2003). Sharing knowledge in knowledge-intensive firm. *Human Resource Management Journal*, *13*(2), 60–75. doi:10.1111/j.1748-8583.2003.tb00091.x

Tackie, H. (2022). *(Dis)Connected: Establishing Social Presence and Intimacy in Teacher–Student Relationships During Emergency Remote Learning*. SAGE Journals.

Tadjer, H., Lafifi, Y., & Seridi-Bouchelaghem, H. (2018). A new approach for assessing Learners in an Online problem-based learning environment. *International Journal of Information and Communication Technology Education*, *14*(4), 18–33. https://doi.org/10.4018/IJICTE.2018100102

Tadjer, H., Lafifi, Y., Seridi-Bouchelaghem, H., & Gülseçen, S. (2020). Improving soft skills based on students' traces in problem-based learning environments. *Interactive Learning Environments*. Advance online publication. doi:10.1080/10494820.2020.1753215

Tamilmani, K., Rana, N. P., & Dwivedi, Y. K. (2018, June). Use of 'habit" is not a habit in understanding individual technology adoption: a review of UTAUT2 based empirical studies. In *International Working Conference on Transfer and Diffusion of IT* (pp. 277-294). Springer.

Tandon, T. (2021, April). What is Bad Bank? Know its Significance, Role and Benefits. *RBI Bulletin*.

Taylor, S., & Todd, P. A. (1995). Understanding information technology usage: A Test of competing models. *Information Systems Research*, *6*(2), 144–176. doi:10.1287/isre.6.2.144

Tchounikine, P. (2009). *Précis de recherche en ingénierie des eiah*. http://membresliglab.imag.fr/tchounikine/Precis.html

Tenenberg, J., Roth, W. M., & Socha, D. (2016). From I-Awareness to We-Awareness in CSCW. *Computer Supported Cooperative Work: CSCW: An International Journal*, *25*(4–5), 235–278. doi:10.100710606-014-9215-0

Terra, R., Valente, M. T., & Anquetil, N. (2016). A lightweight remodularization process based on structural similarity. *2016 X Brazilian Symposium on Software Components, Architectures and Reuse (SBCARS)*, 111–120.

Teruel, M. A., Navarro, E., López-Jaquero, V., Montero, F., & González, P. (2013). CSRML Tool: A Visual Studio Extension for Modeling CSCW Requirements. CEUR Workshop Proceedings.

Teruel, Navarro, López-Jaquero, Montero, & González. (2011). An Extension of i * to Model Requirements for CSCW Systems Applied to Conference Preparation System with Collaborative Reviews. *5th International i* Workshop (iStar'11)*.

Teruel, M. A., Navarro, E., López-Jaquero, V., Montero, F., & González, P. (2014). A CSCW Requirements Engineering CASE Tool: Development and Usability Evaluation. *Information and Software Technology*, *56*(8), 922–949. doi:10.1016/j.infsof.2014.02.009

Teruel, M. A., Navarro, E., López-Jaquero, V., Montero, F., Jaen, J., & González, P. (2012). Analyzing the Understandability of Requirements Engineering Languages for CSCW Systems: A Family of Experiments. *Information and Software Technology*, *54*(11), 1215–1228. doi:10.1016/j.infsof.2012.06.001

Thalesgrpup.com. (2020). *Report. Biometrics for Financial Institutions*. https://www.sc.pages05.net/lp/22466/795954/fs-wp-biometrics-for-financial-institutions.pdf

Thompson, R. L., Higgins, C. A., & Howell, J. M. (1994). Influence of experience on personal computer utilization: Testing a conceptual model. *Journal of Management Information Systems*, *11*(1), 167–187. doi:10.1080/07421222.1994.11518035

Tiamiyu, M. (2005). Prospects of Nigerian book publishing in the electronic age. In F. A. Adesanoye & A. Ojeniyi (Eds.), *Issues in Book Publishing in Nigeria* (pp. 143–157). Heinemann, Nigeria.

Times of India.Com. (2021). *What is Bad Bank and Can It Resolve NPA Woes*. Retrieved from https://timesofindia.indiatimes.com/business/india-business/why-bad-bank-could-be-a-good-move-for-an-ailing-economy/articleshow/80614795.cms

Tip, F., Kiezun, A., & Baumer, D. (2003). Refactoring for Generalization Using Type Constraints. *Proc. SIGPLAN Conf. Object-Oriented Programming, Systems, Languages, and Applications*, 13-26.

Tornatzky, L. G., & Klein, K. J. (1982). Innovation characteristics and innovation adoption-implementation: A meta-analysis of findings. *IEEE Transactions on Engineering Management*, *EM-29*(1), 28–45. doi:10.1109/TEM.1982.6447463

Tourwe, T., & Mens, T. (2003). Identifying Refactoring Opportunities Using Logic Meta Programming. *Proc. European Conf. Software Maintenance and Reeng.*, 91-100.

Tsai, Y. L., & Tsai, C. C. (2018). Digital game-based second-language vocabulary learning and conditions of research designs: A meta-analysis study. *Computers & Education*, *125*, 345–357. doi:10.1016/j.compedu.2018.06.020

Uwalaka, N. M. (2000). *Book publishing performance in the Nigerian Economic Environment* [PhD dissertation]. University of Ibadan, Nigeria.

Van Slyke, C., Ilie, V., Lou, H., & Stafford, T. (2007). Perceived critical mass and the adoption of a communication technology. *European Journal of Information Systems*, *16*(3), 270–283. doi:10.1057/palgrave.ejis.3000680

Van Steen, M., & Tanenbaum, A. S. (2016). A Brief Introduction to Distributed Systems Computing. In Proceedings of Very Large Digital Library (VLDL 2009). Springer. doi:10.100700607-016-0508-7

Van Steen, M., & Tanenbaum, S. (2017). Distributed Systems (3rd ed.). Distributed-sys.net

van Uden-Kraan, C. F., Drossaert, C. H., Taal, E., Seydel, E. R., & van de Laar, M. A. (2008). Self-reported differences in empowerment between lurkers and posters in online patient support groups. *Journal of Medical Internet Research*, *10*(2), e18. doi:10.2196/jmir.992 PMID:18653442

Venkatesh, V., Morris, M. G., Davis, G. B., & Davis, F. D. (2003). User acceptance of information technology: Toward a unified view. *Management Information Systems Quarterly*, *27*(3), 425–478. doi:10.2307/30036540

Venkatesh, V., Thong, J. Y., & Xu, X. (2012). Consumer acceptance and use of information technology: Extending the unified theory of acceptance and use of technology. *Management Information Systems Quarterly*, *36*(1), 157–178. doi:10.2307/41410412

Verma, S. (2022). *Explained: Bad Bank is ready, how will it resolve stressed assets*. Retrieved from https://indianexpress.com/article/explained/explained-bad-bank-stressed-assets-7747007/

Verma, S., & Mathew, G. (2021). *Explained: The Arguments for and Against a Bad Bank*. Indian Express.Com.

Vieira, V., Tedesco, P., & Salgado, A. C. (2010). Using a Metamodel to Design Structural and Behavioral Aspects in Context-Sensitive Groupware. *Proceedings of the 2010 14th International Conference on Computer Supported Cooperative Work in Design, CSCWD 2010.* 10.1109/CSCWD.2010.5472002

Von Krogh, G. (2012). How does social software change knowledge management? Toward a strategic research agenda. *The Journal of Strategic Information Systems, 21*(2), 154–164. doi:10.1016/j.jsis.2012.04.003

Vuorikari, R., Punie, Y., Carretero Gomez S., & Van den Brande, G. (2016). *DigComp 2.0: The digital competence framework for citizens. Update phase 1: The conceptual reference model* (No. JRC101254). Joint Research Centre (Seville site). doi:10.2791/11517

Vygotsky, L. S. (1978). *Mind in society—The development of higher psychological processes.* Harvard University.

Wang, C., Harris, J., & Patterson, P. (2013). The roles of habit, self-efficacy, and satisfaction in driving continued use of self-service technologies: A longitudinal study. *Journal of Service Research, 16*(3), 400–414. doi:10.1177/1094670512473200

Wang, C., Teo, T. S., & Liu, L. (2020). Perceived value and continuance intention in mobile government service in China. *Telematics and Informatics, 48*, 101348. doi:10.1016/j.tele.2020.101348

Wang, Y., Yu, H., Zhu, Z., Zhang, W., & Zhao, Y. (2017). Automatic software refactoring via weighted clustering in method-level networks. *IEEE Transactions on Software Engineering, 44*(3), 2017.

Warren, J. (2010). The Progression of Digital Publishing. *International Journal of the Book, 7*(4). www.googlescholar.com

Watson, A. (2018). *U.S. Digital Publishing Industry - Statistics & Facts.* Statista. https://www.statista.com/topics/1453/digital-publishing/

Weimann, G., & Masri, N. (2020). Research note: spreading hate on TikTok. *Studies in Conflict & Terrorism*, 1-14.

Whelehan, D. F. (2020). Students as Partners: A model to promote student engagement in post-COVID-19 teaching and learning. *All Ireland Journal of Higher Education, 12*(3).

Wigfield, A., Klauda, S. L., & Cambria, J. (2011). *Influences on the development of academic self-regulatory processes.* Academic Press.

Wikepedia.en. (2021). *Bad Bank and U. K. Asset Resolution.* Retrieved from https://en.wikipedia.org/wiki?curid=21296887

Wilson, E. V., & Lankton, N. K. (2010). An integrative model of IT continuance: Applying measures of intention, prior IT use, and habit strength across conditions of sporadic and frequent IT use. DIGIT 2010 Proceedings.

Wilson, E. V., Mao, E., & Lankton, N. K. (2010). The distinct roles of prior IT use and habit strength in predicting continued sporadic use of IT. *Communications of the Association for Information Systems, 27*(12), 185–206. doi:10.17705/1CAIS.02712

WIPO. (2020). *The Global Publishing Industry in 2018.* Geneva: World Intellectual Property Organization. Retrieved from https://www.wipo.int/edocs/pubdocs/en/wipo_pub_1064_2019.pdf

Wohlrab, P., Knauss, E., Steghöfer, J., Maro, S., Anjorin, A., & Pelliccione, P. (2018). Collaborative traceability management: A multiple case study from the perspectives of organization, process, and culture. *Requirements Engineering, 25*(0), 21–45.

Wut, T.-m., & Xu, J. (2021). Person-to-person interactions in online classroom settings under the impact of COVID-19: a social presence theory perspective. *Asia Pacific Education Review*, 371–383.

Yadav, A., & Chavan, P. (2021, Apr.). *ARC's in India: A Study of their Business Operations and Role in NPA Resolution. RBI Bulletin.*

Yang, H., Steensma, H. K., & Ren, T. (2021). State ownership, firm innovation and the moderating role of private-sector competition: The case of China. *Competitiveness Review*, *31*(4), 729–746. doi:10.1108/CR-02-2019-0024

Yoon, C., & Rolland, E. (2015). Understanding continuance use in social networking services. *Journal of Computer Information Systems*, *55*(2), 1–8. doi:10.1080/08874417.2015.11645751

Young, J. (2014). iPolicy: Exploring and evaluating the use of iPads in a social welfare policy course. *Journal of Technology in Human Services*, *32*(1-2), 39–53. doi:10.1080/15228835.2013.860366

Young, J. R. (2009). Teaching with twitter: Not for the faint of heart. *The Chronicle of Higher Education*, *56*, A1–A11.

Yusri, R., Abusitta, A., & Aïmeur, E. (2020). Teens-Online: A Game Theory-Based Collaborative Platform for Privacy Education. *International Journal of Artificial Intelligence in Education*, 1–43.

Yusuf, A. (2012). An Appraisal of Research in Nigeria's University Sector. *Journal of Research in National Development*, *10*(2), 321–330.

Yu, Z. (2019). A Systematic Review on Mobile Technology-Assisted English Learning. *International Journal of e-Collaboration*, *15*(4), 71–88. doi:10.4018/IJeC.2019100105

Yu, Z., & Yi, H. (2020). Acceptance and effectiveness of Rain Classroom in linguistics classes. *International Journal of Mobile and Blended Learning*, *12*(2), 77–90. doi:10.4018/IJMBL.2020040105

Zammuto, R. F., Griffith, T. L., Majchrzak, A., Dougherty, D. J., & Faraj, S. (2007). Information technology and the changing fabric of organization. *Organization Science*, *18*(5), 749–762. doi:10.1287/orsc.1070.0307

Zandkarimi, F., Nakladad, J., Vieten, J., & Geyer-Klingberg, J. (2020). Co-Innovation in a University-Industry Partnership. A Case Study in the Field of Process Mining. *Proceedings of the 32nd International Conference on Advanced Information Systems (ICAIS 2020).*

Zghal, S. (2010). *Contributions à l'alignement d'ontologies OWL par agrégation de similarités* [Ph.D. dissertation]. Tunis Univ, Tunisia.

Zhang, X., Wu, Y., & Liu, S. (2019). Exploring short-form video application addiction: Socio-technical and attachment perspectives. *Telematics and Informatics*, *42*, 101243. doi:10.1016/j.tele.2019.101243

Zhao, J. (2010). School knowledge management framework and strategies: The new perspective on teacher professional development. *Computers in Human Behavior*, *26*(2), 168–175. doi:10.1016/j.chb.2009.10.009

Zhao, J., & Kumar, V. (2022). Technologies and Systems for E-Collaboration during Global Crises. *Pages*, *335*. Advance online publication. doi:10.4018/978-1-7998-9640-1

Zhao, J., & Ordóñez de Pablos, P. (2009). School innovative management model and strategies: The perspective of organizational learning. *Information Systems Management*, *26*(3), 241–251. doi:10.1080/10580530903017781

Zhao, J., & Richards, J. (2021). E-Collaboration Technologies and Strategies for Competitive Advantage amid Challenging Times. *Pages*, *346*. Advance online publication. doi:10.4018/978-1-7998-7764-6

Zhao, Y., & Watterston, J. (2021). The changes we need: Education post COVID-19. *Journal of Educational Change*, *22*(1), 3–12. doi:10.100710833-021-09417-3

Zheng, W., Yu, F., & Wu, Y. J. (2021). Social media on blended learning: The effect of rapport and motivation. *Behaviour & Information Technology*, 1–11. doi:10.1080/0144929X.2021.1909140

Zimmerman, B. J. (2004). Sociocultural influence and students' development of academic self-regulation: A social-cognitive perspective. Big theories revisited, 139-164.

Zimmerman, B. J. (2008). Investigating self-regulation and motivation: Historical background, methodological developments, and future prospects. *American Educational Research Journal*, *45*(1), 166–183.

Zimmerman, B. J., & Schunk, D. H. (Eds.). (2011). *Handbook of self-regulation of learning and performance*. Routledge.

Zolkepli, I. A., & Kamarulzaman, Y. (2015). Social media adoption: The role of media needs and innovation characteristics. *Computers in Human Behavior*, *43*, 189–209. doi:10.1016/j.chb.2014.10.050

About the Contributors

Jingyuan Zhao is a research fellow at University of Toronto, Canada. She is also professor at Beijing Union University (China). She obtained her PhD in Management Science and Engineering from University of Science and Technology of China (China) and completed a postdoctoral program in Management of Technology from University of Quebec at Montreal (Canada). Dr. Zhao's expertise is on management of technology innovation, technology strategy, regional innovation systems and global innovation networks, knowledge management, management information systems, and science and technology policy.

* * *

Igor Alexander Ambalov is a researcher and a lecturer at the Faculty of Digital Technology at Rajapruk University, Thailand. The areas of interest include social research, research methods, information technology, and Android application development using Java (an example project can be found at: https://play.google.com/store/apps/details?id=com.cyberia.radio.AppRadio). https://orcid.org/0000-0002-6481-3305.

Fm. Asikullah is a new researcher, who is interested in labor economics, environmental economics and some particular topics related to business study, especially human resource management. The author has also an appetite for working on other miscellaneous topics.

Rabie Barhoun is a PhD researcher at the Department of Education National, Morocco. His current research interests are access control, privacy & security, collaboration environment, collaboration model, computer network, cloud computing, QoS, and protocol of communication.

Narinder Bhasin is a professor, Amity School of Insurance Banking and Actuarial Science.

Luis Bibbo has a degree in Computer Science and a Master's degree from the National University of La Plata. He participates in research activities in the areas of modeling and formal methods at the LIFIA Laboratory of the Faculty of Informatics, Univeridad Nacionalde la Plata (UNLP). He participates in accredited research projects at UNLP. He has performed training and advisory tasks in both the public and private sectors. He directs work for graduate and postgraduate thesis at the Faculty of Informatics of the UNLP. He is the author of various articles in Conferences and Workshops. He teaches in the area of Software Engineering at the undergraduate and graduate level.

Karima Boussaha is a full Professor in the Department of Mathematics and Computer Science at Oum El Bouaghi University in Algeria. She is obtained her Ph.D. at Annaba University in Algeria since 2016. She is a Member of the Distributed-Intelligent Systems Engineering (DISE) in the Research Laboratory on Computer Science's Complex Systems (ReLa(CS)2) at Oum El Bouaghi University. Her Ph.D. research is based on computer-assisted assessment of learners, application in the programming language field. She holds an HU (Habilitation Universitaire) in Computer Science in 2021 from Oum El Bouaghi University. Her main areas of interest include computer-based/assisted assessment, assessment of procedural knowledge, and assessment in collaborative learning, computer-based/assisted collaborative tutoring, computer-based/assisted collaborative learning, Ontologies, collaboration.

Phonebuson Chakma is a new researcher, who is interested in labor economics, development economics, and environmental economics. He is also able to participate in conversations about today's economic problems.

Junwu Chen is a graduate student of Zhejiang Gongshang University, CCF student member. His main research direction are requirements analysis and service computing.

Khaled Shams Chisty possesses 20 years of experience in the area of undergraduate and graduate level teaching, research and administration management.

Idongesit E. Eteng, in 2013, earned her PhD degree in Computer Science at the University of Ibadan, Oyo State, Nigeria. Her major fields of expertise include Software Engineering, Data Science, Machine Learning, and Database Management and specifying and verifying complex systems using Formal Methods. She is also a public speaker in nurturing young adults to maximize their potentials and actualize their dreams. She is a Senior Lecturer at the Department of Computer Science, University of Calabar, Cross River State, Nigeria, where she has taught since 2006. Before that, she worked at the same University as a Programmer and Systems Analyst. She has supervised several undergraduate and graduate students in the last 5 years. She has presented her research papers in many places, including Ghana, Scotland, London, and the Unites of America, where she collaborated with scholars in computing and other related fields. She has a handful of publications including: A review on effective approach to teaching computer programming to undergraduates in developing countries published by Elsevier in 2022, "Development of an Online Collaboration Tool for Research and Innovation in the University" for International Journal of Management Science and Business Intelligence in 2019, and "A Multi-layered Secured Messaging Protocol for REST-Based Services" for Journal of Internal Technology and Information Management" in 2019, which was also presented at the International Information Management Association & International Conference of Information Technology and Economic Development (IIMA/ICITED) at Prairie View University A & M, Houston, Texas, USA. She has also presented papers in other countries including a paper titled "Detecting Malaria-Prone Areas Using IoT-Based Techniques and Climatic Data" at the Conference of Big Data and Internet of Things, London, the United Kingdom in 2017. She pioneered the development of some computer applications including an expert system for Ebola diagnosis which she presented at the Researchers' Internal Network (RIN) Conference at the University of Cape Coast, Ghana. She has also co-authored a few books with her colleagues at the University of Calabar, Cross River State, Nigeria. Dr (Mrs) Eteng became a member of Computer Professionals of Nigeria (CPN) in 2006, and a member of Nigeria Computer Society (NCS) in 2003.

Alejandro Fernández is a full-time professor at the Faculty of Informatics of the National University of La Plata, in Argentina. He is also a researcher at the Scientific Research Commission (CIC) of the Buenos Aires province and the director of the LIFIA research center. His research interests lie primarily in the intersection of CSCW, knowledge management, and software engineering.

Kamal Gulati is an Associate Professor, Amity School of Insurance Banking and Actuarial Science, Amity University, Noida.

Amira Hanneche is a Software Development Engineer. She completed her Masters in 2017 from Oum el Bouaghi University. Her main areas of interest include CEHL (Computing Environment for Human Learning), learner's assessment, practical works activities, computer-based/assisted collaborative learning, tutoring, computer-based/assisted collaborative tutoring.

Syed Far Abid Hossain is a Senior Lecturer at the College of Business Administration, International University of Business Agriculture and Technology (IUBAT) since 2013. He is pursuing his PhD (Management Science) from the School of Management, Xi'an Jiaotong University, PRC. He holds an MBA degree from the University of Sunderland, UK and a BBA (Marketing) degree from Dhaka University. Mr. Abid authored more than 40 Academic Journal Articles, Conference papers and Book chapters in internationally recognized, peer reviewed and well-indexed Journals from Elsevier, Springer, SAGE, Taylor and Francis, Frontiers, Science Direct, Emerald, MDPI and IGI global. His research interests include academic performance, education psychology, education management, technology in education, women entrepreneurship, innovation and media entrepreneurship. Apart from his current roles at IUBAT, Mr. Abid serves as a regular reviewer of famous journals from reputed publishers including Elsevier, Wiley, Springer, SAGE, Taylor and Francis, Frontiers, Emerald, IGI Global. Mr. Abid is strongly involved with GEPN (Global Education Policy network) for international research collaboration. Till date, Mr. Abid is proudly co-authored with renowned professors and researchers from St. Anthony's College, University of Oxford, UK and many other recognized higher educational institutions from different parts of the world.

Bo Jiang received a Ph.D. degree in computer science from Zhejiang University in 2007. Since 2003, she has been a faculty member and professor in the School of Computer and Information Engineering, Zhejiang Gongshang University. She has a broad research interests in software engineering, requirements engineering, and service computing. She is a member of the IEEE, ACM and CCF. And she is a member of China Cloud Computing Expert Committee, standing member of CCF Cooperative Computing Special Committee.

Tanushree Karmoker is working as a research assistant (RA) at IUBAT University.

Reefat Arefin Khan joined as a Lecturer of College of Business Administration, IUBAT University - International University of Business Agricultural and Technology, Dhaka. Reefat Arefin Khan has been teaching BBA and MBA degrees since 2019. He holds a Master of Business Administration (MBA) from MAHSA university, Malaysia. He was the MBA topper of MAHSA university in 2018. He did his BSc in Accountancy from University of Gloucestershire, London. He has got more than 6-year experience of serving in the education field. In addition, he worked in the finance sector for more than 2 years in Malaysia. He has taken training on "Stress management", "Business research methodology", "Uses of technology for E-commerce" "Management 4.0", "E-Learning and Teaching (CeLT)" and many other business and Education related trainings as well.

G. Aloy Anuja Mary is working as a Professor in the Department of Electronics &Communication Engineering at Vel Tech Rangarajan Dr. Sagunthala R & D Institute of Science and Technology. She graduated in Electronics & Communication Engineering at Sivanthi Aditanar College of Engineering, Tiruchendur, Tamilnadu, India. She secured Master of Engineering in Communication Systems at National engineering College, Kovilpatti, Tamilnadu, India. She graduated Ph.D. in the field of Quantum Cryptography at College of Engineering, Guindy, Chennai, India. She is in teaching profession for more than 16 years. She has presented number of papers in National and International Journals, Conference and Symposiums. Her main area of interest includes Wireless Networks and Quantum Computing.

Salvatore Nizzolino holds a Degree in Language Teaching and various Masters in the fields of Learning Design, Development of Teaching Programs and Knowledge Management. He serves as a Contract Professor for English at the Faculties of Information Engineering / Civil and Industrial Engineering and the Faculty of Economics at "Sapienza" University of Rome (Italy). He serves as a Lecturer and Tutor for the Advanced Course of European Project Management at the Faculty of Economics, "Sapienza" University of Rome. His research interests list Educational Networking, Lifelong Learning, Open Education, EU Projects and Knowledge Management. He is currently attending the Ph.D in eLearning and ICT at Universitat Oberta de Catalunya (Spain).

Samuel Oladimeji is a Ph.D. student of the Department of Computer Science, University of Calabar. He has B.Sc. and M.Sc. degrees in Mechanical Engineering and Computer Science respectively. His main fields of interest lie in Software Engineering, Software Design, Distributed Collaboration, and Knowledge Management. Samuel is currently a Systems Analyst at Caleb University, Lagos and hopes to pursue a lecturing career in the field of Computer Science, particularly focusing on Software Engineering. Aside from his commitments to research, Samuel is passionate about helping young people discover and fulfil their purposes on earth.

Janani P. is working as an Assistant Professor in the Department of Electronics & Communication Engineering at Vel Tech Rangarajan Dr. Sagunthala R & D Institute of Science and Technology. She graduated in Electronics & Communication Engineering at Peri Institute of Technology, Chennai, Tamilnadu, India. She secured Master of Technology VLSI & Embedded Systems Technologies at Vel Tech, Chennai, Tamilnadu, India. She is currently pursuing her Ph.D. in the field of Embedded Wearable technology at Vel Tech, Chennai, India. She is in teaching profession for more than 2 years. She has presented number of papers in National and International Journals, Conference and Symposiums. Her main area of interest includes Embedded systems and Wearable Technologies.

Claudia Pons is a PhD in Computer Science. Full time Researcher and professor at Universidad Nacional de La Plata. Argentina. Expert in Model driven software development and Artificial Intelligence. Director of the information technology research center CAETI at Universidad Abierta Interamericana UAI in Buenos Aires, Argentina.

E. D. Kanmani Ruby received B.E. degree in Electronics and Communication Engineering from Bharathiyar University, Coimbatore, in the year 1998, and M.E. degree in Applied Electronics with university 9th rank from Anna University, Chennai in the year 2005 respectively. She has obtained her doctoral degree in Information and Communication Engineering from Anna University in the year 2013.She has got 22 years of experience in teaching .During her career she has published more than 25 papers in reputed Journals and conferences which includes an International Conference at Las Vegas, USA in 2014 .She has got best faculty award in the year 2007-08 and holds life membership in various professional bodies like ISTE, IETE. Her research area includes Wireless sensor networks, Body area Networks, Communication Networks and Biomedical Instrumentation and Imaging.

Vishnu Kumar S. received his Bachelor's degree in Electronics and Communication Engineering (B.E., E.C.E) from Anna University, Chennai, in the year 2014 and received his Master's in Engineering (M.E., VLSI Design) and Business Administration (M.B.A., Technology Management) in the year 2016 from Anna University, Chennai. He has one-year industrial experience as VLSI verification engineer and 3.8 years of teaching experience. He has published two scientific papers in international journals and two research papers in conference, which also includes an IEEE conference. During his stint as assistant professor, he has received various appreciations for motivating students to do industrial projects. He is an active member of various professional bodies like IFERP, IAENG and IRED. His research area includes In-Vehicle Network Security, Internet of Things and Embedded System Design.

Song Shizhe is a graduate student of Zhejiang Gongshang University, CCF student member. His main research direction are natural language processing and requirements engineering.

Md. Ahmedul Islam Sohan, former graduate of IUBAT, currently works as the Administrative Officer for the MBA department of the educational institution. He has been working in the organization since May 2018. He has completed his graduation from MBA (major in HRM) from IUBAT in 2018 and his Bachelor of Science in Electrical and Electronics Engineering from IUBAT in 2014.

B. Sri is working as an Associate Professor in the Department of Electronics & Communication Engineering at Vel Tech Rangarajan Dr. Sagunthala R & D Institute of Science and Technology. She graduated in Electronics & Communication Engineering at Rajalakshmi Engineering College, Chennai, Tamilnadu, India. She secured Master of Engineering in Embedded Systems Technologies at Vel Tech, Chennai, Tamilnadu, India. She graduated Ph.D. in the field of Wireless Networks at College of Engineering, Guindy, Chennai, India. She is in teaching profession for more than 18 years. She has presented number of papers in National and International Journals, Conference and Symposiums. Her main area of interest includes Wireless Networks, IoT, Cognitive Radio and Wearable Technologies.

Rohit Vashisht is an Assistant Professor in the Department of Computer Science, ABES Engineering College, Ghaziabad, India. He has completed his B.Tech from Ajay Kumar Garg Engineering College, AKTU with silver medal and M.Tech from USICT, GGSIPU, and Delhi with gold medal. He has currently submitted Ph.D Thesis in Jamia Millia Islamia University. His area of interest includes machine learning, sentimental analysis, software engineering and cloud computing. He has teaching experience of 6 years. He is certified as Elite Silver for subject Compiler Design and Operating System by NPTEL.

He has good numbers of publications in reputed international conferences and journals (indexed in scopus, ESCI, SCIE).

K. S. Vinod was born in Chennai, India. He received his B.E. in Electronics and Communication Engineering, from University of Madras at Hindustan College of Engineering, Padur in 1997 and his M.E in Multimedia Technology from Anna University at College of Engineering, Guindy, Chennai in 2006. After his master's, he worked as a software professional mainly in web applications. Since 2012, he has been teaching at Anna University affiliate engineering colleges in the respective departments of Electronics and communication. He is presently teaching at Vel Tech Rangarajan Dr. Sagunthala R & D Institute of Science and Technology, Avadi as Assistant Professor in ECE department. His current research interests include web scraping, wearable technology, wearable security, multimedia databases, machine learning, deep learning, and image & video signal processing.

Ye Wang received the Ph.D. degree in Software Engineering from Zhejiang University in 2013. She is a member of IEICE. She is an associate professor in the School of Computer and Information Engineering, Zhejiang Gongshang University. Her research interests include requirements analysis and service computing.

Zhonggen Yu is professor and Ph.D. Supervisor in Department of English Studies, Faculty of Foreign Studies, Beijing Language and Culture University, Ph.D. in English language, a dual Master-degree holder in applied linguistics and law, and a post-doctoral researcher in psycho-linguistics, has already published over 100 academic papers (mainly peer reviewed international articles) on distinguished journals based on rich teaching and research experiences. His research interest includes educational technologies, language attrition, and language acquisition.

Index

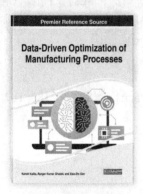
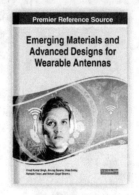

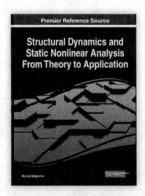

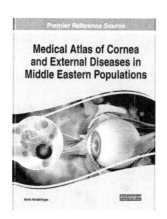
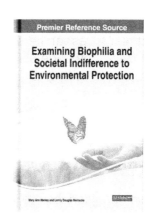
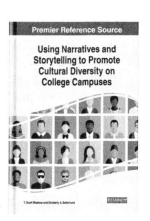

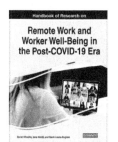

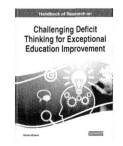